To my grandchildren: Noah, Finlay, Patrick and Erin who I hope someday will have the time to read my story.

Bob Sclater was born, grew up and educated in Kirkwall Orkney. In 1956, at the age of 15, set off to sea, and spent seven years in the Merchant Navy as a deck hand sailing world-wide. He had obtained 2nd Mate, 1st Mate and master mariners foreign going certificates and sailed as an officer for a further 12 years. In 1976, Bob became a marine officer/pilot when the first North Sea Oil came ashore to the Flotta Oil Terminal in Orkney and served in this post for nine years. He got promoted to deputy and then director of harbours with Orkney Islands Council for another 12 years. In 1999, Bob became a local authority councillor for eight years and an honorary sheriff for the past 15 years. He lives in Kirkwall and is married with three grown up children – all working out with Orkney.

Bob Sclater

# THE STORY OF MY
# WORKING LIFE

AUSTIN MACAULEY PUBLISHERS™

LONDON ∗ CAMBRIDGE ∗ NEW YORK ∗ SHARJAH

A CIP catalogue record for this title is available from the British Library.

ISBN 9781398444874 (Paperback)
ISBN 9781398444881 (ePub e-book)

www.austinmacauley.com

First Published 2024
Austin Macauley Publishers Ltd®
1 Canada Square
Canary Wharf
London
E14 5AA

Firstly , the Royal Museums Greenwich, who in 2018 issued a flyer to Merchant Seafarers, "That they wished to enhance their understanding and representation of the Merchant Navy and seeking help to ensure that knowledge is not lost and memoirs not forgotten."

I contacted Ms Lucy Dale, assistant curator and commenced writing my story. She commented favourably on each chapter I sent by stating, "Your career is really fascinating and I have greatly enjoyed what you have sent."

Also, Austin Macauley, who accepted my manuscript with a very positive review.

I would also acknowledge the following not in any specific order as they all played a role in compiling my story one way or another.
U.K. Hydrographic Department, Orkney Islands Council, Dept. Of Harbours, Orkney Ferries, Orkney Towage, Flotta Oil Terminal, BP, NZSCo, P&O GCD, LPR, Lamport + Holt, Moller Line UK, Orkney Photographic, RGIT, DOT, MCA, MAIB, NLB, RNLI, Northlink Ferries, McTay Marine, Wijsmuller Towage, Napier's of Arbroath, Jones of Buckie, Murray Cormack Assoc., Appledore Shipbuilders, Campbeltown Shipbuilders, FBM Shipbuilders, David Abel's Shipbuilders, Alisa Troon Shipbuilders, IMT Consultants, Royal Navy, Orkney Marinas, Foinaven Team, Briggs Marine, Cruise Europe, Tysers insurance brokers, NJPB, HIFB, Hitrans, NI, EI, David Edge, Clydeships, UK and Scottish Governments, J.P. Knight, Wood Group, Chris Howell, Phil English Shipspotting, Jon Wheeler fotoflit

# Part 1

On leaving school at the age of 15 and with no qualifications and little hope of finding a good job in Orkney, I decided that I would head off to sea.

When asked by one of my school teachers what I thought I might do with my life, I said I intended to go to sea. Well, she said, "We will give you some extra maths classes to help as you will need that when you go to sea." Little did I know at the time that this extra tuition would help me in later years.

In September 1956, I set off to Leith Nautical College to learn my skills as a seaman. There were three of us, all friends from Kirkwall, Russel Corsie, John Foulis and myself who caught the MV St Ninian down to Aberdeen then onwards to Leith.

The 15-week preparatory course took place onboard the T.S. Dolphin moored at West Old Dock Leith. Now the site of the Scottish Office.

The T.S. Dolphin had a long and distinguished career in the Royal Navy built in 1882; she saw active service in Egypt, India and Australia. In 1907, she was de-rigged and used as depot ship in Portsmouth. In 1928, she arrived in Leith where she was to be a nautical museum.

In 1944, she eventually became a Merchant Navy training ship and remained so until 1977 when she was towed away from West Old Dock to the shores of Bo'ness where she was beached and burnt just to salvage the copper from her bottom.

Captain Adam Tait, a Shetland Master Mariner, took command in 1944 and set about organising the training programme for up to 80/90 boys as deck boys, catering boys and deck cadets under the control of Leith Nautical College. In 1950, the college opened a course for ship's cooks. My main tutors were Captain Sutherland, an Orkney Master Mariner, and Captain Flockhart.

The majority of boys lived onboard the Dolphin as they came from all parts of Scotland including Orkney and Shetland; there were some local lads who lived at home.

I attended the programme for deck boys, the lowest rank in the Merchant Navy and was trained how to tie knots, box a compass, row a lifeboat, swim, splice rope and all the nautical terminology one would need at sea.

After this intensive 15 weeks' training, I obtained my first ever qualification, a First-Class certificate.

# LEITH NAUTICAL COLLEGE

## Certificate of Merit

Course :— From ___11.9.56___ To ___21.12.56___

ROBERT CHALMERS SCLATER

*having satisfactorily completed the*

## Preparatory Course for Seamen

*has been awarded this ___FIRST___ Class Certificate of proficiency and conduct on the results of his work throughout the session.*

*He attended during ___432___ hours out of a possible ___432___*

*Principal.*

*Chairman of the Governors.*

Leith Nautical College is a Central Institution scheduled under section 34 of the Education (Scotland) Act, 1908.

This certificate is approved by the Scottish Education Department and is issued in respect of the syllabus of work and under the regulations printed on the back hereof.

### NOTE TO HOLDER OF THIS CERTIFICATE.

You must be sure to produce this Certificate at the Mercantile Marine Office when you receive your first Discharge Book.

The Superintendent has been instructed under M.D. Memorandum 5757 of 8/4/48 to enter your period of training in the T.S. "Dolphin," and you must ensure that this is done, as this period will assist towards your qualifying sea time for "Ordinary Seaman and Able Seaman."

# PREPARATORY COURSE FOR SEAMEN

## SYLLABUS OF INSTRUCTION

**Discipline** - - - Physical exercises, squad drill, marks of respect, behaviour on board ship, etc. Boatdrill.

**Arithmetic** - - - Vulgar and decimal fractions, square root. Problems on coinage, reckoning of wages, time and speed of ships, and other nautical applications.

**Mensuration** - - Area of square, rectangle, triangle and circle, surface-area and volume of box shape and cylinder. Problems on sail areas, hatch covers, funnel area, capacity of tanks, holds and bunkers.

**English** - - - Practice in composition of letters, etc.

**Geography** - - - World trade routes, ports and cargoes.

**Nautical Knowledge** - Nautical terms, types of ships, parts of a ship, rigging and working gear. Daily routine on board ship, time keeping by bells, system of watches. Ship cleanliness and hygiene. Magnetic compass—systems of marking cards, boxing the compass, practice on the steering model. Helm orders, lookout, reporting of bearings of ships when on lookout. Navigation lights and rule of the road. Uniform system of buoyage. Leadline, patent log, sounding apparatus. Anchor and cables, windlass and its use.

**Practical** - - - Construction of rope and wire, types of cordage, etc. Usual knots, bends and hitches, whippings, seizings. Splicing in rope and wire, worm, parcel and serve, stoppers. Blocks and tackles, use of purchases. Safe working load. Types of canvas, simple sewing and repairs. Rigging of derricks, description of winches, hatches and cargo gear. To sling a stage and rig a bosun's chair. Proper method of mooring and making lines fast, use of stoppers. Practice in throwing heaving lines. Boatwork. Construction of boats, practical work in launching, pulling and sailing boats. Boat equipment and practice in putting on and adjusting lifejackets. Swimming and lifesaving, methods of resuscitation. Care and maintenance of the ship.

**Signalling** - - - Morse, semaphore and International Code.

## REGULATIONS RELATING TO THE ISSUE OF CERTIFICATES.

In each class there will be a final examination in addition to ordinary class examinations during the session.

There will be two classes of certificate issued—viz., First Class: awarded to students who obtain not less than 80 per cent. of the marks assigned for the whole session's work. Second Class: awarded to students who obtain 60 to 80 per cent. of the total marks.

No student will be granted a certificate who has failed to make at least 75 per cent. of the possible attendances, unless under exceptional circumstances considered by the Principal to merit the award of such certificate.

*The details of the complete syllabus and activities we were put through during our training.*

As I had achieved a First Class Certificate with an 80% pass mark, I was told that I could perhaps go to sea as a deck cadet. Paddy Henderson's, a shipping company in Glasgow, had openings, and I travelled through to have an interview with them…They advised however that being only 15 years old I should go back to college and complete the yearlong course that deck cadets had to carryout onboard the Dolphin. As I had no wish to spend more time at sea school, I thanked them for the interview and said I would just go to sea as a deck boy.

Back in Leith, I reported to the Mercantile Marine office to obtain my discharge book, which is a record of all the vessels seafarers served onboard along with their ability and conduct. I was also issued with a seaman's identity card, which substituted as a passport for merchant seamen.

I applied to The New Zealand Shipping Company for a job and was accepted and informed to go home for Christmas and New Year, and they would contact me when and where to report to them in London.

John and I caught the night train out of Edinburgh to Inverness then onwards to Thurso to catch the MV St Ola home. Russel had already joined a ship and was at sea by then. Being the end of December, the weather was not that good crossing the Pentland Firth, and I was seriously seasick on the trip and wondered what was I thinking of deciding to go to sea as a career.

*The photo shows all the budding seafarers on my course. I am the small chap, middle row, third from the right at only five feet tall and weighing less than eight stones, not really a hardened seaman. Russel is third from right, back row, and John sitting at front right.*

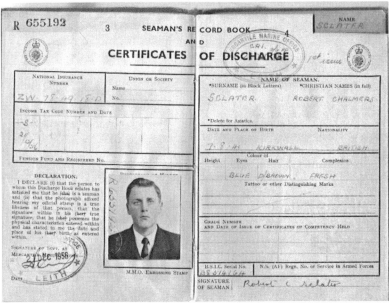

*The TS Dolphin and my first discharge book*

After New Year, I received a telegram to report to the NZSCo agents in Glasgow. They were in fact Paddy Henderson's, the same company I had my interview to go to sea as a cadet so I knew where their offices were in Glasgow.

My father arranged a flight with BEA to fly down from Kirkwall. On arriving in Glasgow, it was too late to go to their offices. The bus from the airport dropped me in St Enoch Square so I booked myself into the station hotel for the night. 'My' pal John Foulis had travelled down by ferry and train, and we met up in Glasgow. We were provided with rail warrants and told to catch the first train to London and report to the NZSCo dock office in Royal Albert Docks the next morning. Arriving at King's Cross in the evening, we had to find a hotel for the night so I booked us into the station hotel. Next morning, we caught the tube to Plaistow station and the bus down to the docks. Remember, I was a scrawny little lad carrying my suitcase with all the working gear required to go to sea. It was still a good walk through the docks to the dock office, and I was very glad to set my case down. In the dock office, we were introduced to Jim Moxley, the shore superintendent (The deck crews on board NZS vessels were knowing as Moxley's Navy) who allocated what vessel you were to serve on. My first ship was to be the MV OTAKI, which was loading general cargo in the Royal Albert Docks and was due to sail for New Zealand within a couple of days. I was told to stay in the Seaman's Mission for the night and report onboard the next day. My friend John was sent to another vessel, and we did not see each other for several years.

*The Royal Docks, Albert Dock is the one on the right of the picture with NZ ships berthed at the top right side as I knew it in 1957.*

*Now London city, Airport*

I climbed up the gangway on 10th January 1957 and found my cabin, which contained four bunks; this was the deck boy/ordinary seamen's accommodation. There were two four-berth cabins for the junior ratings and eight single cabins for the ABs and EDH ratings. The bosun, lamp trimmer (bosuns mate) and the carpenter (chippy) made up the rest of the deck crew.

After storing all my worldly possessions away in my locker and one drawer, I was told that I was now the 'peggy' and was shown to the mess room and instructed that my job was to collect all the meals for the deck crew, and petty officers set the tables, make the tea and wash up after everyone was finished eating. There were two mess rooms, one for the 16 deck crew and a small 5-man mess room for the P.O.s; this included two engine room members, the donkey man and engine room storekeeper along with the bosun, lamp trimmer and chippy.

This was not what I anticipated my job as a seaman would be. I thought that I would be on deck doing nautical work, steering the ship, working with ropes, painting and all the other tasks that I believed seafarers carried out at sea. Anyway, that was not the way a first tripper was expected to learn the ropes; he had to start at the very bottom of the ladder and know his place in the shipboard tradition, which was a hard lesson to start one's career.

Not only did I have to collect all the meals from the galley, clean up after every meal, wash all the dishes, get them ready for the next meal, I also had to scrub the mess room decks along with the alleyways and clean all the toilets and polish brass portholes and all the other brass fittings in the crew's accommodation that were not in the crew cabins.

I officially signed on the ship's articles on 11<sup>th</sup> January, my monthly salary was £12 and 10 shillings a month, and there was a system called an allotment whereby you could send part of your pay home. I sent £5 a month to my mother. We set sail the next day bound for Curacao, Jamaica, then the Panama Canal and onwards to New Zealand. Mid-January in the English Channel is not a very comfortable place to be even on a big ship so once again the seasickness got me.

This of course did not make any difference to my workload. I still had to do all the tasks allocated to me. I was certainly not a happy chap on my first few days at sea. It was a relief to get to my bunk after cleaning up after the evening meal and then dreading the next morning being called at 6:30 to get the breakfast on the table. My seasickness lasted three days and then I got my sea legs, thank goodness. The first few days on board, I was soon to learn the routine of shipboard life. The watch system made up of three watches 12-4, 4-8, and 8-12 was the main routine for all the crewmembers, officers, engineers, greasers, and of course, the deck crew. As I had my duties in the mess room, the watchkeeping did not affect me except for getting meals on the table at the right time for the watchkeepers during the day. The deck watches required two ABs and two ordinary seamen on each watch until the ship was clear of the main shipping lanes then reduced to one AB and two ordinary seamen. Their job was to steer the vessel on two-hour shifts and lookout duties after sunset until daylight. This gave the bosun five ABs (two were on permanent day work) to work on deck during the day washing paint work, painting and overhauling all the cargo running gear and any other task required to keep the vessel in good order. The watchkeepers not steering the vessel also had to work on deck during the day.

The catering staff, stewards, cooks, butcher, baker and galley boy were on day work. The meals were all prepared in the galley, which had a hatch through to the mess room with all the meals placed on the plates and handed through to me, and I placed them in the hot press to keep them warm. I recall the first time I heard of 'tad nabs'; these were the cakes the crew had at smoko a couple of days a week. I was asked if there was any tab nabs and not knowing what they were called said no. I had been given some mince tarts and put them in the hot press, and it was only after smoko that I realised they were the tab nabs; I was learning something new every day. There were also dishes that I was not aware of like curry and rice, something we never had at home; every Friday was fish and chips day with curry for those who did not wish the fish. There were also sheep's brains, and tripe never fancied them.

After the initial three days at sea, I was told that I could earn some overtime in the afternoon by doing some work on deck. This was not a very exciting task, all I had to do was sand and canvas the taff rails. These were the wooden tops of the ship's safety rails around the accommodation; the job entailed having two buckets, one of sand and one of water plus a short length of old canvas hose. You put some water on the rail then some sand and rubbed the mixture back and forth with the piece of canvas. This resulted in removing all the grime on the wood, and when the wet sand was washed off, the wood looked new again. Not a job that would be done at sea anymore; they are now all varnished or made of metal. It was a bit pointless as within a few weeks the wood was back to being tarnished again. At least I got out of the mess room for a couple of hours and was paid the princely sum of three shillings an hour, that's just over 15 pence in today's money. The weather was improving by this time and getting warmer; as we sailed south, the first land I saw was the Azores, all very interesting for a first tripper. Shipboard life was now in a standard routine with various additional activities taking place. Every Wednesday and Saturday, we had the captain's inspection of the ship. Along with his senior officers, they would check the cleanliness of all the accommodation onboard. I did get some help from other ordinary seaman on these days to help with the scrubbing and cleaning of the crew's quarters. This was a very detailed inspection as the captain had a torch, which he shone in every nook and cranny to see if there was any dirt or dust, and if so, a quick reprimand was given, always glad when it was over. We also had fire and boat drills on Fridays; my station on fire drills was bridge messenger. I recall the first ever drill; the captain told me to give his compliments to the chief officer and tell him that he could now cease the fire drill and proceed to lifeboat stations. As I had no idea who the chief officer was, I asked the first man in uniform where I might find the chief officer; after some time, I did find him and pass on the captain's orders. Little did I know at that time that in a few years I would in fact be the chief officer on board the Otaki, a lot of water would pass under the bridge before then and lot of exciting times at sea.

With the weather improving all the time, things did not feel so bad as my first few days onboard. We started to see the yellow weed drifting up from the Caribbean on the Gulf Stream in the Sargossa Sea. Then the flying fish started to be seen skimming across the calm sea; there were pods of porpoises/dolphins also swimming around the ship and the odd spume from a whale all very exciting for a young lad. We eventually sailed into the Caribbean, the islands being the first land for several days; they all looked very lush and green.

*The Flying Fishes*

After a few days at sea, I was to learn about a predecessor of the MV Otaki, which sailed during the First World War. In the officers' dining saloon was a Victoria Cross in a glass case. This was only one of the two VCs won by Merchant Seamen during the war. Captain Bisset Smith was master onboard the older SS Otaki and was involved in a sea battle with a German sea raider in the Atlantic west of the Azores in March 1917. The SS Moewe, a well-armed raider, had already sunk several British Merchant ships and had about 400 POW onboard. The Otaki was very lightly armed and Captain Bisset Smith was told to surrender and stop his ship by the Master of the Moewe. Captain Bisset Smith decided to fight. Unfortunately, although he did damage the German vessel, the Otaki was sunk with the loss of five crewmembers, and Captain Bisset Smith went down with his ship. He was posthumously awarded the VC for his bravery. Several years later, the family put the VC up for sale and the company bought it and placed onboard the OTAKI. I will touch on this story later in my memoirs.

The Otaki arrived in Curacao for bunkers and tied up in Caracas Bay just along the coast from the main town Willemstad, a town I would spend a month in a few years later. There was not very much in Caracas Bay except a swimming pool that was fenced off from the sea. The water was crystal clear, lovely and warm with all kinds of exotic fish swimming very close by.

The bunkering took about 12 hours as I recall then we set sail for Jamaica just over a day's sailing away. The radio in the mess room was on most of the time and the music of the Caribbean was so energetic to listen and made washing dishes a much easier task. The soap used was a hard brick placed in a tin can full of holes over the hot tap, and as the hot water hit the soap, it melted and gave a reasonable amount of lather to wash the dishes but always was left with a scum, not the most hygienic. There was no fresh milk in those days either so I had to make milk from dry powder (chalk and water it was known as). The main milk used in the crew's tea was tinned condensed milk, not the most refreshing. Although scurvy was a thing of the past, every ship had flagons of Board of Trade lime juice for the crew, terrible stuff. There were also salt tablets. I took one once and was instantly sick and never took them again. Anyway, we arrived in Kingston, Jamaica, to load some bananas for New Zealand and playing on the radio was the famous *Banana Boat* song sung by Harry Belafonte, just newly released by him; the words were exactly what we were doing, very apt. Whilst in Kingston, I was to see what real poverty was, the garbage from the mess room and galley was placed in drums on the after deck ready to be taken ashore whilst in port; it was always thrown overboard whilst at sea. On taking my gash bucket down to dump, I found a couple of the dockers going through the garbage and picking out discarded food; it certainly opened my eyes to what life was really like in these islands. I was to see a lot more poverty over my years at sea in many parts of the world.

I did manage a run ashore and went to the seaman's mission that had a nice swimming pool, always loved a swim when I got a chance. Had a walk around Kingston, which was not really a safe place to be on one's own so we made sure there were always a few us together. On one ship I was there later on, one of the crew was mugged in broad daylight on the Main Street.

We then sailed for the Panama Canal about 40 hours' sailing time. I was of course told by the crew to start saving all the stale bread for the mules that helped to pull the ship through the canal. This of course was just a bit of fun as the mules were in fact electrically operated machines that assisted the ship through the locks in the canal. There was always some smart Alec on the ship who tried to make a fool of first trippers, go and ask the lamp trimmer for a sky hook, run up to the mate's office and ask him for a long stand. I never really fell for their tricks. It did however make you understand human nature and how to figure out the genuine people onboard and also the con merchants who loved to take the mickey, and whenever they could swing the lead, the old saying for someone getting out of a job, he should be doing and getting someone else to do it. Being at sea in close proximity with so many seafarers certainly helped me to judge people as to what their true abilities and character were and how to spot a phoney, usually, the one that talked a lot and knew everything and always said that his last ship was always the best.

*Fenced off swimming pool Caracas Bay Curaçao*

We arrived in Panama and started our transit of the canal, which consisted of a series of locks, one set at the Caribbean end and a further two sets at the Pacific end. The first was the Gatun locks; after entering the locks with the assistance of the famous mules, the gate was shut and the water from the lock above was pumped into the one below until the ship had risen up level, with the second lock the gate was opened and the ship then went dead slow ahead into the next lock assisted by the mules who kept the vessel in the middle of the lock there being four mules each side, two forward and two aft port and starboard…

Once the vessel had risen up the four locks, she sailed through Gatun Lake to the next set called Pedro Miguel that consisted of two locks which lowered the ship.

Then onwards to the last set Mira Flores that had three locks down into the Pacific Ocean, the total raising and lowering was 85 feet, total transit about 10 hours depending on other shipping using the canal.

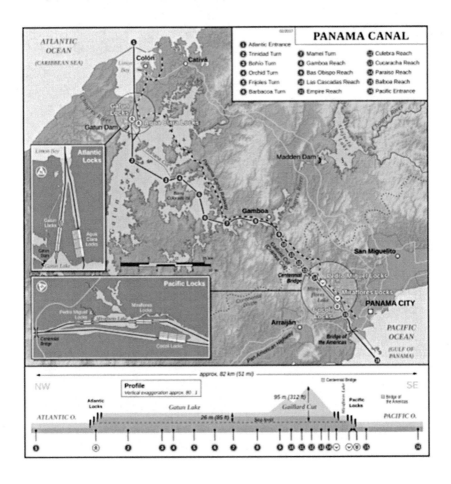

The crew that was not required to steer the vessel through the canal or on standby had the great job of washing down the Otaki with the freshwater from the Gatun Lake. This was a task carried out every time we passed through the canal as it helped to get rid of a lot of salt from the sea water sprayed onboard in bad weather.

The Panama Canal authority place their own crewmen onboard to make fast the mules who are assisted by ship's crew when required. The canal pilots take full control of the ship unlike normal pilotage where the orders are to pilot's advice and master's command, the captain in the canal does not in fact have full command. When I did my first trip through the canal, it was under the control of the USA, but now it is owned and operated by the Panama Government. Of course, a lot of this detail was not known to me when I first went through the canal, but over 20 years at sea and more than 30 times transiting the canal, I was well versed in all aspect of the Panama Canal. The top photo shows the mules that were operating after 1963 with the original black painted mules in the photo below assisting the P&O passenger ship S.S. Oriana through the canal back in the 1950s.

I was in fact on one of the first ships to trial the new Mitsubishi mules in 1963. They were much more efficient and one could do the job of two of the old mules. The operator on the old mules had two control cabs whereas the new mules had one cab in the middle which saved the controller changing cabs every time the ship he had to control was either westbound or eastbound; the new mules were much more powerful and high tech. They helped to cut down the time spent in the locks which greatly increased the efficiency of the canal operations.

After clearing the last set of locks, we headed out the buoyed channel into the Pacific and onwards to New Zealand, which would take between 18 to 19 days' steaming. The only land we saw on the way was the Galápagos Islands off in the distance. The trip across the Pacific was a very pleasant part of my first trip with lovely calm seas and warm weather. I worked on deck most afternoons washing and painting various parts of the ship along with other shipboard tasks.

Once a week, we had a film on deck; this was always a highlight watching a movie under the stars. As the ship required someone on the wheel all the time no automatic steering (iron mike) in those days, I was allowed to learn how to steer the vessel during some of my afternoon duties. A steering certificate was required to obtain an efficient deck hand EDH certificate, which I obtained in 1960. It was very satisfying to come off the wheel and look aft and see the ship's wake to prove you were steering a straight course. We steered using the gyro compass to keep the vessel on the right heading; it was easier and more accurate than the magnetic compasses.

With these balmy days at sea, everyone was getting very suntanned; some of the older hands were brown as berries. I unfortunately having not seen such hot sun in Orkney soon got a bit sunburnt so had to keep my shirt on when out on deck in the afternoon. Shipboard routine continued the same for me on the trip across the Pacific, getting the mess room ready for meals, scrubbing, washing, making 'smoko' morning and afternoons, cleaning up after evening meals. I did enjoy when I finished in the evening after dumping my gash bucket over the aft end, sitting watching the flying fish and occasionally the porpoises close to the ship. Further south, the majestic albatrosses appeared gliding along with their wing tips nearly touching the sea they followed the ship all the way to NZ. They were always on hand to pick up scraps from the garbage thrown overboard. Although it is now illegal to throw anything overboard, the oceans are getting more polluted every year; so much plastics being dumped not only by ships but from many land locations. Although when in port we had to dump our garbage in to garbage barges, they sailed out to deep water and dumped everything into the sea so no wonder the sea is now polluted. Most of my garbage was food scraps so no pollution there.

The day before arrival in New Zealand, the clocks were advanced 24 hours as travelling west the clocks had been retarded every day to ensure that noon occurred at twelve o'clock when the midday sights were taken to calculate our latitude. This meant we were a day behind New Zealand when we reached the

International Date Line; so, we had to jump a day. We got it back on the way home, had two Fridays or whatever day of the week we crossed the International Date Line.

On arrival in Auckland, I was taken off mess room duties and one of the ordinary seamen was given my job. This was a great relief for me after a month looking after the crew. In port, the ordinary seamen were placed on gangway duties on the standard watchkeeping rota 8-12 12-4 and 4-8, they were responsible for keeping the gangway at a safe height for everyone to board and disembark safely, the wharfies in NZ were sticklers on safety. The gangway duties entailed, keeping a check on everyone coming onboard, safety watch during the night, regular checks around the ship, polishing the ship's bell and all outside brass fittings. We also had to make sure that the flags were ready for breaking out at 0800 every morning. This consisted of the stem jack forward the curtesy flag (flag of the country you are, in this case NZ) on the fore mast yard arm, the NZSCo house flag on the main mast and the Red Ensign on the jack staff aft. The flags were rolled up and raised to the truck except the red ensign; the officer of the watch would blow his whistle and each flag was broken out or raised; eight bells were rung on the forward bell; this was carried out by nearly all ships in port. The main UK shipping companies besides NZS were Port Line, Blue Star Line, Shaw Savile and Albion, odd occasion Ben Line.

This flag routine is a thing of the past and would only be carried out now onboard naval vessels in port. This was my duties for most of the time on the NZ coast, what a difference it made having some real seamanship jobs to do. It was also great to get some fresh milk when on the NZ coast; the old chalk and water was banned until we set sail for home.

There was also some work cleaning in the holds of the ship getting ready to load the refrigerated cargo after we were fully discharged. As there was a shortage of manpower from ashore, crewmembers were offered a chance to earn some extra money paid directly by the cleaning companies to help wash and clean all the spaces in the ship's holds, a handy bit of pocket money known as shore pay.

As I recall, although it was sixty years ago, we discharged in Auckland, Napier, Wellington and Lyttelton. We had carried out all kinds of general cargo from cars, cars in boxes (CKD) to be assembled in NZ, buses, railway carriages and locomotives, books, magazines, personal effects of emigrants coming to live in NZ, steel girders and other parts for the Auckland Harbour Bridge (under construction in 1954–59), refrigerators, washing machines and every other thing including the kitchen sink.

Once we completed discharge, the ship was ready to load for the UK. The cargo for the homeward voyage was frozen lamb, butter, cheese, apples, wool, which we loaded in Timaru, Bluff, Nelson and Auckland. The homeward voyage was basically the same route as the outward trip via Panama and Curacao. I was back on mess room duties once again. We arrived back in the UK with Glasgow being our first port where we paid off. I received £55 for the trip with £20 allotment at home.

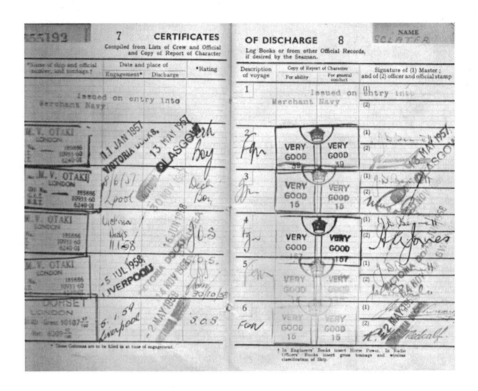

*First page of my discharge book along with vessels and positions I held*

After my second trip whilst home on leave, I found out that an old school friend Norman Muir (Stumper to his friends) had been to the Dolphin, and I said I would try and get him on the same ship as me for his first voyage; the company was happy for this to happen so we sailed together for two trips. Our first trip was once again to NZ with Norman now being the 'peggy'. I was able to shown him the ropes in a better fashion than I received on my first trip. We did the usual discharge and loading in NZ. We visited a few Orcadian cousins of Norman's who had emigrated and lived in Christchurch and Lyttleton. Meeting folk from home was always a treat and I used to enjoy these visits. On our return voyage, we started discharge in Dunkirk and Antwerp. Whilst in Antwerp we took the train up to Brussels to see the World Expo, the first of its kind since before the war. It was quite a sight for two 16-year-olds visiting all the various country's pavilions, and I remember the experience to this day. We also had our first serious hangovers on the Otaki. We had arrived back in Liverpool after our second trip together and decided to go ashore and see if we could get into a pub. We were still only 17 at the time. As we had heard of a drink called a Black and Tan, beer mixed with Guinness, we managed to get away with drinking this in one pub. We staggered back to the ship after only having two of three and were both violently sick and had terrible sore heads the next day. Certainly, learned a lesson on drinking although probably over the years to come did not learn from it.

I did have a few incidents in my early days at sea. The first was my fourth voyage on MV Otaki. One morning whilst on gangway duties in Sydney, I took a very bad pain in my stomach but did nothing about it. Later in the day, as I was still feeling pretty ill, Norman contacted the chief officer about my problem. He in turn contacted the agent who arranged a doctor to come and see me. I was diagnosed with sever appendicitis and taken ashore and had my appendix removed that evening. The doctor came and gave me my appendix in a glass tube to take home; my mother kept it in her glass case for nearly 20 years. The chief officer on my first trip on the Otaki actually died of a burst appendix some years later whilst in command of an NZSCo vessel, not something one should ignore when suffering from unexplained stomach pains.

I was fortunate that this did not happen halfway across the Indian Ocean on the voyage home or I would have been in trouble with the chief officer having to do the operation. I was in hospital for a couple of days then sent to a convalescent home on the outskirts of Sydney at Brighton-le-Sands for five days. This was the area where Captain Cook first landed in Australia back in 1770 in Botany Bay. I recall an Irish motorman was also in the home and asked me for a loan of some money, said he would pay me back in a couple of days, gave him a few pounds he cleared off the next day, and I never saw my money again, another sound lesson was learned in this case, not to lend money to people you don't know, was always wary of the Irish after that. The ship had sailed to Adelaide, and I was flown back to join her for the trip home. I was put on light duties for the voyage home, which made life very easy.

I was pretty good at sign writing by the end of the voyage as I hand-painted all the life belts with the ship's name and port of registry, also all the wooden numbered tags on the bridge which indicted the course to steer by the three compasses.

I was of course by this time a junior ordinary seaman with no mess room duties but on the standard watchkeeping rota so took my turn steering the ship and also lookout duties during the night watches. On the voyage home via the Indian Ocean, I was promoted to senior ordinary seaman. As we came home via the Suez Canal, we stopped in Aden for bunkers. This port was always a highlight for us young seafarers; although we did not get ashore, the locals came out in small rowing boats to sell their wares, everything from transistor radios, toys, binoculars, tea sets, clothing, flipflops, you name it, the 'bum boats', as they were affectionately called, had everything to barter with. The deal was done by shouting to them, and once agreement was reached, they would send up a basket with your purchases, and you would send the money down in the basket. I bought a great number of items to take home to my family.

*Photo of 'bum' boats in Aden. Great fun bartering with the crews.*

We then sailed up the Red Sea to the Suez Canal, another interesting place to see. There are no locks in the Suez as the Mediterranean is at the same level as the Red Sea. My first transit of the canal was during the day so we could see quite a lot of the countryside; on the starboard side was the Sinai desert, sand for miles, but on the port side, it's was quite well cultivated with lots of little hamlets along the canal. I did transit during the night on a couple of voyages when a large searchlight was attached to the bow of the ship to help the canal pilot see the way as there were few navigation lights back in the 50s. There were still some wrecks in the canal from the Suez War in 1956, not the safest place to be during the conflict with Israel over several years. After four trips on the MV Otaki, I decided to try another ship. Joined the MV Dorset in Liverpool and sailed to Australia. I recall leaving Orkney right after New Year to join the ship in Liverpool. Set off at 0800 on 4th January to catch the St Ola across the Pentland Firth and then train down to Liverpool. Had to catch three trains, Thurso to Inverness, Inverness to Glasgow, Glasgow to Liverpool, arrived onboard at 1600 on the 5th, was signed on and sailed that night about 2200 for Australia and would you believe was on the 12-4 watch. I was well and truly glad to get to my bunk after that. It was back to the old sea routine watchkeeping, working on deck and doing all the usual jobs. We sailed through Suez once again, this time at night, surprising how cold it got at night in the canal close to the desert; the canal crew men who looked after the search light were able to sit in the large metal case as the lamp kept them warm. Us seamen on lookout were not so warm standing on the focle head. Whilst in Australia we were anchored close to the Sydney Harbour Bridge for a couple of days awaiting to load so we had a liberty boat laid on to go ashore. It so happened that the steps where we landed to get ashore was just where the Sydney Opera House is now situated, and on the day they laid the foundation stone, I stepped ashore just when they were having the ceremony. After this four months' trip, I thought I would give up the sea and work at home in my father's haulage business as my older brother was due to join the army for his national service, and I would take his job. Unfortunately, or not as the case may be, he never got called up until later in 1959, and I got fed up with home life and headed back to sea in October. At least, I passed my driving test when home, which would have been difficult any other time as I was never home long enough to sit the test. Next page is the MV Otaki and MV Dorset passing under Sydney Harbour Bridge when I was onboard.

In October 1959, I joined the MV Hororata in Liverpool; she was once the largest refrigerated vessel in the world built in 1942 and saw active service during the war. The ship was loading general cargo in Liverpool, and the day before, we sailed a truckload of large 40-gallon drums, arrived they were very solid and heavy, and we were informed by the dockers they came from

Windscale, now known as Sellafield, the atomic installation north of Liverpool. They were stacked on deck and lashed down ready for us departing and heading for New Zealand via Panama. We left Liverpool bound for Curacao, and after a couple of days at sea, we had crossed the 100-fathom line into the Atlantic; the deck crew were told by the bosun to remove the ship's siderails next to these drums and set up a small wooden ramp supplied with them to help run them over the gunwale of the ship's side. They were unlashed and rolled over the side into the Atlantic. The crew doing the task were given rubber gloves and wore rubber aprons to do the job. Always wondered what was in these drums, was it possibly atomic waste material; it was all very hush-hush.

The old routine was the norm onboard steering the ship, lookout duties, overhauling the cargo gear, oiling and greasing the stays on the masts, washing and painting the ship. This is where I came to a sad end, the derricks (booms used for loading and discharging) were lowered into cradles when at sea and were about 10 feet above the main deck when stowed. These were washed before being painted.

I and another ordinary seaman was tasked with the job and got our two buckets of water, one soapy and one fresh tied together to hang over the derrick, you then straddled it and slid along to wash them. I got my two buckets across my one and then took the other two, and just as I went to put them over the derrick, my foot slipped and I ended up on the deck 10 feet below. I was lucky that my back hit the winch underneath on the way down that turned my body so I landed face down on the steel deck. There was a ring bolt on the deck which I landed on, and I severely broke my right arm. I was lucky I was not killed as I could have landed on my head and broken my neck. The chief officer arrived on deck and had a look at my arm and said it looked sprained and would put a splint on it and give me some pain killers; we were still three days away from Curacao so no doctor until then. I was taken off duty and given the odd pain killer and told if my arm was broken, I would know all about it; the chief officer still reckoned it was just a bad sprain. We arrived in Curacao, and the doctor came onboard, took one look at my arm and told me to pack my bags as I must come ashore immediately for treatment and would not be coming back onboard. My arm was now twice it's normal size, all black and blue with the bottom of my wrist adjacent to where the top of my wrist should be and not looking very normal. I was taken to the doctor's surgery where he and his assistant were to set my arm.

He stuck a needle in my wrist, which he broke, took another go and managed to deaden my arm then he took my hand and the assistant my arm, and they pulled against each other until they had my arm looking straight; he then pushed the bones together and slapped a plaster cast around it, and I was then taken to the local hospital in Willemstad where I stayed for five days.

Curacao was part of the Netherland Antilles so Dutch was the main language; of course they have always been fluent English speakers so no problem with speaking to the doctors and nurses and other patients. After the five days, I was checked out and placed in the seaman's mission in Willemstad until a ship could take me home.

This was to take much longer than I thought as there appeared to no ship willing to take me for another three weeks. I spent my time walking around the town watching the shipping coming into Willemstad through the famous swing bridge that cut the town in two when opened. I met some interesting people during my stay in Curacao, seamen who were stuck ashore in the mission for one reason or another. I recall the Dutch seafarers in the mission would enjoy white bread and butter with chocolate vermicelli sprinkled on it for breakfast, tasted very good but only ever tried it in Curacao. We were provided with money from the shipping agents S.E.l Muduro & Sons, and we enjoyed a few Cuba liber, the famous Caribbean drink, when we did have a few guilders to spend. I had to get weekly check-ups with the doctor, and just before I got a ship home, he removed the plaster cast on my arm and gave me instructions on exercises to help strengthen my arm, which still looked in pretty bad shape. I was to buy my first pair of Wrangler jeans in Curacao; this was a must have for most merchant seaman back in the 1950s. I remember coming home from sea and advising a school friend of mine whose family owned a draper's shop in Kirkwall that he should try and get hold of Wrangler clothing to sale in his shop. Many years later, he said I had given him the best advice ever as Wranglers did become a big selling mark in the UK.

*MV Hororata, you can see the height of No 2 hatch derricks quite a distance from the hard steel deck below where I landed luckily not on my head.*

*Curacao Boat Bridge*

Eventually, the Shaw Savile Ship Wairangi homeward bound from New Zealand offered to take me home as a DBS (Distressed British Seaman). Onboard were two Orcadians, Jimmy Brown from Stromness and Jock Hourston from South Ronaldsay. Jimmy was an AB so I had a lot in common with him whereas Jock was third engineering officer so never did speak to him but had a lifelong friendship with Jimmy. I did in fact become friendly with Jock many years later when he was chief engineer on MV St Ola. Also on board was a famous Barra seaman Donald MacNeil, the mad piper as he was known, quite a character; he was reputed to have stood on the top of a samson post on one ship playing the bagpipes, a very dangerous thing to do especially as he was drunk. He was a different person when sober, which he was on the voyage back across the Atlantic. I sailed with a great number of Western Isles seaman, some of the best seamen you could meet. Their only problem was that they tended to enjoy a drink and could get quite tipsy. They would then start singing in the Gaelic; it was something else, not what I would call melodic music, but they seemed to enjoy belting it out in the early hours of the morning after a night on the booze.

Anyway, to get back to my story, we arrived back in London early January, and I made my way home. It took another three months for my arm to get fully better. I was covered by a sick note from the doctor for the duration and received a weekly social security payment of a few pounds. I eventually joined the MV Hinakura in April, some four months after breaking my arm and set sail again for New Zealand on my last trip as ordinary seaman.

The voyage was the same out via Curacao, Panama and across the Pacific, nothing too exciting on the voyage out. Whilst in Wellington I was busy brushing up on my seamanship skills as I was due to sit my EDH certificate when back in the UK. Whilst splicing some wire one of the strands flipped across my eye and just about blinded me. I was sent to the local hospital where the doctor placed a large padded bandage over my eye as there was no way they could do anything with the scratch on my eyeball. I felt quite foolish walking about with this big patch over my eye. It did eventually heal up, but to this day when getting an eye check-up, the optician still comments on the scratch on my eye. Once again, a lucky escape, could have lost my sight and most probably would have ended my career on deck.

After arriving back in the UK and on my way home, I stopped in Aberdeen and took my Efficient Deck Hand (EDH) exams at the Ministry of Transport offices and passed, so I was now no longer an ordinary seaman and with the step up would enjoy a two-berth cabin instead of the ordinary seamen four-berth cabin. I sailed on several ships in this capacity trading back and forth to New Zealand and Australia. We carried general cargo out and mostly refrigerated cargo home, also lots of bales of NZ and Australian wool, which both countries are renowned for.

Since starting this reminiscence, other incidents have popped into my mind; I recall on my second voyage on MV Otaki, we were loading tinned pineapple in Brisbane in to hatch Number 5 right next to the crew accommodation and the wharfies passed a few cases to the crew to savour on the homeward-bound voyage. I really enjoyed them whilst on night watch duties. To this day when I eat tinned pineapple, it brings back memories of that trip. This was totally against the law, but at that time, it was not my problem. It certainly was when I became an officer. I found out just how much pilfering went on by dockers/wharfies in nearly every port over the coming years at sea. I will cover this later on in my story.

My first voyage as EDH was onboard the MV Pipiriki, which I joined in Falmouth dry dock. It was common for NZSco ships to spend time in Falmouth either in dry dock or laid up awaiting cargoes to load or sail light ship out in time for the lamb/fruit seasons in NZ. We did load general cargo in several UK ports bound for NZ. After discharging in NZ, we part loaded frozen lamb, butter, cheese and wool and then completed loading in Hobart Tasmania. This consisted mainly of apples and pears. On the homeward-bound voyage from Hobart, we were crossing the Australian Bight in very heavy weather, and I was tasked with other deck crew to check and secure a deck cargo of apples bound for the military garrison in Aden. After checking that all the bottle screws securing the wire lashing were tightened up, we went to check the locking bars on the forward hatch; whilst doings this a massive wave came over the focle head, and I was washed down the deck, suffered a few bruises but not washed overboard thank goodness, quite a frightening couple of minutes…The cases of apples arrived safely in Aden and were discharged into the Royal Marines landing craft, and I am sure they were very much appreciated.

One other near accident occurred when I was instructed to retrieve the ship's log line. This was the line attached to a rotator and a mileage clock, which was secured to the ship's rail on the stern of the ship, and it gave the distance travelled, not a speedometer as some folk believe. It was usually only streamed on ocean voyages; the clock was read at midday and then reset to zero for the next 24 hours. The watches were still singled up so just three crew on duty, one on the wheel, one on lookout and me on standby. It really was a two-man job as you did require the drum end of the winch to help pull the line in that was 40 fathoms long (240 feet ) and someone to control the winch. On this occasion, there was only me. With some difficulty, I managed to pull the line to the winch, which I had already started running, got the rope around the barrel and started pulling it in. To get the kinks and turns out of it, you paid it out again and then reversed the winch to take it fully in. Just as I tried to do this, my foot caught in a bight of the rope, and I was heading leg first over the barrel. Luckily, the winch window was open, and I managed to reach in and switched it off; otherwise, I would have had my brains knocked out going around the barrel foot first. Never tried that again, never told the officer of the watch either.

*Walkers Cherub Ships log Clock and Rotators*

I mentioned that on watches at sea; there was always a lookout on the focle head during the hours of darkness on some occasions we would run into bad weather. The ship would plunge into the heavy swells that one could encounter and the waves would crash over the bow. Quite frightening not knowing when an extra big wave would hit you, as you hid under the bulwarks. You could not leave your post until the officer of the watch called you or flashed the Aldis lamp to get you off the focle, which on occasions seemed a long time whilst you ducked the waves. We were then stationed on the monkey island above the bridge that was much safer and sheltered. The task of lookout was to ring the ship's bell if you saw a ship/light, one ding for starboard, two for port and three dead ahead. If you met up with a fishing fleet off the Spanish Coast, you could be ringing the bell nonstop. Kept you on your toes when sailing near land but saw very few ships crossing the Pacific. Although most of my time at sea was in lovely warm calm weather, you could encounter some heavy seas in the Atlantic leaving and arriving back in the UK. The South Pacific could also throw up some heavy swells with a southerly weather system. Just missed a couple of hurricanes in the Caribbean did hit the tail ends so heavy seas there as well. The Mediterranean could also throw up quite short heavy seas. The coldest weather was the trip up to New York and Halifax Nova Scotia in December on board the MV Haparangi. As it was nearly Christmas, the ladies from the seaman's mission in New York presented everyone onboard with a present consisting of a pair of warm socks, a housewife sewing kit and a bar of chocolate. It was always nice to pay a visit to the various seamen's missions overseas especially in NZ and Australia. The Flying Angel and British Sailors Society Missions being found in nearly every port. The Chaplin would always try to organise a football match against other ships in port, all good fun. The temperature in New York at that time was 20 degrees below freezing, which made working on deck very difficult. The canvas hatch covers were rock solid when trying to secure them over the hatch's and took a lot of pulling and persuading to get them secured. It was also freezing standing on lookout.

The North Atlantic is not a hospitable or calm ocean at this time of year, very little work done on deck on the trip back to the UK due to heavy seas encountered. No lookout on the focle then that's for sure.

My last voyage on deck was onboard the MV Hauraki where we sailed out to Australia to discharge in Fremantle, Adelaide, Geelong, Melbourne, Brisbane (Christmas there) Townsville (had New Year there) then up to Cairns to complete quite an interesting trip. Was able to visit Green Island and snorkel on the Great Barrier Reef.

We then sailed down to New Zealand to load. Was the first ship to use the all weather loading gantries in Bluff, a big day for the port that allowed ships to load frozen lamb, etc. without stopping for rain. We also loaded cargo in Timaru, Lyttleton, Auckland, New Plymouth and then headed home via Panama, a round the world trip. This would be my last voyage as a deck hand as things were to change on my next leave at home.

My time on deck was very interesting and informative in my early life. Starting off as deck boy standing 5 ft tall and weighing in at less than 8 stone, I had my work cut out in standing up for myself with some quite obnoxious crewmembers. After my first two trips, I grew to 5 ft 10 in and put on about 2 stone in weight so not such a scrawny little guy. It was an eyeopener to meet seamen from all parts of the UK and trying to understand some of the strange accents, scouse, Geordie, cockney and lots of others from around the country. I know my accent Orcadian was difficult so did have to try and change it a bit to be understood. I also became aware of the different lifestyles of crewmembers, the gay community was very prevalent on ships back in those days as a good number of the stewards were of this persuasion. I found them all very likeable and first class at their jobs. It was an eyeopener of course for a lad from the islands, who had never actually been in contact with this type of person before. I recall when in Wellington one trip, two big passenger ships, the Dominican Monarch and the Captain Cook, where most of the catering department were gay. These passenger ships carried out a number of the £10 immigrants from the UK at that time plus other passengers. When in port, together they held a Gala Night known as the D.M. Ball where they all dressed up in their finest dresses and paraded around the hall, quite a sight; of course, it was totally illegal back in the sixties, but the authorities left them alone. Another interesting situation arose when I was waiting to catch the night train up to a Newcastle to join the Haurki. With plenty of time to spare, I had a stroll outside King's Cross station and noticed this very posh car and had a look at it. Just then, this very smart dapper chap in a trilby hat came up and started speaking to me. Asked where I was going so I explained I was waiting for the night train to Newcastle to join my ship. He then said it was his car and would I like a run around London in it to pass the time. I suppose I was a bit naïve, but with a few hours to kill, I thought, yes, why not? So, we set off and saw the interesting sights of London. Then he said would I like to come home for some tea. He seemed a nice chap so I went with him. It turned out once inside his very stylish flat that he also was a homosexual and said he liked me. I told him that I was not interested and that perhaps he should take me back to the station ASAP. I was not frightened of him, and I think he knew this so he drove me back to the station, and I thanked him for the interesting afternoon. A few years later, I saw the press coverage of the Jeremy Thorpe MP case and thought my god that looks really like the guy who picked me up in London. Another lesson learned, be wary of strangers offering gifts/lifts! The above little stories give an idea of what one encountered going to sea.

By 1963, I had circumnavigated the world in both directions sailing through the Panama and Suez Canals and steered ships through both. Travelled across three oceans and sailed more than seven seas. Been to most ports in New Zealand and Australia, called into New York and Halifax NS, Fiji, Jamaica, Curacao and several ports in Europe. Seen some wonderful sights and enjoyed most of my trips. I had chipped, scrapped, washed and painted everything from the top of the main mast to the boot topping on the ship. Oiled and greased wires, blocks, stays and all other running gear on the ship. Holy stoned wooden decks, cleaned brass, spliced wire and ordinary rope and all the other task required by deck hands on board. I felt that now I was the seaman I thought I was when I left the Dolphin, certainly realised that I knew very little about shipboard life when I first went to sea.

Although I mention NZSCo, there was in fact two companies, the FSNCo being the other. The Federal Steam Navigation Company vessels all had English County names whereas the New Zealand Shipping Company's vessel all had Maori names. Cross flags was the term used for both companies; many of the ships were sister ships, the only difference being the funnels. NZSCo were buff whereas the FSNCo were black with a St George's Cross with a black square in the middle. In NZ and Australia, they were affectionately called large Pommy meat boats. Both companies were in fact owned by P&O Ltd.

On the following pages, there are a few photos and certificates of my time on deck. The Brussels Atomium and the photo of Norman and myself brings back happy memories of our visit to Expo 58. The lads with the flag are onboard the MV Pipiriki, average age of deck crew was only 19 years old, I'm the one under the S on the flag. The other photo of splicing wire reminds me of nearly losing my eye. Horse riding in the Australian outback near Bowen Queensland in 1957. Looking smart in gangway boy uniform in Suva Fiji.

Steering Certificate

MERCHANT SHIPPING (CERTIFICATES OF COMPETENCY AS A.B.)
REGULATIONS, 1959

Surname  SCLATER                    Other Names  Robert Chalmers

Discharge Book No.  R.655192        Rating  S.O.S.

R.655192  R Slater        Usual Signature of Seaman

This is to certify that the above-named seaman served as  S.O.S.  from

8.4.60  to  6.8.60

in the  **HINAKURA**  * being a ship  (other than a fishing boat) having a gross tonnage
**183041**  being a sailing ship

**LONDON**
*of 100 tons or more or a sailing ship having a gross tonnage  time took turns at the wheel in steering the ship (apart from periods of instruction)
of 40

for periods amounting in the aggregate to  70 Seventy  hours.
(in words)

*Delete line which is inapplicable.

Date  6.8.60.                                            Master

N.B.—Regulation 4(1)(e) of the above Regulations provides that an applicant for a Certificate of Competency as Able Seaman must, apart
from periods of instruction, have taken turns at the wheel in steering a ship (other than a fishing boat) having a gross tonnage of
100 tons or more or a sailing ship having a gross tonnage of 40 tons or more, for periods totalling at least 10 hours.

Regulation 9(1)(b) provides that the above requirement must be complied with before a seaman can take the qualifying examination
prescribed by Regulation 4(1)(c) and the First Schedule. (This is the examination for which successful candidates receive an Efficient
Deck Hand Certificate).

D99432 58777 M/1683 5M 2/60 FHB 727

*A copy showing details of a paying off chit. Letter required to confirm length of time at sea to sit for Second Mates Foreign Going Certificate.*

No. **53873**

# CERTIFICATE OF QUALIFICATION AS
# AN EFFICIENT DECK HAND.

| Name and Description of Candidate | | | | | |
|---|---|---|---|---|---|
| Name in Full | | Year of Birth | Number of Discharge Book | Height | |
| | | | | ft. | ins. |
| ROBERT CHALMERS SCLATER | | 1941 | R.655192 | | |

| Colour of | | Complexion | Tattoo or other Distinguishing Marks |
|---|---|---|---|
| Eyes | Hair | | |
| Blue | D/Brn. | Fresh | Nil |

This is to Certify that the above-named seaman was examined on the _____14th_____ day of _____October,_____ 19 60 , by an examiner appointed by the Ministry of Transport and Civil Aviation and that he proved to the satisfaction of the examiner that he is an Efficient Deck Hand.

Initials of Issuing Officer

Office Date Stamp

14 OCT 1960

59946.8829.16?

_D.C.Hardgrave_

An Under-Secretary of the Ministry of Transport and Civil Aviation.

Signature of Seaman _R Sclater_

*Atomium Brussels 1958*

# THE NEW ZEALAND SHIPPING COMPANY, LTD.
*(Incorporated in New Zealand)*

# FEDERAL STEAM NAVIGATION COMPANY, LTD.

JBS/GM.

ROYAL ALBERT DOCK, LONDON, E.16

Telephone: ALBERT DOCK 3044   Telegrams: NUZEDOC, ALDOCK, LONDON

### SUPERINTENDENTS' DEPARTMENT

MARINE CREW.      14th May 1963.

TO WHOM IT MAY CONCERN.

THIS IS TO CERTIFY that Mr.ROBERT CHALMERS SCLATER
(Dis.A.No. R.655192) of Town Hall House, Kirkwall, served
on Deck in this Company's vessels, as follows:-

| | | | |
|---|---|---|---|
| 11. 1.57 | 13. 5.57 | m.v."OTAKI" | Deck Boy. |
| 8. 6.57 | 30.11.57 | m.v."OTAKI" | Deck Boy. |
| 11. 1.58 | 16. 6.58 | m.v."OTAKI" | Jun.Ord.Seaman. |
| 5. 7.58 | 14.11.58 | m.v."OTAKI" | Jun.Ord.Seaman. |
| | | (promoted S.O.S. 30.10.58) | |
| 5. 1.59 | 2. 5.59 | s.s."DORSET" | Sen.Ord.Seaman. |
| 31.10.59 | 6.12.59 | s.s."HORORATA" | Sen.Ord.Seaman. |
| 5. 4.60 | 7. 4.60 | m.v."HAPARANGI" | Sen.Ord.Seaman. |
| 8. 4.60 | 10.10.60 | m.v."HINAKURA" | Sen.Ord.Seaman. |
| 16.11.60 | 19.12.60 | m.v."NOTTINGHAM" | E.D.H. |
| 4. 2.61 | 31. 5.61 | s.s."PIPIRIKI" | E.D.H. |
| 19. 7.61 | 9. 1.62 | m.v."HAPARANGI" | E.D.H. |
| 1. 2.62 | 3. 8.62 | m.v."HAPARANGI" | E.D.H. |
| 29. 9.62 | 28. 3.63 | m.v."HAURAKI" | E.D.H. |

During these periods Mr.SCLATER was always satisfactorily
reported upon by the Commanders and Chief Officers under whom
he served in respect of his Conduct, Ability and Sobriety.

Marine Superintendent.

On leaving the Hauraki, little did I know that in just eight years' time I would sail on her again but as second officer with a Master Mariners Foreign-Going Certificate under my belt and also would be on my honeymoon with my wife who I still had to meet…This leads on to my next chapter in my working life.

Whilst home on leave in March/April 1963 my friend John Leslie, who had gone to sea as a deck cadet and had obtained his second mate's ticket, was due to go to Aberdeen to study for his first mate's certificate at Robert Gordon's Institute of Technology and said that I should try for a second mate's ticket. I had also met my future wife on leave at this time and thought that being in Aberdeen studying for my ticket would mean not being away for months and not seeing Anna. We actually met at a students' Easter fancy dress dance in the Cosmo ballroom in Kirkwall. I along with John and two other friends were dressed up as Arabs with our faces completely covered except for our eyes. It was all great fun, and Anna eventually figured out who I was.

So, it was decided that I would go and study for my second mate's certificate. This was quite daunting task as I had a very steep learning curve to understand all the aspects of obtaining this qualification. My old schoolteacher was right; I did need to know a lot about mathematics although this was seven years after leaving school.

John and I sailed down to Aberdeen on the MV St Magnus in May and checked into the seaman's mission in Mearns Street where I would stay until I obtained my Second Mate's Foreign-Going Certificate some six months later. There was a break in July and August when the college was shut for summer holidays. John passed his exams by then so I was on my own for the next few months. This was quite a task for me as all the other students were deck cadets who had been training for this part of their career for at least four years at sea and a further year at college prior to going to sea. Anyway, I got stuck into studying, and with the help of John during the first two months, I soon started to get to grips with all aspects of navigation, rule of the road, chart work, ship design, stability, morse code, semaphore, gyro and magnetic compasses, navigation lights and shapes, buoyage, radar observer and every other aspect of the second mate's course.

The first certificate I obtained during my studies was my radar observer; this was a week's intensive course at the college's radar station on the seafront next to the Bridge of Don tutored by Captain Mackay, one of the most likeable of tutors at the college.

With my radar certificate under my belt, also my First Aid Certificate, I got down to really studying hard; my main tutors were Captain Inch and also Captain Mackay. We attended classes every day, Monday to Friday, and every evening Monday to Thursday, we went back to college to sit old exam papers to get an idea what we could expect for the final exams.

# RADAR OBSERVER
## ON
# MERCHANT SHIPS

*This is to certify that*

NAME ____Robert Chalmers Sclater.____

RANK ____E.D.H.____

CERTIFICATE OF
COMPETENCY, GRADE_____ NO._____ DISCHARGE
BOOK NO. R 655192

DATE AND PLACE OF BIRTH ___7th August, 1941, Kirkwall, Orkney.___

*completed a course of training in Radar Observation, approved by the Ministry of Transport, and passed the examination held by the School Authorities at the conclusion of the course on*

_____24th May, 1963___.

Signed _____ EXAMINER

Signed _____ PRINCIPAL OF SCHOOL

Signature of Holder _____

SEC134 50560 M/2411 60 Pads 2/61 FHB 873

---

No. B.T.17108

## St. Andrew's Ambulance Association

### Special Certificate in First Aid to the Injured
*to meet the requirements of the*
*Ministry of Transport and Civil Aviation*

#### This is to Certify that

ROBERT CHALMERS SCLATER

*has attended a Course of Lectures and Demonstrations on* **First Aid** *to the Injured and has passed the* ___First___ *Examination.*

Head Office:
93-108 North Street,
Charing Cross,
Glasgow, C.2

President
Lecturer
Examiner
Secretary

Date ___14th June, 1963.___

*This Certificate expires three years from date of issue.*

There were three parts written which required at least a 50% pass mark in every paper, but you had to obtain 70% in navigation and chart work with the overall pass mark being 70%; so, you really had to know your stuff.

There was an oral exam covering buoyage, rule of the road and all other aspects relating to seamanship. The signalling test was on morse code, semaphore and the International Code of Signals.

By November, I was ready to sit for my Second Mate's Foreign-Going Certificate. I took my exams in the third week of November and passed. The confirmation of the written exams was delivered to the Marine Office on the Friday, and we were all on tender hooks awaiting the confirmation that we had passed. It was in fact quite a sad day as it was the 22nd of November, 1963, the day John F Kennedy was shot. We did however all go out and have a drink to celebrate obtaining our Second Mate's Certificate. I felt quite good about my achievement as some of the cadets who started studying at the same time as me had still not passed their exams by the time I did.

I was now classed as a seaman who had come up the hawsepipe. The hawsepipe being the pipe where the anchor is attached to the anchor chain and comes over the windlass on the forecastle and down the spurling pipe to the chain locker. On older ships, the crew lived in the forecastle, and it meant that you had climbed up the hawsepipe to become an officer.

Once again however, I was to find out that you did not start as second mate but as third mate, the second mate certificate being the lowest foreign-going certificate one could obtain at that time.

As I had completed my college studies, I returned home for the Christmas and New Year and set about finding a shipping company willing to take a very 'wet behind the ears' third mate with little or no practical experience in this post. I did not wish to return to NZSCo as I would no doubt encounter old shipmates and would find it difficult being an officer in charge of them.

I contacted several shipping companies and eventually was offered a position with the Liverpool based company Lamport + Holt, which traded to South America. My instructions were to report to their offices in Liverpool by 14th January, 1964. I was interviewed by the marine superintendent and sent for a medical and was appointed as third mate on the MV Debrett, which was berthed in Liverpool Docks. The Debrett was slightly different from other ships in appearance as the navigating bridge was actually part of the funnel, which also housed the radio office. The ship was part of the Vestey Group of companies, which included Blue Star Line.

The Debrett was not fitted with a radar due to the fact that one of the Vestey ships had a radar-assisted collision when radar was new on merchant ships. It appeared that the officer on watch did not understand that you had to plot targets to ascertain their course and speed and if they were on collision course. Mr Vestey decided that his ships could do without radar.

As I had never really navigated a ship before, having radar did not concern me that much. Navigators today would not be so happy to do without radar as it is the main stay of collision avoidance and plotting one's course along with satellite navigation systems.

Anyway, I stood by the Debrett in Liverpool for a few days, got my third mate uniform sorted out, bought a second-hand sextant and was ready to go to sea. At last, I had a cabin all to myself; it even had a wash basin in it but no shower, that was a few years away. We did a coastal voyage to Glasgow to load whiskey and other general cargo then back down to Liverpool. This was my first experience of being in charge on the bridge by myself.

Third mates were on the 8-12 watches with the captain on hand to make sure you were not doing anything stupid. It was quite daunting to navigate the ship, taking bearings and plotting the position on the chart; all things I had learned at college but never done in earnest. Also had to keep a good eye on other shipping and change course if a close quarter situation was arising The rule of the road basically required your ship to alter course; if a ship on your starboard side was approaching too close and risk of collision was deemed to exist, you altered course to starboard to let them pass safely ahead of you.

Vessel approaching on the port side had to give way to you. Understanding this aspect was no problem as it was fully taught at college; plus, with my experience on deck steering vessels, I had been responsible for these course alterations when instructed by the officer of the watch.

My job in port was to monitor the loading/discharging of the various cargoes and keep a record in the ship's logbook of the number of hatches being worked along with the dockers working on board and the time of commencing and completing work. A full detailed cargo plan was drawn up showing exactly where everything was in the hold and the various ports where each item was to be discharge. We finalised loading in Liverpool and set off on my first deep sea voyage as a fully certificated deck officer, officially signed-on on 14th February

1964. We sailed down to Northern Spain to Aviles and Feroll where we loaded salt fish, aluminium ingots and some general cargo. We then headed south for Las Palmas for bunkering and onwards to Recife in Brazil.

Once again got into the shipboard routine of watchkeeping as third mate, navigating the ship taken morning and midday sights to confirm our position. The first time I shot the sun with my sextant, the captain was on hand to take the exact time on the chronometer in the chart room to tie in with my sextant angle; the second sight I took was in fact lower than my first, completely impossible as the sun was rising and the angle was getting higher. I had of course only used a sextant at college and was not quite up to taking actual sights. Soon learned how to do it and count the seconds after taking the sight and walking into the chart room to read the chronometer; after a couple of days, I was calculating our position accurately.

The compass error was also regularly checked by taking azimuth and amplitudes bearings of the sun, moon and stars. Once again, we were heading into warm weather, which I had missed being ashore for several months.

Being in charge on the bridge in the evening watch was very pleasant experience and fulfilling; life at sea as an officer was certainly more rewarding than being a deck hand. Your meals were all served in the dining saloon by stewards with no washing dishes or scrubbing decks. Certainly, a new chapter in my life.

We arrived in Recife and discharged the part cargo destined for there. I did have some time clear of duty so managed a run ashore and saw the sights, a lovely city built in the Portuguese style. We then set sail for Montevideo in Uruguay. On the way there, one of the stewards took a sick turn and passed away. The captain decided that instead of keeping his body on ice, we were a fully refrigerated ship, he would bury him at sea, not a very popular decision by the crew who thought he should remain onboard to Montevideo only a few days sailing away. Anyway, the poor steward was prepared for burial at sea and was wrapped in canvas with weights in the bottom to make the body sink. The service was carried out at 1100 hrs and as I was on duty rang down to the engine room to stop the engines, and the captain carried out the burial, and the steward was tipped over the side.

I have seen burials at sea in movies where the body slips gracefully in to the sea; unfortunately, in real life this was not the case as the body tipped over and landed face first with an almighty splash, not a very dignified end. I then put the

52

engines back up to full speed, and we continued our voyage on to Montevideo. Thankfully never experienced a burial at sea again.

Montevideo was another lovely old city, and once again, I was able to have a run ashore, always bought souvenirs when ashore. The wreck of the German Pocket Battleship Graf Spey was marked by a buoy where it was scuttled in December 1939 after the famous sea battle of the River Plate. The anchor and other relics of the ship are just beside the dock gates in Montevideo.

After discharge, we sailed up the River Plate to Buenos Aires in Argentina. This was a very interesting place for a look around and enjoyed the time we spent there. It was also a city where there were a considerable number of armed soldiers and police to be seen, some on the corners of main roads in sand, bagged machine gun emplacements; there was also tanks to be seen stationed outside government buildings. South American countries were very volatile in the 1960s. There was a military coup d'tait in Brazil when we were in Argentina. We had no big problems although we were all issued with Argentine photo passes with our fingerprints on them. The restaurants in both Montevideo and Buenos Aires were renowned for their steaks, which were huge and possibly the best I have ever tasted, so needless to say when ashore always had a steak before going elsewhere in town.

After discharging, we commenced loading of frozen and chilled meat along with bulk grain and other various cargo including the famous Frey Bentos tinned corn beef in Buenos Aires. We then sailed down to Montevideo again to continue loading frozen and chilled beef. Once completed, we sailed back up to Recife to complete loading.

Part of my tasks as third mate was to copy the temperatures of all the refrigerated compartments into a book, which was kept on the bridge. This information, I obtained from the chief refrigeration engineer on a daily basis usually about four o'clock in the afternoon. He was a very nice gentleman and had been at sea for many years, and we always had a good yarn when I went to see him. On the last occasion, the day we were due to set sail for home, he said that he had been on ships where death had occurred and that there was always another death on board following the first. I thought this was a very strange statement to make. Within four hours of him stating this fact, he was killed in a fire that occurred just as we were talking. The ship was getting ready to sail later that evening, and the motorman on duty in the engine room was firing up the boilers to prepare the engine room for departure. Unfortunately, whilst doing this there was a blow back and flames shot into the engine room. The motorman was burnt to death, and the engine room went up in flames. The alleyway next to the engine room where I was sitting with the chief refrigerating engineer was soon full of dark smoke and the fire alarms were activated. All hands went to their fire stations, and the shore authorities were informed. We started fighting the fire, and shortly afterwards, the shore fire brigade arrived. Water was pumped into the engine room. After a few hours, the fire in the engine room was extinguished and the motorman's body recovered. There were still small fires in various parts of the ship adjacent to the engine room, but the worst was over.

The refrigeration plant was down in the engine room, and it was operated using ammonia gas to create the cold air that was pumped through ducting into the various frozen/chilled compartments within the holds of the ship to keep the cargoes at the correct temperatures.

The situation now was that the fire had caused problems with the equipment and the ammonia gases were leaking into the refrigeration plant room. The chief refrigeration engineer wished to enter the plant room to check for any fire damage, but our main breathing apparatus was no longer available as the air tanks had all been used up tackling the main fire. We had also received a breathing apparatus set from a German ship berthed behind us, but this was also no longer useable. There was no way to charge our oxygen bottles as the compressors were in the engine room and of course were out of action. It would also have taken some time to get the German's equipment charged.

He did however have a type of gas mask that he put on, and along with the bosun and myself, we went to check things out. However, he must have taken off his mask or it was not working properly as he collapsed soon after he entered the brine room, and we went in and managed to get him out on deck. Once on deck, it was found that his breathing was very shallow so he was taken to one of the ambulances waiting on the quay, which took him to hospital. Myself and the bosun went back down again to check for any sign of fire, but once again, problems occurred, and the bosun collapsed.

Part of the area where we were was full of water about a foot deep, and I managed to hold him out of the water and shouted for help; a couple of the shore firemen arrived and helped us both onto the outside deck. We were then whisked away in an ambulance with the sirens sounding to hospital where we were given oxygen to help our breathing.

We were both in quite a bad state and covered in soot and grime from the fire so appeared worse than we actually were. After an hour in hospital, we were released and taken back to the ship. On arrival back, we were informed that the chief refrigeration engineer had not been so lucky and died from the ammonia gas.

The fire brigade was stood down later that night and most of the crew were taken ashore to temporary accommodation for the night. The next day, work continued searching for any smouldering fires, which were all dealt with. The problem now was what to do with our frozen and chilled meat with no refrigeration plant working. It was decided that all the meat would be discharge and handed out to the local population. The trucks that took the cargo away were all accompanied by armed guards, the same troops we were told that had carried out the coup d'tait in March. Work was also underway to try and repair the engine room to get the ship back home. One of the company's other ships arrived in port and tied up alongside so their engineers could help with the repairs. They did not stay alongside very long as they got a scare whilst working in the engine room when they got a whiff of ammonia gas. They left the engine room quickly and their ship pulled away and tied up at a berth ahead of us.

Anyway, our own engineers worked hard at getting the engine room back to as normal as possible and eventually patched it up so it was deemed safe to proceed on our homeward voyage, minus our frozen cargo. The bulk grain cargoes in two lower holds had been damaged by water from fighting the fires, but nothing could be done about that until we arrived in Hamburg.

Both the chief refrigeration engineer along with the motorman were buried in a cemetery in Recife, but we were not informed by the agents or the British Consulate about the funeral arrangements. No one from the Debrett attended, and we only found out later from other British seamen who were at the agents and were asked to attend. The crew onboard were very upset at the lack of information and compassion in not being informed about their shipmate's funeral and not able to attend. We never did get to the bottom of this but believe for some unknown reason the captain or the chief engineer withheld the details.

The homeward trip was uneventful, thank goodness, the usual routine taking sights, plotting positions and enjoying the time at sea, once again stopping in Las Palmas for bunkers.

We were also a meteorological reporting ship, which entailed taking observations of weather conditions, wind, wave, swell, clouds, sea and air temperature, dry and wet thermometer readings and any other weather activities. This was then translated into numbers and sent off by the radio operator every six hours day and night to the meteorological office at Bracknell.

We sailed up the English Channel bound for Hamburg; this kept you on your toes, with no radar, everything was done by visual sighting of vessels and bearings by compass. We arrived in Hamburg and commenced unloading the bulk grain that had partly solidified during the voyage home and had to be dug out using pneumatic drills to losing it and allow the grain to be sucked into hoppers and then into barges.

After completing discharge in Hamburg, we set sail once again on an uneventful coastal voyage arriving safely in Liverpool and paid off on 5th June and headed for home. This was quite a baptism of fire for my first trip as an officer. During this voyage, I had met a lot of interesting seafarers and people ashore in the various ports. Witnessed how life was in South America, the rich and the poor, the nice and not so nice, which once again gave me an insight into human behaviour and how people act in dangerous situations. Also had learned my trade as a third mate, quite a daunting task for me, and it would hold me in good stead for the rest of my career at sea. Life however was to get even more interesting as my second voyage was to prove the next episode to follow. The Debrett was scraped in 1964.

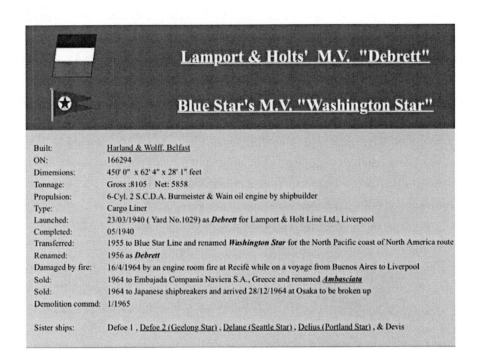

**Lamport & Holts' M.V. "Debrett"**

**Blue Star's M.V. "Washington Star"**

| | |
|---|---|
| Built: | Harland & Wolff, Belfast |
| ON: | 166294 |
| Dimensions: | 450' 0" x 62' 4" x 28' 1" feet |
| Tonnage: | Gross :8105  Net: 5858 |
| Propulsion: | 6-Cyl. 2 S.C.D.A. Burmeister & Wain oil engine by shipbuilder |
| Type: | Cargo Liner |
| Launched: | 23/03/1940 ( Yard No.1029) as *Debrett* for Lamport & Holt Line Ltd., Liverpool |
| Completed: | 05/1940 |
| Transferred: | 1955 to Blue Star Line and renamed *Washington Star* for the North Pacific coast of North America route |
| Renamed: | 1956 as *Debrett* |
| Damaged by fire: | 16/4/1964 by an engine room fire at Recifé while on a voyage from Buenos Aires to Liverpool |
| Sold: | 1964 to Embajada Compania Naviera S.A., Greece and renamed *Ambasciata* |
| Sold: | 1964 to Japanese shipbreakers and arrived 28/12/1964 at Osaka to be broken up |
| Demolition commd: | 1/1965 |
| | |
| Sister ships: | Defoe 1 , Defoe 2 (Geelong Star) , Delane (Seattle Star) , Delius (Portland Star) , & Devis |

After a couple of months at home enjoying the summer and spending time with Anna, I decided I would look for another shipping company sailing in the Far East to broaden my horizons. I contacted Moller Line UK Ltd, a shipping company whose head office was in Hong Kong. They were happy to give me a third mate's position, and I was instructed to report to their offices at Plantation House in London to be allocated a ship. My next ship was to be the Grosvenor Trader discharging cement in Chittagong.

I was provided with an airline ticket that would take me from London to Calcutta on the famous B.O.A.C. Comet airliner then transfer to a Pakistani Airlines flight for a short hope to Chittagong, still East Pakistan in 1964. A very interesting flight stopping in Damascus, Bahrain, New Delhi and finally Calcutta where I had a six-hour stop over. I had departed London at 1330 hrs and arrived in Chittagong at 1700 hrs the next day, quite a long trip. On arrival, I was picked up by the company's shipping agent and taken down to the port to join my ship. As the previous third mate had already departed, I was on duty right away.

The Grosvenor Trader was an old Liberty Ship built in the USA during the Second World War to carry supplies and all types of military equipment from the States to the UK. They were the most basic vessel at sea in those days. The record for building one of these ships was less than a week. The Grosvenor

Trader was built in 1943 in Houston, Texas, in about six weeks. These ships had a deadweight carrying capacity of some 10,000 tons. It was said that if they did manage one trip safely across the Atlantic, then that was payment enough. So many merchant ships were sunk by U-boats in the North Atlantic that these Liberty Ships were an essential part of the war effort. Anyway, I digress a bit from my own story.

As I mentioned, the ship was discharging bags of cement loaded in China and was about halfway through discharge when I arrived. The normal work routine as third mate was to supervise the discharging and note the hatches being worked along with numbers of dockers and times of starting and completing compartments. Also ensuring that everything was done as safe and efficiently as possible.

There were four British officers on board, namely the captain, first, second, and third mates, Indian chief and second engineers, two Chinese engineers and a radio officer, also from India. The deck, engine and catering crewmembers were all from communist China. My previous ships had all been British seafarers, so once again a new experience at sea. I signed articles on 2$^{nd}$ September, 1964, and this would be my home for the next year.

After completing discharge, all holds were cleaned, quite a big job for the shore cleaners, but being in a country with very poor employment, there were dozens of bodies removing every trace of cement, which was not a very nice job. The Grosvenor Trader was basically a tramp ship and was usually on a time or voyage charter carrying a full bulk cargo of one commodity. With no charter on hand when we sailed out of Chittagong, we went to anchor to await orders. This was to take a further 40 days, not a very exciting six weeks. The time was spent on anchor watches or in one's cabin reading a book or listening to the BBC overseas service on your transistor radio. No luxuries on board the Grosvenor Trader, not even an officer's saloon. I did however get to know the ship well and carried a full inventory of all the lifesaving equipment on board, checked all the lifeboats and firefighting equipment so not a wasted period in some respects. There was one item of interest that would play out later in the voyage, this being the story of the .22 rifle left on board by a previous second mate. Whilst on anchor watch one day, the captain came up on the bridge with the gun along with some ammunition. He said he did not want to have a weapon onboard with bullets so decided we would throw some tin cans into the sea and shoot them. This we did and had a bit of fun trying to hit them. The gun was then locked away by the captain and would only be seen again a few months later on a voyage from China to Burma.

After the six weeks at anchor, we received our orders to proceed to Calcutta to load bagged sugar for Saigon in Vietnam. This was only a short voyage, and we sailed up the Hooghly River to berth in Calcutta. The loading was carried out on a round the clock basis so the second mate and myself were on shift duty to supervise the loading. We were only able to part load as there was a draught restriction for transiting the Hooghly. We then proceeded to Visakhapatnam a few days sailing down the east coast of India. Sugar was in fact rationed in India at the time so the dockers were not happy loading the cargo and of course tried to pilfer it.

They certainly managed to steal some, but we kept a tight rein on the loading operations. Once completing loading, we set sail for Vietnam. We sailed across the Bay of Bengal and onwards down the Malacca Strait. At least, the Grosvenor Trader had radar so navigation was easier when near the coast we still took sights when away from land. The Malacca and Singapore Straits were one of the busiest shipping routes in the world so careful watch on other shipping was essential. We stopped in Singapore for bunkers out in the eastern anchorage so no trip ashore. In fact, we never were ashore in Chittagong, Calcutta or Visakhapatnam, working or sleeping all the time. A new second mate joined in Singapore, Duncan Maclean from Tobermory on Mull, said he was related to Alistair Maclean, the famous author, never quite sure if he was kidding. Duncan had started his sea career onboard Puffers, little coastal steamers out of Glasgow to the west coast of Scotland; he was quite a character.

The Grosvenor Trader was a very slow vessel, maximum speed around 10 knots on a good day, and having a triple expansion steam engine was very quiet so sometimes you wondered if you were moving at all with other faster vessel passing you most of the time.

We then sailed up the South China Sea to Saigon. Vietnam was a war zone in late 1964 and navigation up the river was restricted to daylight only, as all the lighted buoys had been destroyed by the Vietcong. With the Saigon River, pilot safely on board, we proceed upriver. It was an interesting trip seeing the Vietnamese farmers working in the fields with their very distinctive conical straw hats.

At one point, we had to slow right down to allow another ship to pass us. As soon as this happened, small boats were seen shooting out from the shore manned by small Vietnamese River 'pirates'. The Grosvenor Trader was fully laden, and as the river was freshwater, our free board was very low, only about 8 ft and very easy for someone to climb onboard with the use of a boat hook. The pilot told us they would try and steel anything they could get their hands on.

This was about 1000 hrs in the morning, and I was on my regular bridge watch. The captain instructed me to go down on deck and chase these guys off the ship. By the time I got down to the main deck, they had already stolen one of the Chinese crewmember's watches by ripping it straight off his wrist. Others were running around picking any item lying on deck and jumping into the river to be picked by the small sampans. Some were just children no more than 12 years old. The crew were also trying to stop this invasion, but they were so agile it was difficult to catch them. The captain left the bridge also and came down on the deck and started shouting at them. Unfortunately, these characters were not frightened, and one ran up to the captain and pulled his watch off his wrist. It was an expensive Rolex watch; to say the captain was upset was an understatement. Anyway, the ship started to increase speed, and the rest of the thieves jumped overboard, and we proceeded up to Saigon, with a not very happy captain. I suppose with hindsight I was taking a chance chasing these guys as they could have stuck a knife in me and jumped over the side and never been caught. We were informed by the agent after we berthed that you could expect street urchins in town to try and rip your watch off your wrist, so on shore leave, we certainly kept a wary eye out for them. Never did have any problem when ashore thank goodness.

As I said, it was a war zone so plenty of military activity. We could see this as we sailed up the river lots of soldiers patrolling the riverbank and further in land through the villages visible from the ship's bridge. These were mostly Vietnamese soldiers although we did see lots of American troops in the city. Ashore in the evening, we noticed that the only US troops in uniform were their military police with the rest in civilian dress usually with an exotic Vietnamese girl on their arms. Across the river where we were berthed was a long flat plain of rice paddy fields and dense wooded areas, and on occasions, you would hear the sound of gunfire and see explosions. The discharging was carried out during the day and part of the evening as there was a curfew from 1100 at night. I did manage a couple of visits ashore but being on duty every other night did restrict shore leave. Saigon was a very French style city with big wide boulevards and with very grand houses and hotels. I recall sitting in the Continental Hotel with its big open veranda bar drinking beer and watching the young Vietnamese on their scooters with the girls, very smart in their national dress. One of the hotels that we had a beer in was blown up just two months after we left. There was also a floating restaurant called the My Canh Café we used to walk past whilst ashore; it was also blown up with the loss of 42 people a few months later. There were stories of American soldiers being caught and butchered by the Vietcong on their way back to their bases after a night out on the town. I read Graham Greene's book and also saw the film *The Quiet American*, it certainly painted the picture of Saigon as I saw it in 1964. We were lucky that nothing happened to us when we were there.

We completed discharge in about two weeks and then the final cleaning of the hatches commenced ready for our next cargo. Just like Chittagong, there were plenty cleaners male and female available to do the job bagging up the loose sugar. I asked one of the supervisors who these people were as they were not dockers; they were all dressed in black pyjamas suits and the distinctive conical straw hats; he said they were all Vietcong and were taking the sweepings home with them, once again not sure if he was winding me up. All of the Vietnamese people I had dealing with were very friendly and showed no animosity to us although I know some were not happy with the US troops being there.

The passage downriver was uneventful until just after we dropped the pilot when the wheel jammed hard to starboard. The ship was just building up speed when the helmsman said he could not steer the ship, and it was swinging rapidly towards the shore. The engines were stopped and the anchor dropped as we were still in shallow water. The engineers went down to the steering compartment and were able to rectify the problem, just lucky again that it had not occurred whilst coming down the river, or we would have ended up on the riverbank amongst the shacks of the pirates we met on the way up.

We were able to continue our voyage to load rice at Sihanoukville in Cambodia just around the corner from Vietnam, a short voyage. The cargo of bagged rice was destined for La Reunion, an island in the Indian Ocean. The rice was in very heavy hessian sacks weighing about 75 kg. The dockers were tough little fellows who carried and stowed the sacks in the hold with wooden dunnage between layers to allow airflow. We were loading 18 hrs a day, and as we were some distance from the town, I never did get ashore.

We sailed down to Singapore to bunker once again. This time however we had a collision whilst under pilotage heading into the Eastern anchorage. I was on the bridge, my usual station whilst entering/leaving port. We were proceeding from the immigration anchorage to the bunkering anchorage when the MV Riverdore was sighted leaving the eastern anchorage. As the normal navigation regulations were expected to apply, we maintained our course and thought the other ship would also stay in the starboard side of the channel, and we would pass port to port. However, this was not the case as the Riverdore on passing the fairway buoy turned to port straight across our bow. Our pilot asked for reduced speed and ordered our ship hard to starboard, and we sounded one short blast in compliance with the collision regulations to inform the other ship of our intentions to avoid a collision.

The first mate along with the carpenter were on the forecastle at their anchor stations. As the risk of collision was becoming more apparent to them, they started walking quickly down the deck, which was a wise precaution. I was instructed by the pilot to put the engines on full astern then emergency full astern but to no avail as we hit the Riverdore just forward of its bridge. As we were fully laden and weighing about 14000 tons and travelling about 4 knots, this was quite a big bang The collision although damaging was not seriously enough to cause any risk of sinking with no injuries to anyone onboard either ship.

The starboard side of the Riverdore had a large gash and our bow was flattened. We continued to anchor and the Riverdore turned around and also went to anchor both to inspect the damage to our ships. It was agreed with the agent that a letter should be handed to the master of the Riverdore holding him fully responsible for the collision and liable for all repairs to the Grosvenor Trader.

I was tasked with delivering this letter and proceeded over to the Riverdore in the agent's launch and was able to see the damage done to the ship. The captain accepted the letter and signed a copy to confirm receipt. We discovered afterwards the reason he took the action he did when sailing outwards from the anchorage. The story was he had been ashore in the yacht club and met up with a Singapore pilot who he asked about sailing from the anchorage without a pilot as it was not a compulsory pilotage area. He was told just weigh anchor proceed out the channel and once past the fairway buoy turn to port and head on your way. This is what he did paying no attention to shipping coming in the channel. Not a very professional act of navigation on his part.

///Grosvenor Trader"

Pointe des Galets,

17th December,    64.

Messrs  Moller Line (U.K.) Limited,
Plantation House,  Rood Lane,
Fenchurch Street,
LONDON,  E.C.3.,

"CONFIDENTIAL REPORT FOR THE ATTENTION OF
THE COMPANY'S SOLICITORS ONLY."

Dear Sirs,

At the request of Captain Veale, I am giving my
observations on the collision with M.V."RIVERDORE" in Singapore
Roads.  As you are aware I am in possession of a 2nd Mate's
Foreign Going Certificate and am fully conversant with the
Collision Regulations.  As Third Officer of the vessel I was on
the Bridge attending to routine duties, with Pilot and Master
on the bridge, proceeding from the Immigration Anchorage towards
the Eastern Roads, at full manoeuvring speed when it was seen
that M.V."RIVERDORE" was leaving the Eastern Roads Anchorage.

The vessel was put at slow ahead and then stopped to
ascertain the intentions of the "RIVERDORE".  We proceeded on our
course at half ahead after we observed that we would pass clear of
the "RIVERDORE", if she kept on her course, being a Port to Port
situation.  The "RIVERDORE" was then observed to alter course to
Port without any sound signals being heard.  We sounded one short
blast and altered course to starboard in accordance with the
Collision Regulations.  As it was then seen that this action would
not clear the "RIVERDORE", the vessel was stopped, then put to full
astern, then Emergency full astern, sound signal also being given
for such action.  I personally heard no sound signals from the
"RIVERDORE", possibly due to my position in the wheelhouse.

My opinion that the maximum speed of S.S. "GROSVENOR
TRADER" was never in excess of 4 knots.

Yours faithfully,

R. Sclater.

R.C. SCLATER
3rd Mate

c c. Hong Kong Office.

JULIUS & CREASY
SOLICITORS, PROCTORS
& NOTARIES PUBLIC,
COLOMBO.

I, ROBERT CHALMERS SCLATER of the motor vessel "Grosvenor Trader" now in the harbour of Colombo in the Island of Ceylon make oath and state as follows :-

1. I am Third Mate of the motor vessel "Grosvenor Trader".

2. On the 25th of November 1964 at 0600 hours I was carrying out routine duties as Third Mate on the bridge when the vessel was approaching the Immigration Anchorage at Singapore harbour.

3. I remained on the bridge and at 0712 hours anchor was aweigh and the vessel proceeded to the eastern roads.

4. It was then noticed that the m.v. "Riverdore" was leaving the eastern anchorage and I received orders from the Master to put the vessel at slow ahead and to stop.

5. At 0719 hours the m.v. "Grosvenor Trader" proceeded at half ahead after it was ascertained that the m.v. "Grosvenor Trader" would pass clear of the m.v. "Riverdore", being a port to port situation.

6. At or about 0722 hours it was observed that the m.v. "Riverdore" was altering course to port but I personally heard no sound signals.

7. On seeing that this action would lead to a close quarter situation, the helm of the m.v. "Grosvenor Trader" was put hard astarboard sounding one short blast.

8. It was then seen that this action would not clear the m.v. "Riverdore" and at 0723 hours I received orders and put the vessel full astern, sounding three short blasts.

9. At 0723½ hours emergency full astern was rung.

10. At 0724 hours the m.v. "Grosvenor Trader" struck the m.v. "Riverdore" on the starboard side.

11. All orders from the Wheelhouse were promptly carried out by me.

```
SWORN and SIGNED at )
              this )
            day of )
               one )
thousand nine hun-  )
dred and sixty five.)
```

                    Before me

                Justice of the Peace
                and as such an officer
                empowered under the
                laws of Ceylon to
                administer oaths.

                                        HSS.

The details are of my official account of the accident.

The bow of our ship was inspected by Lloyd's marine surveyor to ascertain the damage and instruct on repairs required to allow us to proceed on voyage. The local engineering company were tasked to carry out the welding repairs on the bow. It was still quite flattened, but the seaworthiness of the bow was found intact after the welding so were given a Lloyd's certificate to allow us to proceed. The bow was to be repaired at the soonest opportunity when the vessel was next in dry dock. With hindsight, if we had sounded two short blasts and turned to port, we would have missed the Riverdore, providing they did not turn back to starboard. This is of course is contrary to collision regulations, but in some instances, quick thinking can avert an accident. I discovered this in the River Plate a few years later.

We set sail about two days after the accident bound for Port Louise in Mauritius, once again to bunker. The voyage across the Indian Ocean was uneventful. As we were an old tramp ship with a triple expansion steam engine, our speed at best was no more than 10 knots so a very quiet and smooth trip. After bunkering in Mauritius, we sailed to Reunion to discharge. Both islands were very green and lush, both very volcanic looking especially Reunion. The discharging was carried out during the day and evening but no overnight work. I did have a visit ashore a couple of times to see the sights. We were there for Christmas and with no cargo work took a trip to one of the beautiful beaches on the island. Finding a companion to go ashore with was difficult on the Grosvenor Trader with only four of us from the UK and the Chinese and Indian engineers keeping to themselves. We were however tied up next to another British ship in Reunion, and I met up with the third mate onboard, and we went ashore together, which was a nice change. After completing discharge just before New Year, we set course for Lorenzo Marques (Maputo) in Mozambique to load coal. This was a very quick and dirty loading. We tied up alongside a large gantry used to lift the fully laden railway trucks that tipped the coal into the holds. As the gantry was static on the quay the ship had to move up and down the quay to line up with the hatches. We shifted ship about thirty times before we completed loading. Also, the coal had to be trimmed as it was dumped straight into the hold so it had to be moved out towards the ship's side to even up the load. This was done by the dockers using shovels, a long and arduous job also quite hazardous working amongst loose coal and black dust everywhere. These African trimmers had no safety gear, were in bare feet and wearing what could only described as rags on their bodies. I doubt if it would have met health and safety regulations. The ship was also covered in coal dust, certainly glad when we completed loading, which took only 36 hours to load 10,000 tons of coal.

The coal was destined for Colombo in Ceylon (Sri Lanka); we sailed up the Madagascar channel and onwards across the Indian Ocean. Back to normal watchkeeping, taking sights and navigating the ship. The three cargoes we had loaded, sugar, rice, and coal, were all on voyage charters for different charterers. Part of my job was to keep a detailed log of all activities regarding the loading and discharging times, hatches, dockers, weather and any other relevant fact relating to the cargoes. These documents were then forwarded to the charterers and our owners to confirm that the 'charter party' had been fully complied with.

I did mention that the catering staff were all Chinese so the food on board was in their style of cooking. We certainly had Chinese dishes on a regular basis. Every night, you could hear the crew playing Mahjong, what a racket the tiles made. The dining saloon was quite small, only seven of us eating in it. It was also very hot as the main steam lines to the forward winches, both flow and return, were attached to the deck head. As these Liberty Ships were cheaply constructed and built for one trip across the North Atlantic, there was no great thought given to comfort on board especially in tropical climates, certainly no air condition. You had an old fan to blow the hot air around your cabin.

We arrived in Colombo and were tied up between two buoys so no direct access to the shore had to use small liberty boats to go ashore. On arrival in Colombo, a new captain and first mate arrived onboard. The master Captain Shorthouse was from Ireland and the mate Bob Stewart from Scotland; this gave us three Scotsmen onboard, and we all got on well together. We started discharging, but this was a much slower pace than the loading. Barges came alongside, and the coal was shovelled into bamboo baskets holding about 100 kg lifted out of the hold and lowered into them. It took over three weeks to discharge. On the passage from Lorenzo Marques, the second mate and myself decided to build two small canoes out of various bits of dunnage and bamboo left onboard after we discharged the rice. We managed to get some canvas from the stores onboard and painted them to make them watertight. As we had no library onboard, we were always looking for books to read on our long passages at sea. We launched our little canoes in Colombo Harbour and set off with a few books to exchange with another ship close by belonging to a Scottish Shipping Company, Salvesen's of Leith. So, we were right at home as nearly all the crew were Scottish. We had a nice time onboard, changed a few books and paddled back to our ship. Possibly against the port rules as we were not very conspicuous in these small craft. The canoes were not very stable as the first mate found out when he decided to try one out. He was quite a large chap, and as soon as he got in, the canoe overturned, and he ended up in the water. Luckily, he was right next to the gangway so we were able to pull him onboard; he never tried again. These canoes were to play a major role in an incident later on in our voyages.

We completed discharge and then sailed up the east coast of India to Cuddalore to load iron ore for Japan. This was carried out at anchor as at that time there was no port large enough for us to go alongside. The iron ore came out first thing in the morning onboard sailing barges using the morning offshore wind. It was quite a sight to see dozens of sailing vessels heading out from the shore. The iron ore was once again in baskets, these were hooked onto the wire runners attached to the derricks onto the winches and swung across to the side of the hatches and tipped down into the hold. This was a very heavy cargo so its stowage capacity was very low so it was just loaded in a heap in the lower holds. This of course gave the ship a massive GM, the righting moment required to keep the ship stable. We were certainly a very stiff ship as opposed to a very tender ship that has a low GM and has more chance of capsizing with a low righting moment. The sailing barges sailed back to port in the afternoon with the onshore breeze, and we settled down to a quiet night on anchor watches, until they came out the next morning at daylight with the offshore breeze, all very interesting and picturesque. With no shore leave, I spent my time studying for my First Mate's Foreign-Going Certificate as I would be attending college once I had completed my year away.

The second mate was also studying so we helped each other with the formulae and calculations that we would encounter in our exams; we also did this in our spare time on all our long sea passages. On completion of loading, we set sail for Japan, a long sea voyage. We called into Penang for bunkers this time instead of Singapore, another port to add to my list. After about ten days or so at sea, the ship stopped due to engine problems. The chief engineer reported that we were getting low on freshwater, and there was an issue with the water getting to the ship's boilers. We were by this time just north of the Philippines having just passed through the Luzon Strait. He was quite irate about the situation, and it was decided we should head for Naha in Okinawa to top up with freshwater. With the vessel stopped, we were rolling quite badly in the low Pacific swell due to the ship being stiff with the iron ore. We got underway and headed for port.

On arrival, we topped up with freshwater, but by this time, the engineers had to use salt water in the boilers to keep us going. Not a very wise decision as that was the end of boiler tubes as they would have to be replaced due to salt water corrosion.

We arrived in Himeji in the inland Sea of Japan to discharge. This was a high-speed operation; the cargo was out within two days. We then headed to the Hitachi dry dock in Osaka to get our boilers sorted and a new bow fitted. As there was no cargo work, we managed a few trips ashore to see Osaka, one of the larger cities in Japan. Every morning, the workforce in the yard would line up on the quay and carry out 15 minutes of exercise before starting work. They certainly were a very efficient and enthusiastic workforce and got the work done without any problems. Once everything was fixed, we set off again heading for Chin Wang Tao in China. The trip was through the Inland Sea and onwards across the East China sea around the southern tip of South Korea up the Yellow Sea and the Bohai Sea. We were once again to load coal this time for Rangoon in Burma (Myanmar). We had arrived in Chin Wang Tao just before 1st May, 1965; with this being a special day for the Chinese, we were offered a trip to visit the Great Wall of China. The most Eastern end of the Great Wall was our destination. This was the area of the Shanghai Pass, the site of a major battle in the 1644 war between the Ming and Qing Dynasties and a turning point in Chinese history. We were picked up by a minibus outside the dock gates. Whilst waiting for the bus to arrive, the first mate, who had a camera, took it out for a photo, but he soon put it away when an armed guard at the dock gates shouted at him and was walking over removing his pistol from its holster. The agent and other Chinese officials who were there to oversee our visit were quick to tell us that no unauthorised photos were allowed and that the camera would be confiscated after our visit and any pictures taken would be checked and only the ones they thought were suitable returned. The trip to the wall was interesting as there appeared to be very little motorised vehicles on the road, all other traffic were people walking, on bicycles or with animals pulling carts. All the Chinese were dressed in the familiar blue tunics and trousers; this was the time of the Culture Revolution, a very closed country to foreigners, much different from the China we know today. The Chinese were very wary of foreigners so we were under close supervision during the visit. There were no other westerners at the wall during our visit. We arrived at the Great Wall, and as it was the May holiday, there was countless Chinese there especially school children, all dressed the same with little red neckerchiefs marching and singing, quite a lovely sight. I don't think the children had seen foreigners before as they took a great interest in us. We spent a couple of hours walking and climbing the wall and the first mate did manage to get a few pictures developed. These were returned to him a couple of days later along with his camera. The first mate, chief engineer and myself on the wall, the lower is new and looks much tidier than 1965.

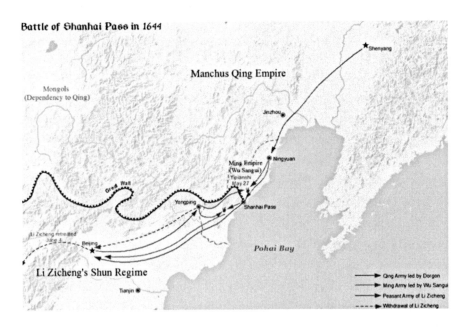

Battle of Shanhai Pass in 1644

Loading continued the conventional way with large buckets lifted onboard by the winches and derricks, very noisy and dirty operation. The trimmers redistributing the coal in the holds were much better clothed than the Africans in Lorenzo Marques. They had hardhats made of bamboo, which looked just like bowler hats and decent footwear. We completed loading and set off on our voyage to Rangoon.

The voyage down the China Sea was uneventful carrying out the usual tasks of navigating the ship, this was to change when we were just over halfway on our voyage to Singapore 150 miles south of the Paracel Islands. I came on the bridge at 0800 to commence my morning watch and relieve the first mate. The captain was on the bridge, and both he and the mate were looking at a small fishing junk lying stopped in the water just off our port side. As it was my normal task to take a sun sight at as near eight o'clock as possible, I carried on with my task. Once I had completed my sight, I went to see what was going on. We had approached quite close to the junk by this time and could see five Chinese crew onboard. The only problem was it appeared that four of them had their hands tied and one was waving frantically to us. The first thought that came to mind was that these were Chinese pirates wanting to attack the ship. As we had no ammunition for the gun we had onboard to defend ourselves (shot it all off in Chittagong several months before), the captain had the radio officer send a CQ radio message to all ships in the area asking for assistance and also if they had guns onboard. A reply was received from a Swedish ship, but it was several hours steaming away. Things were to take an unexpected turn as one of the Chinese fishermen whose hands were tied together jumped into the sea and started swimming towards us. I was sent down onto the main deck and along with some crewmembers put a wooden rope ladder (Jacob's ladder) over the side of the ship. When the fisherman was getting close, I went down the ladder ready to grab him and help him onboard. The ship was rolling gently in the swell so one minute I was up to my chest in water then out of the sea again. I was a bit worried about sharks in the area as on the voyage north to Japan I did witness a hammerhead shark swimming close to the ship in this same area. Anyway, as the fisherman came abreast of me, I grabbed hold of him and managed to get him onto the ladder. I noticed his hands were swollen to double their size with what appeared to cat gut/fishing line attached to a piece of bamboo tied tightly to his hands; he also had a lot of dried blood on his head. I managed to manhandle him up the ladder, and luckily, the second mate appeared and grabbed him from the top of the ladder and pulled him on deck. He was taken up to the bridge where we were to learn the story of what had happened on the junk. The fishermen and the junk were from Hainan, an island a few hundreds of miles north of our position. One of our Chinese stewards came from Hainan and was able to translate for the fisherman; his hands had been untied by then, and he was given water and something to eat. He said that the captain of the junk had been killed by the fisherman who was free on board. He had then overpowered the other four crewmen when they came up from their sleeping quarters below deck. He had knocked them out as they came through the hatch onto the deck, then tied them up and threw them back down into the hold. This had occurred a couple of weeks before, and as they were running out of water, the murderer had taken them on deck that morning and was going to throw them over the side to save himself.

He said the only weapon he had onboard was a knife. It was decided that we would launch our lifeboat and go and capture this murderer and rescue the other three fishermen.

The second mate and myself along with six of our Chinese crew set off to carry out this task. The crew all rigged with hard hats and various weapons, axes and marlinspikes were ready for any trouble. I asked the captain if I could take the .22 rifle that had no ammunition to use as a ploy to encourage the murderer that we meant business.

As we were motoring towards the junk, the other three fishermen decided to jump into the sea and started swimming towards us. We picked them up, and just like the first one, their hands were tied in the same way, and all had head wounds with dried blood. At the same time, a US Air Force transport aircraft came flying over the top of us, no more than 100 feet high. We could see some of the air crew taking photographs as they flew over. There was numerous USAF basis nearby due to the Vietnam War so they must have picked up our CQ and came to check out the situation. We never heard anything more from them. As we approached the fishing junk, the remaining fisherman was waving his arms and holding what looked like a small transistor radio and pointing to it, maybe he thought he was giving us a present. I pointed the .22 rifle at him and motioned for him to jump into the water. He did this quite quickly, and we dragged him onboard and placed him in the bottom of the lifeboat with me pointing the gun at him. Not sure who was the most frightened, me or the murderer as I knew the gun was empty but he didn't. Our own Chinese crewmen untied the fishermen, and we headed back to the Grosvenor Trader. Once everyone was safely back onboard, the three fishermen were given first aid for their injuries; thankfully, most of the cuts had healed over the period but still looked quite nasty. The captain had been in touch with head office in Hong Kong, and we received word to proceed on our voyage to Singapore and take the fishing junk in tow. Once again, the second mate and myself along with a couple of crewmembers boarded the lifeboat still tied up alongside and headed over to the junk. I along with two of the seamen jumped onboard the junk and passed a rope to the lifeboat, and we were towed over to the stern of our ship. A heavy mooring line was passed down to us and made securely to the junk by passing it around its mast. The smell on board of rotting fish and the jerky movement was a bit overpowering and nearly made me sick; I was glad to get back onboard and have a shower and change my uniform for the second time that day, my original being completed soaked after my dip while rescuing the first fisherman. This whole operation had taken up most of the day, and we only got underway again in the afternoon. The murderer was secured on the bridge by the use of a pair of handcuffs, one end attached to his wrist the other attached to a length of wire rope secured around the gyro compass metal stand. A portable bunkbed was found, and this was placed behind the helmsman, and this was where he would remain until he could be put ashore. The mooring line attached to the junk was paid out to a suitable length for towing, and we set off to Singapore a few days' sailing away. With the four fishermen given medical treatment, they were happy to assist our crew on deck by doing a bit of painting. They were placed in spare bunks in the crew's quarters and seemed very happy to be alive. The story of why the murder had occurred came to light as we sailed south. The fisherman who was called Hui Su Lan had been a soldier in the Nationalist Army of Chiang Kia-shek fighting the Communist regime of Mao Zedong in 1947–49. When the communist won the war, Hui Su Lan returned home to what he thought would be the safety of Hainan; he would have been still a young man back then.

After he had been home for some time, he was arrested by the communists and sentenced to 15 years at a rehabilitation commune for fighting with the Nationalist Army. It turned out that the skipper of the fishing junk had betrayed him to the local communist party and this was why he was arrested. After his release, he returned to his village and took up a job as a fisherman.

The junk he was assigned to was skippered by the same man who had betrayed him 15 years before. After a couple days at sea when the other crewmembers were below asleep, he killed the skipper and threw his body overboard in revenge for sending him to prison for 15 years. He then overpowered the other crewmembers, and they drifted for days before we discovered them in an area where it was not normal for small fishing junks to be operating so far from land.

These facts came from conversations he had with the steward on board who came from Hainan and who took his food up to him on the bridge. We did feel a bit sorry for him after hearing his story and had no reason to believe it was untrue. Nevertheless, he was kept secured on the bridge and with an officer on watch; plus, the quartermaster steering the ship right next to him, there was no way he could escape or though we thought. Every morning, Captain Shorthouse would take Hui for a walk on the monkey island above the bridge for some exercise. We also had to take him to the toilet and let him wash himself in the facilities on the bridge deck, always very wary that he did not try to escape.

We were approaching Singapore in the early morning, and it was decided good seamanship to shorten the towline on junk as this was a very busy shipping channel, and we were not the most manoeuvrable of ships. The ship was stopped and the junk was in fact lashed alongside. Unfortunately, this was not a good idea for as soon as we started moving the wash between the two of us caused the junk to capsize and broke adrift. There was nothing that could be done about recovering the junk so it vanished into the dark. A Pan broadcast was sent out to all ships in the area warning them of the hazard of an upturned junk in the eastern approaches to Singapore. We never heard anything more about the junk; it probably sunk or drifted ashore on some island in the area. We arrived in the Singapore anchorage once again ready to take on bunkers and hopefully send our five fishermen ashore to be sent home to Hainan. This was not to be; the agent who had been fully informed of the situation said they would be taken ashore but returned when we sailed as the Singapore authorities wanted nothing to do with them. Shortly afterwards, fully armed police officers boarded and took the five ashore. Just before we were ready to sail to Rangoon, the fully armed police officers took the five back onboard. Hui was taken back onto the bridge and secured behind the quartermaster while the four other lads went back to their cabin. No explanation was given why the Singapore authorities refused entry and repatriation of our five fishermen. The voyage up the Malacca Straits and onwards to the Andaman Sea was uneventful until the night before our arrival in Rangoon Roads. The weather was not very nice as it was just the start of the South West Monsoon period so wind and rain. I was relieved by the second mate at midnight and went down to my cabin to go to my bunk for the night. About 0100, the second mate burst into my cabin and said was the murderer still in his bed when I went off watch. I said yes as I checked on him on a regular basis. I was surprised that the second mate had left the bridge unattended but realised his great concern when he said, "Well, he's not there now." I was out of bunk like a shot, and we both rushed back to the bridge, called the captain and the mate and started a search. All the crew were called, and with all the deck lights switched on, a thorough search was carried out.

We asked the helmsman if he saw anything; of course, he said no even though the guy was lying less than a foot behind him. The splice on the wire rope around the gyro compass had been undone, not a very easy task without a marlinspike. He would still have had one end of the handcuffs attached to him.

It was a bit scary as we were not sure what he might do if cornered with several fire axes attached to the bulkheads in the accommodation that he would have seen whilst being taken through the ship meant he had access to a weapon. He knew full well that we were arriving in Rangoon the next morning and that he would be handed over to the authorities and sent back to China and no doubt executed for the murder of the skipper of the junk. The second mate searched the monkey island and discovered that our two canoes stored up there were gone.

He would have noticed them on his morning walks with the captain and decided to take them and we believe jumped overboard using them as floats, not the most seaworthy craft. The ship was turned around, and we went back on our course to see if we could find him. With the weather and sea conditions being very rough and raining heavily, the chances of seeing him were very slight. We searched for a couple of hours but in the end turned around and set course for Rangoon. We did think afterwards that maybe the Chinese onboard had some sympathy for Hui and assisted in his escape and just maybe had hidden him in their quarters and thrown the canoes overboard to make us think he jumped overboard. We were never to find out what happened to him, but I did feel a lot of sympathy for him and hoped he did survive.

We arrived at the Irrawaddy River pilot station later that morning, picked up our pilot and proceeded up to Rangoon. The first sighting of the city was the large golden dome of the famous Buddhist pagoda, the Shwedagon Paya. As we approached the city, we had to anchor in the river to clear immigration and customs. The mate and carpenter were on the forecastle ready to drop anchor, and I was on the bridge in my usual berthing station. The pilot ordered the anchor to be dropped, but we were going too fast and the anchor chain could not be halted by the windlass, and the chain rattled down the hawsepipe straight into the river, some nine shackles of chain 135 fathoms in length. The other anchor was then dropped and luckily the ship's headway was reduced enough so the anchor did hold this time. We would have been in big trouble if we lost it as well. To say that the captain was not a happy man was an understatement what with losing the junk in Singapore, then Hui the night before and then the anchor problem; he was nearly in tears and who could blame him? After clearing immigration and custom, we proceeded alongside our discharging berth. The local Chinese consulate officials came onboard and met with the four fishermen and advised them that an aircraft was being made available to fly them home directly to Hainan. The local media heard of our story, and this was reported on the radio that afternoon and also in the local newspaper, pity I never kept a copy. The four fishermen were in tears when they left the ship and gave us all a big hug before heading down the gangway. We never heard anything more about them, but hopefully, they would tell the story of how they were saved from certain death by an old British Tramp ship.

*The photos shows the Grosvenor Trader in all her glory. The other of Captain Shorthouse handcuffed to Hui Su Lang on his daily exercise routine on the monkey island (you can see the junk under tow behind) where the canoes where stored. Me on the bridge wing.*

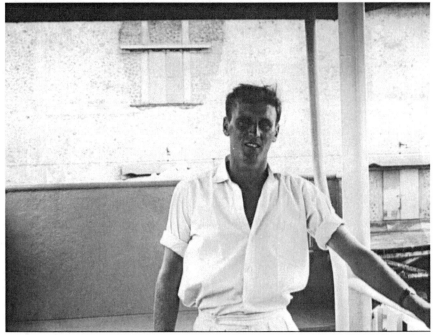

*The first sight you see coming up the Irrawaddy approaching Rangoon.*

We were in Rangoon for a couple of weeks, and once discharging was completed and the holds cleaned, we shifted to another berth to load bagged rice for Colombo. It was back to the usual tasks of supervising the loading which was carried out 18 hours a day so not much chance of shore leave. This was another voyage charter so the usual logging of hatches being worked number of dockers onboard and cargo loaded each day kept me busy. Our lost anchor and chain were recovered from the riverbed and returned safely to the ship.

On our last day in Rangoon, another Moller Line ship tied up in front of us, and I discovered that the master Captain Karl Fiddler came from Orkney. I was invited onboard, and we had a grand evening talking about home over a meal and a few beers. He was the same age as my mother, and they went to school on the island of Stronsay. I had a thumping headache the next day after too many beers, and we sailed that afternoon for Colombo not in the best state of health.

We sailed down to Colombo, thankfully a very uneventful voyage. On arrival in port, we were advised that the cargo of rice had be fumigated and no one was allowed to be onboard during this operation except one officer. In the tropics, there were plenty of bugs and the Colombo authorities were making sure that no foreign pests were on board from Rangoon. Our ship had lots of cockroaches onboard, and you could see lines of little ants on the bulkhead heading for any scrapes of food left lying around; these were things you had to put up with on an old ship with perhaps not just the best hygiene. There were always mosquitos in port so we took paludrine tablets to help keep malaria at bay. They were a real menace at night buzzing around your head and then silence until they bit you.

The captain volunteered to stay onboard during the fumigation so all the officers were taken to the Galle Face Hotel and the crew to another hotel, not sure what it was like, but the Galle Face was certainly luxury compared to our ship. We had a lovely night ashore and went for a swim in the hotel pool. Next day, back to the ship and discharging commenced, all usual tasks carried out. As I enjoyed the Galle Face, I decided that on my days off I would go to the hotel and use the swimming pool. I would walk into the hotel as if I was a guest and use the pool, never had any problem with the staff…We were tied up as usual in Colombo Harbour between two buoys fore and aft, so to get ashore, we had to use the small liberty boat kept alongside. The currency in Ceylon, the rupee, was the only money allowed, and when one requested a sub from the ship, the total amount of rupees was listed on a chit that you had to carry. On going ashore, you could be stopped and searched at the dock gate, and if you had more money than stated on your chit, you were in trouble. Of course, carrying any other currency was strictly illegal. I recall on one occasion, being stopped and searched; I had the exact amount of rupees allowed in my pocket but also a few Singapore dollars hidden in the band of my trousers. We always took other currency ashore as you received a very good rate compared to the rupee. Anyway, the shore customs officials did not find it so I was very relieved and did not try that trick again. We completed discharge and sailed back up to Burma once again to load bagged rice, our first port was Bassein where we loaded at anchor from big barges. As the river was too shallow for a full load, we headed back to Rangoon to top up. Thankfully, this was my last port as the company sent word that as I had completed my year onboard I was to be relieved and flown home. This was not quite straightforward as the Burmese officials would not accept a British seaman's identity card for travelling out of the country. I was to obtain a notarised affidavit to allow me to fly out of Rangoon ( copy below.) This took some time, as I was instructed by the agent where to go and trying to find the notary was a bit daunting in a foreign port, not sure why the ship's agent did not accompany me,. Anyway, I found the address and duly swore the oath and received my travel document. Back to the ship and was given my air tickets and said my farewells to all the officers and crew and headed to the airport for the long flight home.

Stopped in Cairo, saw the Pyramids as we flew in then onwards to Frankfurt and London on a Boeing 707. I had a couple of hours in London then a flight to Edinburgh and onwards to Kirkwall. My parents were unaware of my arrival until I phoned from the airport, no mobile phones or internet back in 1965. I was glad to be back home after a very eventful and exciting year away.

I have attached my affidavit along with certificates of service to cover my time as Third Mate to allow me to sit for my First Mates Foreign Going Certificate. The receipt for my second-hand sextant which cost £35 was quite expensive back in 1964.

**EX-POST-FACTO**

**TRANSIT VISA.**
No. 57 / 69 / 65
Good for transit through Burma
enroute to LONDON
Stay up to 25th August 1965
Valid for ———— months. (25.8.65)
Single Journey only.
within 24/9/65
(CHIT TIN)
Controller
Rangoon of Immigration
Dated 24.8.65 Burma.

Left by B. CAC
On 24-8-65
Asst. Immigration Officer
Rangoon. 24/8/65

Fee Rs. 10- Realised.

Sign Off from Greenare Trader
Stay up to the 25th August 1965

24
(Soe Aung)
1545. 1A
FORE SHORE.

# CERTIFICATE OF WATCH-KEEPING SERVICE.

## For a First Mate's or Master's Certificate.

This is to Certify that Mr Robert Chalmers Sclater
has served on the ~~ss~~ M. V. Debrett
from 14th February 1964 to 5th June 1964
.......................in the capacity of *~~(1st)~~ ~~(2nd)~~
(3rd) Watch-keeping Officer.   During this time
Mr. Sclater
was an officer in $\frac{*(full)}{(effective)}$ charge of a watch for
eight hours out of every twenty-four hours at sea,
except as stated below.

Watches were not doubled at any time during the
voyage.‡

~~Watches were doubled between the following~~
~~dates and at no other times~~ ...........................
~~During this time Mr.~~ ...........................
~~served as the~~ $\frac{*(senior)}{(junior)}$ ~~of two Bridge-keeping~~
~~Officers.§~~

~~An entry to this effect has been made in the Mate's~~
~~log.~~

Signature of Master....................

Date  1ˢᵗ Sept. 1965

* Strike out the words that do not apply.
† "Effective charge of a watch" means responsibility for the watch, confirmed by an entry to this effect in the Mate's log, but it does not preclude
Occasional Supervision by a Senior Officer, provided that that Senior Officer
does not take charge of the watch at any time.
‡ Delete this paragraph if watches were doubled at any time during the
voyage.
§ Delete this paragraph if watches were not doubled at any time during
the voyage.

---

## J. SEWILL LTD.
36, Exchange Street East,
**LIVERPOOL 2.**

Folio ...............
Date Feb 12 1964

| For what required | AMOUNT | | |
|---|---|---|---|
| | £ | s. | d. |
| Mr. R. Slater | | | |
| Town Hall House | | | |
| Kirkwall | | | |
| 1 Second hand Kelvin Hughes | | | |
| Three Circle Micrometer Sextant | | | |
| No. 63170 | | | |
| Ex SB 683 | 35 | — | — |

Signature  ..................

Passed by  12/2/64

# CERTIFICATE OF SERVICE AND CONDUCT.

This is to certify that

Mr. *R. C. Sclater*

has served as *3rd Officer*

in ~~ss~~ M/s *Debrett*

under my command from *14/2/64*

.................. to *5/6/64*

during which period he has conducted himself*

*at all times in a conscientious
and sober manner and
always attentive to his
duties.*

.................. Master.

ss. ..................

Date *1/9/65*

* Here the Master is to insert in his own handwriting his remarks on the conduct, ability and sobriety of the officer.

# CERTIFICATE OF WATCH-KEEPING SERVICE.

## *For a First Mate's or Master's Certificate*

This is to Certify that Mr. ROBERT CHALMERS SCLATER
has served on the ss. "GROSVENOR TRADER"
from 26.8.64 to 26.1.65.

..............................in the capacity of *(1st) (2nd)
(3rd) Watch-keeping Officer. During this time
Mr. SCLATER

was an officer in $\dagger$ *(full) (effective) charge of a watch for
eight hours out of every twenty-four hours at sea,
except as stated below.

Watches were not doubled at any time during
the voyage.‡

~~Watches were doubled between the following~~

~~dates and at no other times~~..............................

~~During this time Mr.~~..............................

~~served as the~~ *(senior) (junior) ~~of two Bridge-keeping~~

~~Officers.§~~

An entry to this effect has been made in the
Mate's log.

*Signature of Master* ..............................

Date 26ᵗʰ January 1965

---

\* Strike out the words that do not apply.

† " Effective charge of a watch " means responsibility for the watch, confirmed by an entry to this effect in the Mate's log, but it does not preclude Occasional Supervision by a Senior Officer, provided that that Senior Officer does not take charge of the watch at any time.

‡ Delete this paragraph if watches were doubled at any time during the voyage.

{Delete this paragraph if watches were not doubled at any time during the voyage.

# CERTIFICATE OF SERVICE AND CONDUCT.

This is to certify that

Mr. R.C. SCLATER

has served as 3rd mate

in ss. "Grosvenor Trader"

under my command from 26th August 1964

to 26th January 1965

during which period he has conducted himself*

in a sober, diligent and competent manner.

_____ Master.

**MASTER**
**S.S. GROSVENOR TRADER**
**OFF No. 301152**

ss. _____

Date 26th January 1965

# CERTIFICATE OF WATCH-KEEPING SERVICE.

### For a First Mate's or Master's Certificate.

This is to Certify that Mr ROBERT CHALMERS SCLATER

has served on the ss. "GROSVENOR TRADER"

from 27 : 1 : 65 to 24 : 8 : 65

.................in the capacity of *(1st) (2nd)

(3rd) Watch-keeping Officer. During this time

Mr. ...... S. C. LATER

was an officer in $\frac{*(full)}{*(effective)}$ charge of a watch for

eight hours out of every twenty-four hours at sea,

except as stated below.

Watches were not doubled at any time during the

voyage.‡

~~Watches were doubled between the following~~

~~dates and at no other times~~...................

~~During this time Mr.~~ ...................

~~served as the~~ $\frac{*(senior)}{(junior)}$ ~~of two Bridge-keeping~~

~~Officers.§~~

An entry to this effect has been made in the Mate's

log.

Signature of Master....................

Date ...... 24ᵀᴴ AUGUST — 1965.

* Strike out the words that do not apply.
‡ "Effective charge of a watch" means responsibility for the watch, confirmed by an entry to this effect in the Mate's log, but it does not preclude Occasional Supervision by a Senior Officer, provided that that Senior Officer does not take charge of the watch at any time.
‡ Delete this paragraph if watches were doubled at any time during the voyage.
§ Delete this paragraph if watches were not doubled at any time during the voyage.

# CERTIFICATE OF SERVICE AND CONDUCT.

This is to certify that

Mr. ....R. C. SCLATER...........................

has served as ...3RD MATE.........................

in ss. "GROSVENOR TRADER"..............

under my command from 27d January

...1965...... to 24d August 1965.....

during which period he has conducted himself*

in an exemplary manner, being
at all times strictly sober
and attentive to his various
duties.

.......................................... Master.

ss. GROSVENOR TRADER

Date 24. 8. 1965.

*MASTER
S.S. GROSVENOR TRADER
OFF No. 301158*

* Here the Master is to insert in his own handwriting his remarks on the
conduct, ability and sobriety of the officer.

# MOLLER LINE (Ü.K.) LIMITED

PLANTATION HOUSE · ROOD LANE
FENCHURCH STREET · LONDON · E.C.3

AND AT THE BALTIC

HEAD OFFICE:
HONG KONG

DIRECTORS:
L. E. TUCKER
J. R. E. HARRISON
A. G. HUTCHINSON
H. H. HOLGATE

OUR REF.  
CREW/1924/65.

YOUR REF.

29th November, 1965.

Mr. R. C. Sclater,
Sailors Home,
Mearns Street,
ABERDEEN.

Dear Sir,

We have pleasure in enclosing our cheque for £107.7.8d. (One hundred and seven pounds seven shillings and eight pence) being balance of study leave pay due to you for the period 4.10.65 to 28.11.65, inclusive.

Details of how this sum is compiled are shown in the attached statement.

Yours faithfully,
For and on behalf of
MOLLER LINE (U.K.) LTD.
(As Agents Only)

L. Lock.

LL/AEF.

---

THIRD OFFICER R. C. SCLATER ex "GROSVENOR TRADER".

STUDY LEAVE PAY.

| | Dr. | Cr. |
|---|---|---|
| 56 days Study Leave pay 4.10.65 to 28.11.65 @ £91.0.0d. per month | | £169.17. 4d. |
| LESS: | | |
| 8 weeks N.I. benefit @ £4.0.0d. per week | £32. 0. 0d. | |
| M.N.O.P.F. on £137.17.4d. @ 1/-d in the £ | 6.17. 8d. | |
| Income Tax @ 'S' coding | 23.12. 0d. | |
| BALANCE: | £107. 7. 8d. | |
| | £169.17. 4d. | £169.17. 4d. |

After arriving home, I rekindled my friendship with Anna who was very happy to see me home after a long year apart. As I was due study leave for my First Mate's Foreign-Going Certificate, I arranged a visit to the Moller Line offices in London to confirm my study leave payments. Anna decided she would like to come with me so we set of to London for a holiday. As I fancied buying a car to use during my six months at home, we toured London to find one. One of the cars that I had taken a fancy to was one I had seen several of whilst in Saigon; it was a French Renault Caravelle, a lovely little red sports car. We found one, but it was left-hand drive; nevertheless, I bought it, and we toured London in it for a few days after I had been to the company's offices to confirm my study leave package. It was quite a daunting task having not driven for over a year and being left-hand drive took a bit of getting used to. We had an enjoyable stay in London visiting all the famous landmarks. Had a night at the theatre to see a Brian Rix farce at the Whitehall Theatre about a Russian ballet dancer defecting to the west. Anyway after our few days in London, we set off down to Bovington Army Camp in Dorset to visit my uncle Harry and family. He was a sergeant major instructor at the UK tank training centre in Bovington. It was quite close to Weymouth so enjoyed driving along the esplanade with the top down on a lovely Sunday morning.

We then started our long drive north all the way to Scrabster to catch the ferry home. We had a lovely holiday and with the weather fine most of the time drove with the hood down. We still talk about our little red sports car and the good time we had. The roads were quiet back in 1965 unlike today so there was no problem with long tail backs on the new motorways as they were then.

*The photo I had of Anna and with me at sea, sitting in our little red sports car.*
*The one of me is at Lake Windermere, one of the many interesting places we stopped on*
*the way north.*

Anyway, after a further two weeks at home, I set off once again to Aberdeen and Robert Gordon's Institute of Technology to study for my First Mate's Ticket. Staying once again at the Seaman's Mission. To sit these exams, you required confirmation of sea time and the certificates on the previous pages were provided as proof. Also, I was entitled to receive study leave pay unlike my second mates where I covered the costs out of my savings. The studying was the same procedure as second mates working Monday to Friday at the college during the day and back in the evenings, Monday to Thursday to go over all past exams' papers. The syllabus was similar to my previous certificate although some of the papers were a bit more detailed especially stability, electricity, engineering, genera ships construction and navigation. The rule of the road and signals were still very much the same. The college closed over the Christmas and New Year so I came home and had a break. After New Year, I applied to sit my exams, and this was completed by end of January, and I passed all three parts written, oral and signals in one go. Now I was fully qualified as a first mate foreign going mariner.

I decided that I did not wish to be away for another year long voyage with Moller Line so wrote once again to The New Zealand Shipping Company to see if I could return as an officer. My application was accepted and was told to report to the Royal Albert Dock offices at the end of February. Once again, I was to find out that in a company like NZS you started as a deck officer on the bottom rung of the ladder. I was to be a junior third officer with three officers above me, the third, second and chief officers and of course the captain. Having served on deck with the company, I knew quite well how regimented and detailed they were in their shipboard operations. Although I was a bit put out by my new position, I soon found out that it was a benefit as once again learned the difference between sailing onboard an old tramp ship and a top-notch liner company. This is not to say that both my other two companies were inefficient, just that things were done in a different fashion in NZS. My first couple of weeks were spent on relieving duties when other officers were home on leave. This was my first and last time onboard a passenger ship; the company had five passenger ships Rangitane, Rangitata, Rangitiki, Rangitoto and Ruhine.

I stood by on the Rangitoto for a week then transferred to the MV Taupo just out of the builder's yard. This was a very new style of vessel with Hallen derricks unlike the conventional cargo gear on all other NZS ships that had fixed derricks; the Hallen was a single boom and operated like a crane. The Taupo also had a very modern sewage system that treated all effluent onboard, and it was said that after treatment, the remaining water was drinkable, never tried it out. In a port like London Docks, the use of onboard toilets was forbidden due to the lack of movement in the dock, and also with most cargoes loaded and discharged into barges, they did not want effluent covering the barges. Toilets were available ashore, not a very handy situation so the Taupo was certainly a great step forward. My duties onboard were supervising loading or discharging depending on what ship I was standing by. I also was to learn how to use a typewriter as every morning a detailed typed report on all activities and shore staff employed, be it dockers or shore maintenance staff, was delivered to the marine superintendent.

After a month standing by several vessels in the London Docks, I was eventually signed on to the MV Sussex to do a coastal voyage discharging in Liverpool and onwards to Glasgow.

This was to turn out to be quite a long stay in Glasgow as it coincided with the 1966 seaman's strike. When we arrived in Glasgow, all the crew were signed off and only a few of us were left onboard to run the ship, all cargo had been discharged by then. There were four third mates plus a second mate and a couple of engineers and an electrician. There was also chief steward who carried out some of the cooking as there was of course no cook onboard. One of the other third mates was another Orcadian Bill Spence, and we have remained good friends ever since. We were tasked with the safety of the ship carrying out safety watches, sounding all the freshwater tanks and bilges and any other duties required whilst a vessel was in port. There was shore staff employed carrying out night watchman duties, although there was always one third mate on duty every night. We were provided with substance money to buy our own food, etc. After a couple of weeks, it was decided that we would commence loading cargo for New Zealand; this was to consist mainly of cases of scotch whisky. The company had shore riggers who came onboard and prepared the ship for loading, and we were tasked with supervising the loading. This as you would expect was no easy task loading whisky in Glasgow. I mentioned before about dockers/wharfies pilfering cargoes, well, this was no exception. It was nigh on impossible to keep an eye on them all the time. The cases were being loaded into the refrigerated lockers onboard so at any one time they could be stacking cases in any four lockers. The pallets of cases were lowered into the hold and then stacked onto wheel barrows and run into the lockers. With the officer on deck watching the loading, it was difficult for any pilfering to take place or though we thought. If the dockers got frustrated, they would just run the wheelbarrow into the ship's side and break a few bottles and then put a mug under the case to catch the whisky running out. Of course, they did in fact steal quite a lot of bottles even with our watchful eye. I know this as we did become friendly with the dockers after a few weeks and were invited to a party at one of their houses one Saturday night. They had a number of bottles of whisky on the table, all of which we had been loading during our stay in Glasgow; we had no proof of course but knew quite well where they came from. Whilst in Glasgow I did manage a weekend at home but not a very happy one as Anna decided that she did not like being tied to a seaman being away for long periods of time so we parted company. This was not the end though; it took another four years before we got back together.

After the seaman's strike ended, I was sent back down to London to continue standby duties on other company ships and did a coastal voyage on the MV Huntingdon. This was the era of the World Cup in the UK so plenty of excitement onboard. Never attended any games but did follow most of the matches. We were in Liverpool for the big game when England won, although being Scottish was still very happy for my shipmates from England when they won the cup. We also visited the Cavern Club whilst in Liverpool, but I don't recall who was playing back then.

After the five months carrying out coasting duties, I was well versed in the operations of NZS and was looking forward to be appointed to a ship heading back to New Zealand. I was given a week's leave and eventually signed on the MV Cumberland on 22nd August, 1966, as junior third mate in Royal Albert Dock and would do eight voyages on her rising to second mate before leaving to study for my Masters Foreign-Going Certificate in 1970. I did my final trip to sea on her in 1975–76 as chief officer, will touch on this later.

*MV Cumberland*

The ship had loaded general cargo in London, and we set off once again bound for New Zealand, some difference from my first departure in 1957 as a deck boy. As I was now only a junior third officer, I was on the 4-8 watch with the chief officer; this I found quite strange as I was used to being on duty by myself. The routine on the 4-8 was slightly different as we both took morning and evening star sights just as daylight was creeping in, and you could still see the stars but also the horizon, something I had not done in the past. It was a very accurate navigation calculation shooting at least five stars with your sextant and plotting the position lines on a chart and where the five position lines crossed you had an accurate position. I really enjoyed this aspect of navigation. I also took morning sights as well and then ran the position line up to midday to cross it with the noon latitude sight. The company was also very keen on keeping a keen eye on the ship's stability so every Sunday at sea we worked out the vessel GM, the righting moment that kept the ship in a stable condition. On the Debrett and the Grosvenor Trader, this was not something calculated on a regular basis. The voyage out to NZ was the same calling at Caracas Bay in Curacao for bunkers then onwards to Panama and then south through the Pacific Ocean. The Cumberland was luxury compared to the Grosvenor Trader and with an all-British crew life was a lot more enjoyable. We played deck tennis and deck quoits; there was also a library onboard and numerous other games available to pass the time. The food onboard was okay but can't say I ever sailed on a ship with exceptional catering, nothing as good as home cooking.

We arrived in Auckland and commenced discharge; the cargo was basically the same as when I sailed on deck a mixture of every item you could think of. In NZ, the wharfies/dockers worked day shift, which meant they started at 0800 and finished at 1700 Monday to Friday and only worked to 1200 on Saturday with no Sunday work. This was a big change for me as on the Grosvenor Trader cargo was worked at least 18 hours a day. There was always of course an officer on duty overnight; this was the task of the two third officers on a night about rota. You did not stay up all night but were on call if required; the gangway boys covered the overnight watches. It was my duty now to blow the whistle at 0800 to break out the flags. The time spent on the NZ coast was a very relaxing and enjoyable time in my sea-going career, and I spent more time seeing the sights than when I was on deck.

My duties were basically the same as my other ships, monitoring the discharging and making sure everything was done in a safe and efficient manner.

We also had to keep a wary eye on the wharfies to stop any pilfering of the cargoes. In the case of high value commodities, we would be stationed down the holds to ensure their safe discharge. It was an ongoing problem in most ports where we handled smaller items of general cargo, which was easy for wharfies/docker to get access to. I must stress, it was not a fulltime problem but was something we certainly had to keep a watch out for.

After discharge was completed and the holds all cleaned, we commenced loading, once again frozen lamb, butter, cheese, fruit, meat, crayfish, wool, casings, tallow and other odds and ends. The cargo of frozen lamb, boxed beef, along with the butter, cheese and fruit (apples and pears) could be destined for several ports and different consignees and every separate parcel of cargo had to be clearly marked either by coloured tape or marking ink.

This was an ongoing task as you could be loading six different hatches with one or two gangs of wharfies in each. It certainly kept you on your toes and very fit climbing up and down the holds to mark everything off. It also required every parcel to be clearly marked on the ship's cargo plan with details of the separation tape/mark used. The cargo plan was kept up to date and on completion of loading detailed coloured copies were sent ahead to head office and the ports where the cargo was to be discharged. The stability and draught of the ship was calculated on a daily basis and worked out for every port of discharge to ensure that the vessel always had a positive GM and that, where possible, the draught of the ship was at the correct depth and trim for each port of discharge. I certainly became an expert in this aspect of loading after a few trips. The second officer was in fact the cargo officer, and he was responsible for the safe loading in conjunction with the captain who kept a close eye on all aspects of the ship's operations. The first mate had an easy task looking after the cleaning of the holds and organising the correct type of dunnage to be placed in every hold/compartment for each type of cargo. The frozen/chilled cargoes required each compartment to have a clear air passage under the cargo to allow the cold air to flow freely to keep the cargoes at the correct temperature. There was always a number of carpenters onboard carrying out this work. They also carried out the shoring up of the cargo to ensure it did not move during voyages between ports.

After this first trip on the Cumberland, I was asked to return for the next voyage, which I was happy to do. By then, I was certainly au fait with the duties of an officer in NZS Co and ready to climb up the promotion list in the company.

I re-joined the Cumberland in London where she was loading general cargo once again for NZ. This time however we were loading the new New Zealand dollar currency as they were in the throes of going decimal. This of course required a careful watch as the boxes of notes were loaded into the sealed refrigerated lockers. There was no chance of any pilfering of this cargo. There was a new second mate on this voyage as the previous one was home studying for his master's ticket. The new second mate was Mike Perfect, a New Zealander whose father had been head postmaster in NZ and was now in charge of the decimal change over in NZ, quite a coincidence that we were loading the money for the changeover.

We sailed out of London bound once again for Curacao, Panama and onwards to NZ. One of the rules onboard NZS ships was that bridge watches were doubled up around the UK coast and continent in the busy shipping lanes. This required two officers on watch at any one time. As I was on watch with the chief officer, we were doubled up; anyway, the other watch was covered by the second and third mates. We were on a four-on-four off routine, and thank goodness, it only lasted a couple of days as by then you were really tired. I could never understand the logic in it as on the Debrett and Grosvenor Trader, there was no way we could do this, and I believe our watchkeeping was much safer than being doubled up with only four hours of duty not enough time to get a decent rest. Once we cleared the English Channel, it was back to the old routine of watchkeeping taking star sights then morning and midday sights working out courses and speeds. We were also weather reporting ships so always busy sending off weather reports. We also received weather data, which we converted into detailed weather maps so always knew what the weather had in store for us.

The voyages at sea were very relaxing, and once in the warm weather and changed out of our thick blue uniforms into whites, we certainly had the best job in the world. The bunkering in Curacao and transiting the Panama Canal broke up the voyage, and then, it was an 18-day sail across the Pacific to NZ. We arrived in Wellington and commenced discharging the new NZ currency with thank goodness no discrepancies in the amount loaded or discharged. Mike's father came down onboard, and I was invited ashore to meet his mother also. Had a nice stay in Wellington and went to the horseracing out in the country with a Mike and his family. Horseracing is a very popular past time in NZ, and every Saturday, there was always someone on the Cumberland offering to place bets at the TAB for you. I was not really into betting so only tried it a couple of times and never won; there was some of the crew who would be betting every week; I don't think any made a fortune.

After discharging, we prepared once again for loading the usual homeward frozen/chilled cargoes of lamb, butter, cheese, wool. This we did in Timaru, Bluff, Port Chalmers, Napier, Auckland. Part of the cargo was destined for Galveston in Texas so this made a nice detour from our usual voyage home. We still came via Panama and Curacao, sailed up the Caribbean and onwards through the Gulf of Mexico to Galveston. When in Galveston, we were discharging at a berth where NASA operation were carried out and a space capsule was lying on the wharf beside us. I have attached a couple of photos on next page of myself, Chief Officer Charlie Turner and Mike alongside the space capsule, and me on the bridge.

After we arrived back in the UK, Mike and the other third mate, John Collins, decided they would love a visit to Orkney so we set this up. As Mike was to study for his master's ticket, he would be staying in the UK for several months so he bought himself a 3.5 litre Jaguar car, very high performance. He and John drove all the way from London to Scrabster to catch the MV St Ola for a week's summer holiday staying with me in Orkney. This was quite an exciting visit for Mike. On his first night, we all went out for a drink and to the local dance hall where he was to meet his future wife. He arranged to drive her home but not being au fait with Orkney roads came to a sharp left-hand bend, which was not sign posted and went straight through a wall and damaged his new car; this was about one in the morning. Luckily, it was in the village where Violet lived, and they managed to get the car to a garage of some friends who were mechanics and were able to repair the car before they were due to depart Orkney. The police did make inquiries about the wall, but we were able to get it repaired without any further police involvement. I think Mike would have been over the drink drive limit so was very lucky in a sense.

My folks visited me three times whilst at sea twice in Liverpool when I was a deck boy and ordinary seaman back in the late nineteen fifties and then in 1968 when I was third mate. Always enjoyed their visits onboard and lunch in the officers saloon even when I was a lowly seaman, happy memories.

*Photo of my dad on the bridge of the Cumberland in Falmouth.*

After a very eventful leave, I was instructed to re-join the Cumberland in Glasgow as senior third officer. Unfortunately, my flight to Glasgow from Orkney was delayed by fog, and when I arrived at Glasgow Docks, the ship had sailed for Liverpool. I had no option but to go to Central Railway Station and wait for the overnight train to Liverpool. There was no problem as the third mate I was relieving was quite happy to pay off in Liverpool. We then completed loading the numerous items of general cargo for NZ. We sailed back down to Curacao, Panama and onwards to NZ. I now had my own watch, the 8-12 same as on the Debrett and Grosvenor Trader so I was happy not to have someone looking over my shoulder all the time on watch. The new junior third mate was now taking the star sights, etc. so my daily navigation was morning and midday sights, which occurred on my watch so made life very easy.

As third officer, I did have extra duties and responsibilities, which kept one busy whilst on watch and even outside watchkeeping duties. As I mentioned, the NZS ships were weather reporting vessels, and I was responsible for this part of shipboard activities. The detailed weather info was kept in a working logbook and transferred to a paper slip, which was handed to the radio officer for transmission to Bracknell. Part of my duty was to transfer all the data from the working log to an official log, which at the end of each voyage was passed onto the met office. Also included in this log was details of the set and drift encountered every 24 hours on ocean passages. This is where the log line came in, which I mentioned when I nearly lost my leg. The position of the ship was ascertained by the midday sights and the distance and course steered in the last 24 hours calculated. This was plotted on the chart then I took the 24-hour reading from the log at midday and the true course steered by the gyro compass. I then plotted this on the chart then joined up the calculated position to this position, which gave me the estimated set and drift over a 24-hour period. The full detailed positions were then inserted into the official met logbook along with my calculated set and drift, which allowed the experts to compile the estimated sea current in the given area. The set being caused by ocean currents and the drift by the wind. If you did a good job with the official met log, you were presented with a prize, which I did receive, see below. There was also quite a considerable amount of paperwork relating to The List of Navigation Lights worldwide and Marine Statutory Instruments to keep updated. I also still kept a log on the hatch temperatures, the frozen and chilled cargoes from the refrigerating department and other tween decks with general cargo by reading thermometers placed in them through mushroom vents above each hold to ensure correct ventilation for the cargo.

We did on occasion carry animals onboard; these were usually dogs going to NZ as their owners were immigrating and had no option but to ship them out. This was great fun for crewmembers who took up the task of feeding them and taking them for walks around the deck. It was always sad when after a month onboard they had to leave, quite emotional for the crew that had taken care of them. We also on one trip carried horses to NZ. On this voyage, a fully trained farrier was onboard to look after them. They were loaded in large horse boxes on deck, and I was supervising the operation when the farrier came up to me and said, "Hi, Bob, how are you?" It was in fact an old shipmate; we sailed together as ordinary seaman onboard the Hinakura back in 1960; his name was John Hayday. It was great to meet him again as we had been cabinmates for several months and were good friends. It turned out that he gave up the sea after a couple of trips and became a fulltime folk singer, back in the 1960s, a very popular genre.

I knew John could sing and play the guitar very well and whilst onboard the Hinakura in Auckland he landed a spot on one of the local TV shows and had great reviews. He told me he had done some busking in London and then had set up The Cornwall Folk Cottage in Newquay with another folk-singing friend. He had also tried his hand as a blacksmith hence his qualifications for looking after the horses. After a while, he decided he would like to immigrate to NZ. As he had experience with horses, he found out about the job and got free passage plus pay to look after them. We arranged to go ashore together that evening, and he took me to a folk club in Soho where Ralph McTell was signing as he was great friend of John and had performed down at his club in Newquay. This was before Ralph became really famous with his song *Streets of London*. John and I spent time together on the voyage out to NZ and had a couple of beers and reminisced about our early days at sea. He also tried to teach me the guitar, which I was not very good at. I will touch on John later on in my story as we did meet up a couple times later on in life.

We discharged in various ports in NZ, and once that was completed, commenced the loading of all the usual cargoes bound for the UK. No detours on the way back either Panama, Curacao and docked in London and managed home for Christmas and New Year, a nice change as I had missed quite a few over the years. Mike Perfect had started his studies at Robert Gordons University in Aberdeen and came up to Orkney for the festive season; he was of course still courting Violet who he had met in the summer and was involved in the car crash. He was possibly one of the funniest guys you could meet and had a very infectious laugh, and you could not help but laugh along with him, great company; my parents loved having him to stay. He returned to NZ after his master's ticket and Violet followed him out with a wedding dress. They were married and lived in NZ for a few years. I will complete Mike's story later on.

After New Year, I was ordered to report once again to the Cumberland berthed in Falmouth. This was a long trip down from Orkney, one end of the country to the other, took more than 24 hours travelling by plane and train. The ship sailed light ship out to NZ, same route and same procedures as previous voyages. We had no cargo to discharge so on arrival once the holds were checked by a Lloyd's surveyor for cleanliness we commenced loading for the UK. Back to monitoring the loading marking off the different parcels of frozen lamb, cheese, butter, etc. Working on the cargo plan which I was responsible for as third mate; the junior third mate also helped with this work. We both were on alternative night duty so shore leave was a bit curtailed. Each night, we had to write up the night orders book with instruction for the gangway boys to ensure they knew what duties they were expected to carry out overnight and who to call in the morning. Any visitors coming onboard required a pass so this we also sanctioned. It was always quite common for the officers to have parties onboard, usually the local nurses enjoyed a night out onboard. The passes however were only until ten o'clock so no big problem in those days with a lot of noise for other crewmembers.

There were a few friends of mine from Orkney that had emigrated to NZ who I met up with quite regularly. Two of them, Ernie Carter and Billy Rendall, both ex-seamen who lived in Auckland with their families. They were both working on a new harbour facility in Auckland and most lunchtimes would come over to the Cumberland for a beer and a sandwich, which the galley staff were happy to provide. I got on well with the catering staff being an ex-deck hand myself.

We completed loading and sailed back to the UK, this being my shortest voyage being only three and a half months. I went home on leave until July and then back to Falmouth to re-join the Cumberland again. The ship was in dry dock undergoing repairs and painting so we had a few weeks in port. Falmouth was a nice little town so always had pleasant runs ashore. With no cargo being loaded had ample time to get ashore during the day. We sailed up to London at the end of July to commence loading for NZ. After bunkering in Curacao, we sailed up to Kingston, Jamaica, to load ortaniques, a cross between an orange and a tangerine.

Just before arrival, we had our usual weekly fire and boat drill stations. On this occasion, the captain told the four deck officers in charge of each lifeboat to give a talk to their boat crews. The talk was to advise everyone of the dangers of going ashore in Kingston and not to be alone or go with any woman whilst ashore. This was the first and last time I ever did this; it was quite embarrassing giving a pep talk to hardened merchant seamen who had seen most of the sights in ports around the world. Mind you, the talk was correct as Kingston was a dangerous place. Unfortunately, I was not to take heed of these words myself and had quite a frightening experience all my own fault as well. After we docked, I had the night off and a few of us decided to visit one of Kingston's famous nightclubs. We had a grand evening listening to Calypso and reggae music and drinking lots of rum and coke. I got slightly worse of the wear and ended up flaked out in a hotel room next to the nightclub. On wakening up the next morning at 5 am, I realised I had to get back to the ship ASAP or I would be in big trouble. I left my room and went downstairs to get out, but the place was locked up tighter than Fort Knox. I was in a quandary; how do I get out. All the windows had bars so no chance of getting out there. I went back upstairs and found a small window that swung inwards; it was pretty small, but being of slim build, I managed to squeeze through and slid down the roof and jumped onto the road. There was no sign of life anywhere. I had a rough idea where I was some two miles from the port so I started walking hoping a taxi might turn up. After a few minutes, I saw a group of Jamaican youths up ahead so having my wits about me turned around and headed quickly down a side street; thankfully, they never spotted me or I would I'm sure been beaten up and mugged. I set off walking and with the sea on my left-hand side knew I was heading in the right direction. It took me over an hour until I finally spotted the Cumberland's funnel in the distance. I was walking down the middle of the road all the way ready to take to my heels if anyone approached me. Thanks goodness, I saw no one, not even a police car all the way back. I think most people kept inside overnight due to the dangerous atmosphere in Kingston. I was mightily relieved to walk through the dock gate and climb up the gangway and drop into my bunk for an hour's sleep before being called at seven to start work. I certainly didn't broadcast this incident or the captain would have given me some dressing down considering his talk before we arrived in port. The old saying God looks after small children and drunken seamen is certainly true in this case, although I was stone cold sober by the time I got back onboard. Probably one of the stupidest and the most dangerous situations I ever found myself in even outweighed the Recife fire, Vietnam War and my other mishaps over the years at sea. This was something that I made sure I never repeated.

We departed Kingston and headed to Panama and onwards to NZ. With no big problems on the way. All the usual activities in NZ, discharging, loading, cargo plans, nights onboard, nights ashore, visiting friends and generally enjoying life.

I had made good friends with the third engineer onboard so when we arrived back in Liverpool and paid off, he invited me to stay with him and his family for a couple of days at his home in Huddersfield. It was the first week in a January so no rush in getting back home as the festive season had passed. We had a good time there, and I hired a car so we could get around. On the Saturday night, we went to the famous Batley Variety Night Club; it was quite a place. We also had a night in Manchester in the town; we had been at sea for over a month so ready to let our hair down. After a few days, Barry decided he would like to come to Orkney for a visit. We booked flights and arrived home for a relaxing time in Orkney. I showed him the sights, and we attended a few parties, and I think he was quite surprised on how good things were up in the frozen north. He flew back after a week, and I settled down to a quieter pace at home. In February, I was instructed to re-join the Cumberland loading in Cardiff once again for NZ. This voyage however was destined to be a double header. This meant we would sail to NZ, discharge then load for the USA and Canada then discharge and reload back down to Australia. After which, we would return to NZ and load for home, a full ten months' voyage. This was known as a MANZ line charter.

The company had decided in 1968 to allow both officers and crews to have bars built onboard. This was a complete change of attitude as in the past liquor onboard was limited to a couple of beers or a bottle of spirits per week at the most. Drink was not something consumed in great quantities at sea; for quite a good reason you certainly did not wish anyone to be under the influence of alcohol on duty. All the necessary equipment and materials for the bars were supplied and the construction was carried out by officers and crew alike. In fact, the officer's bar was constructed by the captain and chief engineer along with some assistance from the carpenter. The bar was in the engineer's lounge, which was much larger than the deck officer's lounge. It was really just like any lounge bar ashore. Payment for drinks was done by signed chits as no money was used. This was all covered by the chief steward who organised the stocking of the bar with designated officers in charge of the bar. It certainly made a big difference when parties were held whilst in port, and there were plenty of them. I think things are different at sea now with most ships being dry with no liquor onboard.

We departed Cardiff and headed out via Curacao and Panama again then the nice quiet voyage across the Pacific to NZ. After discharge, loading of the US and Canadian cargoes commenced. All the usual commodities loaded and off we sailed back across the Pacific to Panama. First port in US was Galveston then onwards to New Orleans where I made my first visit to the famous Bourbon Street. Up the coast to Norfolk, Virginia, Philadelphia, New York. When in New York, a party was organised with some of the ladies working in the NZ Embassy along with their friends from other embassies. One of the NZ girls, Jan Harris, took a fancy to Barry, the third engineer and followed the ship firstly up to Boston then up to Montreal where they got engaged. The wedding was quickly organised to take place on our return to New York on the passage back down the US coast.

We did have a very pleasant voyage up the US coast and to Montreal as it was midsummer so lovely warm but quite humid weather, have fond memories of the trip.

We sailed back down to New York and the big wedding took place in City Hall where I was best man. The ship was berthed in Newark, New Jersey, a good taxi ride or train ride away from downtown New York. As there was a good number of Jan's friends along with several members of the ship's company in attendance, it was agreed that a bus should be hired to get everyone back to the Cumberland for the wedding reception. A very enjoyable day with the catering staff doing a very good buffet onboard. Of course, we were sailing back down the coast in a couple of days so Jan had to remain in New York and did not catch up with Barry for a couple of months until we arrived back in NZ. This was in July, 1969 and the moon landings were taking place on the 21st so we all watched this great occasion on the TV in New York, a nice place to be on that day; actually, it was quite late in the evening when they landed.

We had one incident onboard in Newark when loading, which would result in my attendance in New York for a court appearance some four years later. Whilst loading heavy wooden crates into No 3 hatch one of the longshoremen was injured. It appeared that he was in the wrong place when the crate was swung in towards the underside of the hatch coaming and the crate hit him. He was taken ashore to hospital in an ambulance. At the time, we could not understand why he was where he was when hit as knowing what was being loaded he should not have been in that area. We did think maybe he was pilfering the small items of cargo close to where he was supposed to be working. At the time, the accident was logged, but we thought nothing more about it. I will cover this later on in my story.

We sailed down the coast to Philadelphia and onwards to Newport News next to Norfolk, Virginia. Whilst there we decided to take our motor lifeboat out for a run and motor over to Virginia beach, a lovely sandy holiday area. Along with some of the engineers, I took command and off we sailed. It took over an hour to get there, and I ran the lifeboat on the beach to get all our swimming gear, towels, etc. ashore, dry then backed off and anchored just a few metres of the shore and swam ashore. We had a great time as there was a fun park next to the beach and plenty of food and drink outlets. All good fun; the problem occurred when we arrived back. We had left quite late to motor back so it was getting dark by the time we arrived. Just as we were hoisting the lifeboat into its locking position on the boat deck, this American custom officer came shouting at us to stand still and nobody move, all very dramatic. I did not see a gun, but I'm sure he had one. We all stood aghast and asked what this was all about; the captain was called, and he explained that we were his officers and had been on a day out. It turned out that the customs officers had been informed of smuggling from a ship out at anchor, and as we had steamed past it on our way back, they thought we were taking drugs ashore. It was all sorted out and the custom officer went on his way. We were in fact loading drugs in Newport News, but it was only cigarettes; once again, a very careful watch was kept on the longshoremen during this operation. After completing loading, we set off bound for Panama and onwards across the Pacific to Australia. We discharged in Newcastle, Sydney, Port Kemble, Melbourne, and Adelaide, all ports I had visited before. Nothing too exciting on the Aussie coast, the usual work routine and a few onboard and ashore parties, a very sociable life in port but very quiet and professional at sea.

*My award from the met office, a dangerous night out in Kingston Jamaica, and a wedding in City Hall, New York.*

We departed Adelaide and sailed down to Auckland where Barry was reunited with Jan and was able to meet her father and mother. I was also invited along a couple of days later to meet them. We settled down once again to the old loading routine, checking and marking off cargo, working on the cargo plan and all the other shipboard duties as officer on deck. We sailed down the coast to Napier, Wellington, Nelson, Littleton, Timaru and finally Port Chalmers Port downriver from Dunedin.

In 1969, the cost of transiting the Panama Canal had increased considerably so the company decided to re-route the Cumberland around Cape Horn to save money; the extra cost of fuel outweighed the extra canal transit costs. This was an interesting voyage heading due East out of Port Chalmers bound for the southern tip of South America. It was November that we sailed so the weather was improving in the Southern Ocean so sea conditions were not bad. Never saw another ship until we rounded the Cape and headed north, bound for Las Palmas for bunkers. The voyage at sea was about 26 days. I was on watch when we rounded Cape Horn so was quite proud to be a Cape Horner. We did see lots of little penguins swimming past us as we sailed up past the Falklands. There was also lots of whales and porpoises/dolphins to see on the voyage along with our favourite bird, the Albatross.

After bunkering in Las Palmas, we sailed home to arrive in Hull on 18th December. As there were no flights from Hull and the trains north were limited, four of us bound for Scotland hired a taxi to Glasgow. Not sure what the cost was, but it was certainly the best way to get from A to B at that time. I spent the night in a hotel in Glasgow and managed to catch a flight home the next day. It was great to be home once again for the festive season, and as Barry and Jan had come over to meet his parents, they decided to come to Orkney for Hogmanay. They enjoyed their visit and headed back down to Huddersfield by ferry to Scrabster and then the train from Thurso, quite a long journey especially in January. I was to meet up with them a couple of years later when they had a house in Auckland.

After being home for a month, I received orders to re-join the Cumberland as second mate in Cardiff. This was the next step up the ladder. As second mate, I was responsible for all navigation aspects of the vessel, working out the courses to steer and distances to each port and transferring these onto the relevant navigation chart. Not forgetting to wind the chronometers daily. This was always of course agreed with the captain who had overall command in all ship operations. I also received the chart corrections from the hydrographic department via ship chart agents and spent many hours keeping all the charts up to date. We had quite a large chart portfolio onboard due to the trading routes of the company. I was also responsible for all cargo operations onboard where the cargo was stowed, etc. This included working out the estimated draught of the vessel and the GM for every port we either loaded or discharged at along with the weekly calculations at sea and bunkering estimates. So never a dull moment keeping ever thing up to date. My watch at sea was now the 12-4, the 'graveyard watch' as it was known. By this time, most ships were fitted with automatic steering (iron mike) so no one on the wheel steering anymore. I was fine with this as you had no one on the bridge with you, which I preferred. We still had the lookout on the focle head during the hours of darkness and always a crewmember on call if required. We completed loading in Cardiff and set sail once again for NZ.

The voyage out was a very peaceful trip, and I soon got used to my new position onboard. The daily sight routine meant that I was on the bridge by nine in the morning so no long lie after getting to my bunk every morning about 4:30 am. Once the midday sight was done, I would shoot down to the saloon for my lunch whilst one of the third mates stayed on the bridge. I was always back up before one o'clock to let him get their lunch. There were times at sea when you could get lunch at 11:30, known as seven bells meal and be on the bridge before 12 but this was a bit of a rush. The crew on watches did comply with the seven bells meal times to allow them to relieve other crewmembers on watch. Everything onboard was done in the most efficient manner possible to keep the ship running like clockwork. We arrived in NZ and once discharge was completed, loaded the usual cargo for home. My job now was much more complex as I had to provide the shore cargo supervisors with details of where each parcel of cargo was to be loaded. With six hatches, it was possible to have up to 10 gangs of wharfies loading cargo at any one time. Luckily, the main cargo was frozen lamb so no big problem with stowage factors, all basically the same shape and size so easy to stow. We did have a multitude of different shipper marks on the carcasses destined for different consignees, also different ports and sometimes the ports could be optional. This meant that you had to make sure that each parcel of cargo could be accessible no matter which of the optional ports you went to first. It was normal however to know in advance your first port of discharge and the rota of ports until the final discharge port. We were also loading at several ports so once again had to make sure access was available at the last port of loading for a parcel of cargo that might be for the last port of discharge. As I said before, you also had the problem of making sure the vessel was always in a stable condition with a positive GM. The draught and trim of the vessel was also calculated to make sure it would sail and arrive in port in the best condition as possible. All very taxing work and kept you on your toes and always relieved when everything worked out as you planed. We sailed back to the UK same route as normal with no hiccups on the way so was pleased to arrive back safely in Hull in June…As I was due to go on study leave in September for the start of the autumn course for my Master's Certificate, I decided to stay onboard to do the coastal voyage. This suited me fine as we had a couple of continental ports to discharge at which made a nice cruise around to Hamburg, a night out at the famous beer hall, The Zillertal, onwards to Rotterdam and Antwerp, we finally ended up in London where I paid off. As I had got rid of my little red sports car, I decided to look for a car to do me over my study leave. I met up with the previous second mate who was studying for his master's ticket in London, and he said his next-door neighbour had a car for sale. I thought I would get a good deal for a private cash sale so we agreed a price, and I became a proud owner of a white and black Ford Cortina GT. This was quite a high spec car, and I was very pleased with myself on getting such a good bargain. As I had gathered quite a load of belongings being on the ship for four years, it was much easier having a car to carry everything home. Just one little story before I finish this part of my saga. The weekend before I headed home, I was invited to a party up in London with one of the engineers. This was in a big house in the east end. It was quite a noisy affair with lots of drink and music. After sometime, a few tough-looking chaps arrived and the conversation turned to who they were. They were allegedly part of the Kray twins' gang. Although I had no idea who they were at the time, I realised later on in life who I was rubbing shoulders with, not the best people to be near. The Kray twins being the biggest crooks in London in the 50s and 60s and were jailed a month before the party I attended.

*Cumberland crew enjoying a night ashore in Hamburg, me standing far right with the Zillertal band on stage.*

**The New Zealand Shipping Company Limited**
(incorporated in New Zealand)

**Federal Steam Navigation Company Limited**

Sea Staff Personnel Department

Royal Albert Dock London E16

Telephone 01-283 5220

Telegrams Nuzedoc London E16

KEW/JR/TESTIMONIAL

8th July, 1970

FOR BOARD OF TRADE PURPOSES ONLY

        THIS IS TO CERTIFY that the undermentioned statement of the service of Mr. Robert Chalmers SCLATER in the vessels of this Company is correct and that the Masters under whom he served have satisfactorily reported upon his Conduct, Ability and Sobriety.

        During the service claimed Mr. SCLATER acted in the capacity of 3rd Watchkeeping Officer in sole charge of a watch for eight hours out of every twenty-four hours at sea whilst serving as 3rd Mate, and as 2nd Watchkeeping Officer in sole charge of a watch for eight hours out of every twenty-four hours at sea whilst serving as 2nd Mate. An entry to this effect has been made in the Mate's Log.

| Name of Vessel | Port of Registry and Official No. | Capacity | From | To |
|---|---|---|---|---|
| m.v. SUSSEX | LONDON 183003 | 3rd Mate | 14. 4.66. | 14. 5.66. |
| m.v. HUNTINGDON | LONDON 181898 | 3rd Mate | 7. 7.66. | 28. 7.66. |
| m.v. CUMBERLAND | LONDON 182901 | 3rd Mate | 22. 8.66. | 23. 1.67. |
| m.v. CUMBERLAND | LONDON 182901 | 3rd Mate | 13. 2.67. | 17. 6.67. |
| m.v. CUMBERLAND | LONDON 182901 | 3rd Mate | 12. 8.67. | 19.12.67. |
| m.v. CUMBERLAND | LONDON 182901 | 3rd Mate | 2. 2.68. | 24. 5.68. |
| m.v. CUMBERLAND | LONDON 182901 | 3rd Mate | 26. 7.68. | 4. 1.69. |
| m.v. CUMBERLAND | LONDON 182901 | 3rd Mate | 6. 2.69. | 18.12.69. |
| m.v. CUMBERLAND | LONDON 182901 | 2nd Mate | 26. 1.70. | 11. 5.70. |
| m.v. CUMBERLAND | LONDON 182901 | 2nd Mate | 13. 5.70. | 3. 6.70. |

        During the above periods Mr. SCLATER was not granted Leave of Absence whilst on Articles.

        Watches were doubled on the following dates and at no other times:-

m.v. SUSSEX

        21. 4.66.
        28. 4.66.
         3. 5.66.

m.v. HUNTINGDON

        14. 7.66.
        26. 7.66.

Continued .....

members of the P & O Group

```
27. 8.66.
21. 1.67.
17. 2.67.
16. 6.67.
22. 8.67.
16.12.67.
18.12.67.
 3. 2.68.
13. 2.68.
20. 5.68.
30. 7.68.
20. 8.68.
 3. 1.69.
14. 2.69.
15.12.69.
29. 1.70.
10. 5.70.
14. 5.70.
21. 5.70.
24. 5.70.
26. 5.70.
```

On these dates Mr. SCLATER served as the Junior of two Bridgekeeping Officers whilst serving as 3rd Mate, and as Senior of two Bridgekeeping Officers, whilst serving as 2nd Mate.

*S. Holley.*

Marine Superintendent

I headed home in my new car, left London Docks about 5 am and reached Aberdeen late afternoon. Went and visited John and Moira Leslie, who now lived there as John was involved with the new North Sea oil business and had given up the sea. The next day, I drove up to Scrabster and home on the St Ola, not seasick this time.

Life was to change once again as I met up with Anna who had been away working in a bank in Dundee for the past two years and had come home to work in the local branch again. When I bumped into her, I was just getting into my new car and asked if she wanted a run in it (quite a corny pick-up line). She said yes so that was the start of our romance after four years apart. This was in June, and I had a couple of months at home before attending college. Billy Rendall, one of my friends from NZ, had returned to Orkney with his family and became a fisherman. As I had time on my hands during the day, I spent most weekdays going fishing with him. The main catch being lobsters and crabs. It was a very relaxing and enjoyable two months at home. Rekindling my friendship with Anna and enjoying summer in Orkney. At the same time, my old friend Bill Spence was home and due to go to Aberdeen to study for his Master's Certificate. We discussed where we might stay and put an advert in the P&J, the local Aberdeen paper, looking for accommodation to rent. We received a positive reply from the Woodside House Hotel who had a small cottage next to the hotel in Bucksburn. It sounded perfect for our needs, and the rent was much cheaper than staying in the seaman's mission, which was getting a bit seedy by 1970. We took up the offer and both set off down to Aberdeen to commence our studying. We both had our own cars; Bill had a small MG midget with very little boot space so I carried a lot of his luggage down with me. We sailed over on the St Ola and agreed to meet at John and Moira's house when we arrived in Aberdeen. I arrived first, and we waited some time before Bill turned up. Transpired he had a crash on the way down and his car had a good few dents in it. We then headed down to our new home in Aberdeen, which was ideal, a nice cottage by the River Dee. The owner was a bit concerned when we said we were attending Robert Gordon's College, but after we convinced her we were in fact Merchant Navy Officers studying to be master mariners and not wild university students, she was happy for us to stay. Bill's car had to go for repairs so I drove us in and out to the college until it was fixed. At the same time as we were studying, Bill's girlfriend from Orkney was also studying at Aberdeen University so was very handy for both of them. We all settled down to our studying, which was the most demanding course of my career. The main subjects were similar to Mates, but now, we also had more legal aspects with a full paper on ship master's business. There was also an extra practical part on correcting the deviation on a compass using a 'devioscope'. The rule of the road along with the international code of signals, morse code and semaphore were all the same. Stability along with electronics, engineering, gyro compass, ship construction were all more detailed than previous exams. Navigation and chart work were also slightly more complicated. We no longer went back to the college every evening and instead studied at home in our little cottage. I was quite good at cooking so did the breakfast and evening meal on most days; we had lunch in the college canteen. In October, Anna took some holidays and came down to stay for a week. On the Saturday, we went into Aberdeen and bought an engagement ring as we had agreed to get married before I returned to sea. We kept it a secret all day and went out that evening with Bill and Margaret along with John and Moira for a meal at the Bridge of Dee Motel (no longer there). They were very excited about our news, and we had a splendid evening. We had already phoned both our parents with the news.

*John and me in 1963 heading off to Aberdeen to study for my second mate's ticket.*

*The engagement party, my mother, aunt and Bill at our cottage.*

No. ST 19134

## St. Andrew's Ambulance Association

### Special Certificate in First Aid to the Injured

to meet the requirements of the
Ministry of Transport and Civil Aviation

**This is to Certify that**

Robert Chalmers Sclater

has attended a Course of Lectures and Demonstrations on **First Aid**
to the Injured and has passed the _____Second_____ Examination.

Head Office:
Milton Street,
Glasgow,
C.4

_Daniel Strachan_ .....General Secretary

_____Lecturer

_____ MBUA. _____ Examiner

Date 6th November 1970

_This Certificate expires three years
from date of issue._

We continued with our studies and by November had covered all the syllabus so decided to sit for our Master's Certificate that month. The course was supposed to take six months, but after three, we thought we were ready. We were not in fact fully up to speed and did not pass our written exams although did pass everything else. Not quite so happy but did know where I went wrong in the one paper I failed. As I mentioned, you required. 70% overall pass mark but had to have a 50% pass at least in every paper. I made a complete mess of my ship's construction paper and did not reach the 50% pass mark. I believe if I had achieved 55%, I would have passed overall. Not to worry as still had three months paid study leave so got back down to studying. I did in fact head home early in December as Anna and I had set the date of 8th January for our wedding. Most people these days take more than a year to organise this special event. January is not the usual time of year for weddings so no problem in organising the minister and church along with the hotel for the reception. We had to send out invitations, which was a bit short notice, but we did get it all organised. Ended up with two ministers carrying out wedding ceremony, Anna's minister from South Ronaldsay where she lived and my minister from St Magnus Cathedral, my church in Kirkwall where we got married. The only sad thing about our wedding was my father was quite ill at the time and was unable to attend. We lived in the Town Hall House, which is straight across the street from the cathedral so he was able to see us from his window. Bill was the best man, and we were both kitted out in our best uniforms as you can see from the photos. After a great night, the next day we flew down to Inverness for the weekend, our honeymoon; we were to have an exciting honeymoon two months later when Anna came to sea with me after I had completed my studies, and we sailed to New Zealand. I will cover this later on. I had to sell my car as we did not have much money so it was a tough time for both of us. We caught the train through to Aberdeen on the Sunday, and I was back at college to finish off my studying. We hired a car for the couple of weeks we were in Aberdeen before I could sit my exams again. This I did in January and passed on the 25th with flying colours. We then went down to Edinburgh where I had to attend a radar simulator course, which was required before I could receive my Master's Certificate. Anna's brother and his wife lived in Edinburgh at the time so very handy during the day for Anna whilst I was at the radar school in Leith. I managed a visit onboard my old training ship, the TS Dolphin, still in West Old Dock. I had come a long way in the past 14 years. After completing this course in Leith, we headed home for a couple of weeks' holidays until I received instructions to report to the Hinakura in Liverpool. The company by this time allowed officers of my rank to take their wives to sea with them so this was great. We flew down to Liverpool and stayed the first night in the Merchant Navy Hotel then next morning went down to Liverpool Docks. The second mate's cabin only had a single bunk so the carpenter started work that morning to convert it into a double bunk without any great problem. We only stayed on the ship for a few days then were ordered to join the Hauraki in Avonmouth, which was loading for New Zealand. We arrived onboard and settled in, and I started my usual onboard tasks of sorting the navigation requirements to get us safely to NZ.

*The photo of Anna and I newly married Bill best man and Elizabeth Anna's sister in law bride's maid. 08/01/71.*

# CERTIFICATE OF COMPETENCY

AS

# MASTER

OF A FOREIGN-GOING SHIP

No. *111219*

To    - *Robert Chalmers Sclater* -

WHEREAS you have been found duly qualified to fulfil the duties of Master of a Foreign-going Ship in the Merchant Navy, the Board of Trade in exercise of their powers under the Merchant Shipping Acts and of all other powers enabling them in that behalf hereby grant you this Certificate of Competency.

Dated this   *25th*   day of   *March*    19 *71*

Countersigned

_____
Registrar General

An Under Secretary of the Board of Trade.

REGISTERED AT THE OFFICE OF THE REGISTRAR GENERAL OF SHIPPING AND SEAMEN.

---

Signature of the person to whom this Certificate is issued _____

Year of Birth: NINETEEN HUNDRED AND *Forty one*

Place of Birth *Kirkwall, Orkney*

This Certificate is given upon an Examination passed on the *25th* day of *January* 19 *71*

Issued at the Port of *Kirkwall*

on the *10th* day of *August* 19 *71*

_____ Supt.

If any person forges or fraudulently alters, or assists in forging or fraudulently altering, or procures to be forged or fraudulently altered any Certificate of Competency, or an Official Copy of any such Certificate, or makes, assists in making, or procures to be made, any false Representation for the Purpose of procuring either for himself or for any other person a Certificate of Competency; or fraudulently uses a Certificate or Copy of a Certificate of Competency which has been forged, altered, cancelled or suspended, or to which he is not entitled; or fraudulently lends his Certificate of Competency or allows it to be used by any other person, that person shall in respect of each offence be guilty of a Misdemeanour.—Section 104 of the Merchant Shipping Act. 1894.

NOTE.—Any person finding this Certificate must send it to the Registrar General of Shipping and Seamen, Cardiff, CF5 2YS, postage unpaid.

202913 6/68 873

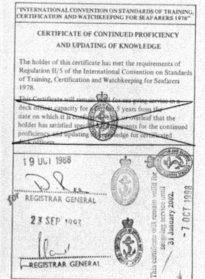

"INTERNATIONAL CONVENTION ON STANDARDS OF TRAINING, CERTIFICATION AND WATCHKEEPING FOR SEAFARERS 1978"

CERTIFICATE OF CONTINUED PROFICIENCY AND UPDATING OF KNOWLEDGE

The holder of this certificate has met the requirements of Regulation II/5 of the International Convention on Standards of Training, Certification and Watchkeeping for Seafarers 1978.

This Certificate will remain ... for sea-going service in a deck officer capacity for ... 5 years from the date on which it is ... overleaf that the holder has satisfied spe... ...ents for the continued proficiency and updating ... ...ledge for certificated officers.

19 OCT 1988

REGISTRAR GENERAL

23 SEP 1993

REGISTRAR GENERAL

---

*My radar certificate and master's certificate.*

# Part 2

It was quite surreal joining Hauraki, the last ship I had sailed on as an EDH in 1963, and now back onboard her as Second Officer with a Master's ticket and married.

We sailed out of Avonmouth on the 13 March bound for Curacao, Panama, and New Zealand. This was our honeymoon, although it was a working one for me, but having Anna onboard certainly was like no other voyage I had been on. Our cabin was our dayroom plus bedroom with only a sink. There was a cadets' toilet and shower room next to our cabin that was made available to Anna; there were no cadets on board.

These older vessels were not really suitable for wives other than the most senior officers who had en-suite facilities. We were, however, quite happy with our lot. The master on this voyage was Captain Jamie Laidlaw from Biggar in the borders of Scotland and quite a character to sail with. He was known as "Rock-hopping Laidlaw".

If there was an island on the route, he would head for it even if it meant a slight detour from the recognised course, normally taken on ocean voyages. This did give me extra work, calculating the course and distances to take on each leg of our voyage but it did make the trip more interesting for everyone onboard, seeing places you would not normally see.

He was also a great man for looking for more cargo to load than what was allocated by the company's offices in each loading port in New Zealand. By this time, the company had also done away with the junior third officer's post on all their vessels, so only three deck officers now. This did entail extra duties for me, as I was now required to do nights onboard duty taking turns with the third mate, a bit of a bind with Anna onboard.

This did curtail our ability to go ashore in the evenings when we wanted. Also, I would now still have to mark off cargo and draw up the cargo plan, the tasks usually done by the two third mates. One positive thing about the reduction was we could not double up watches. The four hours on and four hours off routine was, in my mind, more dangerous due to lack of sleep.

The first land as usual after leaving the UK was the Azores and then across the Atlantic into the Saragossa Sea, very interesting for Anna to see the yellow weed coming up on the gulf stream. Plenty of flying fish and dolphins to see. We entered the Caribbean via the channel between the islands of Guadeloupe and Dominica with our usual stopover in Caracas Bay for bunkers.

Nothing much to see there but a nice walk ashore to the old fenced off swimming pool and then up to one of Captain Morgan's old forts overlooking the bay. We then sailed onwards to the Panama Canal, a very fascinating place to see no matter how many times you transited. Anna who had only travelled abroad to Norway a couple of years before, found these new places very exciting and was really enjoying her first trip on sea.

We had a very pleasant voyage across the Pacific Ocean first passing the Galapagos then onwards towards the French Polynesian islands, Tahiti and Moorea were stunning sights. The photos below MV Hauraki and a copy of the track chart showing our voyage out and back highlighting the many islands we sailed past.

*MV Hauraki*

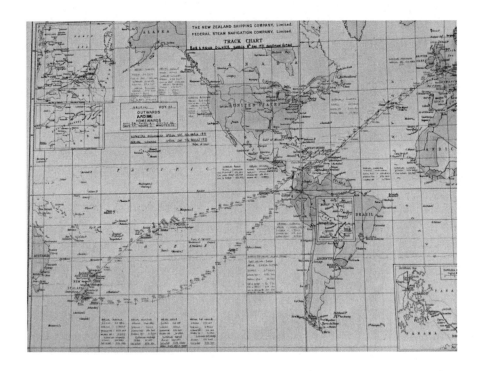

*Track Chart*

After noon each day, I placed a track chart in the officer's and crew's quarters to let them know our position; also the clock changes each night. This ensured mid-day was at 12 noon for our sights.

Courses and distances on two separate voyages showing how Captain Laidlaw's routes were very different from the normal tracks taken.

M.V. HAURAKI       AT SEA     26-3-71

BALBOA TO TAURANGA

| | | Co. | Dist. | To Go. |
|---|---|---|---|---|
| From Fairway Buoy | | | | 6774.2 |
| to Taboguilla ils lt | brg 252 x.5ml | 162 | 3.1 | 6771.1 |
| to Cabo Mala lt | brg 287x 5.9ml | 197 | 86.0 | 6685.1 |
| to Frales Del Sur | brg 315x5.5ml 7 17.80 05 | 225 | 14.3 | 6670.8 |
| to Cape Norte | brg 185x6.oml 0 30s 89 20w | 230 | 727.2 | 5943.6 |
| to Pta Wreck Lt Ho | brg 143 x 5.0ml | 233 | 24.5 | 5919.1 |
| to Cabo Rosa | brg 349 x 4.5ml 01 07s 91 09w | 259 | 90.8 | 5828.3 |
| to Pukapuka | brg 344 x 3.0ml 14 52s 138 48w | 254 | 2960.3 | 2868.0 |
| to Takume | brg 180 x 4.9ml 15 40s 142 10w | 256 | 202.5 | 2665.5 |
| to Twr. Kauehi ils | brg 180 x 6.2ml 15 40s 145 09w | 270 | 172.4 | 2493.1 |
| to Niau ils | brg 332 x 5.5ml 16 15s 146 18w | 242 | 75.4 | 2417.7 |
| to Venus Pt Lt | brg 151x 1.4ml 17 28s 149 30w | 248½ | 198.8 | 2218.9 |
| to Motu Tehiri ils | brg 159 x 2.5ml | 249 | 7.2 | 2211.7 |
| to Nuvpere Pt | brg 340 x 2.2ml 17 37 149 47w | 236 | 10.6 | 2201.1 |
| to Mauke ils | Posn 20 16s 157 20w | 250 | 459.4 | 1741.7 |
| to Raratonga ils | Posn 21 20s 159 44w | 245 | 149.9 | 1591.u8 |
| to Tauranga | Posn 37 36s 176 11e | 232 | 1591.8 | |

Charts: 1299, 3111, 1929, 4023, 1375, 785, 3664, 998, 2683, 1382, 1158, 993,
1264, 788, NZ 11, NZ 541, 3633, 2527, 3332, NZ 5412.

      Steaming Times:  @ 14kts .......483 42m
                       @ 14½kts ......467h 12m      12m
                       @ 15 kts ......451 24
                       @ 15½kts ......437h 00m
                       @ 16kts ....... 421h 27m

      Clocks to beretarded 67hrs 00mins  and advanced 24hrs 00mins

THE NEW ZEALAND SHIPPING Co., LTD.
FEDERAL STEAM NAVIGATION Co., LTD.

## Balboa to Auckland

| | | Co. | Dist. | TO Go |
|---|---|---|---|---|
| Fm. Fairway Buoy | | | | 6569.2 |
| to Taboguilla Is. lt | brg 252 @ 1.6 mls | 162 | 3.1 | 6566.1 |
| to Cabo Mala Lt | brg 287 @ 6.0 mls | 197 | 86.0 | 6480.1 |
| to Frailes del Sur Lt | brg 301 @ 9.2 mls | 211 | 12.5 | 6467.6 |
| to Posn. off Culpeppa Is | brg 156 @ 7.0 mls 01 46 N 92 04 W | 246 | 796.9 | 5670.7 |
| to Posn 10m off Rapa Is. | 27 26 S 144 24 W | 240 | 3512.1 | 2158.6 |
| to Posn off Cuvier Is lt | brg 165 @ 3.4 mls 36 23 S 175 46 E | 255 | 2105.0 | 53.6 |
| to Channel Is Lt. | brg 352 @ 0.8 ml | 262 | 21.2 | 32.4 |
| to The Noises Lt | brg 145 @ 4.3 mls | 235 | 22.4 | 10.0 |
| to Rangitoto Bn. | brg 134 @ 0.8 ml | 224 | 10.0 | |

Charts: 1299, 1300, 1929, 2145, 3318, 1375, 4023, 788, 786, 1375, 783, 992,
29, 780, 3633, 3797, 3565, N.Z. 532, 5322, 11, 52.

Steaming Time: @ 18  kts.........365h 00m
@ 18½ kts.........355h 00m
@ 19  kts.........345h 54m
@ 19½ kts.........336h 30m
@ 20  kts.........328h 24m

Clocks: Retard 07h 00m and Advanced 24h 00m

## PORT CHALMERS to BALBOA

| | | Co. | Dist | To Go |
|---|---|---|---|---|
| FromTairoa Hd. Lt.  brg 190 x 1.5ml | 45 45 S 170 44E | | | 6662.5 |
| to Posn off Bounty Island | 47 35 S 179 00 E | 108 | 361.6 | 6300.9 |
| to Posn. B. | 47 38 S 170 00 E | 090½ | 444.9 | 5856.0 |
| to Posn. C. | 47 05 S 160 00 W | 085½ | 407.8 | 5448.2 |
| to Posn. D. | 45 30 S 150 00 W | 077 | 424.5 | 5023.7 |
| to Posn. E. | 43 00 S 140 00 W | 070¾ | 456.4 | 4567.3 |
| to Posn. F. | 39 25 S 130 00 W | 064½ | 501.4 | 4065.9 |
| to Posn. G. | 34 03 S 120 00 W | 056 | 580.2 | 3485.7 |
| to Posn. H.  off Easter Island | 27 30 S 110 00 W | 052¾ | 650.0 | 2835.7 |
| to Posn. I. | 18 50 S 100 00 W | 046¾ | 759.8 | 2075.9 |
| to Posn. J. | 08 30 S 90 00 W | 043½ | 853.0 | 1222.9 |
| to Posn. K.  off Malpelo Island | 04 00 N 81 35 W | 034 | 905.3 | 317.6 |
| to Cabo Malo brg 292 x 3.5 ml | 07 27 N 79 57 W | 025 | 228.3 | 89.3 |
| to Taboguilla Island brg 289 x 1.0 ml | | 019 | 85.5 | 3.8 |
| to Fairway Buoy | | 000 | 3.8 | |

Charts: N.Z. 6612, 2532, 3634, N.Z. 11,1022, 788, 789, 783, 1386, 4023,

3318, 396, 1929, 1300, 1299, 3111, 5098.

Steaming Times:  @  14  kts ...... 475h 54m

@  14½ kts ...... 459h 30m

@  15  kts ...... 444h 12m

@  15 ½ kts ...... 429h 51m

@  16  kts ...... 416h 24m

### Port Chalmers to Balboa

| | | Co | Dist. | To Go |
|---|---|---|---|---|
| Fm Posn off Tiaroa Head | 45 45 S 170 44 E | | | 6736.4 |
| to Posn off Bounty Island | 47 38 S 179 11 E | 108 | 367.1 | 6369.3 |
| to Posn off Easter Island | 27 18 S 109 36 W | Var. | 3473.1 | 2896.2 |
| to Posn off Easter Island | 27 06 S 109 12 W | 061 | 24.6 | 2871.6 |
| to Posn off Ia La Plata | 01 24 S 81 12 W | 046¾ | 2238.8 | 632.8 |
| to Posn off Pta Galera | 01 00N 80 12 W | 023 | 156.2 | 476.6 |
| to Posn off Cabo Malo | 07 27 N 79 57 W | 002 | 387.3 | 89.3 |
| to Taboguilla Island brg 289 x 1.0 ml | | 019 | 85.5 | 3.8 |
| to Fairway buoy | | 000 | 3.8 | |

When we arrived in Tauranga, we discovered that my old fried Ernie Carter and his family now lived there. It was great for Anna to have Dorothy to visit during the day when I was on duty. Ernie also loaned us his car so we could take a trip to Rotorua to see the hot springs, which was a couple of hours drive away.

It was nice to be in port and meeting up with people from home. After Tauranga, we sailed up to Auckland to complete discharge and start loading our homeward bound cargo. Jan and Barry Beaumont now lived in Auckland, so we also met up with them. I also managed to track down my old friend John Hayday living in Auckland as well. He invited us over to his house for a meal and we caught up on his life stories since I last saw him on the Cumberland.

I was of course busy now, sorting out our loading plan so not really much shore leave and also having to do nights onboard, not very exciting for Anna at times. We were to load in Napier, and port Chalmers as well as Auckland. It was a 6-port discharge with a couple of options on which port came first on the continent. The ports were Dunkirk, Antwerp, Flushing, Rotterdam and Hamburg finishing off in London.

This was quite a task as Captain Laidlaw was ashore most days looking for more cargo to load. Anyway, we sailed down the coast to Napier, then onto port Chalmers to finish off. We did have quite a nice time as there was no Saturday afternoon or Sunday working and the wharfies knocked off at five o'clock which was fine.

We certainly managed to see quite a lot of New Zealand during our visit and met some nice people along the way. The loading progressed well and I managed to load everything in a ship shape manner with every port's draught and GM worked out.

I think this was the largest cargo ever loaded on one of the "h" boats. We had every hatch full even the tonnage hatch. On top of every hatch was hundreds of bales of wool and on deck alongside no's 2,3,4,5 barrels of casings and tallow. I was informed a few months later that Captain Laidlaw carried a copy of the cargo plan to show anyone interested just how much cargo we carried.

Of course, I had the task of ensuring that everything fitted and was accessible for discharge in the correct port rotation. You can see from the track chart that the route home was a great circle with us sailing further south and heading towards Easter Island.This was something quite new as in all my previous voyages we never sailed this route. We arrived in Panama and back to Curacao for bunkers, then onwards to Dunkirk. Captain Laidlaw went home on leave from there and another Scotsman, Captain Roddy Michael took over.

It was a nice voyage around the continent calling into Antwerp, Flushing, Rotterdam and Hamburg. Anna and I managed ashore in all the ports and enjoyed sightseeing and the night life. I think Hamburg was an eye opener to Anna. A night out in the Reeperbahn was always an experience. We eventually sailed into London on 7 August (my birthday) and paid off and flew home. I can say without contradiction that not many married couples had a honeymoon like ours.

*The photos of Anna ready for boat drill, relaxing in the sun, Gaillard's cut-Panama Canal, Captain Morgan's fort-Curacao, Pania of the reef-Napier (Māori legend), Hagen Beck Tier Park (zoo)-Hamburg.*

When we arrived home, we did not own a house, so we ended up staying with Anna's folk for a time, then at my folk's flat in the town hall, not really what we wanted. We looked for places to rent but could find nothing suitable.

After a few weeks at home, I was contacted by the company and advised that I had been chosen to attend a very high profile two-week shipboard management course at S. S. Stephenson & Partner's headquarters in Hazelmere in Buckinghamshire.

The main aspect was to do with a new system of planned maintenance onboard ships. Also, more up to date management techniques. The attendees all NZSCo Officers: captains, chief engineers, chief officers, second engineers, one chief steward and I was the only Second officer.

I found the course very enlightening and enjoyed the company of both the lecturers and the other officers.

*The photo of the happy band who attended along with our lectures. I am back row fourth from the right.*

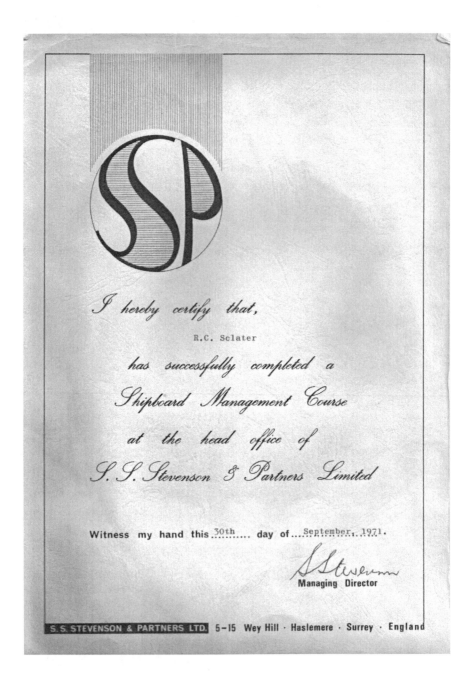

I hereby certify that,

R.C. Sclater

has successfully completed a

Shipboard Management Course

at the head office of

S. S. Stevenson & Partners Limited

Witness my hand this ...30th.... day of ...September, 1971.

Managing Director

S. S. STEVENSON & PARTNERS LTD. 5-15 Wey Hill · Haslemere · Surrey · England

*The Copy of My Certificate*

When the course finished, I had a night in London prior to flying home.

I phoned Anna and she told me that there was a house for sale in South Ronaldson and that we must buy it as staying with her parents was just not an option when I returned to sea. When I arrived home, we picked up the keys from the local bank manager and had a look at Springbank.

It was an old farm house with six acres of the land overlooking St Margaret's Hope and lovely views of Scapa Flow and the Hoy hills. The house had been renovated by a couple from down in England who were to retire there. Unfortunately, the husband died before they could move in and the house had been empty for over a year.

We ascertained the price and managed to get it reduced to £3,500 and bought it within a week. Back in the early seventies, you could only get a mortgage at two and a half times your salary. I did not earn enough but luckily; I had a life insurance policy taken out whilst standing by NZ ships in London in 1966.

The Clydesdale bank gave us a mortgage and used my insurance policy as collateral. It was a wise move I made in 1966. We set to and managed to buy some furniture and laid carpets and moved in within a week. This was to be our home for the next nine years.

At the end of November, I returned to sea and Anna went back to her old job in the Clydesdale bank and lived in rented accommodation in Kirkwall during the week. This, due to the fact that Anna did not have a driving licence and had to use the bus on the 13 miles journey to Kirkwall. Her folks lived in Widewall South Ronaldsay just over a mile from Springbank, so this was very handy for her at the weekends.

My new ship was the MV Wild Auk being built in Bergen for a new consortium of P&O and Lauritzen Reefers, a Danish shipping company specialising in fast fruit carrying vessels. The new company was known as Lauritzen Peninsular Reefers.

I flew down to Newcastle and joined the Norwegian ferry the MV Leda and sailed to Bergen via Stavanger. There were a couple of engineers also on the way to join our new ship. After arriving in Bergen, I was taken to a B&B as the ship was still under construction in the ship yard and not yet suitable to live onboard.

The next morning I reported onboard and met the chief officer. We were the only two deck officers onboard. I had a busy time sorting out all the navigation equipment, charts, nautical publications and everything on the bridge to make us ready for sea. I also had the stability calculations to study and compile the necessary paperwork to ensure safe loading of the vessel.

The ship yard did supply very detailed written stability calculations which were a great help. This work took some time and I was engaged in this for over a week. I was still living ashore and catching the bus down to the shipyard each day.

The other crew members standing by were in other accommodations, one of them was Jack Anderson, a chief engineer who had been on the course in Hazelmere. So nice to meet up with him again. We were eventually allowed to stay onboard and I moved into my cabin which was very well appointed with en-suite facilities.

By this time, other crew members were arriving from the UK and another deck officer reported onboard he was a second mate as well but I was the senior of the two and he took up the responsibility of the third mate. We all worked hard to get everything in order prior to carrying out sea trials and acceptance trials.

By this time the new captain and all officers and crew were onboard. The sea trials took place in the fjords outside Bergen. We had a slight problem as the holds on the vessel were not fully cleaned and this was an essential requirement as our first cargo was to load oranges and grape fruit from Israel for Europe.

The shipyard work force volunteered along with some of their office staff to carry out this cleaning whilst we were on sea trials. Being the ship's cargo officer, I was in charge of this work. This was quite a big job as each deck in the hold had removable wooden gratings to allow the flow of cold air to the cargo be it refrigerated or chilled.

Every grating was lifted and the deck underneath swept clean. There were five hatches with 19 decks in total, a long process. So instead of being present on the bridge during trials, I was down the hatches. It did cause me a bit of concern as I was not fully au fait with all the new navigation equipment onboard. I soon figured it all out prior to our final departure from Bergen.

I was also happy with the hatch cleaning so everything was in order for sailing and for loading our first cargo. I recall that after completing the cleaning of the ships holds, I reported to the captain that everything was in order. The trials had just been completed at about 1700 in the afternoon and I was instructed to go down and change the ensigns to confirm that the Wild Auk was now part of the British merchant navy.

I proceeded aft and started lowering the Norwegian ensign and making ready the red duster; it was dark and blowing quite hard which made the task quite difficult as I did not want to drop either of the flags on the deck. The fact was that representatives of the ship yard along with an official of NZS were watching.

This official, quite an arrogant chap, shouted come on 3/O get the flags sorted. As I was not the third mate, although still in a boiler suit, and had a tough day climbing up and down hatches, I was not in the best frame of mind to have someone shout at me. I just managed to keep my temper, gave him a look that would kill and carried on with sorting out the flags. Could have been my last days in NZS if I had thrown the flag at him.

We departed Bergen a couple of days after sea trials bound for Flushing to Bunker. We sailed early evening and into a force ten storm. It certainly gave the Wild Auk a baptism of what was to come during her maiden voyage. During my first 12/4 watch, we received a mayday call from a vessel in distress due to the ferocious weather.

Unfortunately, we were some 100 miles away so really unable to help as we were not making much headway anyway. I believe the vessel eventually reported it was safe, so no harm done. We arrived in Flushing and bunkered in a few hours then sailed to load our first cargo in the port of Haifa in Israel. This was changed to Ashdod on our voyage out.

The Wild Auk was quite a fast vessel as you can see from the ship's details on the next page. There was no doubling up of watches on this ship; one officer per watch. You certainly were kept on your toes sailing down the English Channel as you were overtaking every ship and had to keep a close watch on crossing ferries and fishing boats as we were travelling at nearly 25 knots (28 mph).

This was quite a difference from the Grosvenor Trader that steamed along about nine knots if you were lucky. We arrived in Ashdod, Israel just after Christmas day to commence loading oranges and grapefruit for Antwerp and Rotterdam. Before arrival in Ashdod, the port authorities were very cautious on ships approaching Israel and once we made contact, we were instructed to put our helm hard over to starboard and then after a couple of minutes return to our course for arrival at the pilot station.

Israel was still on a war footing with the Arab countries, so they made sure no unidentified vessels approached their coast line. The loading of the cargo was quite straight forward as all the boxes of oranges and grapefruit were the same size, so easy stowage. The other second mate and myself had our work cut out as we had to open all the hatches which were all electrically operated. Once each deck was filled, we had to close each hatch top to allow the next deck to be loaded.

The stevedores were not allowed to operate the electrical units used for operating the small winches in each compartment, although they did help to replace the wooden gratings in each deck.

We completed loading without any problems and set sail for Antwerp. It was our wedding anniversary on the 8 January and we were off the Portuguese coast so I called Anna on the ships radio to wish her happy anniversary. It was a terrible line and you had to say 'over' once you spoke, so never tried that again.

*The M.V. Wild Auk on trials still flying the Norwegian ensign.*
*The ship was built by a/s Bergens Mekaniske Verksteder in Bergen, Norway.*
*Signal letters G, O, X, S.*
*Manoeuvring Speeds-Dead Slow-6kts Slow Ahead-10kts Half Ahead-15kts Full Ahead-*
*18kts*
*Certainly, kept the pilot on his toes with these speeds coming into port.*
*Length-154 metres; Beam-21 metres; Summer draft-9 metres.*
*Gross tonnage-9601; Nett tonnage-5317; Displacement-18278 tons; Deadweight-*
*12078 tons.*

Although the ship was handed over, there was still a lot of painting not completed due to the heavy rain encountered in Bergen during the winter months. We, therefore, had painters from the yard onboard to Ashdod to complete the painting. The weather on route was good so the ship was all painted by the time we arrived in Israel.

We had an uneventful discharge of our oranges and grapefruit in Antwerp and Rotterdam and were ready to sail back to Israel within a week. The next loading ports were to be Haifa and Ashdod. The cargo, once again, oranges and grapefruit for Philadelphia and Halifax. We did manage a look ashore but there was not a lot to see in either port.

After leaving Ashdod, we stopped in Augusta, in Sicily, for bunkers. The weather in the Mediterranean in January could be quite rough and we knocked one of our echo sounder transducers out of the bottom of the ship by going too fast in the short heavy swell encountered in the Mediterranean. We did have two, so were still classed as sea worthy.

After clearing the strait of Gibraltar, we headed across the North Atlantic to the USA. The first two days was fine and we kept up our speed of 22/23 knots. The weather conditions deteriorated quite quickly and we were punching into another force ten storm. The engines were slowed down and we battered our way for two days into swells of 30/40 feet.

Once the depression was passed, we picked up speed and arrived safely in Philadelphia. The weather again, not pleasant, down to about ten degrees below. The discharge went without any problems, then we sailed up to Halifax, Canada with the remainder of the fruit. Discharging was very fast, so only a couple of days in port kept us busy opening and closing hatches etc.

We headed back across to Ashdod again to load the same cargo for Halifax, Nova Scotia. On the passage through the straits of Gibraltar, we notched up the fastest speed on the voyage, just over 27 knots (31 mph). After loading in Ashdod, we called into Augusta for bunkers, then onwards to Canada. Another heavy sea crossing and then we arrived in Halifax, still ten degrees below, and this was in March.

We completed discharge and were due to sail down to West Palm beach in Florida for our next cargo. The weather was so bad with storm force winds, snow and freezing temperatures which resulted in departure being delayed for 24 hours. We eventually sailed and within the next 24 hours temperatures had gone from ten degrees below to 15 degrees above. I was informed just prior to departing Halifax that I would be relieved in West Palm beach and be going home on leave on 31 March.

I flew down to Miami and caught a flight to London and home to Orkney. It was really a very interesting and challenging period of my life at sea.

To be the responsible officer, in charge of navigation and cargo operations in a new vessel carrying chilled cargoes at high speed required one to be fully on top of the job. Although I had been onboard, the MV Taupo, a new vessel, in 1966, I was only a junior third officer and only onboard for a couple of days.

After a very well-earned two months leave and with plenty of work to do around Springbank, I was happy to return to sea. Anna was to accompany me once again. We flew down to Liverpool and joined the MV Tongariro on 31 May. We were to sail light ship down to Montevideo and Buenos Aires to load refrigerated and general cargo once again for continental discharge.

The voyage down to Montevideo was very relaxing, although Anna had to put up with me going on watch at midnight and climbing back into our bunk at four in the morning. The Tongariro was a sister ship of the Taupo, built in 1966, so still quite new and we had en-suite facilities much better than the Hauraki.

On arrival in Montevideo, we tied up close to a vessel which had been in collision with an oil tanker on passage down the river plate a couple of weeks before our arrival. This was the MV Royston Grange, a Holder Brothers' vessel carrying frozen and chilled meat and butter from buenos Aires to London.

The Liberian registered tanker loaded with 20000 tons of crude oil was on passage up the river plate, both had pilots onboard but it was thick fog and dark at 0530 in the morning. Everyone on the Royston Grange was killed in the collision, a total of 61 crew, the pilot and 12 passengers of which six were female and one 5-year-old child. On board the tanker MV Tien Chee, eight crew members were killed.

The findings of the accident board were that the tanker had moved into the centre of channel to deeper water, which pushed the Royston Grange further towards the shallower starboard side of the channel. This caused her to bounce off the bank and hit the tanker which exploded causing a massive ball of fire that engulfed the Royston grange.

It was also stated that the cargo of butter would have caught fire and as it was highly inflammable, would have created intense heat. The freon gas used by the refrigeration plant may also have caused carbon monoxide fumes which would have been lethal. The findings also stated that the channel was not properly dredged and not deep enough for fully laden vessels due to the build of slit coming down the river. I will touch on this in a later paragraph.

It certainly was not a very pleasant sights witnessing the burnt-out shell of the Royston Grange and knowing that so many lives were lost onboard her. Some of our own Western Isles crew members had lost friends on the ship. It also brought back sad memories of the fire onboard the MV Debrett in Recife and the ammonia gas refrigeration plant.

We were to load chilled and refrigerated beef in Montevideo and as usual, spent the working day opening and closing hatches drawing up cargo plans and supervising the loading. As I had been in Montevideo on the Debrett, I knew the city reasonably well, so no problem going ashore.

One thing that we did was to head for one of the famous steak restaurants a must in this port. Each T-bone steak was the size of a roast beef lunch for four. I never did manage to eat the whole thing; they came with chips and beef tomatoes. The head stevedore was a very outgoing chap and invited Anna and I along with the chief electrician and his wife ashore one evening for a meal and then to a night club; this once again was an eye opener for them.

The club had a floor show, what appeared to be glamour's female dancers and they did look good until you realised how big they were. It was a transvestite show something quite big in South America. There was other wives onboard and two children. It was common back in the seventies for wives to sail with their husbands. Even the Bosun had his wife with him, a German lady who was renowned for sunbathing topless and she was not a young lady either. Always interesting topics going on at sea.

We sailed up to Buenos Aires to continue loading and had a nice time ashore there as well. There was lovely leather clothes and souvenirs to be bought, so we ended up with new leather coats and a cow hide to take home. Of course we also had more steak dinners when ashore.

The last night in port I was due to be called early to get things ready for the final days loading, finalising the cargo plans and getting charts in order for departure. For some reason, I decided to leave the cabin door unlocked when we went to our bed that evening.

At about five o'clock in the morning, Anna woke up and thought she heard the door but no light came on, a few seconds later she saw a body crawling across the floor and shouted out. I was out of the bunk like a bullet and caught this chap just outside our door. He was not one of the crew and I instructed him to get off the ship.

As I was only wearing pyjama bottoms, I ran back into the cabin got my uniform on and shot down to the gangway and got hold of the shore night watchman. We searched the ship and caught this fellow in the crew's quarters. We got hold of him and contacted the port security who came and took him away.

We should have searched him as it turned out a couple of the crew found their watches were missing when they got up in the morning. Anna was quite distraught and I promised never to leave the cabin door unlocked again.

Mind you it could have been more serious as the robber could have attacked me when I apprehended him.

*The photo of Tongariro, fine looking vessels. There were four vessels of this design the Taupo, Tongariro, Tekoa, and Westmorland. This was quite a transition from the older 'h' class ships of NZSCo. & FSNCo. With the one Halen Derrick replacing two conventional Derricks at each hatch, plus a green hull instead of the old black and red.*

*The two passes required by the authorities in Buenos Aires to allow you to go ashore. You will see that Anna is classed as a stewardess.*

*The artist impression of the Taupo.*

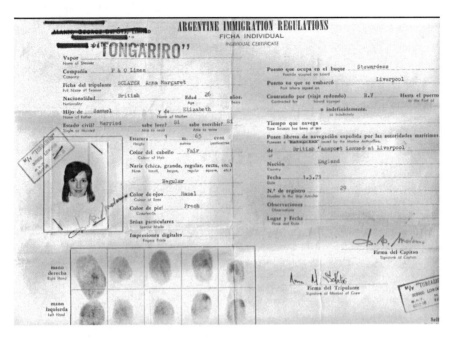

## ARGENTINE IMMIGRATION REGULATIONS
### FICHA INDIVIDUAL
INDIVIDUAL CERTIFICATE

**"TONGARIRO"**

Vapor — Name of Steamer

Compañía — P & O Lines — Company

Ficha del tripulante — SCLATER Anna Margaret — Full Name of Seaman

Nacionalidad — British — Nationality — Edad 26 años — Age — Years

Hijo de — Samuel — y de — Elizabeth — Name of Father — Name of Mother

Estado civil — Married — sabe leer? si — sabe escribir? si — Single or Married — Able to read — Able to write

Estatura — 1 m. 65 cent. — Height — metres — centimetres

Color del cabello — Fair — Colour of Hair

Nariz (chica, grande, regular, recta, etc.) — Nose (small, large, regular, square, etc.) — Regular

Color de ojos — Hazel — Colour of Eyes

Color de piel — Fresh — Complexion

Señas particulares — Special Marks

Impresiones digitales — Finger Prints

mano derecha — Right Hand

mano izquierda — Left Hand

Puesto que ocupa en el buque — Stewardess — Position occupied on board

Puerto en que se embarcó — Liverpool — Port where signed on

Contratado por (viaje redondo) — R.V. — Hasta el puerto — Contracted for — round voyage — to the Port of — o indefinidamente — or indefinitely

Tiempo que navega — Time Seaman has been at sea

Posee libreta de navegación expedida por las autoridades marítimas — Possesses a Passport issued by the Marine Authorities — de — British Passport issued at Liverpool — of

Nación — England — Country

Fecha — 1.3.71 — Date

N.º de registro — 29 — Number in the Ship Articles

Observaciones — Observations

Lugar y Fecha — Place and Date

Firma del Capitán — Signature of Captain

Anne M. Sclater — Firma del Tripulante — Signature of Member of Crew

---

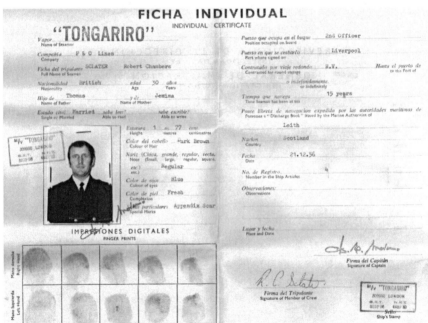

## FICHA INDIVIDUAL
### INDIVIDUAL CERTIFICATE

**"TONGARIRO"**

Vapor — Name of Steamer

Compañía — P & O Lines — Company

Ficha del tripulante — SCLATER Robert Chambers — Full Name of Seaman

Nacionalidad — British — Edad 30 años — Nationality — Age — Years

Hijo de — Thomas — y de — Jemima — Name of Father — Name of Mother

Estado civil — Married — sabe leer? — sabe escribir? — Single or Married — Able to read — Able to write

Estatura — 1 m. 77 cent. — Height — metres — centimetres

Color del cabello — Dark Brown — Colour of Hair

Nariz (Chica, grande, regular, recta, etc.) — Nose (small, large, regular, square, etc.) — Regular

Color de ojos — Blue — Colour of eyes

Color de piel — Fresh — Complexion

Señas particulares — Appendix Scar — Special Marks

### IMPRESIONES DIGITALES
FINGER PRINTS

Mano derecha — Right Hand

Mano izquierda — Left Hand

Puesto que ocupa en el buque — 2nd Officer — Position occupied on board

Puerto en que se embarcó — Liverpool — Port where signed on

Contratado por viaje redondo — R.V. — Hasta el puerto de — Contracted for round voyage — to the Port of — o indefinidamente — or indefinitely

Tiempo que navega — 15 years — Time Seaman has been at sea

Posee libreta de navegación expedida por las autoridades marítimas de — Possesses a "Discharge Book" issued by the Marine Authorities of — Leith

Nación — Scotland — Country

Fecha — 21.12.56 — Date

No. de Registro — 4 — Number in the Ship Articles

Observaciones — Observations

Lugar y fecha — Place and Date

Firma del Capitán — Signature of Captain

R. C. Sclater — Firma del Tripulante — Signature of Member of Crew

M/v "TONGARIRO" — 309990 LONDON — Ship's Stamp

We completed loading in Buenos Aires and sailed late evening bound for Rotterdam. I was on my usual 12/4 watch on the bridge along with the pilot, captain and helmsman, heading down river. At about the same spot as the Royston Grange had its accident the helmsman reported that the ship was not responding to the helm and was drifting to port even with the wheel hard to starboard.

We were navigating in the starboard side of the channel as per normal shipping regulations. Another vessel was heading up river and if we were unable to steer the right course chances were, we could collide. Both pilots being fully aware of the previous collision contacted each other on VHF and it was agreed that instead of passing port to port we would cut across his bows and pass starboard to starboard.

Fortunately, we were far enough away from each other before we passed and this manoeuvre was carried out safely. We believed that the Tongariro had in fact touched the silted up river bank, just like the Royston Grange, and this made us unable to keep the correct heading in the channel.

I did mention previously about the collision between the Grosvenor trader and the Riverdore in Singapore when, if we had altered course to port on that occasion also, we would have not collided. Hindsight is a great thing but also quick thinking is also essential in a difficult situation. Lessons learned by mistakes always hold you in good stead for the future.

We had an uneventful voyage to Rotterdam, lazy days at sea for the wives and kids onboard. My daily routine was up just before midnight to take over my watch, always ten minutes early, if possible, good seafaring practice always relieve before the hour. Providing there was no shipping in the area, I would spend most of my watch correcting charts and updating nautical publications.

The hydrographic department of the navy issued notices to mariners and statutory instruments on a regular basis which contained all the information to keep all our charts and publications up to date. This was a very necessary requirement as it highlighted any navigational dangers and new navigation lights and buoys along with traffic separation zones, something that was coming into operation during the 1960/70.

They introduced a new chart correcting system which consisted of transparencies of each chart corrections which when laid on the chart, made the task much easier. Dealing with a worldwide chart folio kept you quite busy. As the officer in charge of the gyro compass, I also spent time ensuring it was working correctly. It certainly made your grave yard watch pass quickly with all this work also, of course, keeping a good look out for other shipping. At four o'clock after writing up the ships log, you retired to your bunk but was up again by eight for breakfast and on the bridge to take morning sights.

At nine every morning, I would wind up the two chronometers and get a time check via the radio officer. The chronometer was an essential tool in navigation as you had to have the exact Greenwich Mean Time of when you took your sight. The other tools being a nautical almanac, Norie's tables, and most of all your sextant.

Navigating by the sun every day was a rewarding exercise when at mid-day you were able to plot your exact position on the chart, work out the distance and speed over the past 24 hours and then calculate your course and distance to mid-day the next day and also how far to your next port of call. In this day and age, all done by satellite, press a button and you know exactly where you are. Electronic charts that I am sure will be updated automatically with corrections.

I still think the old way was much more rewarding. I did have plenty of free time during the day to relax and spend time with Anna. We arrived in Rotterdam and commenced discharge with no problems with the cargo. Then on to Hamburg another trouble-free discharge.

Of course we had another run ashore to take in the night life of this great city. We also did some sightseeing during the day. After Hamburg, we went across to London to complete discharge. We then sailed down to Falmouth for annual repairs and surveys. The crew paid off ships articles and most of them headed on leave.

As Anna and I had been on the ship for only two months we decided to stay for the next voyage. Whilst in Falmouth, we hired a car one weekend and toured Cornwall, visited Newquay and of course lands' end, can't say we were impressed with these tourist destinations. Falmouth was one of the nicest places in Cornwall and reminded us a lot of home.

After about a week, we signed on articles and set sail for New Zealand once again, light ship. This was the usual track down to Curacao but this time we bunkered in Willemstad, not Caracas Bay, made a nice change and a chance to have a run ashore. I was able to show Anna where I spent my month in the Seaman's mission back in 1959. We went onwards to Panama and across the Pacific to Auckland. We met up with old friends there and then sailed down to Napier and onwards to Timaru.

The head stevedore's wife in Timaru took Anna out for a tour of the countryside. She also had her very young baby with them and part of their trip took them past a couple of the vineyards in the area. I don't think they drank a lot but Anna said it was great fun. We still have a bottle of eldered wine bought on that trip.

*Eldered Wine*

After Timaru it was down to Bluff to complete loading using the all-weather loading gantries that I had first seen used back in 1963. We were, of course, loading mostly frozen lamb on this voyage along with the usual bales of wool and other animal by-products. Once again, we managed to have a weekend off the ship and hired a car and set off on the Saturday morning bound for Queenstown.

We headed first to see lake Wanaka just over a 3-hour drive through spectacular countryside. We then headed down to Queenstown. On the way, we passed a little town called Arrowtown and visited a museum. Whilst looking around, the curator noticed we were looking at a spinning wheel and asked if we knew where it came from, of course we said no. Well, she said it had come all the way from the Orkney islands. She was quite aghast when we told her that's where we came from.

We then headed to Queenstown and spent the night in a hotel, quite a change from onboard ship. Next day we headed back towards Bluff, stopping off in Invercargill, the most southerly large town in South Island. There is a big long sandy beach called Oreti beach close to Invercargill that we took a run down to see. There were lots of cars driving on the beach which went on for miles.

I was to discover later that this was the beach where the fastest Indian (a motor bike) owned by Burt Munro practiced on before he broke a world record for speed in the USA. We returned to the ship in Bluff and I got back to my duties sorting out the cargo plan and setting the course for our voyage home. The usual track back via Panama and curacao with an uneventful trip with nice balmy weather.

Anna had a slight problem on the way home with a sick bug. We had been given a present of bottled peaches from our friends in Napier Mr and Mrs Bob Organ. Anna thought she had a bit of food poisoning from them but we then figured out she was, in fact, pregnant. We never told anyone as you were not allowed to be onboard if you were pregnant.

Our first port in the UK was Avonmouth, just across the Bristol channel from Cardiff where Bill Spence was studying for a nautical degree at Cardiff university. Margaret and Bill were married by this time and we got in touch with them from the ship. Bill came over in his little MG sports car and took us over for a visit with them one evening, it was nice to see them and we had a good night although unfortunately for Bill having to drive us back to the Tongariro not able to drink.

The ship once again paid off in Avonmouth but Anna and I remained onboard for the coastal voyage to make sure I had enough leave to stay home for Christmas and New Year. We then sailed up to Southampton to complete discharge. We paid off on 3 November and headed home for a couple of months leave after a very interesting second trip for Anna and excellent news that she was expecting our first child.

*My sextant bought second hand in Liverpool in March 1964 still in working condition. The wooden carrying case was very distinctive and always carried as hand luggage when flying.*

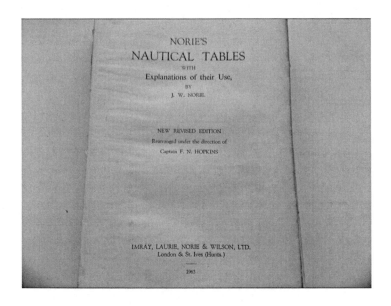

*A well-used copy of Norie's Tables.*

When we arrived home, I was informed that I required a new discharge book as the old one was out of date. I had 33 stamped discharges in my old book the first being as deck boy on the MV Otaki that I joined back in January 1957. As you can see on the next two pages. the first entry in my new book was January 1973 as second officer on the MV Otaki, quite an achievement in just 16 years. All the discharges now were under P&O general cargo division, although the funnels were not changed for another year to the P&O logo.

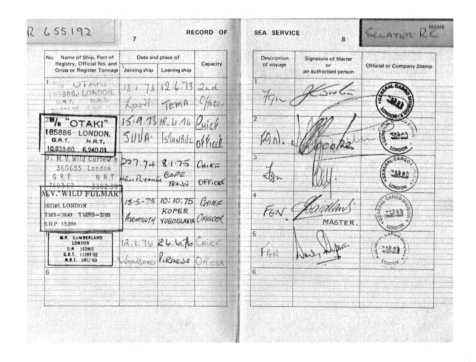

After New Year, I was contacted by head office and informed that I was required to fly to New York to attend a legal case regarding the Longshoreman that was injured onboard the MV Cumberland back in July 1969. I was to travel to London and leave my seagoing gear there and then fly to New York only with essential clothes for three days.

I also required a USA visa so after checking in at head office, I attended the US embassy and was issued with a 10-year visa. Then back to head office for update on the case and collect my flight tickets and instructions on accommodation and contacts in New York. Whilst at head office, I was asked how married life was going. I said that everything was just grand and that we were expecting our first baby in June that year.

'Well,' said Mr Fisher, the head of fleet personnel, 'we will certainly try to have you home for the birth'. My next ship was to be the Otaki, loading general cargo in Liverpool bound for Australia that I would join on return from the USA. I headed to the airport and flew to New York where I was met by one of the legal team representing the shipping company namely Kirlin, Campbell and Keating. I was booked into one of New York's finest hotels, the commodore right next to Grand Central station.

I was picked up the following morning to attend a briefing with our lawyers to go over my recollection of the accident. They also gave me an idea on what to expect the next day at the hearing. The hearing was held at the court house and I was questioned in detail by the complainant's lawyers. I explained that as far as I was concerned, the Longshoreman should not have been in the area of the hold where he was struck by the wooden crate.

I explained that if he had been carrying out his work as required, he should have been fully aware of what his colleagues loading the cargo were doing. In my estimation, he was not watching what was happening with the large crate being swung across the hold to a position under the coaming to its final resting place. Of course my testimony did not go down well with his lawyers but as far as I was concerned it was true.

There was one point that I did not highlight because I could not prove it in court and that was, we believed the Longshoreman, was in fact, in the act of pilfering cargo when he was hit by the crate as we found evidence of boxes being tampered with when we checked the hatch after he was taken ashore. I could have been charged with slander if I had said this and ended up facing claims for defamation of character.

I never did find out what happened but I have no doubt that the US courts would have awarded the Longshoreman considerable compensation as he was unable to work after the accident which happened some three and half years before. The only people who saw what really happened were his work mates down the hold and doubt very much that they would have told the whole truth.

I arrived in New York late evening on the 10 January and departed late evening on the 12. My flight was from JFK airport back to Manchester. From there, I caught a train to Liverpool and joined the MV Otaki in Liverpool docks. It was a strange feeling climbing up the gangway of a ship I had spent two years on as deck boy and ordinary seaman, and now as a senior officer.

The ship was loading for Australia and I got back to my duties of sorting out the charts required for the voyage, which this time was sailing via Cape Town instead of going through the Suez Canal, due to troubles in the Middle East. This was my first time on this route, so it was an interesting task calculating our courses and distances.

We sailed from Liverpool, late January bound for Lisbon, Portugal to load more general cargo, only in port for a day, so no shore leave as I was busy supervising the loading. Our next port was cape town for bunkers, we always topped up our fresh water every chance we could.

We sailed across the Indian ocean to the port of Dampier in Western Australia. This was where most of the iron ore was exported from Australia. so quite a lot of red dust alighted on the ship, it was also extremely hot there. Then onwards to Adelaide, Melbourne, Sydney, and Brisbane. We then headed down to New Plymouth in New Zealand to commence loading.

We sailed round the coast to Nelson, Lyttleton and finally Auckland. Part of the cargo was for Durban, South Africa and Tema in Ghana; the main cargo being for the UK. As I was concerned about the arrival of our new baby due on 12 June and the added time the discharging at these additional ports would take, there was no way I would be home in time for the birth. I wrote to the company and received a positive reply from Bill Fisher.

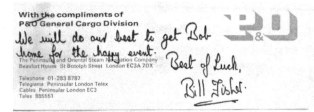

With the compliments of
P&O General Cargo Division

*We will do our best to get Bob home for the happy event.*

*Best of Luck,*
*Bill Fisher.*

The Peninsular and Oriental Steam Navigation Company
Beaufort House St Botolph Street London EC3A 7DX

Telephone 01-283 8787
Telegrams Peninsular London Telex
Cables Peninsular London EC3
Telex 885551

Mr. R.C. Sclater,
Second Officer,
m.v. "OTAKI"

3078                         GCD/FP/O/WF/MG    3.5.1973

Dear Mr. Sclater,

  Thank you for your letter of the 15th April 1973, requesting transfer to a vessel to enable you to be in the U.K. in time for the expected birth of your first child on or about 12th June 1973.

  As you will recall prior to leaving U.K. there was every possibility that the "OTAKI" would be home before this date but, according to our latest information, your arrival U.K. is now approximately 18th June 1973 in Sheerness. Unfortunately between receiving your letter and "OTAKI's" departure New Zealand there have not been any vessels on the New Zealand coast which would arrive U.K. intime for your wife's confinement.

  We appreciate that we made a commitment on this matter prior to your departure from U.K. and in the circumstances, provided we have a suitable Deck Officer available, we will endeavour to arrange to relieve you in Tema for U.K. leave.

  We extend our best wishes to Mrs. Sclater and yourself on her confinement.

    Yours sincerely,

    W. Fisher
    Fleet Personnel Department.

cc: Master m.v. "OTAKI"

cc: AFM 'B' Fleet
cc: Mrs. R.C. Sclater

Anyway, we set sail for Durban from Auckland, not a very common route but a very relaxing voyage until we were close to Durban. The seas along the east side of South Africa can be quite rough due to the Agulhas current which runs along the 100-fathom line down the coast and meets up with swells coming up the coast from the Southern Ocean.

It has been known to create rouge waves of 30 metres or more. We did not hit that height but did get a battering. A Ben Line vessel, the MV Ben Cruachan was not so lucky as a couple of weeks prior to our arrival in Durban, she hit a rogue wave that bent her in two and was nearly sunk. She was still tied up in Durban when we arrived being safely towed in after the disaster. We spoke to some of the crew members who highlighted how the disaster occurred.

The vessel was one of Ben Lines fast liner service ships, steaming at 21 knots, and the captain who was on his last voyage wished to do as fast a voyage as possible back from the far east to the UK. They said he kept the vessel going at high speed into the heavy seas. The engineer on watch phoned the bridge several times, as he was concerned about the pounding the vessel was taking with the high seas, and asked when the bridge would order the engines to be slowed down.

No order was received and the vessel then hit the rogue wave and buried its bow into the sea and did not rise up out of it. The weight of the water bent the forward part of the ship and she nearly sank. No one was injured and the ship stayed afloat and was eventually towed into Durban. We learned our lesson onboard the Wild Auk which was an even faster vessel than the Ben Cruachan, whilst crossing the North Atlantic in the winter of 1972.

We slowed down to below ten knots and still had waves hitting the bridge windows, so not a wise move to steam at high speed into heavy seas. I read that between 1981 and 1991, over 30 large vessels had either been sunk or badly damaged on the east side of South Africa in this area. I have no reason to doubt the story told to us by the crew onboard the Ben Cruachan that the master refused to slow down.

I never heard if this was reported in the official findings that the vessel was travelling at excessive speed into heavy seas or just blamed being caught by the rogue wave. Every seafarer worth his salt knew that this part of the world was renowned for freak waves, so really no excuse for not being careful. Reminds me of the Titanic. She also was steaming at high speed when she hit an iceberg, once again a captain trying to achieve a goal but at what cost.

*Ben Cruachan after the Accident*

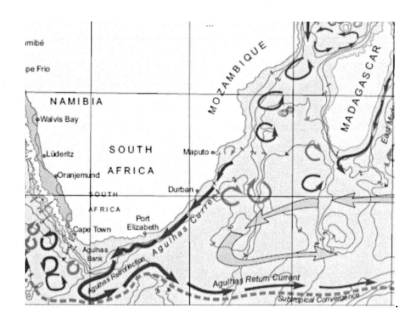

*Area of Treacherous Seas*

Anyway, we discharged our small cargo of bagged powdered milk and then sailed round to cape town to bunker. This took only just over a day, then we set sail for Tema. By this time, I had received word that I would be relieved in Tema and flown home for the birth of our new baby. I paid off on the 12 June the day the baby was due.

I spent the night in a hotel in Accra, then a flight home via Lagos, Geneva, London, Edinburgh and Kirkwall. Luckily, our daughter Esther delayed her appearance until 17 June, three days after my arrival, good timing. This was a new experience for us but with both being at home to start the baby learning curve, we coped quick well.

The big problem was to come when in September I received orders to re-join the MV Otaki as chief officer in Suva Fiji. I was to leave Anna and Esther at home for the next seven months, not a very happy experience. Thanks goodness Anna had passed her driving test by then.

I flew out from London via New York, San Francisco, Hawaii landing at Nadia airport in Fiji. I then caught an internal flight to Suva. On the flight out we landed in New York and had to go through immigration and passport control then back on the flight to San Francisco back off the flight, clear passport control and immigration all just a complete waste of time. USA certainly has a strange way of making people feel welcome even when just transiting their country. I took up my duties as chief officer straight away and settled down to my new position.

The company had altered things once again and the responsibility of cargo operations had been removed from the second mate's duties and I was back in charge of all aspects of discharging and loading cargoes. This also entailed the stability calculations etc, all the tasks I was responsible for over the past couple of years as second mate.

The shipping company had now changed completely and was now known as P&O General Cargo Division. All NZSCo vessels had been changed to the, FSNCo livery a couple of years before. P&O Strath services, Cargo vessels along with all other subsidiaries were also taken under the umbrella of P&O GCD. This gave a total cargo fleet of over 100 vessels.

Although all deck officers in the fleet were fully up to speed on loading general cargo, they were not all acquaint with refrigerated cargo which did cause some concern. Anyway, I digress from taking up my new post as chief officer on the Otaki.

Whilst in Suva, I met up with my old friend John Hayday who was carrying out under water work in Suva harbour. He certainly was a jack of all trades. We had a couple of beers together and caught up on old times. After a couple of days discharging, we sailed round to Lautoka right next to Nadia airport, if the company had waited a couple days in flying me out, I could have saved the flight to Suva.

We then headed down to Auckland to discharge the rest of our cargo. At this time, we had no indication of where or what we were to load and in which ports. On arrival in Auckland, the Captain left the vessel and we were to await the arrival of a new captain who we were informed was an ex P&O passenger ship master. I was therefore, now in charge until his arrival. During this period I was contacted by Peter Hojsgaard, General Manager of Lauritzen Peninsular Reefers.

He wished to know if the Otaki could load several thousand tons of frozen lamb for the Persian Gulf. This was over the phone when I was ashore one Saturday afternoon at a friend's house. He somehow got the phone number from the duty officer onboard the Otaki.

Quite a surprise, as I had never met him and thought it might be someone having me on. Anyway, I said, 'Yes of course we can but could we meet onboard as soon as possible to discuss this and also to contact head office in Auckland'. This was done and we were informed by head office that our next voyage would be to the Gulf.

After discharging in Auckland we commenced loading for Karachi, Muscat, Dubai, and Khorramshahr in Iran. The new captain arrived onboard in Auckland along with his wife and 10-year-old daughter. It was back to the usual work load of planning the loading sequences and making sure everything was in the right compartment for an efficient discharge in each port.

Most of the frozen cargo was Muslim killed lamb they all had a red MK stamped on each carcass. We also had two chilled lockers full of eggs for Dubai, along with other bits and pieces including bales of wool. We sailed from NZ bound for Karachi, all new ports for me. Once again, the usual activities at sea now on the 4-8 watch, back to star sights morning and evening and of course now in charge of all deck work.

Regular meetings with the bosun and carpenter to get everything ship shape on our voyage across the Indian ocean. Discharge went smoothly in Karachi and then we anchored off Muscat in Oman. The port was not big enough for us, so we discharged into barges. Then up into the gulf to Dubai. It was a very small port and not the bustling metropolis it is today.

Then onwards up the Shat-al-Arab to Khorramshahr. This was our main discharge port and we had quite a long time in port. At first, we had to anchor in the river to await our berth. The river was quite narrow and on each tide the vessel swung to meet the rising or falling tide.

This resulted in us standing by both fore and aft with the engines on standby to push the ship away from the bank of the river. The border between Iran and Iraq was the middle of the river, so your bow would be in Iran and your stern in Iraq.

Once we did start discharging, I became quite friendly with the manager in charge of both the agents Gray Mackenzie and the stevedores a Mr Jimmy Linton. He was a large jovial man and we were invited a few times to his house for lunch and sometimes dinner. He was a great entertainer and met up with lots of nice people working in various embassies and banks in Khorramshahr.

This was a great treat as there was not much to do ashore. We completed discharge and set sail for Australia stopping off in Colombo for bunkers. Our first port in Australia was Brisbane, so our voyage took us south of Indonesia into the Timor Sea on wards to the Torres straits where we picked up the Great Barrier Reef pilot.

The pilot remained onboard until we picked up the Brisbane River pilot. Normal watches were kept on the passage and it was a very interesting trip down the reef. I had, of course, sailed up and down to Bowen, Port Alma, Townsville and Cairns when on deck.

We arrived in Brisbane to commence loading for Istanbul-Turkey, Constanta-Romania, Piraeus-Greece, and Genoa-Italy. A considerable amount of the cargo were items being sent back home by immigrants who had settled in Australia. I have no idea what was in the crates, but they were certainly not small. We also loaded rutile sand, a very dense commodity used in paints, plastic and paper production. This was bound for Romania, also loaded ingots of lead.

When in Brisbane, we were struck by tropical cyclone Wanda with winds up to 100 mph and torrential rain. It has since been reported that it was the worst flood in Brisbane in the past 50 years. The death toll was 16 with 300 injured, 8000 homes destroyed and total cost of damage put at $980a million.

The wharf where we were berthed was completely under water and of course cargo work was stopped for several days. During the storm, I was called by the night watchman and advised the police were onboard, worried about an old dredger/barge that had broken from its moorings and was heading down river. I got up and went out on the after deck with the police to watch this vessel coming down the river.

It came in sight and it was heading straight for us. We went down onto the wharf and it struck just a few metres behind our stern. We jumped onboard and grabbed mooring lines on its deck and managed to secure it alongside. We were very lucky that it had drifted out of the main flow of the current and was not travelling too fast when it hit the wharf. That was the only excitement we had, although we did see lots of debris coming down the river.

Once the cyclone had passed and the river water receded, we got back to loading again. I did manage a trip down to the Gold coast and had a swim and a bit of body surfing. It was only an hour's bus ride from Brisbane. We also managed to dine out a couple of times at the famous steak restaurant at Breakfast Creek nearly as good as Montevideo.

After completing our loading in Brisbane, we set off down the coast to Sydney, then onwards to Melbourne. Once again, loading all kinds of cargo from refrigerated meat and lamb to personnel effects, bales of wool etc. Whilst in Melbourne, we were asked to carry the ashes of an old gentleman and scatter them in the straits of Gibraltar on our passage into the Mediterranean.

We set sail from Melbourne bound for Fremantle to complete loading. Whilst in Fremantle, I was head hunted by the main stevedore company's boss asking me if I would like to come and join their company and work in Australia. This was quite an offer and he actually gave me the application form and said just sign the bottom and the job is yours. Unfortunately, I was not in a position to accept as I explained to him that I was married and would have to consult with my wife. I said I would contact him after I had discussed it with her.

Very difficult being at the other side of the world, no internet back then. I did not, in fact, take the job as things were to change over the next two years with the oil industry operations in the North Sea, that I will cover later.

We set sail for Durban as there was still problems regarding the Suez Canal, so we were to sail round the Cape of Good Hope. This was quite a long way out of our way as we were heading for Istanbul right at the opposite end of the Mediterranean. No problems on the voyage even the Agulhas current was quite peaceful.

Just lazy days at sea doing all the tasks required up at 4 am and back to my bunk at 9 pm. When we were approaching the straits of Gibraltar, I called the captain and asked about the ashes we were to scatter going through the strait. He went down to his cabin and came back up with them. This was about seven in the morning.

I expected him to give me the casket so I could go down aft and open it up and scatter the ashes. Instead, he walked onto the bridge wing and threw the box which was still in its brown paper wrapping over the side.

To say Captain Cooke was a bit eccentric was an understatement. I did manage to work with him but he was like no other captain I had sailed with before. I did sail with another P&O passenger captain on my last voyage will touch on him later. On arrival in Istanbul, I was to pay off and go home on leave.

CAPTAIN EN COWDRY
or
CAPTAIN DUCAN HOLIDAY
25 HENRY ST
FREMANTLE

MERCANTILE STEVEDORES (W.A.)

APPLICATION FOR EMPLOYMENT

POSITION FOR WHICH APPLYING: ............................................

NAME IN FULL: ............................................

ADDRESS: ............................................

............................Tel.Number...........

DATE OF BIRTH: ............................................

PRESENT AGE: ............................................

MARRIED OR SINGLE: ............................................

NUMBER OF CHILDREN: ............................................

REFERENCES: ............................................

............................................

............................................

............................................

WHERE LAST EMPLOYED: ............................................

PERIOD OF LAST EMPLOYMENT: ............................................

EXPERIENCE: ............................................

............................................

............................................

............................................

Date..................... .........................

Signature of Applicant

*My application form for post in Fremantle.*

163

*Captain Cooke and Myself, and Peter Hojsgaard's Business Card*

I arrived home on 19 April having been away for nearly seven months, so very happy to get back to Anna and Esther who was now growing into a little girl, not the baby I had left behind. It was great to be home for her first birthday and with it, being summer catching up with all the jobs around the house.

Like all good things, they come to an end and three months later, I was informed that I would be flying out to New Zealand to join the Wild Curlew in New Plymouth. I said my farewells at Kirkwall airport and headed down to London to catch my flight to NZ. We flew east bound, via Bahrain, Singapore changed planes in Sydney and flew onwards to Wellington. On arrival in Wellington, I was informed that the Wild Curlew was delayed outside New Plymouth due to bad weather and that the airport was also closed.

This meant a night in an hotel in Wellington. I was not unduly concerned as I was tired after the long journey out. The next day, I caught my flight to New Plymouth but the ship was still storm stead outside, so another night in an hotel. The following day, everything was back to normal and I relieved the chief officer and he headed home.

The ship had been loading round the NZ coast and was topping off in New Plymouth. The cargo was all destined once again for Khorramshahr. We set sail and this time headed via the Great Barrier reef and Torres Strait roughly the same trip we took coming down from Khorramshahr to Brisbane on the Otaki.

Once again, the same delays in discharging in Khorramshahr lying at anchor in the river until a berth was available. We had some crew changes once we got alongside a new captain, an ex-P&O passenger master, new second and third officers. The second officer, Billy Phimister had Orkney connections and the third officer, John Mackay came from Helmsdale. It made a nice change having these two onboard. Captain Fields was also a pleasure to sail with, a real gentleman could see how he would have charmed the passenger on the big P&O liners. Jimmy Linton was very kind and we had a few visits ashore to his house for lunch. The discharge went without a hitch and we sailed once again back to New Zealand bound for Napier to load back to Khorramshahr and Basra.

We took the reciprocal course back to NZ, although this time we sailed outside the Great Barrier Reef so no pilot required this time. We arrived in Napier, commenced loading our frozen cargo of lamb, butter, cheese, then onwards to Lyttleton to finish off. Whilst in Lyttleton, I discovered that my friend Captain John Leslie and his wife Moira were in port onboard a bank line ship.

John had given up the North Sea oil work and returned to sea to obtain a command. It was nice to meet up with them and we had a couple dinners, one onboard their ship and one on the Wild Curlew. Then we sailed back up to the Gulf on the same route outside the Great Barrier Reef onwards through the Torres Straits, south of Indonesia round Ceylon, through the straits of Hormoz to the Shatt al-Arab.

The same procedure on discharging as previous ones although only part cargo for Iran. With Jimmy Linton being involved in most shipping activities in Khorramshahr, he asked me to carry out a Lloyds damaged cargo survey, onboard an Iranian vessel the MV Arya Naz lying just behind us in port. My report and fee for this work is on the next page. It would be some years before I would carry out marine surveys again, this will be highlighted much later on in my story. We completed our discharge in Khorramshahr and headed up to Basra which was further up river. The discharging went quite smoothly with no big problems. After completing discharge, we received orders to set course for Santos in Brazil to load soya for South Africa. This was something quite different from loading refrigerated cargo.

*The MV Wild Curlew probably the finest ship I sailed on.*

<u>Survey Carried Out Onboard the M.V. ARYA NAZ</u>

<u>No 2 Berth Khorramshahr A.M. 20-11-74</u>

Approximately 150 bags of Milk Powder stowed in No 3 L.H. of the above vessel were found by me to be damaged.

Of the above number 80/100 bags will possibly be contaminated with Paper Starch which was stowed on top of the Milk Powder. The Paper Starch being discharged in Kuwait.

The other 50/70 bags of Milk Powder were found to be broken on the outside covering only, the polythene bag inside being intact.

The covering used to seperate the Paper Starch from the Milk Powder was found to have been dragged out of place thus leaving about 50% of the stow uncovered. The covering used being plastic paper (polythene).

R.C. Sclater, Master Mariner
Cert. No 111219.

## RECEIPT

D. V. No. .............................

Date ..24th November, 1974.

Khorramshahr,

Received from Messrs GRAY MACKENZIE & Co. Ltd,

the sum of Rls ......... 7000.- Surveyor's Fee
410.- 5½% Incometax
7410.-

( Rials ..Seven thousand Four

hundred and Ten only)

on account of ...damage to cargo in Hatch No.3 L/H m .v." ARYA NAZ "

Capt., R.C. Sclater,

Signature R·C Sclat

Lloyd's Survey Report No.74/377

*My simple survey and fee paid, good money for doing very little.*

| From :- | Lyttleton   to   Khorramshahr<br>Course | Distance | To Go |
|---|---|---|---|
| Pilot<br>to: | | | 9182 |
| Godley Hd.Lt. brg.330 @ 0.8'<br>to: | 076 | 3 | 9182 279 |
| Kaikoura Pen.La.Lt. brg.304 @ 10'<br>to | 036 | 79.8 | 9099.2 |
| Cape Campbell Lt. brg.296 @ 5.8'<br>to | 026 | 49.8 | 9049.4 |
| Brothers Lt. brg.256 @ 5.4'<br>to | 009 | 41.8 | 9007.6 |
| Postion"A" 20 S. 156 40 E<br>to | 324 | 1564.4 | 7443.2 |
| Postion"B" 9 22 S.146 E.<br>to | 316 | 891.1 | 6552.1 |
| Bramble Cay brg.326 @ 3.3'<br>to      ( via recommended track) | 275 | 124.5 | 6427.6 |
| Carpentaria Lt. V/L. brg.029 @ 6.5'<br>to | Var. | 218.0 | 6209.6 |
| Cape Wessel Lt.Ho. brg.180 @ 10.0'<br>to | 270 | 254.0 | 5955.6 |
| Meatij Miarang Lt.Ho. brg.010 @ 10.0'<br>to | 286 | 513.5 | 5442.1 |
| Pta.Horo brg.356 @ 4.8'<br>to | 280 | 77.6 | 5364.5 |
| Ngo.Tutun Pt. brg.349 @ 6.0'<br>to | 266 | 95.5 | 5269.0 |
| Ipa. Penla Pt. brg.358 @ 14.0'<br>to | 259 | 239.0 | 5030.0 |
| Talonan Pt. brg.008? 12.2'<br>to | 268 | 278.0 | 4752.0 |
| Pakis Pt. brg.010 @ 17.4'<br>to | 278 | 307.7 | 4444.3 |
| Pt. Genteng brg.050 @ 19.0'<br>to | 280 | 344.4 | 4099.9 |
| Postion"C" 5 40 S. 102 E. off(Engana Is.)<br>to | 295 | 275.2 | 3824.7 |
| Galle Hd. Lt. Ho. brg036 @ 6.2'<br>to | 298 | 1493.2 | 2331.5 |
| Valinjam Lt.Ho.brg.049 @ 9.2'<br>to | 306 | 248.5 | 2083.0 |
| Tangasseri Pt. Lt. Ho. brg.062 @ 10.8'<br>to | 322 | 33.5 | 2049.5 |
| Ras Al.Kuh. Lt. brg.047 @ 6.0'<br>to | 313 | 1500.0 | 549.5 |
| Little Guoin Lt. Ho.brg.301 @ 2.2'<br>to | 320 | 55.3 | 494.2 |
| Little Guoin Lt Ho.brg.087 @ 1.8'<br>to | 285 | 3.8 | 490.4 |
| Jas Tunb Lt.brg.172 @ 3.2'<br>to | 262 | 67.0 | 423.4 |
| Jas Guais Lt.brg.004 @ 6.9'<br>to | 274 | 71.5 | 351.9 |
| Cable Bank Lt. V/L.brg.202 @ 7.8'<br>to | 292 | 80.6 | 271.3 |
| Lt. V/L.Fl 15 sec.brg.032 @ 3.6'<br>to | 302 | 75.3 | 196.0 |
| Shatt.Al.Arab. Lt. V/L.brg.224 @ 2.5'<br>to | 314 | 163.0 | 33.0 |
| Pilot | Buoyed Channel | 33.0 | — |

*The courses and distances from Lyttleton to Khorramshahr, quite a long voyage at sea.*

We sailed down the African coast, no pirates back then thank goodness. Round the cape of good hope once again the weather was good to us no heavy seas. Onwards across the Atlantic to arrive in Santos. We commenced loading our bagged cargo which was quite straight forward. We had Christmas in Santos, so did have a day without any cargo work.

There was another company ship in port, the Wild Fulmar, little did I know at the time that this would be my next ship. I did go onboard her as I had sailed with her Captain on the UK coast onboard the Tongariro. I did think at the time that the ship was not in a good state of repair, unlike the Wild Curlew which was spike and span.

We thought we might still be alongside for New Year but managed to convince the stevedores to speed up loading so we could get away without another day's delay. We sailed on the 31 bound for cape town where I was to be relieved and flown home. I signed off articles on 8 January, our 4th wedding anniversary. I flew from Cape Town up to Johannesburg and changed planes there.

Whilst waiting in departures, I was having a drink at the bar, I had my sextant in its box. Sitting beside me along the bar were a few other chaps who asked what ship I was off as they recognised my sextant box. I told them my ship and that I left her in Cape Town. They then asked where I was from. I told them Orkney.

They were all fishermen heading to join their fishing boat in Cape Town and said that they used to call into St Helena and did I know an Orkney man called George Rouse who worked there? I did in fact know him but not very well back then. They said that when I got home to give him their regards, can't recall any names but I did in fact let George know I had met friends of his in Johannesburg. It is a small world sometimes.

Anyway, I caught my flight home via Frankfurt, London, Aberdeen and onwards to Kirkwall. It was great to be home and had a very enjoyable four months leave, making friends with Esther who did not know who I was, just known as "the man" for the first few days. The shipping company by this time allowed senior officers to take their wives and children, so I applied to take Anna and Esther on the next voyage.

This was granted and we headed of for Avonmouth to join the Wild Fulmar, another of the Lauritzen Peninsular Reefers. The ship had arrived from NZ and the chief officer seemed quite disorganised as everything was in a mess, the cabin and the paper work. Anna and Esther could not get into the cabin to unpack as he had not even packed his belongs when we arrived.

I told him to just get his gear together and I would sort everything out. Eventually, he took the hint that I was not impressed with him and he packed his gear and left. The new master joined at the same time. It was our old friend Captain Jammie Laidlaw with who we did our honeymoon voyage on the MV Hauraki. I knew it was going to be another interesting trip with him in command.

After discharging in Avonmouth, we sailed to Rotterdam and Hamburg to complete discharge. We managed a few trips ashore with Esther, although she remembers nothing about them now. Our next cargo was to load grain in Port La Palice, La Rochelle in France bound for Pointe Noire in the Republic of Congo. The voyage down the channel and into the Bay of Biscay was a bit rough but Esther coped very well she just sat down on the cabin deck and was never sea sick.

There was three other wives onboard which was very nice for Anna and Esther. The Port of La Palice was a nice place and we managed ashore to see the local carnival, all very picturesque. We loaded our bags of grain and headed down to West Africa another pleasant trip at sea. Whilst tied up in Pointe Noire, a Latvian research ship struck our stern when berthing.

It seemed her engines did not go astern when they should, so hit us with quite a bang and dented our stern. We had a survey carried out and we were advised that the damage must be repaired before sailing. The engineers on the Latvian vessel carried out the task so no costs to anyone. We were changing the hull colour of the ship so this worked in well with the repairs.

Just prior to completing discharge the agent came onboard to ask the captain if we could help with a party of tourist on a safari trip through the Congo who were afraid to continue onwards to South Africa. This was due to the volatile situation in the area with warring factions on their route. Contact was made with head office and they agreed we could take the group.

They had two land rovers and there was about ten tourists plus their guides. We managed to find spare accommodation onboard and loaded the two land rovers and set sail for Port Elizabeth. On the voyage round to Port Elizabeth we had Esther's 2nd birthday party. We had a few presents for her and the cook made her a nice birthday cake.

When we did arrive in port, the safari party were allowed to disembark, they had, however with them, two small monkeys and a baby crocodile which we allowed them to take onboard. The authorities would not allow them to be taken ashore and we were advised that they should be put down before we left port. A vet arrived onboard and carried out the procedure by lethal injection.

I recall taking him up to the forecastle store room where they were kept in their cages. He picked up the small crocodile and said you must be careful they don't bite you, which it did and caught his fingers, he stuck the needle in it quite quickly. We were to keep the bodies onboard until out at sea and then dispose of them.

Our cargo this time was oranges and lemons for Bordeaux and Le Havre in France. The holds had been thoroughly cleaned both in Pointe Noire where all the loose grain was swept up by our deck crew on the voyage down to Port Elizabeth. Ado Safari Park was close to Port Elizabeth so the agent organised a trip out to see the wild life.

Plenty of elephants, rhinoceros, emus, and other animals in the park. We then set sail for cape town to complete loading our cargo. On the way round, I disposed off the little bodies into the sea, quite sad as the group should have left them in the wild. We anchored off Cape Town on arrival and then eventually berthed to complete loading.

I never managed ashore but Anna and Esther did go ashore with other crew members. South Africa was never a safe place to be ashore alone. Back at sea again for a pleasant voyage up to Bordeaux. We did not berth in Bordeaux itself but in a small port further down the river Gironde. There was a nice little town just up from the jetty that we visited.

One afternoon, when we were ashore the Tour de France cycle race came through and we saw some of the riders. After part discharge, we headed round to Le Havre to finish off. Esther had a small accident whilst there. She was coming onto the bridge of the ship when the radio officer gave her a fright and she jumped back and fell down the stairs.

She did not appear to be hurt but to be on the safe side, I took her ashore for a check-up. The doctor found her to be ok, just a bit of a limp in one of her legs which soon got better. You certainly had to be extra careful with young children onboard ship.

Our next voyage was to Ecuador to load bananas for Italy and Yugoslavia. The usual track across the Atlantic to curacao and onwards through Panama Canal. Our first loading port was Esmeralda where we loaded at anchor from barges. We took a trip ashore in a dugout canoe to visit this small town situated on the north coast of Ecuador.

The locals were very taken with Esther, with her blond hair and blue eyes. They came running across the street to look at her. I don't think it was a big place for tourists. There was, however, some souvenirs to purchase from the stevedores who came out to load the bananas. Everyone bought ponchos and wooden trinkets.

We then sailed down to Porto Bolivar for the rest of the cargo. The boxes of bananas were loaded in a very unique manner by the dockers running up and down wooden gangways carrying them on their shoulders into each hold it was quite a quick method. Once again, the agents took us for a tour of the countryside and up to a banana plantation. It was all very primitive, the way they air sealed the plastic bags of bananas with domestic vacuum cleaners.

The mosquitos were lethal there and they certainly loved biting Esther. Our cargo was destined for Civitavecchia, Italy and Koper in Yugoslavia.

Not looking her best in this photo, taken some time after I had left the ship. The hull colours and change of funnel were carried out during my time onboard so all the paint work was fresh and new by the time I left. Not sure why they changed when you see how good the Wild Fulmar looks all white.

*Wild Fulmar*

*The Photos of Spring bank, South Ronaldsay, our home for nine years. Keeping fit onboard. At anchor off Cape Town with Table Mountain in the back ground. Carnival in La Rochell, Esther's 2nd birthday and on the phone to the captain. Our cabin onboard had a day room bedroom with en-suite facilities; it was luxury compared to our honeymoon voyage on the Hauraki.*

The usual voyage back via Panama and Curacao without any problems. We certainly had plenty bananas to eat on the way. Any boxes that were appearing to be ripening when the hatches were checked by the refrigeration engineer were taken out. I should highlight that all the bananas were green when loaded and carried at chilled temperatures.

One thing about sailing on these reefer ships, the cargoes were either in boxes or sacks of the same size, easy storage plus a full cargo of each commodity so nothing extra for Captain Laidlaw to get his hands on, so this made loading very easy. Esther got on well with everyone onboard as she could talk quite well for a two-year-old.

At the dining table, we sat with the captain who also talked a lot. One lunch time, Captain Laidlaw said, 'You're a blether Esther Sclater.' She came right back at him and said, 'You're a blether to Captain Laidlaw. It gave everyone a laugh. She also was able to say Civitavecchia, not the easiest words to pronounce. We also spoke about going to Yugoslavia. She would pipe up and say 'Me go Slavia to'.

Our first port was, in fact, Augusta in Sicily to Bunker. This meant when we left Augusta, we sailed up through the strait of Messina quite an interesting passage between mainland Italy and Sicily. As usual, Captain Laidlaw made sure we saw all the sights travelling up the coast.

After our part discharge in Civitavecchia, we sailed back down the coast via the Strait of Messina and round into the Adriatic onwards to Koper in the north of Yugoslavia. This was a lovely little town and we enjoyed our time there. Our next voyage was back across the Atlantic to Curacao and through the Panama to load bananas this time in Puerto Armuelles just south of the border between Panama and Costa Rico.

The port was quite open to a southerly swell, so the mooring arrangements were such that the vessel was tied to the jetty but also to mooring buoys to keep us from direct contact to the wharf. Whilst there, Anna and Esther along with the other wives and some of the crew were taken by the agent on a bus run into Costa Rico.

I was too busy working to go on the trip. Anyway, we completed loading and set sail once again bound for Koper where we would be leaving the ship and heading home on leave. We had one frightening incident onboard caused by the steering gear jamming hard to starboard whilst in a busy shipping lane in the Adriatic.

I was down for my evening meal having been relieved by the captain when we felt the ship starting to list dramatically; this due to our speed of some 21 knots with the wheel hard over. I knew something was wrong so quickly headed to the bridge where the captain had put the engines on stop.

It takes some time for a ship to lose way but luckily, we were not too close to any other vessels. By this time the engineers were checking everything and I went down after to check the steering gear. There we discovered that one of the emergency steering gear buttons had got stuck into the main steering gear controls and caused it to jam.

This was soon put right and we managed to get everything back to normal and continue on our way. We eventually arrived in Koper and signed off. We had over an hour's taxi ride through lovely countryside to catch our flight home from Ljubljana now in Slovenia. We flew to London and onwards to Kirkwall via Aberdeen.

It was great to be home for a nice long leave. Esther was a bit confused when we arrived and asked could she go into the other cabins in the house. She still thought she was on the ship where you did not go into anyone else's cabin unless you were invited. She soon got back to normal and happy to have so much space to run around in.

After two months at home the company informed me that I must attend two courses, one a firefighting course and the other a ship's captain's medical training course. These were to be held in Leith and Liverpool. The first was a very intensive fire course at Macdonald Road fire station and lasted four days.

After several lectures we were then involved in hands on firefighting and the use of breathing apparatus in the mock up ship's accommodation block. This was no easy course as the inside of the module was set alight by the use of burning barrels which contributed to intense heat and smoke similar to that in a real fire. We were instructed on the use of water and foam to extinguish the fires also whilst using breathing apparatus.

One test resulted in everyone going into the module which was full of smoke and pitch dark without any breathing apparatus and told to crawl along the floor keeping our noses as close to the ground as possible to get what air there was available. This was quite frightening and not very pleasant.

There were firemen in breathing apparatus stationed along the route; we had to crawl ready to get anyone out who panicked.

The module had side panels that could be opened to stick one's head out into fresh air, none of our team required this. Another exercise was to run to the top of the training tower about eight floors up with breathing apparatus on, this was hard going and you needed to be fit. The final day, we had a real full-scale exercise and I recall at the end of the day, the top of my ears were all blistered due to the mental clips on my breathing apparatus getting so hot.

The firemen in charge did say that some of our training was out with of their training due to health and safety regulations. It was certainly an interesting course that I would have liked to have taken prior to the fire on the Debrett. I might have done things differently back then with the knowledge I learned at Macdonald Road.

I was, of course, quite up to speed on firefighting onboard ship as we had regular fire drill and boat drill at sea and in port. Nothing so intensive as what the professional firemen put us through. The next course was in Liverpool run by the department of trade and industry. The lecturers were all practising doctors so a very interesting course covering all aspects of medical problems one could face at sea.

We did practice carrying out injections but only on oranges, we tied ever type of bandage, put on splints, things I had already done on previous courses. We learned about tropical diseases, pregnancy, heart disease you name it we covered it. Some of the details shown were quite graphic not for the squeamish. At the end of the week, we took a written and practical examination which thankfully I passed. Certainly could tell a sprained wrist from a broken arm!

# mntb

merchant navy training board
this is to certify that

fire fighting
training
certificate

name ROBERT CHALMERS SCLATER,

rank CHIEF OFFICER        discharge book no. R655192.

certificate of
competency, grade (if any) MASTER (F.G.)  no. 111219.

date and place of birth  7·8·41    KIRKWALL

satisfactorily completed a merchant navy fire fighting course approved by the
department of trade and industry at Macdonald Road Fire Station, Leith, Scotland

from  2·12·75        to    5·12·75

D.J. Wright

chief fire officer

signature of holder

secretary
merchant navy training board

date of issue    5·12·75

---

7333

DEPARTMENT OF TRADE AND INDUSTRY

SHIP CAPTAIN'S MEDICAL TRAINING CERTIFICATE

THIS IS TO CERTIFY THAT

NAME      Robert Chalmers SCLATER

RANK          Chief Officer.

CERTIFICATE OF
COMPETENCY, GRADE  Master FG No. 111219  DISCHARGE 655192
BOOK No. R

DATE AND PLACE OF BIRTH   7·8·41   Kirkwall

completed a Ship Captain's Medical Training Course, approved by the Department of Trade and
Industry, and passed the examination held at the conclusion of the course on 12/12/ 19 75.

Signed

EXAMINER

Signature of Holder    R. Sclater    Signed

PRINCIPAL OF SCHOOL

Date of issue  12th December 1975

---

I mentioned earlier about North Sea oil and the impact it would have on my
life. Occidental, a US based oil company had discovered oil east of Orkney and
decided to bring the oil ashore by pipeline to the island of Flotta in Orkney. As
this would entail the use of large oil tankers to export the oil from their terminal,

marine pilots would be required to carry out the task of safely piloting these tankers into and out of Scapa Flow.

I had, in fact, written to Occidental when this was first muted to ask about marine positions with them. At that time, they said that they would maybe operate their pilots out of wick and Thurso on the Scottish mainland. There was no harbour authority in Orkney when Occidental first started negotiations with Orkney County Council. It was common practice in other oil ports for the operator to use his own staff as pilots/mooring/loading masters.

In 1974, the government had brought in legislation to create Orkney islands Council, an amalgamation of Kirkwall and Stromness town Councils and Orkney County Council under one umbrella. The new Council took up office on 16 May 1975. The Councils were fully aware of the impact of oil on the islands and the revenue that would result from this lucrative industry.

They started drawing up the Orkney County Council Act 1974 and this was passing through parliament to create a harbour and pilotage authority in Orkney. The Act would pass control of all the piers and harbours within Orkney to the local Council authority, the only exception being St. Margaret's Hope who wished to remain independent.

With this Act passed, it gave the Council in Orkney the powers to create a harbour and pilotage district covering Scapa Flow where the oil terminal was being built.

It also meant that Orkney County Council soon to become Orkney islands Council would in fact, employ pilots not the oil company. They advertised for a harbour master in 1974 to put together, everything required to operate an efficient oil port.

Captain Duncan Robertson who was a depute harbour master on the Humber was appointed along with Captain Harry Banks, an ex-river Thames pilot as his depute in early 1975. At the end of 1975, they advertised for marine officers in the local paper, The Orcadian. This was in December whilst I was still home on leave and I duly applied for one of the positions which would also take in the role of pilot.

As I was due back at sea at the beginning of January, I was invited for an interview with Captain Robertson and Captain Banks which took place on 31 December. I received a positive response and was advised to keep them informed on when I would be home after my next voyage.

Construction of the Flotta Oil Terminal had commenced in 1974 but the North Sea oil from the Piper and Claymore Fields was not expected to be flowing until late in 1976. This meant that the posts of marine officers/pilots were not required to be filled until late September at the Earliest. On the next couple of pages are my firefighting and ship's captain medical certificates and my application form for the marine officer's post.

I departed home on 9 of January, day after our fifth wedding anniversary, and was bound to join my old ship the MV Cumberland in New Zealand. My flights took me down to London onwards to Bahrain, Singapore, Perth, Sydney and Christchurch. I changed to an internal flight up to Auckland.

The Cumberland was berthed in Whangarei, 100 miles north of Auckland so I stayed the night in an hotel there to catch up on some sleep as my body clock was 12 hours out of sync. The next morning the local company manager picked me up in his car and we had a lovely 2-hour drive through the scenic New Zealand countryside.

Here I was back on the first ship I sailed to NZ as a very junior officer back in 1966 now second in command, nine years later. I stowed my gear and went to meet the captain. He had been a P&O passenger ship master for many years and not really a cargo ship man. Never the less, I was to get on quite well with him although he did have a slight health problem and weighed in at only eight stone so not very robust.

The company had changed a lot over the years since becoming P&O GCD, we now had a second mate with a second mate's ticket and a third mate with no qualifications. When I first joined as an officer, the first mate had a master's ticket and 2$^{nd}$ and two third mates had first mates certificates.

Anyway, that was the way things were so just had to get on with it. We did however, have two deck cadets which certainly helped when loading cargo. I settled down and started sorting out our loading plan as the ship had already completed discharging.

Our cargo was bound for Valletta-Malta, Lattikia-Syria, Limassol-Cyprus Piraeus-Greece, Genoa-Italy and finally London-UK. Our cargo was the usual frozen lamb, butter, cheese, fruit, bales of wool and every other animal by-product produced in NZ, even had a large container of honey. I also had my first meeting with the bosun and we discussed the planned maintenance of the ship whilst on the NZ coast.

It was normal practice to paint the hull and funnel when in port and also general maintenance not carried out at sea. The ship was not in too bad shape and I found the bosun a very competent seaman. We completed our part, loading in Whangarei then sailed down to Auckland.

The Captain was a very lenient chap as he allowed the third mate to take his girlfriend on the voyage down the coast. I did think that this gave a very bad example to crew members and was not impressed with his decision. The third mate of course had been on the ship for several months with the Captain so had a good rapport with him. It was to come back and bite the Captain later in the voyage.

After Auckland, we sailed down to Napier where we had a collision with the small harbour tug the 'Mahia' who was to assist in our berthing. The tug came in alongside the break of the focle head to pass up a tow line. We tried to pass a heaving line down to the tug to attach to the tow line, unfortunately, they were unable to pick it up. The skipper then moved ahead right under the bow of the ship and once again we passed the heaving line down to him.

Due to interaction between the ship and the tug, she was drawn in to the ships side. The skipper put his wheel hard over to starboard and increased speed to clear our bow. This was a mistake as the stern of the tug was being pushed against our bow and the twisting moment resulted in the tug swinging under our bow. I contacted the bridge and told them to go full astern but as it happened so quickly nothing could be done.

The tug listed to starboard and swung right around our bow once the stern lifted of our ships side it steamed clear but nearly tipped over. Once clear, it limped away to its berth with considerable damage. The next day, I went over with the Lloyds surveyor to see the 'Mahia' at the local shipyard slipway, to see the damage to its hull and propellor.

In 1977, I received a request from P&O to give them my thoughts on the incident. The letter on the following page from P&O strath services thanking me for my report on the incident. This was another port where I was offered a job by the Lloyds surveyor but explained I was in fact hoping to obtain a pilot's position at home.

# P&O Strath Services

Captain R.C. Sclater
Springbank
South Ronaldsay
Orkney

| telephone ext. | your reference | our reference | date |
| --- | --- | --- | --- |
| 2031 | | GCD/I&C/ARS/PAW | 24 October 1977 |

Dear Sir,

**m.v. "CUMBERLAND" Contact with Tug "MAHIA"**
**on 4th February 1976.**

We were indeed pleased to receive your letter of 17th
inst. together with the enclosures and certainly consider
that the professional answer written by you in response
to the questions posed by the Company's Solicitors will
be to good effect particularly as you were stationed in
the foxle-head, and looking straight down at the tug.
Further it has probably not been rbought out earlier that
the Tug Master made a starboard helm before the tug was
clear of our bow and so pushing his stern hard against
the starboard bow of the "CUMBERLAND" this making matters
even worse.

Your very clear recollection of the course of events in
this unfortunate matter is much appreciated and we thank
you for your willing assistance in our efforts in dealing
with the case.

Yours faithfully,
for P&O STRATH SERVICES LIMITED

A.R. Stewart

P&O Strath Services Limited
Beaufort House, St Botolph Street, London EC3A 7DX
Telephone 01-283 8787 Telex 885551

Managers of the General Cargo Division of The Peninsular and Oriental Steam Navigation Company
Registered Office P&O Building, Leadenhall Street, London EC3V 4QL   Registered Number 21693 England

We completed our part load in Napier then headed down to Timaru. We collided with one of the all-weather loading gantries whilst berthing. It was unfortunate as we were under the control of a new pilot learning the ropes with a senior pilot supervising. No damage to ship but quite a dent in the gantry. Then onwards to port Chalmers with another slight incident here prior to arrival.

Our radar had broken down and in those days, there was only one radar onboard. It was thick fog so no exact position of where we were. I came on watch at 0400 and we worked on a DR (dead reckoning) position and steamed along at slow speed as we could not pick up the pilot until daylight. About 0600, we reckoned we were close to Taiaroa head using DF (direction finder) bearings which were not very accurate.

The fog was slowly lifting and the next thing we saw was the cliffs of the headland straight ahead of us. We had, in fact, over shot the entrance. Luckily, we were steaming at slow speed so the engines were quickly stopped and put full astern. It was quite deep water close in, so were able to navigate safely away from the cliffs.

The fog cleared and we headed for the pilot launch. The radar was repaired when we arrived in port. We completed loading in port Chalmers and then set sail for Fremantle in Western Australia for bunkers. During this leg of the voyage resulted in us finding two stowaways onboard. I mentioned the Captain allowing the third mate to have his girlfriend onboard. Well, two of the stewards went one better and decided to take theirs on the voyage home.

We were carrying out the weekly accommodation inspection (down to once a week now) when one of the crew said to check the lockers in the steward's cabins. The Captain left me to it so I went into the cabin, opened the locker doors and found the two girls. The agent in Fremantle was informed and arrangements were made to repatriate them back to New Zealand.

We were lucky that we had to bunker in Fremantle otherwise they would have been onboard until Malta. No way they would have been taken off in Aden, our next port or in the Suez canal. The two stewards were duly reprimanded and logged a few days' pay. On board, we had two ship's log books, the bridge log that covered all aspects of shipboard activities relating to navigation noon position star sight position bearing and distances of light houses headlands etc.

Loading discharging cargo which holds were in use time of commencing/finishing, weather and sea conditions and any other eventuality which required reporting. The ships log was a full record of the ship's life during every voyage and one of the most important documents on board. The other log book was the official log book. This contained details required under the various merchant shipping acts such as time of boat and fire drills accommodation inspections and the fines placed on crew members who had committed a misdemeanour.

Hence the term a crew member was logged. We also had an oil record book covering the pumping of engine room bilges through the oily water separator. The time and position of commencing pumping and finishing was kept in this book. The information was also in the ship's log. I have strayed a bit again, but as I had not mentioned log books before, thought it was a good time to do it.

We arrived in Fremantle and the two stowaways were taken away. No idea what happened to them. We then set sail for Aden where we bunkered and then onwards to Suez. I did mention my concerns for the Captain and his ill health. Quite regularly, he would come into the dinning saloon for his meal, order it and as soon as it was placed in front of him, he would appear to be going to be sick and head out of the saloon without touching his food.

He was a bit of a recluse and I only went into his cabin to discuss ship's business. He was not a sociable man, very unusual onboard ship, I believe he did have a drinking problem but hid it quite well. On the day we arrived in Suez, he came on the bridge and looked like death and I did think he was on his last legs.

Anyway, he went down to his cabin and came back up just as we were picking up the pilot and appeared to have a new lease of life and back to some sense of normality. A great relief to me.

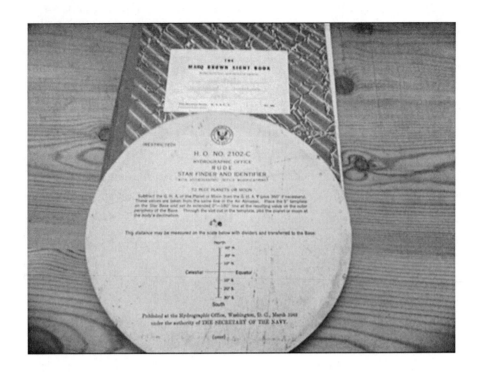

*Just A Bit of Further Information Regarding Navigation.*
*Essential items for calculating morning and evening star sights. The rude star finder and identifier allowed you to calculate the bearing and altitude of the stars you were to 'shoot' with your sextant. Normally, you would try for five stars to give you a good 'cocked hat' when plotting the five position lines which you were lying on. Knowing the true bearing and altitude allowed you to have the sextant set at as near as possible the stars altitude as the sight had to be taken at twilight and the horizon still visible. It could be quite tricky getting them all done before it got too dark or too light in the morning.*

I only found out when joining the ship in New Zealand that it was loading for the Mediterranean and not back to the UK. This would result in another five months voyage for me. I therefore, contacted head office and requested if Anna and Esther could join the Cumberland in Malta for the rest of the voyage. I was very pleased to receive a positive reply.

We transited the Suez canal without any problems and set sail for Valletta. Anna and Esther were due to fly out and join the ship in Malta. The agent received their flight details and we both went out to the airport to meet them on a flight from London. All the passengers disembarked but no sign of Anna and Esther.

I was really very concerned on where they had got to, so was the agent as there had been no information from the company or from the airline to explain why they were not on the flight. The agent and I met every flight coming in from London that evening, still no sign. The next morning the agent came onboard and gave me the news on where they were and why they missed their flight.

The air traffic controllers in France had been on strike and this had delayed flights in the UK and Anna and Esther missed their connection in London.

BA had rerouted them from Heathrow through to Gatwick but they missed that flight also and had to have a night in a hotel. They were booked to fly out the next day via Rome where they had to change aircraft. This was quite a trial for them both, with Esther still only two years old and all their luggage and a push chair.

Anna had managed to phone the company in London, thank goodness, to let them know the situation. I was very relieved to get the news but not happy with the French air traffic controllers. We met the flight from Rome and were very pleased to see them walking into the terminal building. We were all very relieved and happy to get settled into our cabin onboard the Cumberland.

We stayed in Valletta for a further two days so had a chance for some sightseeing. Then sailed over to Latakia in Syria. No alongside berth, so we discharged into barges at anchor and it took us two weeks to discharge. The anchorage was quite open to the prevailing sea conditions and we did drag our anchor and had to vacate the anchorage and steam for a night and day until the weather improved.

The big problem was the anchorage was full of other shipping so you could not afford to drag your anchor or you might collide with other vessels. Quite a boring time but there was always things going on onboard. It was common to have BBQs on deck and also even fancy-dress parties. There was a few other wives and children onboard so quite a happy group of people.

We then proceeded to Limassol which was a lovely Greek Cypriot city. The agent had organised a deal with one of the local tourist hotels, the Apolonia beach hotel which allowed us to use their swimming pool and facilities whilst in port. This was excellent and most afternoons we went to the hotel. Whilst in Limassol, there was serious troubles in Lebanon and the UK government had dispatched a royal navy warship to evacuate non-essential British residents.

The US navy carried out a much larger evacuation in July the same year. The royal navy vessel took the evacuees to Limassol and a few were put up in the Apolonia hotel. We met some of them and one young girl got on well with Esther and loved playing with her in the pool. I think they were only too happy to be away from war torn Beirut. After completing discharge, we sailed up to Piraeus which would be our last port. We stayed at anchor for nearly two weeks as there was no alongside berth available.

We did get ashore with a liberty boat but it could be quite hairy getting back onboard as the anchorage once again was quite open to the sea. Always carried Esther up and down the gangway to board and disembark from the launch. We eventually berthed and were to stay in Piraeus for another two weeks. The old Captain left and a new one joined; thank goodness he was an NZSCo master so things got back to normal onboard. Esther had her third birthday onboard so we had a nice party and cake for the occasion.

We had a very pleasant stay in port and visited Athens and the acropolis and other tourist attractions. Quite a few afternoons were spent at Vouliagmeni beach, a very popular seaside resort outside Athens. On one of our visits to the acropolis we met a young Greek student who wished to practice her English so we spoke to her for some time. She then asked if she could write to us and of course we agreed and we are still in touch, 43 years later.

Only one incident in Piraeus when Anna had an accident ashore whilst attending the dentist. After she finished her treatment, she was going down the marble stairs with Esther in her arms when she slipped and fell down the stairs and hit her head with a crack on the marble floor. Not sure how she did it but managed to turn round and had Esther on her chest when she hit the floor.

We took her to a doctor's surgery next door who put metal clamps instead of stitches in her head where it was bleeding. Thanks goodness Anna was made of strong stuff or she could have fractured her skull. Esther was none the worse after the fall but Anna had headaches for a few days after. During one of our walks round Piraeus Marina, we came across Jacques Cousteau's research vessel the 'Calypso'. Unfortunately, he was not onboard at the time, but was fascinating to see his famous ship.

I had kept in contact with Captain Robertson regarding the position of marine officer as I had expected to be back in Orkney by May. He assured me that there was no problem as things were not progressing as quickly as he thought and the oil terminal would not be up and running until December. As I had been onboard the Cumberland for over five months, I was due to go on leave.

I signed off on 26 June and this was to be my last trip to sea. We packed up our suitcases and were taken to Athens airport to fly home. The day after we left Athens airport, an air France flight departed Tel Aviv bound for Athens to pick up 58 more passengers bound for Paris. Unfortunately, they also picked up four hijackers. We had departed the afternoon the day before so could have rubbed shoulders with the hijacker checking out the airport.

After it departed, the hijackers took over and flew the plane via Benghazi to Entebbe. This was the famous hijack that the Israeli commandos successfully saved most of the hostages in their daring raid in Uganda. We were thankful that it was not a British airways flight they decided to hijack.

We arrived back in a London and stayed the night at Heathrow it was 1976 the hottest summer in the UK for many years. The temperatures in London were considerably higher than what we had left in Athens. The hotel room was like a hot house. We were happy to get our flight north the next morning to slightly cooler climate in Orkney.

*The photos of our enjoyable days in the Mediterranean. Steering the ship. Fancy dress night onboard. Beside the pool at Apolonia beach hotel. Day out at the Acropolis. On deck with one of our old ships the Tongararo. In the back ground, in full, P&O livery. In a pedalo, at Vouliagmeni beach.*

Once we arrived home and settled into normal life ashore, I contacted Orkney Harbours Authority to let them know I was available for another interview. I had also received a letter from Occidental dated 20<sup>th</sup> May concerning a post as loading master at the terminal. They must have retained a copy of my letter sent two years earlier asking about employment as a pilot.

It was very satisfying to be invited for two interviews. I attended the first one at the Harbours Department, just three days after arriving home and was offered the position as Marine Officer. Occidental arranged an interview a couple of days later at the Flotta Oil Terminal.

They did offer me the post but advised me that the position of loading master would not be filled until possible November and I should return to sea until then. I had no wish to return to sea and as the Harbours Department was happy to employ me at the end of my leave period on 27 September, I decided to take up their offer. This was to be the next challenge in my working life.

I had set off as a young lad of 15 years old in September 1956 to attend the TS Dolphin as a trainee deck boy without any preconception of what the future might hold. My qualifications on leaving school amounted to nothing and therefore, did not have any great ambitions on where my sea career would take me.

Now exactly 20 years later, I held the highest qualification required at sea to be in command of any UK merchant vessel, not too bad an achievement. During my time at sea, I had seen many interesting countries, learned the ropes as a seaman and then as a deck officer. I had sailed with some interesting characters and some not so nice. I had been involved in fires, collisions, murder, suicide, war zones, pirates, sea rescues and many other incidents highlighted in my story. I had certainly achieved much more than I ever expected and thankful for the help I received from the late Captain John Leslie who convinced me to sit for my second mates ticket.

My story will continue with my time as a first class authorised pilot, then as deputy director of a harbours and onwards to director of harbours with Orkney islands Council and finally as a Councillor myself and chairman of the harbour authority.

# OCCIDENTAL OF BRITAIN, INC.

(Subsidiary of Occidental Petroleum Corporation)    (Incorporated in U.S.A.)

Hyde Park House,
60 Knightsbridge,
London SW1X 7JX
Telephone: 01 235 4321
Telex: 918124

127 Causewayend,
Aberdeen,
AB2 3TP
Telephone: 0224 572561
Telex: 73340

P.O. Box 14,
Kirkwall,
Orkney
Telephone:
Telex:

Please reply to ......KIRKWALL.......

Mr. R.C. Sclater,
Springbank,
South Ronaldsay,
Orkney

9th July 1976

Dear Sir,

I thank you for giving of your time to come to Flotta and
fully understand that a post as a Marine Officer offers a wider scope.

I can only wish you every success and look forward to
meeting you again once you have taken up your position with the Local
Authority - and settle  down to a more regular home life.

Yours faithfully,
for OCCIDENTAL OF BRITAIN INC.,

M. Gunn
Marine Superintendant.

# ORKNEY ISLANDS COUNCIL

## DEPARTMENT OF HARBOURS

Broad Street, Kirkwall, Orkney, KW15 1DH

**Director:**-Capt. D. O. Robertson, M.R.I.N., M.N.I.

Tel.: (0856) 3218  35353  Ext 65

YOUR REF.:

OUR REF.: 75/54.R/ET

1st July 1976

Captain R.C. Sclater,
Springbank,
South Ronaldsay,
Orkney.

Dear Sir,

Marine Officers.

This letter will serve to confirm information given to you at your
second interview yesterday that your application has been successful
and I offer you a post as Marine Officer with the Orkney Islands
Council Harbour Authority commencing 27th September 1976.   As was
explained this appointment is subject to a successful medical
examination by the Council's Doctor which has been arranged through
this office.

The salary for the post will be £5,583 rising to £6,063 by three
annual increments, to which falls to be added an Islands Allowance
of £183.   The salary takes into account the requirement to operate
on a watch keeping basis involving a working week of 40 hours.
The allocation of the hours of work will be as laid down by the
Director of Harbours.   Duties will include pilotage, watch keeping,
patrol and such other duties as may be prescribed by the Director.

Uniform will be provided and must be worn on duty.   Telephone rental
will be paid by the Council.

The N.J.C. Scheme for Principal Officers will apply where this does
not conflict with the aforementioned conditions.   The holiday
entitlement is 22 working days i.e. 4 weeks, plus public holidays.

I will be obliged if you will confirm your acceptance of this post.

Yours faithfully,

D. O. Robertson,
Director of Harbours.

*The Letters from Occidental and Orkney Islands*
*Council Harbours Department*

# Part 3

After a lovely summer on leave, I took up my new post as a marine officer with the Orkney Islands Council's Department Of Harbours on 27 September 1976. Part of my new position would require me to pilot vessels in both of the new pilotage areas set up by the Orkney County Council Act 1974 and Orkney PILOTAGE ORDER 1976. I therefore ordered a full set of admiralty charts covering Orkney to familiarise myself with these areas.

Being a local Orcadian, I did have a rough idea of the topography and seascape of Orkney which was a help. My new work place was a couple of portacabins situated at Scapa beach where eventually the main headquarters for the Harbours Department would be built.

There was to be six marine officers and I was the fourth to be employed. The first one being the ex-Kirkwall harbour master Captain Billy Sinclair, the only one of the six who had hands on pilotage experience in Orkney waters. There were two ex-pilots who had worked in the oil port of Kharg island in Iran.

I was the only one of the first four with no hands-on pilotage experience. There were two others to join later, one an ex-ferry master Captain Gray and the other an ex-harbour master from Scrabster Captain Cowie, who also had some pilotage experience.

The oil terminal was still under construction with no oil expected to be flowing until late December. This then gave me a chance to get to know the pilotage districts, navigation marks, lights, depths, along with all the other essential information required to pilot vessels safely into and out of port.

Although there were no large tankers to be piloted there was, however, lots of smaller coastal traffic to be conducted into and out of both the Scapa Flow and Kirkwall pilotage areas. I, therefore, started a very quick familiarisation with the art of piloting. It was to take a few weeks before I actually piloted a vessel by myself, I did, however, accompany the other more experienced pilots when they were carrying out this task.

Our piloting was to get very interesting after we had been in post for a couple of weeks. This was due to the accident in September 1976 when the aircraft carrier US's JFK lost one of its tomcat aircraft overboard just north of Orkney. The US were very keen to salvage the aircraft and its missiles.

A German salvage vessel the 'Taurus' was chartered to carry out the task. Her first port prior to commencing work was Kirkwall where she came under pilotage and I, along with one of the pilots boarded her just inside the pilotage area.

She was to come intro Kirkwall a couple of times during the salvage operations due to weather related problems and to pick up equipment. It gave everyone some extra training in piloting into and out of Kirkwall. There was other smaller vessels assisting that also came into Kirkwall. It was quite an exciting period.

Above: The German Salvage vessel 'Taurus' pulls the stricken F-14 from the watery depths. Photos: US Archives.

The multi million dollar jet, eagerly watched by a Russian trawler, still had the missile which at that time was a revolutionary weapon still on the secret list, so it had to be recovered at all cost.

It an epic operation costing $1.5 the German salvage ship 'Taurus' towed the F-14 to shallow water between Egilsay and Shapinsay and both the aircraft and the missile over a period of nearly two months were recovered, though the F-14 which was more or less undamaged when it reached the seabed, had been battered to pieces and was a total wreck.

The other vessels, we learned our trade, were small coastal tankers discharging petrol, diesel, heating oil and jet2aircraft fuel into the two oil installations one in Kirkwall and another located above Scapa pier. We also had a small tanker taking diesel to the Flotta oil terminal which berthed at Sutherland pier, a very small stone jetty could be a job if arriving at night as the pier had very poor lighting.

There was also a number of small coasters bringing various cargoes for discharge into Kirkwall and Stromness. Some required pilotage and others were either exempt or did not wish to use pilots providing they were under the required pilotage regulations. We worked 9 to 5 Monday to Friday and on call out with these hours if a pilot was required.

With six of us, this made our work load quite relaxed. We had a rota for covering out of normal working hours. Details of all shipping was provided by the local shipping agents so we knew well in advance which vessels required pilots. The department had bought three pilot launches, one second hand the' Kirkwall bay' quite a basic little motor launch for use in the Kirkwall pilotage area.

The other two designed by Murray Cormack associates naval architects, were talisman 49 hull, state of the art pilot boats, the 'Scapa patrol' and 'Scapa pilot'. The crews on the pilot launches were mostly local fishermen and seamen with plenty of experience in Orkney waters, and capable of boarding and landing pilots safely to/from the large oil and gas tankers that were to operate to the Flotta Oil Terminal.

*Scapa pilot and Scapa patrol, first two pilot launches built in 1976.*

At the same time, the Council were in discussion with JP Knight Ltd, a towage company, with head offices in Rochester, Kent. They also operated JP Knight Caledonia Ltd in the port of Invergordon. A contract was signed with them and the Orkney Towage Company was set up in 1976. The shares being 51% Orkney Islands Council and 49% JP Knight Ltd. The first two tugs were the Mt Kessock and Mt Kinloch both of about 35-ton bollard pull.

The tugs were on a bare boat charter which meant that Orkney Towage would man, maintain, and operate the tugs and pay JP Knight an annual fee for their use. JP Knight provided a local manager, Albert Slater who set about employing mostly local skippers and seamen to man the tugs. There was also two experienced tug skippers one from Rochester, Captain Don Beathal and one from Invergordon, Captain Fraser Forbes who helped to train the new skippers and crews.

I will cover the towage operation and financial situation in much more detail later on in my story. As I was only a marine officer/pilot back in 1976, I had no locus in their operation. I certainly made big changes when I finally took over responsibility for Orkney towage. During the three months prior to the first oil arriving, we spent countless hours travelling around Scapa Flow, Pentland firth and surrounding areas getting to know the district and understanding the strong tidal flows in the firth.

We also spent time at the Flotta Oil Terminal getting to know our counterparts the new mooring/loading masters. The Harbours Department had also constructed a remote radar installation to cover the approaches to the Pentland firth situated on sandy hill in South Ronaldsay with a microwave link to our portacabin control room.

There was also a radar installed next to the control room covering Scapa flow itself. This was not a state-of-the-art VTS setup. The two radars were 16-inch Decca ship's radars, so plotting of shipping was basic China graph pencil to ascertain their course and speed, of course, we were a fixed unit so need to apply our course and speed.

The control room was fitted with VHF radios to contact vessels and to give out any navigation information and the daily weather forecasts. By the end of December, we were all up to speed and awaiting our first oil tanker due at the beginning of January.

The berthing arrangements at the terminal consisted of two Single Point Mooring Towers (SPMS) and one alongside jetty. The Single Point Towers could accommodate tankers up to 200000 tonnes and the jetty up to 150000 tonnes. The jetty could also handle both ethane and propane gas carriers. The Single Point Moorings were ready for use by December but the jetty would not be up and running until August 1977.

The first vessel to arrive was the French registered tanker the Mt Dolabella which we boarded east of the Pentland firth at 0950hrs, 5 January 1977. There were four of us who boarded, Captain Banks the pilot, Captain Dunn one of the ex-Kharg island pilots, myself and my old friend Captain Bill Spence now operating John Jolly, the main shipping agent in Orkney.

The Mt Dolabella was taken to anchor and was advised that it would berth to the Single Point Mooring on Sunday 9 January. This resulted in some of the pilots and mooring masters boarding the pilot launch at Scapa pier to set out to witness the first oil tanker berthing at the Flotta Oil Terminal, a flag ship day for all concerned.

The pilot in charge of the berthing was Captain Banks, the pilotage superintendent.

There were three hoses attached to the ship's manifolds, two loading and one for de-ballasting. No ballast water was pumped over board all ballast went to a dedicated ballast reception tank at the terminal; this ballast water was put through a ballast treatment plant prior to being pumped into the Pentland firth.

Occidental (oxy) was a consortium of four oil companies, Occidental the main partner, Texaco, Union Texas, and Phillips Petroleum. The first oil came ashore via a pipeline from the piper and claymore North Sea Oil Fields sector in December 1976. There were several other fields in this sector that would come on stream as time went on. These are all highlighted on the oil map on one of the following pages.

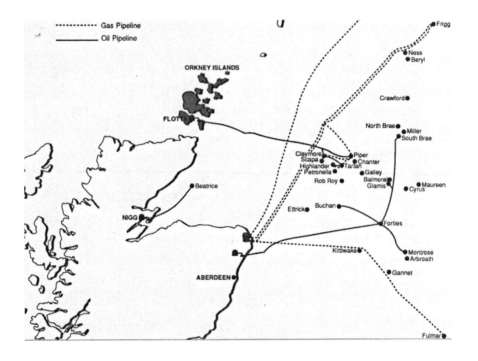

*Flotta Oil Terminal*

The berthing to the SPM was quite a straight forward manoeuvre with two tugs made fast, one on each bow, ready to push or pull the tanker into position with the SPM right ahead. The vessel steamed at slow speed into the wind as the floating hoses were lying down wind with an oxy workboat pulling them clear of the approach.

The mooring master on the focle was in direct contact by radio giving distances from the SPM to the pilot on the bridge. A ship's rope was passed down to another oxy work boat who then attached it to the main mooring messenger which was then pulled onboard. The messenger was attached to the mooring chain that would hold the tanker safely to the SPM during loading.

Depending on the tankers lay out the chain was either shackled to wire strops already placed around the mooring bits on the focle or the chain caught directly into a fixed mooring clamp. Although the first berthing took over three hours, after a few months we reduced this mooring time considerably.

Unmooring was also quite simple. The messenger line on the chain was taking to the windlass drum end and the weight taken of the chain sometimes by giving the ship a touch ahead on its engines. The clamp or wire strops were

201

removed and the chain lowered into the water. With a tug lying on the port bow ready to push the loaded tanker away from the floating hoses the vessel was put astern and manoeuvred safely away from the SPM.

The mooring master along with his mooring crew and berthing equipment disembarked as soon as the vessel was clear off the SPM. The tanker then proceeded out of port with the pilot disembarking in Hoxa sound and the tanker increasing to full sea speed for entering the Pentland firth. The two tugs escorted the tanker outwards until well clear of the channel.

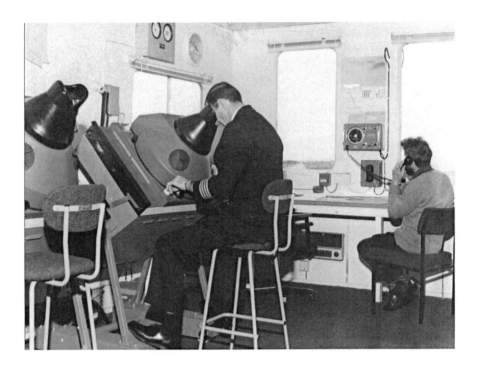

*Photo of Captain Mike Milbank on radar and Captain Billy Sinclair on VHF radio in our portacabin control room.*

As soon as the Mt Dolabella arrived, we went onto a watch keeping system of 8-hour shifts. This was quite a commitment as there was only six of us and we were giving 24-hour watch keeping, plus 24-hour pilotage cover for what was to become a very busy port operation.

Our rota consisted of three night, three day and three evening shifts, then three days off; pilotage covered three first call and three second call for 18 days. This put us well over our contracted 40 hours a week. This resulted in some heated debate and several letters to UK Pilots Association (union) and the Local Government Nation Joint Council, to get overtime payments for the extra hours. I was now, along with Captain Sinclair, the pilots' representatives on the Orkney Pilotage Districts Committee and a member of the Pilotage Examining Board. A copy of my pilots' authorisation is also on the following pages.

I never was a great union man and was not really happy having to go down this route by complaining in this fashion. However, as the pilot's representative I had no option but to see it through. The pilots were all members of the United Kingdom Pilots Association (UKPA) essential to cover your pilot's licence in any legal action and also to assist in any disputes.

## ORKNEY PILOTAGE DISTRICT

No. 111219

The Orkney Islands Council, as Pilotage Authority for the Orkney Pilotage District, in pursuance and by virtue of the powers given them for that purpose in and by the Pilotage Act, 1913, and of all other powers them enabling having first duly examined

ROBERT CHALMERS SCLATER

of SPRINGBANK, SOUTH RONALDSAY, ORKNEY aged 35 years

and having, upon such examination, found the said ROBERT CHALMERS SCLATER

to be a fit and competent Person, duly skilled to act as a Pilot for the purpose of conducting Ships, sailing, navigating, and passing within the limits hereinafter mentioned, DO hereby appoint and licence the said ROBERT

CHALMERS SCLATER to act as a Pilot, for the purpose of conducting Ships within The Orkney Harbour Authority Area for Scapa Flow bounded as follows: Commencing at the Out Taings point on Hoy; thence in a straight line to Breckness on Mainland; thence in a generally eastern direction following the line of low later on the southern boundaries of Mainland to the northern end of the northernmost Churchill Barrier; thence in a generally southerly direction following the western sides of the four Churchill Barriers and the lines of low water on the western boundaries of the islands of South Ronaldsay (other than Swona) to Brough Ness; thence in a generally westerly direction by a straight line to the southernmost part of Swona and a straight line from that point to Brims Ness on South Walls on the island of Hoy; thence following the line of low water on the western and northern sides of Aith Hope and the seaward boundaries of South Walls and of Hoy to the point of commencement; together with that area of the Pentland Firth enclosed by a line drawn due south (true), three miles from Tor Ness Lighthouse, thence in an east-south-easterly direction to Muckle Skerry Lighthouse and thence in a northerly direction to the south-eastern extremity of Old Head; and within the Orkney Harbour Authority area for Wide Firth/Shapinsay Sound area bounded as follows:

Commencing at Harpy Taing on Mainland; thence in a straight line to Stromberry on Shapinsay; thence following the line of low water on the southern boundary of Shapinsay to Backaness; thence in a straight line to Rerwick Point on Mainland; thence in a generally westerly and north-easterly direction following the line of low water on part of the northern boundary of Mainland to the point of commencement. And this Licence (if the same shall not be revoked or suspended in the meantime, as in the said Act provided), is to continue in force up to and until the 31st day of July next ensuing the date of these Presents, but no longer, unless renewed from time to time by Endorsement hereon. Provided always that the said Pilot shall so long comply with all the Byelaws and Regulations made or to be made by the said Council.

This Licence shall not authorise or empower the said ROBERT CHALMERS SCLATER

to take charge as a Pilot of any Ship or Vessel drawing more than FEET WATER (except when an upper draught Pilot is not available to offer his services)

Given under the Common Seal of The Orkney Islands Council at County Offices, Kirkwall, this 17th day of February 1977

Clerk to the Pilotage Authority

I had been a member of the Seaman's Union from December 1956 whilst on deck as it was classed as a 'closed shop union' so you had to be a member. I was also a member of the Merchant Navy Officers and Airline Pilots Union. This once again gave legal cover in case of accidents that may threaten your ticket.

We did win our case and the department realised that there was no way it could operate the port with only six marine officers/pilots and advertised for an additional four marine officer/pilots. We also received overtime payments but not as much as we asked. One reason being that whilst on pilotage duty, we were allowed to stay at home and only come on duty when a vessel required a pilot. This gave us considerable free time.

Back in the seventies, the majority of pilots in UK ports were self-employed and paid for each act of pilotage. We, however, were fully employed with all the benefits this provided. The Pilotage Act of 1987 was to change the self-employed status and I will cover this later in the story.

Although I was piloting tankers from the start, I was supervised for the first few pilotage acts by Captain Banks, the pilotage superintendent. I also accompanied other pilots when I was off duty to get more experience for when I would be on my own and in full charge of the berthing and un-berthing of tankers. By March, I was up and running and happy to be on my own and not having someone looking over my shoulder.

This was, of course, a very unique situation as only one pilot Captain Sinclair had ever piloted ships in the area, so everyone was on a fast-learning curve. Normally in ports, pilots could take over a year to reach the position of a first-class pilot, handling ships of all sizes and drafts. With the Pentland firth being one of the most dangerous stretches of water around the UK due to the very fast tidal flow (at times up to 16 knots) not a place where you could be complacent when first boarding and getting up to the bridge.

The next few months were very satisfying and rewarding, piloting ships of all shapes and sizes safely into and out of port. The tanker operations began to build up and a copy of my acts over the first couple of years are shown on the next pages. I had one slight accident in my early days, the details are on the page out of my old note book. The Mt Teglholm was a small coastal tanker berthed in Kirkwall and the Captain was keen to sail although it was blowing a gale.

LET GO. FROM TANKER BERTH  AT MID-NIGHT
COMING ASTERN  WIND CANTED STERN
INTO ISLANDER  HAD TO TURN
SHORT ROUND OFF TANKER BERTH
ON DOING THIS. STERN TOUCHED
BANK AND V/L STUCK UNTIL.
0100hrs.  KIRKWALL BAY ASSISTED
WITH PUSHING off STERN.
ANCHORED AT 0115hrs TO CHECK
bound FOR ANY DAMAGE,
NOTHING VISIBLE AT PRESENT
STAYING AT ANCHOR TO CHECK IN
DAYLIGHT. ALSO BAD WEATHER
OUTSIDE

+ CSW WOOLSTON    855   SCATR   650,294
CSDO WOOLSTON    855
HERMAN SHUR    499
JEN TRADER    399
A.P. WARRIOR    1529
HAMILTON MILLER    1537

| Date | Vessel | Movement | Tonnage |
|---|---|---|---|
| 24/2 - | MARIE FORSYTH | TO ANCHOR | 42,789 |
| 25/3 - | DAPHNE | TO ANCHOR | 39,481 |
| 24/3 | MARIE FORSYTH | TO SEA | 42,789 |
| 28/3 | DAPHNE | SPM-2 | 39,481 |
| 28/3 | DAPHNE | TO SEA | 39,481 |
| 3/4 | KURUSHIMA MARU | SPM 2 | 44,774 |
| 4/4 | FORTUNA | TO ANCHOR | 35,930 |
| 5/4 | FORTUNA | ANCHOR-ANCHOR | 35,930 BAD WEATHER |
| 6/4 | FORTUNA | SPM 2 | 35,930 |
| 6/4 | FORTUNA | TO ANCHOR | 35,930 BAD WEATHER |
| 7/4 | NACELLA | TO ANCHOR | 60,275 |
| 7/4 | FORTUNA | SPM 2 | 35,930 |
| 9/4 | NACELLA | SPM 2 | 60,275 |
| 9/4 | FORTUNA | ANCHOR-TO SEA | 35,930 |
| 10/4 | NACELLA | TO SEA | 60,275 |
| 9/5 | DOLABELLA | TO SEA | 41,506 |
| 9/5 | OCEANUS | TO SEA | 67,534 |
| 11/5 | NISO | TO SEA | 62,845 |
| 21/5 | ALMARE QUARTA | SPM 2 | 59,319 |
| 23/5 | ALMARE QUARTA | TO SEA | 59,319 (935743) |

The wind caught the bow of the ship when we let go and pushed the stern in towards the local ferry, the MV Islander. I had no option but to try and turn the tanker round in a very tight area, but the stern touched the bank and got stuck. With the helm hard to port and a touch ahead on the engines with the pilot boat pushing, the stern lifted off the side of the channel.

No damage was done and the Captain decided to wait for better weather before sailing. It was good experience but not something that ever happened again during my time as a pilot. There was also an incident at the SPM when the Mt Nacella broke the mooring chain in storm force winds.

The tug on standby was made fast to the bow and held the tanker steady until a pilot arrived and also to uncouple the loading hoses. It resulted in an oil spill of some 70 barrels (7 tonnes) of crude oil, the largest in the terminal's history. This made everyone have a rethink on the actual mooring arrangements.

The system in the beginning consisted of a chain which had no elasticity so when the vessel was moving back and forth there was no stretching of the chain and it parted. It was agreed that the mooring should incorporate a nylon rope between the chain links to give some movement.

It was also agreed that a tug would be attached to the stern of the tanker to keep a steady strain on the mooring. On the next pages, details out of my old note book and a few photos and details regarding the Flotta Terminal operations. I will cover some of these later in my story.

I was the pilot on the first vessel the Mt Messidor to berth at the jetty, although the berthing itself was carried out by Captain Milbank who had more experience berthing large tankers. Prior to the jetty becoming operational, it was agreed that the two tugs Kessock and Kinloch did not have sufficient bollard pull to handle large tankers berthing to the jetty. An additional tug, the Mt Kintore with steering kort nozzles and with 40 tons+, bollard pull was placed on bare boat charter with Orkney Towage Ltd.

| Date | Vessel | | Tonnage | | Date | Vessel | | Tonnage |
|---|---|---|---|---|---|---|---|---|
| 15/6 | TIISKERI (2nd sms)(skerry) | S.P.M.1/S.P.M.2 | 64,357 | | 2/10 | ESSO ANTWERP. | S.P.M. 2 | 42,094 |
| 14/6 | TIISKERI | TO SEA | 62,357 | | 7/10 | ESSO TORINO | S.P.M.1 | 39,270 |
| 30/6 | KURUSHIMA MARU | S.P.M. 2 | 44,773 | | 7/10 | ESSO TORINO | To Jetty | 39,270 |
| 2/7 | KURUSHIMA MARU | TO SEA | 44,773 | | 8/10 | ESSO TORINO | S.P.M.1 | 39,270 |
| 7/7 | KURUSHIMA MARU | S.P.M. 2 | 44,773 | | 8/10 | NEVERITA | TO SEA | 57,905 |
| 7/7 | NEVERITA (large)(skerry) | ANCHOR. | 57,905 | | 13/10 | ESSO TORINO | (1st NIGHT) JETTY. | 39,270 |
| 24/7 | KURUSHIMA MARU | TO SEA | 44,773 | | 2/11 | NACELLA. | (6 mth skerry) JETTY | 60,275 |
| 25/7 | ESSO WARWICKSHIRE | S.P.M.2 | 48,049 | | 3/11 | NACELLA | TO SEA | 60,275 |
| 24/7 | ESSO WARWICKSHIRE | To SEA | 48,049 | | 5/11 | ESSO TORINO | TO SEA | 39,270 |
| 1/8 | ESSO ANTWERP | S.P.M.1 WARWICK | 42,094 | | 8/11 | ESSO TORINO | To ANCHOR | 39,270 |
| 8/8 | ESSO ANTWERP | S.P.M 1 | 42,094 | | 9/11 | ESSO TORINO | JETTY | 39,270 |
| 19/8 | MESSIDOR | (1st on setting) END of FLOTTA. | 48,054 | | 20/11 | DOLABELLA | JETTY | 41,506 |
| 19/8 | POITOU | TO SEA | 69,016 | | 21/11 | ESSO TORINO | JC | 39,270 |
| 24/8 | ESSO ANTWERP | TO SEA | 42,094 | | 22/11 | DOLABELLA | TO SEA | 41,506 |
| 30/8 | ESSO ANTWERP | JETTY | 42,094 | | 31/12 | ESSO ANTWERP | TO SEA | 42,094 |
| 31/8 | ESSO WARWICKSHIRE | JETTY | 48,049 | | 1978 | TOTAL = 55 ACTS | | 254,545 +++ |
| 30/9 | ESSO WARWICKSHIRE | JETTY | 48,049 | | 5/1 | ESSO ANTWERP | L.P.G. | 42,094 |
| 1/10 | ESSO WARWICKSHIRE | TO SEA | 48,049 | | 9/1 | NEVERITA. | Jetty. | 57,905 |
| 1/10 | ESSO TORINO | JETTY | 39,270 | | 10/11 | ESSO PARIS | S.P.M.1 | 96,226 |
| 2/10 | ESSO TORINO | TO SEA | 39,270 | | 9/1 | ESSO CARDIFF | TO SEA | 31,720 |

*We had a log book in the control room with ever act of pilotage logged, so I discontinued my own record.*

Just a sample of the pilotage acts I carried out in my first couple of years to the Oil Terminal. I did not keep a record of other acts as they were also all logged in the control room log. On following page, Nacella at pilot station, ESSO Antwerp heading to SPM with tug on starboard bow, tanker with Kintore towing on the stern keeping steady strain on the mooring chain, Mobil Astral at SPM, and my radiotelephony certificate required to use VHF radios in control room.

The Mt Keston was the relief tug and was based in Invergordon. It stood by when the Kintore, Kessock and Kinloch went on annual refit to JP Knights dry dock facilities in Ostend Belgium. The three tugs are shown alongside Scapa pier. I will cover the details of refits and bare boat charters later in my story when the full financial implications of these provisions were made aware to me.

No. **MT/5156**

## UNITED KINGDOM OF GREAT BRITAIN AND NORTHERN IRELAND

### RESTRICTED CERTIFICATE OF COMPETENCE IN RADIOTELEPHONY

This is to certify that, under the provisions of Section 7(1) of the Wireless Telegraphy Act, 1949, and the Radio Regulations annexed to the International Telecommunications Convention, Malaga Torremolinos, 1973.

Mr. ROBERT CHALMERS SCLATER

has been examined in Radiotelephony and has passed in:—

(a) Practical knowledge of the adjustment of radiotelephone apparatus.

(b) Practical knowledge of radiotelephone operation and procedure.

(c) Sending and receiving spoken messages correctly by telephone.

(d) General knowledge of the regulations applying to radiotelephone communications and particularly of that part of those regulations relating to the safety of life.

It is also certified hereby that the holder has made a declaration that he will preserve the secrecy of correspondence.

Signature of Examining Officer...................................................

MPT 105

Date.........................................

Dear Sir,

<u>m.t. NEVERITA – arrived Scapa Flow</u>

<u>7th July, 1977.</u>

On behalf of Shell International Marine Limited, and Captain C. Clausen of m.t. NEVERITA, we should like to record our appreciation of the pilotage service rendered to this tanker when she arrived at Scapa Flow on 7th July, 1977.

As you may know, this is Captain Clausen's first visit to Scapa Flow; for this reason he requested that the Pilot embark outside the limits of the compulsory area, in a position to the north-east of Muckle Skerry where the tidal streams are appreciably weaker than those experienced at the limits of your area, and where there is ample room to manoeuvre. We are happy to report that Captain Clausen's request was fulfilled in a very satisfactory way.

In conclusion may we say how pleased we are to be able to write in this vein, but more importantly, we feel that the safe operation of vessels into Scapa Flow has been enhanced by your kind co-operation.

Yours faithfully,
For John Jolly,

(AS AGENTS ONLY)

*Copy of letter from the Captain of the MV Neverita via John Jolly thanking me for the pilotage from east of the Pentland Firth to the Flotta Terminal in July 1977. This was due to the fact that it was the ships first visit and it was thick fog, could hardly see 100 feet from the bridge. I was happy when Bill Spence passed me a copy, nice to know that the job you were doing was appreciated.*

The Pentland firth could be a tricky place to navigate outside slack water. The Mt Nacella, sister ship of the Neverita, was caught when she sailed out into a strong ebb tide. When her bow was just past Swona island, she wished to turn to port and head eastwards in the firth. The ebb tide caught her bow and with her stern still in the eddy, she was unable to turn and ended up going hard to starboard and headed westwards until she could turn safely and head back through the firth.

We always advised captains on the tidal flow prior to departure so they were fully aware what to expect when proceeding outwards. We always tried to get them to sail at slack water. If they did wish to sail earlier, we advised that if proceeding eastwards, try to sail when the tide was flowing and to keep well to the west side of Swona island.

When sailing out to the west, the ebb tide was the most advantageous although, providing the ship was building up to full sea speed with the east flowing tide, they would manage but would encounter a reduction in speed through the water due to the tide. As pilots, we certainly became aware just how strong the tides could be and it was not uncommon when boarding a tanker to find that we had to have the ship steering with some 20 to 30 degrees of set to maintain the desired course.

The tides certainly kept you on your toes. The sea conditions could be quite ferocious in the firth if the wind was against the tide. With a westerly swell against an ebb tide, it was not uncommon for the tanker to bury its bow into the sea. We always warned masters of this prior to sailing. If, of course, the weather was too bad, pilotage would be suspended. This, more so, for arriving vessels as boarding was quite dangerous.

Vessels departing were not such a problem as we could disembark reasonable safely in Hoxa Sound. Did get a few soakings with the sea coming up between the pilot launch and the ships side when stepping off the pilot ladder. When boarding, we always had the pilot ladder on the lee side so not much sea but the tanker could be rolling in any swell.

It could be a very daunting experience especially in the middle of winter and pitch dark heading out into the Pentland Firth in gale force winds to board safely and then take full control of a very large vessel. You had to be fit and agile doing the job. After boarding the tanker, we proceeded inwards and once we were abeam of Nevi Skerry, the oil terminal mooring/loading masters along with their loading crew would board.

They then lifted onboard a large wooden box containing all the necessary equipment for mooring and loading at the SPM. No requirement for this if proceeding to the jetty. After a few months, I stopped using the two tugs forward, one on each bow when berthing to the SPM as one tug on the starboard bow could handle the ship without any problems.

The second tug I had made fast aft ready to put a strain on the mooring chain as soon as we were safely moored to the SPM. This also saved the oxy work boat from pulling the floating hoses a long way from the tower on the tankers port side. This reduced our berthing time pilot onboard to all fast to one and a half hours, half the time taken on the first mooring of the Dolabella.

Although our main purpose was to handle tankers to the terminal we also were required to cover all other shipping as I mentioned previously. In the summer months, there was a number of cruise vessels visiting Orkney mostly anchoring in Kirkwall bay, as the alongside berths were too shallow for them.

In the summer of 1977, I had an interesting pilotage act when I was asked to pilot the SS Uganda on a cruise around the island of Shapinsay and the Green Holms. The reason being that there was insufficient buses available on Orkney at that time to take all the passengers on a tour of the mainland.

I said that I would do it and prior to her arrival checked out my charts and laid out the courses for the trip. There was an interesting talk given over the ship's tannoy system by Lord Birsay a well-known Orcadian on the trip round the island. The main passengers on board were all members of historic Scotland. I had already piloted a tanker to the SPM earlier the same morning and then proceeded out to pilot the Uganda to Kirkwall Bay anchorage at 0800hrs.

A number of the passenger went ashore by ships lifeboats and visited the various archaeological sites on Orkney. The Orkney Islands Shipping Company ferry MV Orcadia came alongside and transported a number of passengers to the island of Shapinsay to visit Balfour castle. Once everyone was safely ashore and the lifeboats back onboard we set of on our short cruise.

I must point out that I had never sailed in this area before and it was outside the pilotage district, I never mentioned this fact to the Captain. The trip went fine and we returned safely back to anchor. We picked up all the other passengers and sailed out at 1800hrs. It had been a long interesting day and I enjoyed my experience on the SS Uganda.

Many years later, the renewable tidal industry were setting up their tidal machines in the area we had sailed with the Uganda. A tug towing a tidal device out to the sight hit the bottom in an uncharted shoal. The depth was less than the draft of the Uganda so we were very lucky we did not hit it on our mini cruise.

*MV UGANDA is my interesting cruise around Shapinsay*

*The island of Shapinsay and Green Holms are shown on the Orkney Island's map.*

In summer 1977, one of the pilots, Captain Dunn decided he did not wish to continue working in Orkney and headed back to the Middle East. With our four new marine officers plus an extra replacement, we now had five new trainee pilots to get up to speed. They took up watch keeping duties in the control room and when on free time accompanied existing pilots on all vessels to learn the ropes in the Orkney pilotage districts.

This was no problem for the first few weeks but as the new pilots had to gain hands-on experience we had to supervise their ship handling. As they were all master mariners and some with pilotage experience, the task was reasonably straight forward. It did reduce my job satisfactions, not being the hands-on pilot but still fully responsible for the actions of the trainee pilot.

I did have one frightening experience whilst supervising one of the new pilots. The Mt Esso Torino was moored to SPM1 and the weather conditions were deteriorating so the oil terminal marine staff requested that we move her to the jetty. This was no easy task with the wind gusting up to 40 knots. I, along with the trainee pilot, boarded the ship at the SPM and unmoored her and proceeded to the jetty with the trainee in charge.

Being the supervising pilot, I always tried not to interfere with the trainees handling of the vessels. However, on this occasion, I realised that he had lost control and we were heading for the inside of the jetty due to the strong NW wind. I took over control and put the engines up to full ahead and the helm hard to starboard.

The forward tug had been made fast by this time as we were very close to the jetty, I instructed the tug to commence pulling the bow away from the jetty. He, of course, was having his own difficulties with the wind and also as I was increasing speed affecting his control of the tug. Luckily, I took over command just in time as we narrowly missed the end of jetty and steamed off to anchor.

In hindsight, I probably should have done that instead of attempting to berth at the jetty. Closest shave I ever had berthing to the terminal which could have been a disaster and knocked the jetty out of action for months. The trainee pilot also learned a lesson that day to take early action in a bad situation. The Esso Torino was eventually berthed again to the SPM to complete loading.

On her next visit, she was the first tanker to berth at night to jetty which I carried out myself with no trainee. The next few months, we continued with our piloting and control room duties without any big mishaps. The training programme of the new pilots went without a hitch and soon we had ten marine officers/pilots covering the work load.

It once again became apparent that covering the control room 24/7 and providing 2 pilots 24/7 there was no way that ten officers could cover this and take the leave due. It was decided that to cover the work load with the increase in tanker traffic, this required 15 marine officers/pilots to cover the operational requirements of the department.

The advert for the addition five officers was placed in the relevant publications and five new trainees were appointed. Back to supervising these new pilots once again. By this time, the new harbour authority building was being constructed next to our portacabin. I should mention that the director and his depute along with office staff had moved from their offices in the town hall out to additional portacabins attached to our control room early in 1977.

Everything was taking shape and our duties were not quite so demanding as they were in the first six months of operations. We now worked a rota of nine days on duty in the control room and nine days duty pilot. This then gave us 18 days free of duty each month. The nine days on pilotage duty spent at home on instant call out gave considerable free time.

You could, of course, be out at two o'clock in the morning piloting a large tanker then have a cruise ship at eight and back to sailing a tanker by late afternoon. It was a very interesting and enjoyable experience being in command of so many different types of vessels. The oil terminal was also by now processing ethane and propane natural gas so we were soon to be handling this type of traffic to jetty.

*The Esso Torino where I had a lucky escape by taking control from the trainee pilot just in time to avert the ship hitting the inside of the Flotta Terminal jetty.*

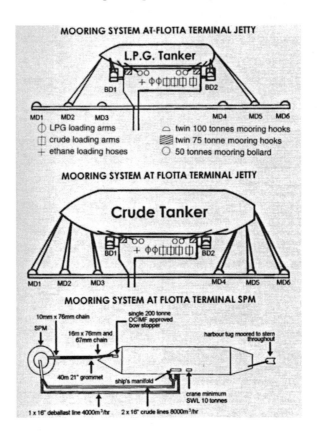

In the summer of 1977, our pilot launch the 'Kirkwall Bay' was stolen from its berth in Kirkwall harbour and taken out to sea. The culprits were not seaman and did not open the water-cooling system for the engines and the launch caught fire and sank in the approaches to Kirkwall bay.

This did cause us a problem as the two launches at Scapa had to be on station 24/7 so we had to use small fishing boats for quite some time to board and land from shipping into and out of Kirkwall harbour. The fishing boat we used was the 'Misty Isle' owned by none other than my old ship mate Norman Muir (stumper). He had given up the sea many years before. This was our pilot vessel for the next couple of years. The Harbours Department ordered a new larger pilot launch once again designed by Murray, Cormack associates with a north 58 hull to operate in Scapa Flow but it did not arrive until 1980.

The tankers using Flotta were to become very regular visitors and we became quite friendly with the masters onboard. Captain Hans Lutz was master of the Mt Nacella and we became very good friends. Whenever he got the opportunity, he would come ashore with me and I showed him the interesting sites in Orkney.

He also arranged a couple of evening functions in the local hotels for the off-duty pilots, mooring masters and their wives. He was a very genuine and generous man. He invited my niece who was studying German at university to visit his family in Germany which she did. Some of the tankers called into Flotta over 100 times, so it was like meeting old friends every time you arrived on the ship's bridge.

On 30th November 1978 we had a lovely addition to our family when our son Andrew was born (St. Andrews day). My shift rota worked in well as I was off duty on the happy occasion. It did, of course, make some difference to our sleep patterns as I still had night shifts to cover, but we coped fine, much better than having to go back to sea. Esther was now five years old and at school.

It was an eventful day also at Sullom Voe, the oil terminal in Shetland as the first oil tanker loaded there on the 30th November. On the 22nd of December, I piloted the 200000-ton tanker the Mt Esso Bernicia to SPM2. The master and crew onboard were excited as after completing discharge of their Flotta crude, they were heading to Sullom Voe. Little did they know that it would not be a happy occasion.

The ship arrived on the 30<sup>th</sup> December and whilst berthing, one of the after tugs caught fire and let go from the tanker. The pilot was unable to control the Esso Bernicia and she struck the jetty and ruptured her fuel tanks spilling 1200 tons of bunker oil into the sea. This could have happened to me on the Esso Torino which not only had fuel in her tanks but was half loaded with Flotta crude, but we were lucky and managed to avert a collision.

Another tanker that I piloted out of Scapa Flow on 11 September 1978 was to hit the headlines shortly afterwards. The Mt Christos Bitas ran ashore on the Pembrokeshire coast on 12 October on passage from Rotterdam to Belfast. She spilt 4000 tons of crude but managed to re-float herself and continued on passage.

However, she was still spilling oil so she was stopped and two other oil tankers came alongside and pumped her cargo into their tanks. The Christos Bitas was classed as a total loss and taken out into the Atlantic and scuttled. Roughly in the same area, we dumped the drums of 'toxic waste' back in 1959.

One of the essential requirements of an efficient pilot was to be fully aware of the tidal conditions in the area you were piloting. The tidal flow in the Pentland firth were based on high water dover. I copied the tidal map in my note book along with the dover tides, this was a very handy tool. As both Kirkwall and

Scapa Flow were secondary ports, there was no tides available in handy form for them.

During my control room duties, especially on night shifts, I set to and drew up tide tables for both areas. Scapa flow high water was based on Widewall and was roughly an hour difference from Kirkwall. I have shown these tables on the next page. It took the department two years before they produced tide table booklets to cover these areas.

I also had a note of all navigation lights in my little book. The new harbours authority building was being completed and the new launch the Scapa pathfinder was well under construction. A couple of both on following pages.

The marine officers/pilots employed by 1978 were Captains Cowie, Gray, Irving, Jones, Mackie, Milbank, Moore, Norton, Proctor, Richmond, Sclater, Sinclair, Sutherland, Walker and Welch.

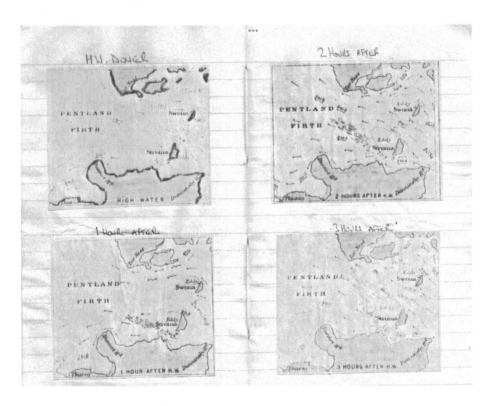

*Ebb tide in Pentland firth running westwards.*

KIRKWALL — JANUARY

| Day | Time | Ht | Day | Time | Ht |
|---|---|---|---|---|---|
| 1st SUN | 0229 | 8·0 | 9TH MON | 0402 | 1·5 |
| | 0857 | 4·3 | | 1013 | 10·3 |
| | 1432 | 8·5 | | 1635 | 0·9 |
| | 2055 | 2·6 | | 2245 | 10·2 |
| 2nd MON | 0327 | 7·7 | 10TH TUES | 0452 | 1·4 |
| | 0908 | 3·7 | | 1053 | 10·7 |
| | 1532 | 8·2 | | 1721 | 0·5 |
| | 2151 | 3·1 | | 2331 | 10·2 |
| 3rd TUES | 0431 | 7·6 | 11TH WED | 0538 | 1·5 |
| | 1011 | 3·8 | | 1137 | 10·6 |
| | 1642 | 7·9 | | 1811 | 0·5 |
| | 2257 | 2·8 | | | |
| 4TH WED | 0543 | 7·6 | 12TH THUR | 0019 | 9·9 |
| | 1126 | 3·6 | | 0622 | 1·9 |
| | 1758 | 8·0 | | 1223 | 10·4 |
| | | | | 1856 | 1·3 |
| 5TH THUR | 0008 | 2·5 | 13TH FRI | 0108 | 9·4 |
| | 0650 | 8·1 | | 0705 | 2·3 |
| | 1240 | 3·2 | | 1310 | 9·9 |
| | 1910 | 8·6 | | 1940 | 1·4 |
| 6TH FRI | 0116 | 2·2 | 14TH SAT | 0159 | 8·7 |
| | 0752 | 8·7 | | 0747 | 2·8 |
| | 1347 | 2·6 | | 1400 | 9·4 |
| | 2016 | 9·0 | | 2025 | 2·1 |
| 7TH SAT | 0216 | 1·7 | 15TH SUN | 0251 | 8·1 |
| | 0846 | 9·4 | | 0334 | 3·1 |
| | 1446 | 1·7 | | 1455 | 8·6 |
| | 2110 | 9·5 | | 2118 | 2·6 |
| 8TH SUN | 0310 | 1·9 | | | |
| | 0931 | 9·9 | | | |
| | 1540 | 1·4 | | | |
| | 2158 | 10·6 | | | |

Flood tide commenced roughly six hours before HW Dover and gave an easterly flowing stream. The tidal flow was at its strongest three hours before and three hours after HW Dover. I produced a larger scale copy of these maps that were set into a glass covered frame and situated behind the duty officers console and were updated every day so he knew the tides at any given hour.

Kirkwall tides with depths alongside at lat. The tanker berth is just outside the basin on the west side quite a restricted berth and not a lot of leeway in strong wind as I found out with the Mt Teglholm. I calculated the tides (note all hand written ) for the first two years and copies were made available to all harbour staff and shipping agents.

The Widewall tides covered Scapa flow and Stromness harbour. Sutherland pier a very basic stone structure with no lights made it difficult when berthing small tankers delivering diesel oil to the Flotta oil terminal.

221

WESTSIDE SUTHERLAND (Pier) Soundings AT L.A.T.

On next page, the new pilot launch Scapa Pathfinder on station in 1980. Boarding a tanker in calm weather in the Pentland firth. In the early days, we had three methods of boarding the one shown with the ship's gangway. The other vessel just had a pilot ladder quite a long climb on these large tankers.

Some ships had pilot hoists but they were not the safest as you were dependant on the crew man operating the lift. Could find yourself going down instead of up. These were discontinued due to safety reasons.

I had one slight problem boarding when the crew man kept his foot on the bottom of the ladder lying on the launch's deck when I was climbing up. The launch pulled away from the ship's side and the ladder was lifted of the side of the tanker with me hanging on for dear life. Luckily, when they realised what was happening the crewman let go of the ladder and I landed heavily onto the ship's side. Thankfully, I had a good hold of the ladder.

222

The next couple of years were uneventful with the piloting of numerous large oil tankers, ethane and propane gas carriers at Flotta. The cruise ship trade was increasing so the summer months when they visited could be quite busy. The liners arrived first thing in the morning and sailed late afternoon giving the cruise passengers an opportunity to visit a few of the many interesting sites in Orkney.

We also had visits from sailing ships, always fun to pilot them although they did have engines for berthing Regular visits from naval ships, some requested pilots although they were all exempt from pilotage. I had an interesting pilotage of a German submarine into Kirkwall pier. It was quite difficult to jump onto its rounded hull from the pilot launch.

Standing on the conning tower was something new. The Captain invited me down to see through the sub and we had a nice glass of snaps to round off the visit. We had, by this time, one of the smaller pilot launches, Scapa patrol in Kirkwall, to cover pilotage much more comfortable and speedier than the Misty Isle.

One other interesting occurrence was the arrival of a US navy task force into Scapa flow. It also consisted of an aircraft carrier and several destroyers and smaller naval vessels. I did not pilot any as I was on control room duty. The morning after their arrival, there was to be an official visit by Admiral Moses, the Task Force Commander.

It was a very foggy day and the Admiral set off in the carriers launch to head for Scapa pier. On board was an RN liaison officer based in Orkney. The shore party awaiting the launch contacted me to see if I could locate the launch on the harbour radar as they were well overdue. I could not pick it up, so instructed the pilot launch to proceed out to try and find them.

After a short while the pilot boat picked them up on their radar and reported that they were away off course and heading in the wrong direction. The pilot boat then escorted them into Scapa pier still in thick fog. We were surprised that they had made no radio contact and should have been aware that their trip from the carrier was taking far longer than expected.

It turned out that they were steering with a magnetic compass that had been badly affected by some metal parts on the launch and the deviation caused the compass reading to be widely inaccurate. I think Admiral Moses would have given the officers in charge of the launch quite a dressing down. We heard later that the incident had been sent round all US navy ships about the Admiral who lost his way in Scapa flow.

Scapa flow was of course, one of the most famous naval anchorages and bases in the UK during both World Wars. Admiral Jellicoe set off with his fleet from Scapa in 1916 to engage with the Germans at the battle of Jutland. Lord

Kitchener sailed on HMS Hampshire from Scapa and was lost at sea when the ship hit a German mine off Marwick head in June 1916. HMS Vanguard blew up in July 1917 with the loss of over 843 crew. The sunken wreck was close to the Flotta terminal jetty but we thought that there was sufficient water over the remains not to worry deep laden tankers sailing from the jetty.

One of our tug skippers was testing his echo sounder one day and discovered a piece of wreckage on the seabed with only 14 metres clearance, loaded tankers sailing had over this draught when departing. A lighted navigation buoy was promptly put in place, another lucky escape.

*HMS Vanguard war grave buoy*

There was also a small bunkering tanker sunk just to the west of the jetty with its own lighted navigation buoy. Back to history, the German grand fleet arrived in Scapa flow in November 1918 and 74 vessels lay at anchor until 21 June 1919 when they were scuttled.

HMS Royal Oak was torpedoed whilst lying at anchor in Scapa flow by the German submarine U47 on the night 13/14 October 1939 with the loss of 833 crew. I will touch on some of the above later in my story.

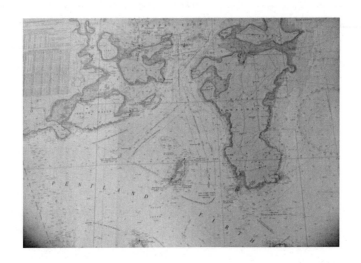

*Pentland firth and approaches to Scapa flow. Will cover the pilotage areas shown also navigation channels and notes on navigation later on in my story.*

*Photo of ethane carrier MV Quentin along with her sister ship the MV Borthwick operated on the route at the same time so a very regular service back and forth to Heroya in Norway. They had some pretty bad crossing in the winter months not uncommon for their ETAs at the pilot station to be adjusted by several hours on the short hop across the North Sea.*

*Great practice piloting these small vessels to the LPG jetty. These ships used to transport the Christmas trees from Norway, gifted from Orkney's Twin Council Hordaland and Grimstad, the birth place of St Magnus Orkney's patron saint every year.*

The harbour building and pilot launches were all based at Scapa pier which was 15 miles from Springbank our home in south Ronaldsay. This required a half hour drive every time I was either on control room duty or to board the pilot launch and proceed to sea.

The winter months could be quite bad especially when crossing the Churchill barriers, these were causeways joining the four South Isles. It was not uncommon for large waves to break over them in strong winds. Also, in snowy conditions the roads could be quite treacherous. If you were on midnight to eight or on call for a tanker at three in the morning, not very easy driving conditions. I never missed a watch or ship but we decided to move into Kirkwall in November 1979.

We bought our new home 'Korsgarth in Kirkwall just five minutes' drive to the harbour offices, certainly made life much easier for me. There was a new school recently built very close to our house that Esther attended. Everything was settling down and I was enjoying my job at home and not having to go back to sea.

On 28 November 1980 we had another happy addition to the family when our second daughter Joanna was born. Still on shift duties, so spent a good lot of time at home during the day helping out with the children. Could be a slight problem when on night shift, getting peace and quiet to sleep during the day.

In January 1984, we were all placed on an ARPA course at Glasgow College Of Nautical Studies (copy of certificate on next page) mainly for use whilst piloting as our old 16-inch Decca radars had no automatic plotting system. It was also required to keep our master's certificate up to date. In just three years' time, we did have a modern VTS in place which I was instrumental in acquiring when I became pilotage superintendent.

EXN 84

No. GLA 032

DEPARTMENT OF TRADE

AUTOMATIC RADAR PLOTTING AIDS COURSE CERTIFICATE

THIS IS TO CERTIFY THAT

NAME R C Sclater     RANK Pilot

DATE AND PLACE OF BIRTH 07 08 '41 Kirkwall

CERTIFICATE OF COMPETENCY     DISCHARGE BOOK NO.

CLASS Masters NO.     R 655192

satisfactorily completed a simulator training course, approved by the Department of Trade, in the operational use of
AUTOMATIC RADAR PLOTTINGS AIDS at Glasgow College of Nautical Studies

Date 27 January 19 84     Signed [signature]
                                          Principal of College

Signature of Holder [signature]

V4862

In May 1984, the pilot boat crews went on a work to rule which caused problems for boarding and landing from vessels as we were a 24/7 operation. As pilots' representatives, I had to write to the pilotage authority to try and mediate and get the crews back on a normal footing.

The tug crews also went on strike for better conditions earlier in our operations and we ended up berthing tankers to the SPMs without the use of tugs. The Oxy work boats assisted in the berthing. I only did it once and then they were back to normal, no berthing to the jetty when they were on strike.

The department was not very good at providing any outside training and in September 1984, we the pilots, decided that some overboard recovery training should be carried out. The pilot launches were equipped with hydraulic lifting arms on either side to allow a person to be recovered safely from the water but never been used in anger.

As the pilot's representative, I obtained agreement and funding through the director to bring the UKPA's safety representative to Orkney to run man overboard drills. Captain Mike Irving arrived in Orkney to carry out the training for pilots and launch crews. This required volunteers to jump into Scapa flow to be rescued.

As the pilot's rep and also as I had just completed lifesaving training, I was happy to be the guinea pig. A couple of photos on the next pages with me in the water, wearing a survival suit, and lying in the water awaiting rescue. My two medals bronze medallion and award of merit from the royal lifesaving society. I had obtained a bronze medallion at the Dolphin back in 1956. My lifesaving training was carried out at the Kirkwall swimming pool in 1983.

*Being lifted out of the water by mechanical hoist. We tried other methods of recovery but trying to lift a body out of the water by hand was nearly impossible. It was also advisable to lift the person out as level as possible and not in a straight up and down position which could cause problems with loss of blood to the brain. It was a very worthwhile exercise and lots of lessons were learned.*

A few weeks after the exercise, one of the pilots did fall in when disembarking from a tanker at anchor. The pilot launch drifted away from the tanker's side just as he was to jump onto it. Missed his footing and landed in the water. The crew were quick to react and had him out in three minutes. They said that the training received made the recovery much quicker.

We also carried out these exercises in the dark to test our strobe lights on our life jackets that we wore when boarding and landing from all ships. No photographs of these as it was dark.

A number of the harbours staff were RNLI coxswains and crew, so were highly trained in rescue techniques. The pilot launch training programme was also of great benefit to them.

*The photos of Churchill barriers in bad weather. Made life quite difficult if you had to cross to get to work. The barriers were built after the sinking of HMS Royal Oak to cut off the entrance used by U47. I have some other stories relating to the barriers that I will cover later.*

*Certainly a frightening experience when caught with a large wave. The metal safety rails were not fitted when I was travelling back and forth in the seventies. Not very good condition for your car being covered in salt water.*

One point that I just remembered was the signing of the Official Secret Act. Back in the seventies and eighties the cold war was still evident in the minds of the mod. In this instance, they had a special department covering all UK ports. Orkney being no exception, the mod had every port allocated a dedicated mariner to take charge in the event of hostilities.

I was allocated Kirkwall harbour with other pilots given other ports and piers in Orkney. We therefore all had to sign the Act. We had several training briefs both in Orkney and Shetland where the basic outline of what our responsibilities would be. The system was disbanded a few years later. It was an interesting experience.

# Official Secrets Acts...

**Declaration** To be signed by members of Government Departments on appointment and, where desirable, by non-civil servants on first being given access to Government information.

My attention has been drawn to the provisions of the Official Secrets Acts set out on the back of this document and I am fully aware of the serious consequences which may follow any breach of those provisions.

I understand that the sections of the Official Secrets Acts set out on the back of this document cover material published in a speech, lecture, or radio or television broadcast, or in the Press or in book form. I am aware that I should not divulge any information gained by me as a result of my appointment to any unauthorised person, either orally or in writing, without the previous official sanction in writing of the Department appointing me, to which written application should be made and two copies of the proposed publication be forwarded. I understand also that I am liable to be prosecuted if I publish without official sanction any information I may acquire in the course of my tenure of an official appointment (unless it has already officially been made public) or retain without official sanction any sketch, plan, model, article, note or official documents which are no longer needed for my official duties, and that these provisions apply not only during the period of my appointment but also after my appointment has ceased. I also understand that I must surrender any documents, etc., referred to in section 2 (1) of the Act if I am transferred from one post to another, save such as have been issued to me for my personal retention.

Signed *R. C. Sclater*

Surname *(Block letters)* SCLATER

Forename(s) ROBERT CHALMERS

Date 11Th MARCH 1983

*Copy of My Signed Official Secret*

One thing I wanted to do was to highlight my work colleagues at the Flotta Terminal.

They were for most of my time: Captain Max Gunn marine superintendent, Captain Arthur Porteous deputy marine superintendent, the mooring masters/loading masters: Captains John Legget, Ian Mackenzie, Ken O'Connor, John Railston, Jim Harvey, Charlie Olsen, John Wareham, Alistair Mackenzie, Arthur Batty and Roger Henry.

My old friend Mike perfect returned to Orkney with his Orkney wife Violet and two daughters and he became a mooring master for a couple of years prior to returning to New Zealand to take up command of the Wellington to Picton ferries. It was great to meet up with them after several years.

1985 was to be an eventful year for me in more ways than one. Unfortunately, my father passed away in February which was a big shock. He had always been very proud of my achievements in the marine world and followed my progress through the ranks with great interest. When he was only nineteen, he emigrated to Canada. He spent five years there and used to tell us great stories of his working life back in the nineteen twenties from grave digger to lumberjack and farm worker. I think that is where I inherited my wanderlust from.

Also in February, the Director of Harbours decided he was going to retire later in the year. Application details were advertised in the local press and I duly sent in my application. I was not very confident on being appointed as I believed that his depute Captain Harry Banks would be in pole position for the post. Anyway I received confirmation that I was on the short list for the post and should attend the interview on 5 April which would be carried out by all 24 of the Orkney Islands Councillors.

The strange thing about the post was the salary set at £18870-£20319 some £4800 less than what I was earning as a pilot. I always knew that the depute was on a lower scale than the pilots which I always thought very odd. This post was for the director, responsible for the whole department and to receive a lower salary than his staff was not acceptable. Anyway, I attended the interviews along with Captain Banks and one other Orkney mariner.

As I expected Captain Banks was appointed to the post. However sometime after the interviews I was contacted by the chief executive of the Council and offered the deputy's post. This is where things got interesting when I explained that I would be happy to take up the post but would request that I remain on my present salary. I pointed out that I would be willing to carry on as a stand by pilot in the event of sickness cover or training new pilots.

This was agreed and of course the knock-on effect was that I could not earn more than the director so his salary was increased by another £6000. I know that Captain Banks would not have attempted to get his salary increased although he knew quite well what the marine officers/pilots were earning. Everything was eventually agreed and I was set to take up my post in November 1985.

I am not sure why Captain Robertson put the new salary for the post so much lower than he was earning before he retired as he was certainly on a much higher salary than the pilots at the time. He was not a happy man when he was told what salary Harry and I were to receive when he retired. When I eventually received confirmation, the other pilots were also put out and said if they had known what the salary was they would have applied.

I told them quite clearly they had the same opportunity as me to apply and then put forward a logical case to maintain their salary. Once again a lesson learned, stick up for yourself because no one else will, especially when it comes to money. Captain Banks of course came out a winner without doing anything.

Over the coming years, I would certainly justify my salary by making savings and procuring additional revenue from winning new oil field contracts we were also shortly to take over the running and upgrading of the internal ferry services. Of course, here I was taking up a more responsible position with no increase in salary.

One great positive was not having to do anymore shift duties although I was on call 24/7 in the event of any accidents or oil pollution incidents. The rest of that year went past quickly and I took up my new post on 1 November. I was appointed a Deputy Launching Authority (DLA) with the RNLI at the same time. Esther, Andrew, and Joanna were now all at school so life became a bit easier for Anna. We did however, buy a golden retriever puppy which was just as much work as the children, great company though.

The Norwegian sail training vessel "Sorlandet" that I piloted from the Pentland firth through Scapa flow into Stromness harbour, one of the interesting tasks I carried out during my pilotage days. We had a number of sail training vessels visiting every year.

HMS Orkney an island class patrol vessel that was a regular visitor to Orkney. Had the privilege to pilot her into Kirkwall and Stromness. She was exempt from pilotage being royal navy but the Captains were always happy to take a pilot. I met a few Captains during my time as pilot and attended numerous functions onboard.

The BP Warrior one of the many coastal oil tankers bringing fuel oil to Orkney. All required to take pilots. All petrol was discharge into the oil tanks at Scapa pier. The oil tanks in Kirkwall were close to residential areas so no highly inflammable product allowed to be stored there.

My time as a pilot was another interesting and enjoyable period in my career and I learned some valuable lessons and new experiences during the nine years in the post. I was quite happy, however, to be facing a new challenge as deputy director and pilotage superintendent.

*The photos of some of the ships piloted outside the Flotta terminal tankers.*

# Part 4

I started my new post on 1 November 1985 and settled into my big new office on the second floor of the harbour authority building with a mammoth task of getting to grips with the job in hand. This was to be once again a steep learning curve as the post covered a multitude of responsibilities. In 1985, THE ORKNEY ISLANDS COUNCIL were in the early stages of upgrading the piers and harbours to accommodate roll on roll off ferries.

The first upgrade had already taken place for the islands of Hoy and Flotta where new link span facilities were constructed. The new service was operated from Houton in Orphir to Flotta pier and Lyness pier in Hoy. Two second hand small ro/ro ferries were purchased one from Faroes and one from Shetland.

At this time, the ships were run by Orkney Islands Shipping Company under the control of the UK government's Scottish office in Edinburgh. The piers all came under the Harbours Department control. When I commenced my duties as depute we were in the process of constructing new hard ramp facilities for a service between the islands of Rousey, Egilsay, and Wyre to Tingwall in Rendall.

A new ro/ro ferry contract was in the process of being placed at David Abel's ship yard in Bristol. These islands had a very basic ferry service prior to this date with only a small passenger launch run by the Flaws family residents of Wyre. There was a once-a-week service provided by OISCO, cargo ferry the MV Islander.

The reason I highlight this now is that the Scottish office had informed Orkney Islands Council that the ferry service was to be handed over to them to upgrade and operate from 1987. I recall one of the Councillors arriving at my office and asking if we were capable of taking over this responsibility.

I said that of course we could and would be happy to take up the challenge. The Orkney Islands Shipping Company had offices in Kirkwall with a local manager and shore staff to run the existing ferries. These were the two small ro/ro ferries Hoy Head and Lywara Bay serving the south isles. The MV Orcadia was the main passenger lift on lift off ferry servicing the north isles along with the 12-passenger cargo vessel, the MV Islander.

Serving the island of Shapinsay was a small passenger launch, the Clytus. The MV Islander provided the lift on lift off cargo service to Shapinsay also. The small launch, the Golden Mariana carried out a summer service from Kirkwall to Rapness in the south of Westray. Operating out of Stromness was a small privately run launch service to the island of Graemsay and to Moaness pier in North Hoy. This then was to be a big task for us.

Our priority in the first years was the construction of the hard ramp facilities in Rousey, Egilsay, Wyre and Tingwall being constructed by Lilly Constructions Ltd. The Councils engineering department was the lead on the terminal construction. The harbours department were to carry out the design, tendering, and supervising the construction of the new ferries.to achieve the required infrastructure and ferries. We had to convince the UK government's Scottish office that additional funding had to be provided. I will cover these issues later, as my story progresses.

*The photos of the MV Islander, MV Orcadia at Kirkwall pier, Clytus and the Hoy Head, the Lywara Bay was basically the same design and size. As you can see from these details it was a very basic ferry service and by 1987 it had to start improving.*

The motor launch Clytus that ran a passenger and parcel service from Kirkwall to Shapinsay. Work had started on the construction of the hard ramp alongside the west pier for the new Shapinsay/Kirkwall service. Note the cannons sunk into the end of the pier as bollards, I have a story on them later.

MV Hoy Head the first inter island ro/ro ferry. The Lywara bay was of similar design and size. The hoy head was built in the Faroes in 1973 and the Lywara bay built in Norway in 1970. I must shake my head when I look at this, a new ro/ro service but the shipping company decided to purchase old second-hand vessels already too small for the route.

The Scottish office officials certainly did not go out of their way to provide what was needed. What should have been provided was new vessels to operate an efficient service. The service commenced in 1983 within seven years, we managed to agree contracts for two new vessels.

The Golden Mariana was operated on the Kirkwall to Rapness in Westray route by Norse Atlantic ferries who also had an old Scilly isles, ferry the MV Syllingar that provided a lift on lift off service to Shetland between 1984-5. The company went into receivership in August 1985 and Orkney Islands Council acquired the golden Mariana and continued with the Rapness service in the summer months, the MV Syllingar was sold. It did, however, result in the main ferry company P&O Scottish ferries deciding to recommence a ro/ro link between Aberdeen, Kirkwall and Lerwick in 1988 something that was long overdue.

Back to oil related shipping activities, at the beginning of December 1985 we were contacted by John Jolly, the shipping agents regarding the request from the Finnish shipping company Neste Oy who wished to carry out a ship-to-ship transfer in Scapa flow. A VLCC, the Mt Zenit Kraka, carrying 346000 tonnes of Arabian crude wished to transfer this oil into two other tankers the, Mt Tiiskeri and Mt Jaarli to ship to Finland.

Meetings were eventually held with representatives from Neste Oy and agreement reached on the operation and the harbour charges that would apply. This was to be the largest ship ever to enter Scapa flow with a loaded draft of some 22 metres. The depths in Scapa flow were certainly deep enough to handle the ship but to make sure there were no obstacles in the channel, I carried out a survey using the pilot launch's echo sounder to confirm this.

It was a very basic survey but did give us confidence that we could safely navigate the Zenit Kraka to the designated anchorage. There had been one previous ship-to-ship, about five years before, but with a smaller amount of crude oil transferred. The harbour charges were also much higher than what we negotiated with Neste Oy.

We believed the higher charges in the past had discouraged other STS transfers taking place. The Zenit Krakar arrived in the western approaches to the Pentland firth at slack water on the morning of 23 December. I, along with the duty pilot, boarded the vessel and we proceeded to the anchorage in Scapa flow without any problems.

The ship anchored at 1230 hrs and the large Yokohama Fenders were towed into place. The operations was carried out by Fender Care, a world-renowned expert in ship-to-ship operations. The Mt Tiiskeri was then made fast on the Zenit Krakar's port side and the discharging hoses connected. The berthing operation took just over three hours to complete. The details on the next couple of pages highlight the operation in more detail.

I boarded the Zenit Kraka every day to check on the discharging and mooring arrangements to confirm everything was carried out in line with our detailed safety requirements. The ship-to-ship operations in Scapa flow are much more frequent nowadays but we were the pioneers of this activity back in the nineteen eighties/nineties. The problem we had back then was the restriction on pumping ballast water into Scapa flow.

New designs of segregated ballast tanks now allow tankers to discharge straight into the flow where in the past they had to part load and then proceed out to sea to get rid of ballast water before returning to complete the transfer. In the Zenit Kraka operation the two receiving vessels pumped their ballast back into the Zenit Kraka saving them the requirement to go out of port to get rid of ballast water. Not every tanker was capable of transferring ballast water between vessels.

*Photo of the Zenit Kraka with the Mt Tiiskeri moored alongside. Note the tug made fast aft to keep vessel on steady heading during berthing.*

*Myself sitting at the steering console on the Zenit Kraka.*

At the start of 1986, it was back to normal work with a lot of new ideas circulating in my head. First of all, I started looking at the possibility of upgrading our out-of-date radar monitoring system and installing a Vessel Tracking System (VTS). After making enquiries with the relevant providers of this type of equipment, I set too and produced a report to the Orkney Islands Council's Harbours Committee outlining my proposals and the estimated costs involved.

Dealing with the Council did take some time to get agreement as it had to pass through the various committees, then to a full Council meeting for ratification. I received the go ahead and the contract to supply the new equipment was to be placed with the Norwegian company Kongsberg's technical department, Norcontrol, specialising in this field.

We had several on site meetings and the final details were ironed out and the go ahead given. The new state of the art VTS would eventually be installed the following year. This was very similar to air traffic control with each vessel acquired on the system and named with course and speed instantly displayed. More info, later.

Also, at this time, the bare boat charter with JP Knights relating to the three Orkney towage tugs was due for renewal and a new charter was being looked at. I had my concerns regarding the initial costs and the way the company was run and thought that purchasing new tugs and taking them under Orkney towage ownership was a much more costs effective way of managing the towage operation in Scapa flow.

I always thought that the three tugs were under powered and not as manoeuvrable as the new breed of tugs on the market at this time. Orkney towage had a marine superintendent supplied by J P Knight who had been in Orkney since towage operations commenced. He was Captain Bethel from Rochester who had helped train the tug crews back in 1976-7.

In 1986, the company appointed one of the tug skippers as an assistant marine superintendent to take over, as Captain Bethel was due to retire later that year. The new superintendent Captain David Shearer was very keen also to see new tugs purchased and for the company to cease the bare boat charter which was a very expensive way to charter vessels.

Back in 1976, with the Council having very little experience in this type of activity, I suppose it was the easiest and logical way to get the port up and running. Of course in the early days money seemed to be no object. Although I was not a director of the company, with Captain Banks being the executive director, he was quite happy to let both David and myself progress with our ideas on the design and purchase of new tugs and for me to produce a report to Orkney Islands Council, the lead share holder in the company to get our proposals accepted.

This we did and visited several other ports to study their towage operations. We were helped by the Marine Superintendent Gerry Banks of Clyde Towing, the company involved with Shetland towage at Sullom Voe. After a few months, we were in a position to report to the Council on the way forward.

Of course JP Knight had also been busy drawing up plans for new tugs to be bare boat charted to Orkney towage. They had engaged the services of one of the world's leading towage companies Wijsmuller, based in Ijmuiden, Holland. Both sides presented their proposals with Wijsmuller's tugs certainly being the most suitable for operating in the Orkney area.

The main purpose of course, was the decision on whether or not the Council should continue with the chartering of JP Knights tugs or we should take on the task ourself. We would of course, still have the involvement of the Knights as they were our partners in the towage company. The Harbours Committee considered both presentations and agreed by just one vote that Orkney towage should no longer bare boat charter the tugs from Knights but to look at purchasing new tugs and consider the most advantageous method of funding them.

I was surprised at the Harbour Committee meeting just how many Councillors were willing to back JP Knight in continuing with their original agreement when the figures showed the actual costs to Orkney Islands Council were extremely high. The annual refits alone were way beyond anything one would expect with each tug going away every year for at least six weeks with no tendering from other ship yards to carry out the work.

The ship yard in Ostend was owned by JP Knight and the refit costs were additional to the bare boat charter fee. The Mt Keston covering during the refits was also on a daily rate with the tug on refit still on charter. After the meeting, we discussed the way forward and agreed that the Wijsmuller tug design was the best and that we should engage their expertise in the final design and tendering for the tugs. This was to take another few months with visits to other ports operating the Wijsmuller tug design. The funding arrangements for their purchase was also to be undertaken. We also decided that the towage company required a dedicated engineering superintendent based full time in Orkney. He would also be required to supervise the building of the new tugs at the nominated shipyard.

The main contact with Wijsmuller was their General Manager Sven Aarts, one of the most dedicated towage experts one could meet. He was only too happy to agree to carry out the consultancy work. We did, of course, have to dispense with the services of Gerry Banks of Clyde Towing but we did want the best and we were confident that we would get this from Wijsmuller.

The new engineering superintendent was Bill Braby, one of the tug chief engineers. I should mention that we were only purchasing two new tugs and that they would carry out the work of the three existing tugs as they were to be much more powerful and manoeuvrable. Sven Aarts invited David and I to Ijmuiden to witness the Wijsmuller tugs handling vessel to the port of Amsterdam.

We also visited the oil ports of Sture and Mongstad in Norway where similar tugs to the two we were having built operated. The tender documents for the two tugs was issued in 1988 to several shipyards and the contract placed with Mctay Marine in Bromborough on the Wirral. The tugs would be completed by the end of 1989 when the charter for the Kessock and Kinloch would cease. The two tugs would be purchased under a leasing agreement with Hambros bank in London who specialised in this type of transaction.

The UK government gave special financial help with the building of vessels in UK yards so the deal was very good for the Council. There would be an eight-and-a-half-year payment agreement where the main payments would cover the costs of the tugs plus interest. At the end of the leasing agreement, a small yearly 'peppercorn' payment would be paid to the bank.

This was much more satisfactory and financially favourable than the old bare boat charter. The towage company, if they so wished could pay a small amount to take full ownership of the tugs unlike the bare boat charter where the tugs had to be returned in first class condition to the owners a win-win situation for them. This you can see from my notes on the previous page. I have moved ahead quite a bit with my story regarding the towage company but thought it best to cover this one issue in one go. I will touch on the building of tugs at Mctay Marine and also the annual refits as my story progresses. On the next page details of the Mt Einar and Mt Erlend. Named after Norse Earls and prominent in Orkney history. You can see in the details that we did eventually get agreement for a new third tug. Will cover this once again as we progress.

**ORKNEY TOWAGE COMPANY LTD.**
HARBOUR AUTHORITY BUILDING · SCAPA · ORKNEY · KW15 1SD
TELEPHONE (0856) 873636                    FAX (0856) 873012
MOBILE 0850 709431                          TELEX 75475 SPLICE G

## M.T. "EINAR" and "ERLEND"

| | | | |
|---|---|---|---|
| LENGTH O.A. | 31.5 m | FUEL CAPACITY | 91.0 tonnes |
| BREADTH MLD | 10.0 m | F.W. CAPACITY | 50.0 tonnes |
| SUMMER DRAUGHT | 4.78 m | DISPERSANT CAPACITY | 11.7 tonnes |
| TRIAL SPEED | 12.8 knots | FOAM CAPACITY | 11.1 tonnes |
| B.P. AHEAD | 53 tonnes | B.P. ASTERN | 48 tonnes |

**MAIN ENGINES** — 2 off RUSTON 6RK270M developing 1492 KW each at 900 rpm

**PROPULSION** — 2 off AQUAMASTER US2001/UNIT
driven through twin disc M.C.D. unit

**GENERATORS** — 2 off 150 KW Alternator driven by Volvo TMD 122A
1 of 48 KW Alternator driven by Lister CS6M

**DECK MACHINERY** — Hydraulic Norwinch anchor windlass/tow winch
30 tons at 12.5 m/mins
Hydraulic Norwinch tow winch 30 tons at 12.5 m/mins
Effer knuckle boom hydraulic crane 12 tonnes metre

**FIRE PUMPS** — 2 of 360 m3/hour at 135 m head driven by Volvo TMD 122A
supplying 1 remote and 2 hand operated monitors.

**LLOYDS CLASS:** — + 100 A1 TUG + LMC UMS; D.O.T. CLASS IX

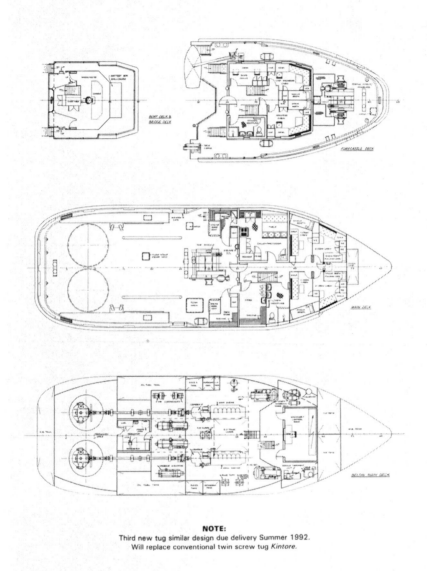

**NOTE:**
Third new tug similar design due delivery Summer 1992.
Will replace conventional twin screw tug *Kintore.*

So with the tugs sorted out over the 1986-9 period, I will progress with other interesting activities relating to my responsibilities. The involvement of the Harbours Department with the delegated responsibility for the internal shipping services was to be quite an undertaking. The Council had firstly to obtain agreement with the various island communities involved on what their preferred options were in relation to the siting of ro/ro ferry terminals be they link span or hard ramp facilities.

The four outer isles Westray, Eday, Stronsay, and Sanday were requesting link span facilities. This would require a large extension to Kirkwall pier to accommodate a link span for the new ferries. Shapinsay was to have hard ramp facilities at Balfour village with a service direct to Kirkwall where a hard ramp would be installed on the west side of the West pier.

The two other outer isles Papa Westray and North Ronaldsay were not included in the provision of new facilities at this time. Meetings were held between the elected Councillors, officials and the various island communities and eventually agreement was reached on where best to site the facilities. We still had to get agreement from the UK government's Scottish office on these preferred options.

In this respect Michael Ancram MP, the Undersecretary of State at the Scottish office, responsible for local government was to make a visit to Orkney to study the proposals and also to carry out a site visit to see the areas where new harbour facilities were proposed. I was tasked by the Council's chief executive to arrange the site visit.

This I did by, firstly chartering one of Logan Air's Islander aircraft to fly the party out over the North isles to see the four areas where the linkspan facilities should be installed. Two were at existing piers namely Eday and Stronsay with two new harbours being constructed at Loth in Sanday and Rapness in Westray. This was to give the shortest distances between these ports and Kirkwall the main destination for these services.

After our flight, we landed at Stronsay airfield and proceeded to Whitehall village where I had one of the pilot launches waiting. We then set off and headed for Rapness, Loth, Backaland pier in Eday and onwards to Shapinsay. This gave the Undersecretary a chance to see the whole picture from the sea.

After arrival back in Kirkwall, a meeting with the full Council was held and he agreed on the proposals submitted and the go ahead was to be given to construct all the necessary harbour facilities and the relevant ferries to operate the service. This was to be a very expensive operation running into tens of millions of pounds, the biggest investment in Orkneys local government history.

By mid-1986, the tender for the new ferry to service Rousey, Egilsay and Wyre was placed with a David Ables shipyard in Bristol. The Napier company of Arbroath naval architects were appointed to draw up the specification and tender documents and also supervise the building of the ferry which would be named "Eynhallow". The map on the following page shows all the relevant ports, piers and jetties mentioned in my story.

The residents of Stronsay were offered the alternative of a new link span facility in St Catherine's bay on the west side of the island which would have provided a shorter route to/from Kirkwall. They, however, decided that they wished the service to operate to the existing harbour in Whitehall village a more sheltered harbour. The relevant departments within Orkney Islands Council settled down to drawing up the designs and documentation necessary to progress the new terminals and ferries required.

The first ferry to be placed on this tender list was the new Shapinsay ferry. The Napier Company were once again appointed by the Department of Harbours to carry out the design and issuing the tender documents to the various shipyards capable of building the ferry. The successful bid was tendered by Yorkshire Drydock of Hull. The main hull being constructed at their yard with the fitting out carried out at Jones of Buckie. By this time, the Eynhallow was in service so our new fleet was progressing.

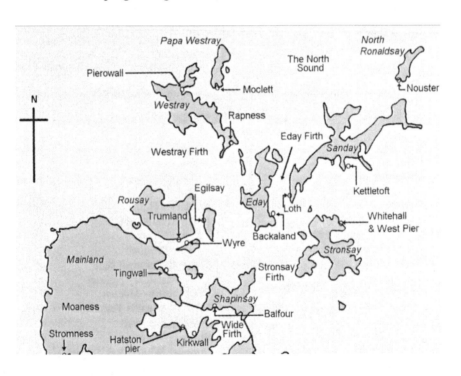

*The North isles showing all the various piers and harbours. The Kirkwall and Wide Firth harbour and pilotage area is also clearly marked.*

*The South isles showing the large harbour and pilotage area of Scapa Flow along with Stromness harbour and the various ro/ro piers and Graemsay and Moaness the two piers served by the private passenger launch operator.*

*The first new ferry in our fleet. I would be responsible for the introduction of a further eight new ferries of various sizes and designs along with three new tugs, two pilot launches, one oil pollution vessel and one small motor launch for the marine biology unit over the coming nine years.*

Part of my responsibilities as Deputy Director was Deputy Oil Pollution Officer. As I had very little hands-on experience in this field, I was happy to attend two detailed training courses run by the Wood Group on board their dedicated oil pollution vessel the MV Fasgadair, the certificates on the following pages show my attendance in 1986 and advance training course in 1987.

*The photo show some of the attendees onboard our small oil pollution craft with the Fasgadair in the back ground.*

One of our lecturers on the course was my old friend Captain Fraser Forbes, the tug skipper from Invergordon who helped train our tug skippers back in 1976-8. He is standing in the stern with me on his right-hand side also standing. It looks like a cold day, but weather plays no part when an oil pollution incident might occur, so you work with the elements to get things cleaned up or preferably have in place procedures to reduce the changes of one happening.

*T*his is to certify that

Captain R. C. Sclater

*of*

Orkney Islands Council

*successfully completed the*

# Wood Group
# Environmental Services Ltd
# Oil Pollution
# Prevention and Clearance
# Training Course

*held onboard*

## M.V. Fasgadair

*from* 13th May, 1986          *to* 16th May, 1986

_____          _____
Senior Lecturer                          General Manager

*This is to certify that*

Captain R C Sclater

*of*

Orkney Islands Council

*successfully completed the*

# Wood Group
# Environmental Services Ltd
# Advanced Oil Pollution
# Prevention and Clearance
# Training Course

*held onboard*

## M.V. Fasgadair

*from* 9 June 1987                    *to* 12 June 1987

_____          _____
Senior Lecturer                              General Manager

We learned some interesting lessons on both courses. It also let you know how difficult it is to clean up after an oil spill and just how small a percentage of oil can be retrieved from the sea even with state-of-the-art oil recovery equipment. We certainly were strongly advised that oil dispersant spray should only be used as a last resort as it introduced more chemicals into the environment and were quite damaging. Between the two courses I was involved in, the last big oil spill in Scapa flow when 45 bbls of oil was split from the Mt Eva at SPM1 on 19 January. I had just returned from Norway and ended up Beach Commander in charge of clean up ops. On Glimps, Holm and Burray for nearly two weeks. A very difficult task without much success, although no oil birds. I am jumping back and forth with my story but as I had many hats to wear, it is difficult to try and get it all in chronological order.

Back to my VTS plans where Norcontrol were progressing well with the project. In January 1987, I travelled over to Kongsberg's head offices in Horten just south of Oslo to carry out the owner's acceptance trials. This was an interesting couple of days as the equipment was of very high quality and the detail of Scapa flow and approaches were way ahead of anything I had ever seen.

The two main business managers dealing with the project from the UK were Brian Schnabel and Graham Greener (a descendant of the famous Greener Shotgun family). The technical side was carried out by Kongsberg's specialist in the main factory. The test all went well and it was agreed that the equipment would be installed at the harbour authority building later in 1987.

This work took some time to complete but by summer we had everything up and running. This gave the duty marine offices instant and accurate details of all vessels operating within range of our two radars, one on Sandy Hill in South Ronaldsay, the main coverage of the approaches to the Pentland firth and the local radar next to the control room.

1987 was a big year in Orkney being the 850th anniversary of the building of St Magnus Cathedral with visits planned by Queen Elizabeth 2, the queen mother and King Olav V of Norway. This gave me an idea that we could ask King Olav to carry out the official switching on of the new Norcontrol system as it was Norwegian. This was not agreed as it was put forward that the queen should do the honours after her dedication of the new stained-glass window above the west door in the cathedral on the Sunday morning.

This was a busy time with lots of security being carried out both at the harbour offices and Kirkwall harbour. King Olav was arriving in his royal yacht the "Norge" and would anchor in Kirkwall bay and come ashore by launch. The official switching on of the new equipment went according to plan and both Anna and I were presented to the Queen and I also managed to convince the powers that be to allow my daughter Joanna to present the Queen with a bouquet of flowers.

All very exciting for everyone at the harbours. A couple of days later, King Olav's royal yacht arrived and he came ashore in his own launch. We escorted him into the corn slip with the pilot launch and Kirkwall lifeboat where the Queen Mother was waiting to greet him. They then adjourned to St Magnus Cathedral where the Queen Mother and King Olav unveiled a tapestry presented by the King and the people of Norway.

The following day we had a visit from King Olav to the harbour offices who took great interest in the new VTS radar operations being a very experienced seafarer himself. During this big occasion, we also had a visit of a Norwegian sail training vessel the Christian Radich that had attended the 800 anniversary back in 1937.

Onboard in 1987 was one of the original cadets who had sailed into Kirkwall in 1937 which was quite an honour. The crew attended the Cathedral on Sunday which made it a very Norwegian occasion. Orkney was part of Norway until 1472 when it was annexed to Scotland due to King Christian I of Norway failing to pay his daughter Margaret's dowry to king James III of Scotland on their marriage.

My main role in these royal visits was to ensure that everything was in place and looking shipshape and no hiccups along the way. The stair well in the harbour building was more like a fire escape and very uninteresting with plain painted concrete walls. To improve the area, I searched for photos of all the various shipping operations that had occurred over the past years. I then brought them to St Combs, the Council's handicapped day centre in Kirkwall where they carried out framing of photos.

It took me a couple of months but in the end the stair well looked more like an art gallery which gave the director, Captain Banks items to discuss with the Queen as they moved up to the control room. Anna, Joanna and myself remained at the front door to present the bouquet when the royal party returned. The Queen's standard was also to be broken out on her arrival, so I made arrangements for one of the leading sea cadets to carry out this honour.

There were so many little details to sort out and in most cases when they do, everyone thinks how easy the visit went, preplanning and dedication to a task is a must if you want satisfaction after the event is over and done with. The photos on the next few pages relate to the royal visit and the 850 years anniversary of St. Magnus Cathedral.

*Anna and I being introduced, we did have a brief conversation regarding my position. I recall her majesty saying "So you are the deputy director" in a way that I thought my reputation was already known to her, which I doubt.*

*Joanna waiting patiently for the queen. There, at last, with the bouquet passed over without a hitch, watched by proud parents. Lord lieutenant and Captain Banks also in attendance.*

*King Olav checking out the VTS, along with photo of radar picture transferred to Norcontrol tracking and identifier console.*

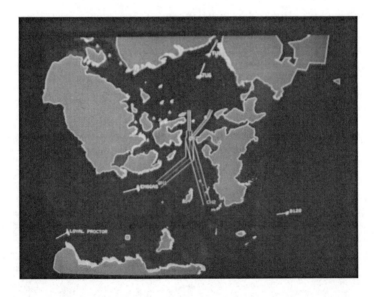

*Presenting an Orkney Islands Council plaque to Captain of Christian Radich, with my friend Captain Bill Spence, the Norwegian Consul in Orkney. We had a lovely dinner onboard the ship with our wives that evening, with good plain Norwegian fare washed down with plenty of Aquivit. On following page, the Christian Radich alongside Kirkwall pier fully dressed with St Magnus Cathedral in the background.*

In 1987, the UK government brought in a new Pilotage Act which related to changes in how pilots in the UK should be employed. In several pilotage districts, they were in fact self employed but this Act was to change this. As we in Orkney were already employed, the changes did not effect us the same. As pilotage superintendent, it was my task to draw up the New Orkney Islands Council pilotage direction 1988.

The only big changes were the harbour and pilotage limits in the Scapa flow area, also the pilotage committee was disbanded. This came under the Council Harbour Committee. In the original Orkney County Council Act 1975, the pilotage district was set well south of the Harbour area in the Pentland firth. It was decided that the harbour area and pilotage area should be the same. This was agreed and all new pilotage authorisations highlighted this change as you can see from both of my own pilotage authorisations.

The Orkney Islands Shipping Company situation was moving ahead and by late in 1987, the ferry services manager Alan Bullen and his assistant Alistair Learmonth became directly employed by OIC Harbours Department. All other employees of the shippping company remained as they were albeit under the control of Orkney Islands Council.

The main ferry operations were still maintained in the shipping company offices in Kirkwall with regular meetings between harbours and shipping company staff. The details of the new outer north isles ferries was an ongoing topic. Once again, as Napiers of Arbroath Navel Architects, we're engaged to draw up the necessary documentation to go put to tender.

I should mention by this time, the Eynhallow had arrived from the builders with little pomp and ceremony and was ready to commence the Rousay, Egilsay and Wyre to Tingwall service. The crew for the ferry was the ferrymen who operated the original launch service, members of the Flaws family from the island of Wyre, very competent ship handlers.

The design of the new ro/ro ferries resulted in some long detailed discussions on their size and carrying capacity and also the costs involved. Once again Councillors were very reluctant in spending money and seemed to be afraid of the scottish office officials when it came to asking for a decent settlement.

As I was still only the depute director my voice was not really listened to. In the end, we did, however, convince the relevant Councillors that these new ferries had to be at least 45 metres in length not the 37 metres they wanted and that the design should be of a much more modern vessel than they seemed was required.

In the end, a design was agreed and 1/50 models of the two ferries were constructed and tank test were carried out in Holland to ascertain the sea keeping qualities and abilities of the ships in heavy weather. The design met all expectations although the figure allocated to build both ferries was set very low in my opinion.

Tender documents were issued to several ship yards within Europe and the UK and the successful bidder was in fact Mactay Marine of Bromborough, the same company building the two new tugs. This made things easier in a way as attending building meetings with the yard, I was able to cover all four vessels, albeit the tugs were well advanced before the ferry construction commenced.

By this time we were into 1988 and things were progressing well with the construction of the new harbour facilities. I must not forget we still had a harbour to run and meetings with Occidental at Flotta and at the harbours was a regular occurrence. The ports of Stromness and Kirkwall were also having improvements, so plenty to keep you on your toes.

On the next pages, the new Orkney Pilotage Direction 1988. I did have to go over the contents with the legal department of OIC and the Council's parliamentary agents just to ensure the legal terminology was acceptable. Also, my basic sea survival certificate, last one.

*Sail Training Vessel "Christian Radich"*

# ORKNEY ISLANDS COUNCIL

## THE ORKNEY PILOTAGE DIRECTION 1988

## COMPETENT HARBOUR AUTHORITY

*Sea Survival Certificate*

### SUMMARY OF CONTENTS

*New Pilots Authorisation complying with new Pilotage Direction. Renewed until 1988/89 when I no longer carried out pilotage duties.*

# ORKNEY HARBOUR AREAS

No. 111219

The Orkney Islands Council, as Competent Harbour Authority for the Orkney Harbour Authority Areas, in pursuance and by virtue of the powers given it for that purpose in and by the Pilotage Act, 1987, and of all other
powers enabling it, having first duly examined ........................ ROBERT CHALMERS SCLATER ........................

of ........ KORSGARTH, HIGH STREET, KIRKWALL, ORKNEY ........................................ aged ........ 47 ........ years

and having, upon such examination, found the said ........................ ROBERT CHALMERS SCLATER ........................

........................................................................ to be a fit and competent Person, duly skilled to act as a Pilot for the purpose of conducting Ships, sailing, navigating and passing within the limits hereinafter mentioned or outside the limits if he is acting in terms of Section 22 of the above mentioned Act DO hereby appoint and authorise the said ........ ROBERT CHALMERS SCLATER ........................

........................................................................ to act as a Pilot, for the purpose of conducting Ships within the Competent Harbour Authority Area for Scapa Flow bounded as follows: Commencing at the Out Taings point on Hoy; thence in a straight line to Breckness on Mainland; thence in a generally eastern direction following the line of low water on the southern boundaries of Mainland to the northern end of the northernmost Churchill Barrier; thence in a generally southerly direction following the western sides of the four Churchill Barriers and the lines of low water on the western boundaries of the islands of South Ronaldsay (other than Swona) to Brough Ness; thence in a generally westerly direction by a straight line to the southernmost part of Swona and a straight line from that point to Brims Ness on South Walls on the island of Hoy; thence following the line of low water on the western and northern sides of Aith Hope and the seaward boundaries of South Walls and of Hoy to the point of commencement; and within the Competent Harbour Authority Area for Wide Firth/Shapinsay Sound area bounded as follows:.

Commencing at Harpy Taing on Mainland; thence in a straight line to Strombery on Shapinsay; thence following the line of low water on the southern boundary of Shapinsay to Hacksness; thence in a straight line to Rerwick Point on Mainland; thence in a generally westerly and north-easterly direction following the line of low water on part of the northern boundary of Mainland to the point of commencement. And this Authorisation shall, if not revoked or suspended in terms of the said Act, continue in force until the holder reaches his 65th birthday, provided always that the said Pilot shall so long comply with all the Byelaws and Regulations made or to be made by the said Competent Harbour Authority.

This Authorisation shall not authorise or empower the said ........................ ROBERT CHALMERS SCLATER ........................

........................................................................ to take charge as a Pilot of any Ship or Vessel

drawing more than ................................................ METRES WATER (except when an upper draught Pilot is not available to offer his services).

Given under the Common Seal of The Orkney Islands Council

of Council Offices, Kirkwall, this ........................ First ........................

day of ........................ October ........................ 19 88

Chief Executive

RENEWED THIS

| | | | | |
|---|---|---|---|---|
| 1st | day of | August | 19 77 | H. A. Graeme Pabley |
| | | | | Clerk to the Pilotage Authority |
| 7th | day of | August | 1978 | H. A. Graeme Pabley |
| | | | | Clerk to the Pilotage Authority |
| 23rd | day of | August | 19 79 | H. A. Graeme Pabley |
| | | | | Clerk to the Pilotage Authority |
| 25th | day of | August | 1980 | H. A. Graeme Pabley |
| | | | | Clerk to the Pilotage Authority |
| 12th | day of | August | 1981 | H. A. Graeme Pabley |
| | | | | Clerk to the Pilotage Authority |
| 9th | day of | August | 1982 | H. A. Graeme Pabley |
| | | | | Clerk to the Pilotage Authority |
| 3rd | day of | August | 19 83 | H. A. Graeme Pabley |
| | | | | Clerk to the Pilotage Authority |
| 31st | day of | August | 1984 | H. A. Graeme Pabley |
| | | | | Clerk to the Pilotage Authority |
| 15 | day of | August | 19 85 | |
| | | | | Clerk to the Pilotage Authority |
| 31st | day of | August | 1986 | R. M. |
| | | | | Clerk to the Pilotage Authority |
| 31st | day of | August | 19 87 | R. M. |
| | | | | Clerk to the Pilotage Authority |
| 31st | day of August | | 1988 | R. M. |
| | | | | Clerk to the Pilotage Authority |

No. 385

ORKNEY ISLANDS COUNCIL EDUCATION DEPARTMENT

# BASIC SEA SURVIVAL COURSE

### THIS IS TO CERTIFY THAT

NAME   CAPTAIN   ROBERT C. SCLATER

DISCHARGE BOOK NO.   DEPUTO HARBOUR MASTER

O.I.C. HARBOURS.

satisfactorily completed a Basic Sea Survival Course, including Wet Drill, approved by
the Merchant Navy Training Board and the Department of Trade.

Date of Course 25 November 1987

R. C. Sclater.
Holding Certificate

M.N.T.B. Approved Instructor

R. L. Sutherland.
Course Organiser:

NOTE:—Details of this certificate should be entered in holder's  Discharge Book by
THE  SUPERINTENDENT  OF  A  MERCANTILE  MARINE  OFFICE  at the earliest opportunity.

In summer 1988, we went on a holiday to Canada and the USA to visit family. Whilst in Detroit on 7 July, when we came down for breakfast my cousin asked if we knew the Piper Alpha Oil Field in the North Sea.

'Of course', I said, 'it provides the main pipe line link for the crude oil processed at Occidental's Flotta oil terminal'.

'Well,' he said, 'come and have a look at the news.'

The pictures were to say the least horrific, with the platform engulfed in flames. It certainly was a dreadful sight. We were to be in the US and Canada for another couple of weeks so could only follow the crisis on the television. On arrival home, it was back to work and coming to terms with the implications of the Piper Alpha disaster.

With the loss of 167 lives and the destruction of the platform, the impact on the community was devastating. It was still unclear at the time what Occidental would do regarding the replacement of the system. The terminal was shut down with no oil flowing, so the harbour staff were concerned for their jobs. It would be a couple of months until Occidental were in a position to decide just what the future held as far as their operations in the North Sea would be.

The accommodation module on Piper Alpha where approximately half of the platform staff were lost was still at the bottom of the North Sea. Captain Banks and I met up with Occidental's management and were advised in September that when the module was retrieved from the seabed it would be taken to Flotta to recover the 87 bodies of those who had perished inside the module.

The large crane barge DB102 was to carry out the recovery. Just prior to everything being in place, I was invited to fly out to the Crane barge along with Captain Max Gunn, Depute Terminal Manager to oversee the loading of the module onto a barge that would be towed from the piper platform to Flotta. We boarded a helicopter at the Flotta terminal and traveled out to the DB102

On arrival, we were given a briefing on progress and advised the module would be lifted the next day. We witnessed the Rov's attaching the lifting cables and heavy shackles ready for the big lift. It was a sobering sight to see the module break the surface the next day and landed on the deck of the DB102

As the weather at the time was unpredictable, it was agreed that instead of transferring the module to the barge lying alongside, it would remain onboard and the DB102 would proceed to Scapa flow prior to the transfer. Captain Gunn and myself then flew back to Flotta to confirm arrangements for the arrival of the module.

The DB102 arrived at slack water in the Pentland firth as it was not a very manouverable vessel with the pilot already onboard. It then proceeded to anchor and the module was successfully transferred to the receiving barge and brought alongside the LPG jetty at the Flotta oil terminal. The difficult task of recovering the bodies was then carried out.

It was a very sad saga in the history of the North Sea oil operations where the only problems we had encountered were small oil spills. It certainly made you realise just how dangerous things could be out onboard these oil installations. The accident did cause a big problem for Occidental, but they persevered and were able to bypass the Piper Oil pipe line and resume production from Claymore, Tartan, and the other smaller fields in area.

It was a great relief to everyone in Orkney employed directly or indirectly with the oil terminal operations. There were no redundancies and things slowly got back to normal albeit with reduced through put due to Piper being off line. The remains of Piper Alpha were in fact blown up and sunk to the bottom of the North Sea, a sad end.

Early in 1989, Captain Banks announced he was to retire in June and leave Orkney. This was very interesting and of course I was happy to throw my hat in the ring once again to obtain the top job in the Harbours Department. It was to take the Council until May to advertise the post. I will cover the application and interview as the rest of my story unfolds.

At this time, the construction and tendering for the new ferries and tugs were progressing well along with the harbour and pier infrastructures. So, never a dull moment. There was one big problem relating to the ferries and that was the annual refits they had to comply with under the various Merchant Shipping Acts.

There were no suitable shipyards in Orkney capable of carrying out this work so they either went to shipyards on the Morayshire Coast or up to Shetland. With the ferries away, a replacement ferry was required. The Hoy Head and Lywara Bay were covered by a relief Shetland Islands Council ferry, the Fivla and the Enyhallow by a Caledonia Macbraine ferry, the Cana. This was not really a very satisfactory situation as we were dependant on other companies and if one of their ferries was out of action, we would not get their relief vessel.

This resulted in considerable debate and a few proposals were put forward. As the South isles ferries operated to a link span facility and the Eynhallow and the Shapinsay operated to a hard ramp; these vessels were not compatible. What we required was a dual purpose ferry capable of operating to both types of facility.The directors of the shipping company proposed we carry out alterations to either the Lywara Bay or the Hoy Head to achieve a dual purpose vessel. This gives you an idea how difficult it was working with Councillors who seemed to have no concept of ship design or the costs involved. The OISCO did have a marine advisor appointed by the Scottish office, an ex-cunard passenger ship master Captain Pat Morrish who advised the board on shipping matters.There was no marine or engineering superintendents in the company in 1989. All the refits were handled by John Pirie Engineering Consultatants once again appointed by the OISCO. This was to change, but at this time during the transition period, things were as they were prior to 1987.

I was in contact with Maurice Napier and his staff who were busy with the Shapinsay and the two new ferries to be named Earl Thorfinn and Earl Siguard and posed the question on the dual purpose ferry. I have included on the next page my views sent to the chief executive regarding this project. What really worried me was the fact that Councillors were happy to waste £1200 on consultants to get an answer to something I already knew the answer to.

## MEMO

FROM: Capt. R C Sclater
Depute Director of Harbours
REF: E.7.S/PB

TO: Mr R H Gilbert
Chief Executive and Director of Finance
REF: 5th April 1989

PROPOSED CONVERSION OF 'LYRAWA BAY' OR 'HOY HEAD' INTO A DUAL PURPOSE VESSEL

1. 'LYRAWA BAY' : BUILT 1970

It is the considered opinion of The Napier Company and ourselves that it is not feasible to convert this vessel into a dual purpose vessel on the grounds of its age and lack of carrying capacity (only 19 tonnes), and also because any conversion would probably cost more than the vessel is worth, as is shown by the details relating to the 'HOY HEAD'.

2. 'HOY HEAD' : BUILT 1973

The cost to convert the 'HOY HEAD' would be in the region of £400,000. This is made up of the following figures, for the bow ramp and forward steelwork alone:-

| | |
|---|---|
| New forward ramp (weight 16 tonnes) | £ 45,000 |
| Installation costs | 8,000 |
| Steelwork forward | 50,000 |
| Sundry work, piping, painting etc | 20,000 |
| | £123,000 |

By carrying out this work on the vessel, she would not then comply with Department of Transport regulations. In order to meet these requirements and to improve the draught, trim, recover lost deadweight, minimum bow height and forward draught requirements, the vessel would have to be lengthened and a new forward end fitted on landing craft lines. The existing short link span ramp would also have to be replaced. The following figures relate to the total costs:-

| | |
|---|---|
| New 5.0 metre mid section | £130,000 |
| New forward end | 60,000 |
| New bow ramps | 62,000 |
| Installation costs | 10,000 |
| Heighten forward lounge | 35,000 |
| * Rewiring etc | 30,000 |
| * Structural fire protection | 25,000 |
| * Increased scantlings repair work etc | 25,000 |
| * Pipework | 12,000 |
| * Drawings, D.O.T. fees damaged stability | 25,000 |
| TOTAL ESTIMATED COST | £414,000 |

* Due to major conversion, vessel would have to comply with latest Department of Transport regulations.

The above figures may be on the high side but even at half the cost it is still
much too high. I would therefore like to recommend that the request to carry out
a complete feasibility study at a cost of £1,200 should be refused by the
Committee and that we should instead push ahead with our plans for building a
specialised dual purpose vessel.


Depute Director of Harbours

Note : Attached are details received from The Napier Company.


Fortunately, the committee agreed with our recommendations and the go
ahead was given to proceed with the design and funding for the new ferry. Two
of the senior Councillors met with a Scottish office official but failed to get
funding. However, an approach was made to the ERDF (European Regional
Development Fund) and with our very positive and robust application they
agreed funding.

With this achievement, it meant that the Scottish office would also be willing
to match some of the cost. One of Maurice Napier's naval architects who I had
been dealing with, Neil Patterson had set up his own naval architect business so
I requested the Council to allow us to appoint him as our main designer and
advisor. This was agreed and we proceeded with drawing up the relevant
documentation ready to go out for tender in early 1990.

The work load on the department was increasing but we managed to maintain
a professional and competent working schedule to meet all the demands placed
on us.

Following the Mt Eva oil spill back in January 1987, we realised that the oil
pollution plans we had in place were not really fit for purpose. It was also found
that liaison between all interested parties as far as the environment was
concerned needed updating. In this instance, the department set up the Oil
Pollution Liasion Committee; in the past this type of liasion was very ad hoc.

This was a great step forward by including the harbours own marine biology
unit (contracted from Dundee University), RSPB, SNH, coast guard, Occidental,

Environmental Department of the Council, and the Council's direct labour organisation (the main work force in the event of an oil spill). It was strange that the oil operations had been ongoing since 1977 but no proper group was in place to discuss the ways and means of handling an oil spill. There was, of course, oil spill contigency plans in place.

The oil terminal had its own plan along with a full warehouse of oil pollution equipment, I think in the beginning this was thought to be all that was required and the terminal staff would look after any oil pollution incident. The only oil spill equipment held at the harbours was two 20 ton tanker trailers containing oil dispersant. The committee met on a regular basis and a much better liasion was had with the environmental bodies, something that was missing in the past. I will touch on the Marine Biology Unit and Oil Spill Contingency plans later.

Also in 1988-9, a new ferry was being proposed for the Pentland firth route operating from Burwick in South Ronaldsay to Gills Bay on the Caithness side of the firth. The company behind the scheme consisted of local business men. Their plan was to run in competition against the existing route between Stromness and Scrabster. The main lifeline ferries were operated by P&O scottish ferries and subsidised by the scottish office.

The new ferry would not receive any subsidy. Work commenced on building harbour facilities at both ports with no funding from OIC or the UK government. The proposed service was in my mind, a bit ambitious and the ferry route, not what I believed to be a safe passage especially in the winter months. I made my thoughts clear to Orkney Islands Council but as it was a private operator and not the Harbour Department's responsibility, the project continued.

A new ferry was also being constructed for the service and it would come into operation by summer 1989. We did, of course, have regular meetings with the company registered as Orkney Ferries at the time. The terminal at Burwick was inside our harbour area although the Council had leased the area to the them, it still required our involvement as local light house authority and also to ensure the harbour works were up to standard. This will also highlight in my story as we progress.

ORKNEY ISLANDS COUNCIL
DEPARTMENT OF HARBOURS

APPLICATION FOR APPOINTMENT OF DIRECTOR OF HARBOURS

Advertised in .....Lloyd's List.................

Surname .....Sclater..................................

Christian Names .....Robert Chalmers...................

Address .......'Korsgarth', High Street, Kirkwall, Orkney, KW15 1AZ..........

.................................................................

Tel No. .....K. 2359.............. Date of Birth ....7th August 1941........

Name & Address    1. ...Capt. H A Banks....... 2. ...Capt. M Gunn...........

of each Referee      ...Director of Harbours....    ...Deputy Terminal Manager..

                     ...Harbour Authority Building    ...Occidental Petroleum (Caledonia)

                     ...Scapa, Orkney, KW15 1SD..    ...Flotta Terminal, Flotta,...

                                                     Stromness, Orkney, KW15 3NP

PROFESSIONAL TRAINING (INCLUDING APPRENTICESHIPS)

| Dates (From - To) | College etc | Type of Course | Qualifications Gained |
|---|---|---|---|
| 11.9.56 - 21.12.56 | Leith Nautical College | Preparatory Course for Seamen | First Class Certificate |
| 20.5.63 - 24.5.63 | Robert Gordons Institute of Technology (RGIT) | Radar Observer | Certificate |
| May - November 1963 | R.G.I.T. | 2nd Mate Foreign | Certificate |
| October - January 1965/66 | R.G.I.T. | 1st Mate Foreign | Certificate |
| September - January 1970/71 | R.G.I.T. | Master Foreign Going | Certificate |
| 1.2.71 - 5.2.71 | Leith Nautical College | Radar Simulator | Certificate |
| 16.9.71 - 30.9.71 | S.S. Stevenson | Shipboard Management | Certificate |
| 2.12.75 - 5.12.75 | MacDonald Road Fire Station | Fire Fighting | Certificate |
| 8.12.75 - 12.12.75 | Department of Trade | Ship Captains Medical Training | Certificate |
| 24.1.84 - 27.1.84 | Glasgow Nautical College | A.R.P.A. | Certificate |
| 13.5.86 - 16.5.86 | Wood Group Environmental Services Limited | Oil Pollution Prevention and Clearance Course | Certificate |
| 9.6.86 - 12.6.86 | As above | Advanced OP Course | Certificate |

POST OF DIRECTOR OF HARBOURS

To support my application for the above position, I believe that the following details are relevant.

I have held the position of Depute Director of Harbours and Pilotage Superintendent for the past $3\frac{1}{2}$ years and in this capacity I have ensured that a high standard of safety and efficiency has been maintained in all aspects of harbour operations throughout the Orkney Harbour Areas. I work in close co-operation with Occidental personnel to ensure that all safety procedures relating to tanker operations are maintained at all times and that the threat of oil pollution is kept to a minimum. Since taking up this post, a great deal of new developments, improvements and changes have taken place within the Department of Harbours, which I have been fortunate to be deeply involved in and, to highlight these points, I would mention the following:-

1.  Installation of new radar surveillance system;
2.  Drafting and bringing into operation The Orkney Pilotage Direction 1988;
3.  New oil pollution plans, equipment and meetings;
4.  New harbour developments;
5.  Short sea crossing;
6.  Acquisition of Orkney Islands Shipping Company;
7.  Design, tendering and building supervision of new vessels for Orkney Islands Shipping Company;
8.  Design, tendering and building supervision of new tugs for Orkney Towage Company Limited;
9.  Fish farms - Works Licences;
10. New emergency plans and explosives licences;
11. Installation of new weighbridges; and
12. Tanker lightening operations.

A considerable amount of new legislation has also become law recently especially in light of the 'Herald of Free Enterprise' disaster, which regulations encompass: Safety of Life at Sea, Weighing of Goods Vehicles and Other Cargo, Vessel Stability, Dangerous Substances in Harbour Areas, Prevention of Pollution, Reception Facilities, Food and Environmental Protection, Dock Regulations, Pilotage etc. I ensure that these, along with all other relevant Acts and Regulations are complied with in so far as they apply to the Harbours Department's role within Orkney Islands Council's framework.

There are of course the continuing day to day operations of the Harbours Department and in carrying out my duties I maintain a close working relationship with other departments within the Council and with various governmental and official bodies, namely:- Northern Lighthouse Board, Department of Transport (various sections), Hydrographer of the Navy, Scottish Development Department, Crown Estate Commissioners, Department of Agriculture and Fisheries, Ministry for Agriculture and Fisheries, Department of Trade and Industry, H.M. Customs and Excise, H.M. Coastguard and other harbour authorities throughout the U.K. with special links with Sullom Voe, Lerwick and Invergordon.

I regularly/

I regularly attend meetings of the Transportation Committee and Orkney Islands Shipping Company and have produced and presented numerous reports connected with the Council's marine activities. I subsequently ensure that any decisions reached relating to the Department of Harbours are carried out.

I hold the following positions:-

Assistant Oil Pollution Officer for the Orkney Islands Area;
Member of the Pilotage Examining Body as laid down in The Orkney Pilotage Direction 1988;
1st Class Authorised Pilot for the Orkney Harbour Areas;
Safety Inspector under the Health and Safety at Work etc Act 1974;
Deputy Group Manager for Orkney in the Department of Transport's Port and Shipping Organisation;
Deputy Launching Authority R.N.L.I. for the Kirkwall Lifeboat; and
Member of the Nautical Institute.

Prior to taking up my position as Depute Director of Harbours I was employed as a Marine Officer and 1st Class Pilot with Orkney Islands Council's Department of Harbours, for 9 years. In this respect I was the longest serving Pilots' Representative on the Orkney Pilotage Committee.

My outside interests are swimming, gardening, D.I.Y. and walking my dog. I am a committee member of the Parents and Friends Association of the 1st Kirkwall Company Boys Brigade and the Kirkwall Amateur Swimming Club, an official time keeper for the Scottish Amateur Swimming Association and an elder of St. Magnus Cathedral.

I reside in Kirkwall and I am married with two daughters and a son.


..........................
Capt. R C SCLATER M.N.I.

# ORKNEY ISLANDS COUNCIL

Council Offices, School Place, Kirkwall, Orkney, KW15 1NY

**Chief Executive and Director of Finance:-** Ronald H. Gilbert, I.P.F.A., F.R.V.A.

Tel. [0856] 3535
Telex: 75475

Fax. No. [0856] 4615

YOUR REF:

OUR REF:    RHG/CB

6th October 1989

PRIVATE AND CONFIDENTIAL

Captain R.C. Sclater,
Korsgarth,
High Street,
Kirkwall.

Dear Captain Sclater,

### Post of Director of Harbours

I have pleasure in confirming your appointment as Director of
Harbours as from 28th June 1989.  Your salary will be based on
JNC Chief Officials Scale £28,314-£30,330 with a starting salary
of £28,314 increasing by three annual increments.  A special
responsibility payment of £6,000 per annum and an Islands
Allowance of £708 per annum are also payable.

Your duties will include overall responsibility for the running
of the Department of Harbours and for the exercise of the
Council's functions as Harbour Authority.  You will be expected
to provide advice to the Islands Council on all marine matters as
determined by the Chief Executive and to maintain overall
supervision of the affairs of the Orkney Islands Shipping Company
Limited.

The Director of Harbours is also ex-officio a Council-appointed
Director of the Orkney Towage Company Limited and you will be
responsible to the Board of Directors for the efficient operation
of the tugs and their crews.

You will also be responsible to the Council as Oil Pollution
Officer for the Orkney Islands Area.

Yours sincerely,

Chief Executive

cc:  Mr. G. Gray

9th October 1989                                                RCS/MHS

Mr R H Gilbert
Chief Executive
Orkney Islands Council
Council Offices
KIRKWALL.

Dear Mr Gilbert

POST OF DIRECTOR OF HARBOURS

I wish to acknowledge receipt of your letter of 6th October 1989, confirming my
appointment as Director of Harbours.

Yours sincerely


Capt R C SCLATER
Director of Harbours


*The details of my application for the Director's Post which gives a rough
resume of my story.*

So, that was me at the top of my career with a very busy few years ahead of
me. You will note the Council was not the very quickest of organisations when
it came to correspondence or advertising for posts. The post was advertised on 9
May with interviews advised on 6 June to take place on 28 June. Captain Banks
held his leaving party on 30 June and sailed out of Orkney on the same evening
to his new home on the Moray Coast.

There were six candidates including myself interviewed for the post. Three
from out of Orkney and two of the existing pilots. Not sure what would have
happened if any of these others were appointed with no Director to carry out a
hand over. Thank goodness it was me.

Of course, I was on my own now and had to settle down and advertise for a
depute. This would take until September with the administration department
responsible for advertising for senior positions in the Council. We in the
Department Of Harbour, got on with things and any new jobs were advertised
and interviews set up as quickly as possible. We made sure everyone in the

department knew what was expected of them, punctuality, politeness, and efficiency in their jobs was essential.

# Part 5

On Monday 3 July, I settled down in my new office to come to grips with my responsibilities as Director of Harbours with Orkney Island Council. Having been depute for nearly four years and already heavily involved with all aspects of the department's work, the task was much easier than starting from scratch.

Of course my first task was to advertise my old post to have someone in place to help with my workload. This process was to take a couple of months due to the time taken to place adverts in the local press and other marine publications.

In July, the new ferry the MV Shapinsay was nearing completion and would be delivered by the third week of July. As there had been no naming ceremony for the Eynhallow, it was decided to have an official naming of the Shapinsay. To this end, it was agreed that the ferry would be named at Balfour pier, on the island of Shapinsay on 22 July by Mrs J Sinclair, wife of the chairman of the Transportation Committee of the Council.

It was my task to organise the ceremony and send out the invitation in consultation with the chief executive and the chairman of the transportation committee. Everything was in place by Thursday 20th with the local Shapinsay community organising the buffet reception after the naming.

The Shapinsay was all set to sail up from Buckie but had engine problems and would therefore, not arrive on time for the naming. This was a setback as I had to inform every one of the problems and reschedule the naming for the following Saturday 29th. This was achieved and the ferry arrived home on Monday 24th with all the preparations set for the 22nd now all in place for the 29th.

All the invited guests along with the Salvation Army Brass Band departed Kirkwall onboard the Shapinsay on the Saturday morning for the official naming. I had two bottles of champagne all ready for the naming, and just as well, the first bottle exploded before we attached it to the bow of the ferry. This was due to Jim Mitchell putting a small grove on the bottle with a glass cutter to ensure the bottle broke on impact. It actually blew up in my hands.

We quickly retrieved the other bottle but did not try scratching it and it took a couple of goes hitting the bow before it broke. My daughter Joanna was on hand to present Mrs Sinclair with a bouquet of flowers. After a lovely buffet at the community centre, all the guests from the mainland returned to the ferry for the trip back to Kirkwall. A good day was had by all and the hiccups along the way forgotten.

*MV Shapinsay. Joanna presented the flowers hence the invitation to her*

**The Convener, Mr E. R. Eunson**
*requests the pleasure of the Company of*

Miss Joanna Sclater

**at the Naming Ceremony of m.v. Shapinsay**
at
**Balfour Pier, Shapinsay on Saturday, 22nd July, 1989**
**at 3 p.m.**
*and thereafter to Refreshments at The Community Centre*
THE VESSEL WILL BE NAMED BY MRS J. SINCLAIR, HAQUOY

R.S.V.P.
The Chief Executive,
Orkney Islands Council,
School Place,
Kirkwall.

Guests leave on m.v. Shapinsay
from Kirkwall at 2.15 p.m.
from Shapinsay at 4.30 p.m.
Please show this Invitation for boarding

THE DIRECTORS OF ORKNEY FERRIES plc
*cordially invite*

*Capt. and Mrs R. Sclater*

to be present at
The Naming Ceremony of their New Ferry for Orkney
on Tuesday 4th July 1989, at 11 a.m.
in Kirkwall, Orkney

*RSVP*
Ken Brookman
General Manager
Orkney Ferries plc
Burwick
South Ronaldsay
tel: 0856 83 343

*Please present
this card on arrival
at the quayside.*

The short sea crossing ro/ro service between Burwick in South Ronaldsay and Gills Bay in Caithness was progressing by July 1989. The company had built a new ro/ro ferry and had it officially named Varagen at Scapa pier on 4th July the same week, I took up my new post.

As the new link-span facilities were still under construction the vessel was laid up in St Margaret's hope for a month. There was a song made about the ferry to the tune of a "pub with no beer" namely the "ship with no pier". Eventually the make shift facilities at Gills Bay were in place with a floating linkspan with two Dolphins for the vessel to moor alongside. Not the very safest harbours with no shelter from the westerly swell and seas in the area.

The ferry started operating from the harbour authority ro/ro terminal at Houton in Scapa flow to Gills Bay on 15 August. Not the most prestigious start to this new service. On Saturday 16 September, I received a phone call from one of the skippers of the Varagen to tell me the link span at Gills Bay had broken adrift due to the strong winds and heavy westerly swell that evening and was floating upside down.

On the Sunday morning, I set off with the Council's Director of Engineering onboard our pilot launch to check on the situation. It was still blowing a gale and we had a bumpy trip across the Pentland firth. The link span was still attached to the shore connection, but upside down and would be out of action for some time. We then set off to Burwick to check on the facilities there. Fortunately everything was intact and no damage.

Burwick at this time was still a long way from completion as there was considerable dredging to be carried out and the breakwater was only half built. Orkney Ferries Plc was now in dire straits as they had no money to continue. They put forward a proposal to Orkney Islands Council to take over the task of completing the terminals.

Councillors, in their wisdom, agreed to take over the project as several Councillors were very keen to see the project up and running. In my mind, the whole concept was fraught with danger as the sea conditions around the entrance to Burwick had treacherous tidal flow and heavy confused seas at certain states of the tide. I had pointed this out to the Council that in the winter months and in the dark, it would be a daunting task taking a ferry into a Burwick, but to no avail.

Anyway, the Council took up the challenge which caused considerable disagreement with the other Councillor. I recall a meeting with senior Councillors and officials discussing the costs to get the two harbours up to department of transport requirements.

The costs put forward was over £5 million, so they said that let's tell the Council it will cost just £3 million and once we have started the extra can be added as it will be too late to stop. I was astonished at this but having already put my negative point forward about the scheme, my views were discounted. The project was agreed by the Council and handed to the Harbours and Engineering Departments to oversee the construction of the two terminals.

I attended several meetings with the department of transport surveyors who clearly stated that both ports must be fully protected, dredged and safe for ferry operations. I also had meetings with the Northern Light House Board on the navigation aids and leading lights required. All these items came at a cost.

The estimates for the completion of the terminals by the engineers were a way too low and eventually, after the Council had thrown millions into the project they pulled the plug and everything was mothballed. The Varagen was laid up in Grangemouth, I will come back to her later in my story.

Back to more mundane topics, by the end of August we were able to draw up a short leet for the depute post and set the interviews for early September.

There were three applicants, two existing pilots and one assistant harbour master from the Clyde. Following the interviews Captain Bob Moore was appointed.

Captain Moore had joined the department in 1977 and was fully up to speed with all harbour aspects of the post in relation to pilotage and control room operations. Bob had actually been at the TS Dolphin with me back in 1956, although he was attending as a deck cadet on the one-year course.

He had carried out his first four years at sea as an officer cadet with Clan Line, an Scottish shipping company operating mainly to the far east. The big difference at this time was that I would certainly not be taking a back seat unlike Captain Banks who was happy to let me take responsibility for the efficient running of the department.

He would arrive at 9 o'clock in the morning and be heading home with a copy of Lloyd's list under his arm at 5 o'clock and his parting words, if anything was happening "it'll sort itself out" and away he went. Of course, things did get sorted but not without detailed planning and intervention to make sure it did.

I suppose as a new broom, I wished to get things done in the department which I was not able to do, as Harry was only too happy to let things drift along and have as easy a life as possible. Not that we were at loggerheads as we worked well together and the department did run efficiently but there were many aspects that could be done better in my opinion, and I was determined to prove my point.

One of these issues was the insurance cover for all the vessels coming under our control. The pilot launches were insured through the Council's insurers commercial union with the annual premiums renewals paid each year without query. The ferries were with a Dundee based insurance company. The towage company vessels were covered by the London-based marine insurance brokers Tyser&Co.

I had met the Tyser brokers through JP Knights and made contact with them to see if we could draw up a fleet policy both for hull and machinery and P&I (protection and indemnity) to cover our existing vessel and also the new tugs and ferries under construction.

My main contact was Norman Proctor, a very highly respected broker in the Lloyds insurance market in London. Norman was only too happy to take up our business and I forwarded all the details of our existing fleet along with information of the two new tugs and the new north isles ferries. Following the quotes from Tyser&Co, I submitted a report to the Transportation Committee and also Orkney towage board on the premiums proposed.

I should mention the towage company cover was not part of Orkney Islands Council fleet policy being a separate limited company. It still helped with the fleet cover as all the vessels were covered by the same Lloyd's names and gave a larger policy which helped to reduce premiums. We certainly made savings and with new vessels still to be added over the next few years, made my job much easier by using the expertise of Tysers.

They also carried out all claims through the head of their claims department Mike Cairns. It was one of the best decisions made in my first year as director. I have shown on the following pages a couple of the fleet premium lists in 1996, the only years I have copies of.

### Orkney Islands Council
### Hull & Machinery/Increased Value
### 12 months at 16th August 1996

Conditions of Insurance as per our cover note dated 19th August 1996.

| Name | GRT/BLT | Value £ | Deductible £ | Rate % | Premium £ |
|---|---|---|---|---|---|
| **A) Hull and Machinery** | | | | | |
| 1) Earl Thorfinn | 771/1990 | 3,200,000 | 10,000 | 0.425 | |
| 2) Earl Sigurd | 771/1990 | 3,200,000 | 10,000 | 0.425 | |
| 3) Varagen | 928/1989 | 3,000,000 | 10,000 | 0.450 | |
| 4) Thorsvoe | 385/1991 | 2,000,000 | 7,500 | 0.450 | |
| 5) Hoy Head | 358/1994 | 2,000,000 | 7,500 | 0.450 | |
| 6) Shapinsay | 199/1989 | 1,400,000 | 7,500 | 0.450 | |
| 7) Eynhallow | 79/1987 | 750,000 | 5,000 | 0.500 | |
| 8) Graemsay | 82/1996 | 800,000 | 3,750 | 0.450 | |
| 9) Golden Mariana | 33/1973 | 250,000 | 2,500 | 0.500 | |
| 10) Scapa Lass | 42/1992 | 570,000 | 2,500 | 0.425 | |
| 11) Scapa Pathfinder | 43/1979 | 700,000 | 2,500 | 0.425 | |
| 12) Kirkwall Bay | 56/1992 | 500,000 | 2,500 | 0.425 | |
| 13) Scapa Pioneer | 32/1993 | 900,000 | 2,500 | 0.425 | |
| 14) Scapa Pilot | 33/1975 | 350,000 | 2,500 | 0.425 | |
| 15) Scapa Protector | /1994 | 25,000 | 500 | 0.500 | |
| **B) Increased Value** | | | | | |
| 1) Earl Thorfinn | Amount | 800,000 | | 0.165 | |
| 2) Earl Sigurd | Amount | 800,000 | | 0.165 | |
| 3) Varagen | Amount | 750,000 | | 0.165 | |

TOTAL PREMIUM PAYABLE

Orkney Towage Company Limited

9th April 1996

Hull and Machinery
12 months from 1st April 1996

Conditions of Insurance as per Cover Note dated 9th April 1996.

**To Premium:**

| | | | | |
|---|---|---|---|---|
| "Einar" | £ 3,150,000 @ 0.5285% | = | £ | ▬▬▬ |
| "Erland" | £ 3,150,000 @ 0.5285% | = | £ | ▬▬▬ |
| "Harald" | £ 3,500,000 @ 0.5285% | = | £ | ▬▬▬ |
| | Total Premium | = | £ | ▬▬▬ |
| | Less Owners Discount 9.5% | | £ | ▬▬▬ |
| | **Total Premium Due** | = | £ | ▬▬▬ |

**Premium due on or before 15th May 1996.**

After the Piper Alpha accident, oil through put at the terminal dropped (as can be seen from the information on one of the following pages). When it started to increase we were informed that our port operators liability insurance premiums were to go up.

The insurance company Willis, Faber and Dumas informed us that due to the increase in through put in 1991 compared to the two previous years our premiums were to rise. They never reduced them when we had the reduction in oil supply because of the Piper Alpha disaster.

The department of legal services had handled this aspect of insurance up to this time. I contacted Norman Proctor and asked if he could get a quote for this cover.

'No problem,' he said and within a week, our premiums dropped by some £18000 for the same cover. I also had Norman obtain cover for our nine link spans in case of damage.

During this time, I was also involved in obtaining all the necessary paper work to register our new vessels, with the UK register of shipping this included confirmation of the names chosen for each ship. The legal department also played a role in this aspect of the registration.

The shipbuilders supplied the craving and marking note confirming the vessels official number (on) and NRT net registered tonnage. This info was cut into the main beam of all UK vessel. The official name was inscribed on each bow along with the name and port of registry on the stern.

Telex : 76642 Napier G
Fax : 0241-71712

# THE
# NAPIER COMPANY
(ARBROATH) LTD.
NAVAL ARCHITECTS/MARINE CONSULTANTS

WEST GRIMSBY STREET
ARBROATH DD11 1PF
SCOTLAND

FACSIMILE MESSAGE

TO FAX NUMBER    0856-3012
DATE             23rd May 1989
FOR              Orkney Islands Council
ATTENTION        Capt. R. Sclater
FROM             B.S. Cotton
NO. OF PAGES (inclusive of message page) 2
PLEASE ADVISE IF NOT CLEAR AND WE WILL REFAX/TELEX TO YOU.

## 45m RO-RO VESSELS - OUTER NORTH ISLES

Dear Sirs,

Thank you for your letter dated 16th May requesting a detailed report covering various extras asked for by the Department of Transport and Lloyds.

MC12    $CO_2$ to BTU Space - This item has been recommended to be fitted by the D.O.T. and although not a rule it was decided to comply with this for the safety of the vessel.

MC13    Modification to Volvo Engine - Volvo engines were uprated after the specification was written. After the contract was signed it was found that this new size of engine had not been given a Lloyd's Class Certificate and the size above would have to be fitted.

MC23    Larger Embarkations Doors - McTay have included this as a D.O.T. item in error although it could be included for M.A.F.F.S. as it was widened to allow cattle to pass whilst the linkspans were being completed.

MC41    Standby Pumps - Required by the D.O.T. for the main engine gearbox lubricating oil system.

MC47    Pump Casings - The D.O.T. required the fire pump to be increased in size and to make all pumps compatible it was decided to fit them all the same size.

MC48    Skeg Modifications - The original design was for a single plate skeg. Lloyds asked for the skeg to be double plated as they thought this vessel was a bit too big for a single plate skeg.

MC53    Two Urinals - Asked for by D.O.T. in excess to the toilets etc. specified.

MC63    $CO_2$ vs Halon in Engine Room - $CO_2$ is only recommended by the D.O.T. because it is more ozone friendly than halon. It was decided to comply with this as conversion may be required in future years.

MC66    Ventilation to Vehicle Space - This item was unexpected because this space is open to the aft end and has washports at Main Deck level, but D.O.T. insisted on this fan being fitted to extract car fumes. This fan can be used for supplying air to the cattle when carried.

| Modification Number | | | Credit | Extra | |
|---|---|---|---|---|---|
| 10 | Flow Censor | | | 1120 | |
| 12 | CO2 to B.T.U. Space | B.O.T. | | 4800 | |
| 13 | Volvo Engine | Lloyds | | 490 | |
| 18 | Crane Cab (see Mod 68) | | | | |
| 19 | Fuel Meter | | 2200 | | |
| 23 | Shell Door | | | 2400 | |
| 25 | Passenger Access Door | | 1850 | | |
| 26 | Officer Cabin | | | 5750 | |
| 29 | Immersion Heater | | | 300 | |
| 34 | Docking Hatch | | 2500 | | |
| 41 | Standby Pumps to Gearboxes etc | B.O.T. | | 3200 | |
| 44 | Crane (see Mod 60) | | | 8500 | |
| 47 | Pumps | | | 1200 | |
| 48 | Skeg | Lloyds | | 5800 | |
| 52 | Emerg Lights | | 545 | | |
| 53 | Gents Toilet | B.O.T. | | 1050 | |
| 57 | Hyd Pumps for Crane | | | 1025 | |
| 58 | Bollards for Fairleads | | | 2950 | |
| 59 | Belting | | 3600 | | |
| 60 | Crane | | 2500 | | |
| 61 | Galley Equip | | | 606 | |
| 62 | Computer | | 6000? | | Check and Advise |
| 63 | Co2 Engine Room | B.O.T. | | 4300 | |
| 65 | Wheelhouse across Bridge Front | | | 16250 | |
| 66 | Ventilation | B.O.T. | | 8900 | |
| 67 | *Gyro Compass | B.O.T. | | 16275 | |
| 68 | Crane Cab | | | 600 | |
| 70 | Drench System Pump | B.O.T. | | 8200 | |
| 71 | Sailor R501 | B.O.T. | | 1244 | |
| 72 | M.F. Transceiver | B.O.T. | | 5200 | |
| 73 | Waterproof VHF | B.O.T. | | 50 | |
| 74 | Navtex Receiver | B.O.T. | | 1452 | |
| 75 | Decca Navigator Receiver | B.O.T. | | 2430 | |
| 76 | Stabilised Radar Gyro Compass | B.O.T. | | 1250 | |
| 77 | *Direction Finder Unit Type STC-ADF-790 | B.O.T. | | 8640 | |
| | Additional Insulation | B.O.T. | | 35000 | Approx |
| | | | 19195 | 148982 | |

```
                              148982
                               19195
                              129787

B.O.T. Extras                 101991
Lloyds Extras                   6290
                              108281
```

*The details on the two new ferries relating to the extra costs at the shipyard relate to when I was still deputy.*

This aspect of the building programme with the ferries and the tugs was an ongoing problem you had to keep a very careful watch on what the shipyard was doing. I attended several meetings with our naval architect, Brian Cotton of Napier's also Sven Aarts and Kes Krot of Wijsmuller.

These meetings at Mctay Marine could be quite difficult trying to reach agreement on the extra costs always came in far too high.

The tugs were also encountering extras but we managed to keep them in check, thanks to the Wijsmuller team. I, of course, had to report all these problems back to The Transportation Committee, The Towage Company Board and The Scottish Office to get clearance to pay the extra costs, no easy task dealing with Councillors.

The work load had certainly increased since my initial appointment as deputy back in 1985. It was a great challenge and I'm sure many seafarers would have loved to be in my position. The ferry service manager Alan Bullen who had played a major role in the early stages of the new ro/ro service retired shortly after I took over as director. His assistant manager Alistair Learmonth took up the post.

Captain Morrish, the Scottish office representative on the Orkney Islands Shipping Co Board also decided to retire as the company now came under Orkney Islands Council remit and his services were no longer required. The minute of the transportation study group on the previous pages gives an indication on how the department wished to progress in relation to the ferries and the department itself. It was a time for change and with a new team, I was confident we could achieve our goals.

By the end of 1989, the two new tugs were nearing completion and would be on station by January. The Kessock and Kinloch were now ready for their off-hire surveys carried out in Ostend. I attended the Kessock survey and it was during the big gale on 25 January, quite a day. It was quite a costly affair with the tug being fully refurbished.

Once again, a naming ceremony was proposed and I set to drawing up the invitation list and the programme for the occasion. The date set was 2nd February at Scapa pier. The Mt Einar was to be named by Mrs E Eunson, wife of the convenor of Orkney Islands Council and Mrs J Tait, wife of the vice convenor to name the Mt Erland, both Councillors being directors of the towage company.

The tugs duly arrived home after successful trials on the river Mersey next to Mctay Marine shipyard in Bromborough on the Wirral. The new tugs were certainly a great leap forward compared to the Kessock and Kinloch more power, versatility and manoeuvrability with a design that would cope with the rough sea conditions in Orkney waters.

The only problem being their berth alongside Scapa pier was not really suitable for these larger tugs. I therefore, submitted a report to the transportation committee outlining the problem and recommended that the pier be extended and dredged to meet the requirements of the new tugs. This was agreed and the engineering department carried out the design for a 50-metre extension along with dredging.

At this time discussions on moving the oil storage facilities of S&J D Robertson's in Kirkwall and dispensing with oil discharging manifolds on Kirkwall pier were being muted. This gave us an opportunity to progress this controversial topic by involving the other oil company Highland fuels operating their oil reception tankage at Scapa pier.

The facilities in Kirkwall handled diesel, heating oil and jet a1(aircraft fuel). The facilities at Scapa handled all petrol imports. The two companies had a working agreement on distribution of diesel, heating oil and petrol. There was sufficient tankage at the Scapa depot to handle all fuels coming into Orkney with capacity for well over a month's supply.

We held several meetings with both companies and highland fuels agreed to progress with cleaning out and preparing their additional oil tanks not in use to be available if agreement could be reached with BP. The extension to Scapa pier required an additional pipe line along with a new manifold to handle the four oil products to be discharged.

The work on the pier and at highland fuels was completed but unfortunately, S&J D Robertson (BP pulled out of the negotiations and instead, refurbished their oil tanks in Kirkwall much to our dismay. In 2018, the oil company operating the Kirkwall oil depot eventually agreed to move all its fuel oil operation through Scapa.

At least our efforts back in 1990 were not all in vain, but it took 28 years to achieve. The only fuel coming in to Kirkwall in 2018 was fuel for the power station. I have digressed again but it did relate to the Scapa pier extension for our new tugs.

The naming ceremony was all set to take place on Friday 2nd February with everything in place. Unfortunately, on the Thursday night we were hit by a severe southerly gale with the sea breaking over the pier. This was a very difficult situation with normally the guests standing on the pier to witness the naming.

The decision was made to have all guests attend in the harbour authority building and only have the naming party onboard each tug. The naming would be carried out from the bridge of each tug with the champagne bottles being released from the bridge window to strike the opposite tug. The ceremony would be relayed by VHF radio to the harbour building so everyone could hear the ceremony. Everything went fine and an enjoyable buffet followed in the harbour offices with towage director's dinner in the evening.

## THE DIRECTORS OF ORKNEY TOWAGE COMPANY Ltd.

request the pleasure of the company of

..........*Captain + Mrs R. C. Sclater*..........

at the NAMING CEREMONIES of M.T. *EINAR* and M.T. *ERLEND*

at

*SCAPA PIER on FRIDAY, 2nd FEBRUARY 1990 at 12.30 p.m.*

and thereafter to a Buffet Lunch at the Harbour Authority Building

The M.T. *EINAR* will be named by MRS E. EUNSON
The M.T. *ERLEND* will be named by MRS J. TAIT

R.S.V.P.
Executive Director,
Orkney Towage Co.,
Harbour Authority Building,
Scapa. Tel. 0856 - 3636

*The weather conditions on the Thursday night prior to the naming. It had calmed down a bit by the Friday still not safe on the pier. The naming of the tugs was a unique naming with the two ladies their husbands and the minister who blessed the tugs all safely stationed on the bridge of each tug. Harbour authority building first on right of photo. The guests could see the tugs from the windows of the building.*

Although we were to reduce to two tugs, I managed to put forward an argument to keep the Kintore on station for an extra few months to see how we could operate with just two tugs. This gave a strong case to build a third new tug and this was achieved by 1994, more details later.

During my time as a pilot I did think that having to carry out watch duties as a marine officer in the control room was a bit of a waste as there was no need for an authorised pilot to carry out this task. My view was that a marine officer with a master foreign going certificate could carry out this duty without being a pilot.

It would also mean that a pilot would do piloting duties and not spend a considerable amount of his duties sitting in the control room. It would result in a reduction of pilots to ten and have five marine officers who could train for pilotage duties if they so wished. Also when a pilot retired or left the department then they could be first in line for the post. I put this proposal to the Council and received a positive response.

My main concern at the time was the age of when a pilot should retire. I was of the opinion that that once a pilot reached the age of 60, he should no longer continue due to the dangerous aspect of the job. We had the opportunity to carry out these changes with Captain Moore's position becoming vacant and at least four other pilots reaching or past the age of 60 by the end of 1990.

There would be savings in salary as the marine officers would receive considerably less than the pilots. I was also proposing the appointment of an assistant oil pollution officer who would also stand in as a marine officer in the event of sickness. Some of the pilots, of course, were not very happy with my proposals, although it was a win-win situation for them.

With no fixed office duties and piloting vessels on a more regular basis and the opportunity to retire on full pension at 60 and at home when not piloting was in my mind, the best of both worlds. By the 1 January 1991, we had the new scheme basically in place and had appointed the assistant oil pollution/marine officer.

Some of the pilots were not in agreement with these proposals and we had several meetings to outline the various benefits to them. It took them sometime to arrange for their union to meet us and put forward their objections. They did not have a very strong case and the union representative told me afterwards that they could not understand the attitude of the pilots as they were of the opinion that this was a very positive deal. Things settled down and the majority accepted the deal and I know that as time went by and pilots reached the age of 60, they realised just what a good deal I had achieved for them; some however, never did. Today, this would not be allowed with new legislation relating to retirement.

The harbour works were continuing at pace with new link spans being put on place at the four north isles terminals and Kirkwall pier. At the same time, work was being carried out in Kirkwall basin. The basin was an ideal place for a new berth for the RNLI lifeboat and the piling and dredging would provide this much needed facility.

I should mention that there were three lifeboat stations in Orkney namely Kirkwall, Stromness, and Longhope. The latter two stations still had their lifeboats out at moorings. This was not the safest practice, as the crew had to proceed out to the lifeboat in a small motor launch to board in bad weather and in the dark was a daunting task, plus the time taken to get underway.

As a member of the Kirkwall Lifeboat Committee and a Deputy Launching Authority, I had several meetings with the powers that be within the RNLI. We agreed that progress should be made to have all three lifeboats provided with alongside berths. The first was to be the Kirkwall station with the new works in the basin providing an ideal sheltered berth on the west pier.

With a new extension being constructed on the south pier in Stromness a new lifeboat berth would be provided. The Longhope berth would take a few years longer to achieve. The Kirkwall facilities were all completed in summer of 1990 and the new shore station officially opened by the Princess royal on 14 July.

*Having a chat with the Princess Royal.*

*Kirkwall RNLI lifeboat station, West pier in 2019, not a great deal different from 1990, only the floating pontoon and gangway for safer and quicker access to the lifeboat.*

*My son Andrew opening the car door outside Kirkwall Town Hall.*

The two new ferries being constructed at Mctay Marine were progressing well. The Earl Sigurd had been towed round to Mctay Marine's subsidiary yard at Methil in Fife to be fitted out with; the Earl Thorfinn being completed at the yard in Bromborough. This meant travelling to two yards to attend meetings with our consultants and Mctay management.

The first ferry ready for acceptance trials was the Earl Thorfinn which I attended in the river Mersey. The trails went well with a few defects that the yard rectified and the ferry was ready for sailing up to Orkney. The crew were all up to speed having been onboard for some time and happy to be sailing home. There was quite a reception when the ferry did arrive alongside at Kirkwall pier with a great number of experts casting a critical eye at the ship.

*Arrival of Earl Thorfinn escorted by Orcadia, Islander, pilot launch, & Lifeboat.*

The Earl Sigurd was not ready for a few weeks and I attended once again for the trials in the Firth of Forth. Not such a positive sea trial as there were some 100 faults to be rectified. This would take another couple of weeks before she arrived home. I did not attend at the yard again as our consultants along with our engineering superintendent, the master and chief engineer were all onboard to confirm all faults were completed.

The naming ceremony for the ferries was set for 24 November at Kirkwall pier. The Earl Thorfinn to be named by Mrs J Scott, wife of the OISCO. Chairman and the Earl Sigurd by Mrs G Stevenson, Vice-chair. Once again, it was my task to make the necessary arrangements send out invitations. As it was mid-November we were worried about the weather. Fortunately, the Saturday turned out very nice and the naming went off without a hitch.

We had the two ferries tied up side by side with the two champagne bottles ready for their ribbons to be cut. There were a great number of guests as representatives from all the north isles were invited along with Councillors, officials and wives. A very successful buffet was provided onboard in the vehicle deck under cover.

## THE CONVENER OF ORKNEY ISLANDS COUNCIL

requests the pleasure of the company of

Capt & Mrs R C Sclater

at the NAMING CEREMONIES of M.V. *EARL THORFINN*
and M.V. *EARL SIGURD*

at

*KIRKWALL PIER on SATURDAY, 24th NOVEMBER 1990 at 12 noon*

The M.V. *EARL THORFINN* will be named by MRS J. SCOTT
The M.V. *EARL SIGURD* will be named by MRS G. STEVENSON

Finger Buffet on board following naming

R.S.V.P.
Director of Harbours,
Harbour Authority Building,
Scapa. Tel. 0856 - 3636

I should point out at this time that none of the ro/ro link spans were ready for the start of the service. Both ferries were fitted with cranes so the lift on lift off service continued for some time. When the new pier facilities were completed, opening ceremonies were also carried out at the four island terminals. The two older ferries the MV Orcadia and MV Islander were put on the market for sale through ship brokers and successful buyers were found.

I should also mention that both the ferries were purchased through a leasing agreement with Hambros bank on similar conditions as the two new tugs. In this instance, however, the Council had received full payment through the Scottish office grant and the ERDF (European Regional Development Fund) so the annual leasing payments were no problem for the Council's finance department.

*The photo of MV Earl Sigurd. The Earl Thorfinn was a sister ship with all details similar. The company was renamed Orkney Ferries early in the nineteen nineties.*

This was not the end of our new build programme as mentioned earlier, a dual-purpose ferry was required to cover the inner north isles and the south isles during refits and breakdowns. The naval architects IMT Marine Consultants were employed to carry out the design and tendering for the vessel. The documents were forwarded to 14 ship yards and the winning tender was received from Campbelltown shipyard in Argyle and Bute, tender details on following pages.

This was to be an interesting construction experience with the design for the vessel to operate successfully to hard ramps and link spans. The yard were very keen to prove their ability to meet our requirements and the vessel was completed in summer 1991. Once again, a naming ceremony was arranged and the invitations and the vessel details are on the next page. The ferry was to be named Thorsvoe, the name being chosen by local school children in the south isles.

The Harbours Department were also looking at new vessels out with the ferries and tugs. I always felt that a new pilot launch come work boat would be an asset with all the new harbour facilities requiring maintenance.

We contacted Murray Cormack; the architects involved in the design of our three pilot launches. They were happy to take up the challenge and designed a steel hulled pilot/tug/work launch to meet our requirements. The successful tender was won by Jones Buckie shipyard where the MV Shapinsay was fitted out. The shipyard was quite well known to us as they carried out the annual refits for our south isles' ferries.

I mentioned before our marine biology unit part of Dundee University which we paid an annual contract fee. In 1990, they stated that their costs were increasing and the annual payments were to increase by some 30%. I had discussions with the head of the biology unit at Scapa, Alex Simpson and asked if he would wish to become a direct employee of the Harbours Department and cut our ties with the Dundee University.

We worked out the costs of employing Alex and his assistant and the equipment required to carry out their monitoring of Orkney waters, especially Scapa flow due to the oil terminal activities. We came up with a reasonably accurate figure that showed we could, in fact, carry out the same work at much reduced sum than what the University was offering.

I submitted a report to Orkney Islands Council and it was agreed we would set up our own marine biology unit and dispense with our links to Dundee. The head of the biology unit, was not very happy with our decision but it was his own fault for trying to increase the costs by so much. He was so upset he sent some of his staff up to Orkney to take away equipment from the unit during an overnight raid. I only found out the next day after they had departed on the ferry that this had happened. I contacted him and said we were not impressed by his tactics and wished to meet with him to discuss the "robbery" as I believed a considerable amount of the documents and equipment taken had been paid for by the Council. I agreed to meet him in Aberdeen and arranged with my contacts at Aberdeen harbour board to allow us the use of their offices for this meeting. A representative of the Council's legal department attended with me and we eventually agreed that they could retain the documents and equipment they took but everything else remaining at Scapa would be in our ownership. A reasonable outcome, and to my mind we did the right thing as the biology unit was now part of Harbours Department and free to carry out more diverse duties and much more cost effective.

The unit was set prior to the oil terminal operations to ensure a monitoring system was in place that covered the before and after periods of an oil pollution. We made a saving of £80000 by taking over the unit, not a bad decision.

**IMT MARINE CONSULTANTS LTD.**
Naval Architects and Marine Engineers
THE BOAT HOUSE, 42a HILL STREET, ARBROATH DD11 1AB SCOTLAND
TEL. 0241-78370 FAX 0241-78373

FAX Nº- 0856·3012

ATTN:- CAPT. R.C. SCLATER - DIRECTOR OF HARBOURS


SUBJECT:- PROPOSED DUAL PURPOSE FERRY


ATTACHED TO THIS FAX IS A COPY OF THE LIST OF YARDS INVITED
TO TENDER FOR THE ABOVE VESSEL.
THE TENDER DOCUMENTS WILL BE POSTED WEDENSDAY 25TH. APRIL
AND WE WILL FORWARD A TYPED LIST OF THE YARDS, WITH NAMES,
ADDRESSES, PHONE & FAX NUMBERS ETC., ALONG WITH COPIES OF
THE TENDER DOCUMENTS.
WE HAVE INCLUDED A COPY OF THE 'CONTRACT' FOR "SHAPINSAY" WITH
THE "SHAPINSAY" CONTRACT DETAILS. LEFT BLANK.


*The details of shipyards tendering for MV Thorsvoe new hard ramp/ linkspan duel*
*purpose and stand by ferry.*


PROPOSED DUAL PURPOSE FERRY.              23·04-90


LIST OF YARDS QUOTING (DELIVERY SPRING/SUMMER 1991)   2 OF 2


1.  THE YORKSHIRE DRYDOCK CO. LTD, HULL
2.  JONES BUCKIE SHIPYARD LTD., BUCKIE
3.  HERD & MACKENZIE LTD., BUCKIE
4.  CAMPBELTOWN SHIPYARD LTD., CAMPBELTOWN
5.  RICHARD DUNSTONS (HESSLE) LTD.
6.  FERGUSON SHIPBUILDERS LTD.
7.  F.B.M. MARINE LTD., ISLE OF WIGHT
8.  AILSA - PERTH SHIPBUILDERS LTD., TROON
9.  APPLEDORE SHIPBUILDERS LTD., APPLEDORE, DEVON
10. A & P APPLEDORE (ABERDEEN) LTD., ABERDEEN.
11. AARDING MACHINEFABRIEK B.V., NUNSPEET, THE NETHERLANDS
12. PSA TRANSPORT LTD. LONDON (FOR WISŁA & UTSKA SHIPYARDS POLAND)
13. WILLY NESSIT, NORWAY (FOR SOUTH NORWAY SHIPYARDS ASSOC.).
14. P/F TÓRSHAVNAR SKIPASMIDJA, FAROE ISLES.

## THE CONVENER OF ORKNEY ISLANDS COUNCIL

requests the pleasure of the company of

*Capt. and Mrs R. C. Sclater*

at the NAMING CEREMONY of M.V. *THORSVOE*

at

*LYNESS PIER on MONDAY, 16th SEPTEMBER 1991 at 12 noon*

The M.V. *THORSVOE* will be named by COUNCILLOR MRS MAIRHI TRICKETT

**Guest of Honour Commissioner Bruce Millan, EEC**

Finger Buffet following naming

R.S.V.P.
Director of Harbours,
Harbour Authority Building,
Scapa Tel 0856 - 3636

M.V. *THORSVOE*
Dep. Houton 1100 hrs
Dep. Lyness 1400 hrs

You will note that the guest of honour was EEC commissioner Bruce Milan. The reason being that we had put forward a strong case to the EEC for grant funding for the ferry which we were successful in obtaining. This was a small gesture on our part of thanking them for the grant. The naming went off well with no problem with the bottle of champagne breaking on impact with the bow. I still carried a spare, just in case which I then presented to Councillor Trickett along with a framed photo of the MV Thorsvoe and the cork of the bottle used in the ceremony. I always did some fancy rope work with red, white and blue ribbons to set off the bottle. Every lady naming our vessels was presented with a framed photo of the vessel along with the decorated champagne cork.

*Thorsvoe*

*Decorated ever Champagne bottle used in naming ceremonies.*

Kirkwall bay alongside cross berth in Kirkwall basin. Multi-purpose vessel used for pilotage towage and general work boat fitted with small crane. The Scapa patrol was sold on the arrival of the Kirkwall bay.

The Kirkwall bay was officially named by the managing director of Jones shipyard. I did not attend but our craft superintendent did.

*The Kirkwall Bay*

The other vessels under construction at this time was an oil pollution catamaran, the Scapa lass. The department in consultation with Occidental had agreed in 1990 to set up a fund to cover the purchase of new oil pollution equipment. The department had very limited resources but the terminal was well equipped.

It was agreed to increase the harbour charges for all tankers by 3p per grt and use this money to purchase equipment. With the average vessels grt at 40,000 this gave us about £150000per annum to help with our purchases. The one item recommended, which was quite expensive was the new oil pollution vessel.

It was agreed to go ahead with the contract with part of the funding coming from the harbour equalisation fund.

This was a fund set up jointly with the Flotta terminal operators and the Council by charging all tankers using Flotta slightly more per GRT (gross registered tonnage) than other ports to ensure when oil through put decreased, there would be sufficient funds to keep the port operating even at a loss.

The fund was very healthy in 1991 with the prospect of oil flowing for several more years to come, so no problem with funding. The contract was awarded to a shipyard specialising in this type of vessel based in Portland Dorset. The Scapa lass was owned by OIC but operated by Occidental.

*Scapa Lass*

*Oil pollution equipment store at Flotta Oil Terminal*

In 1991, Occidental decided to dispose of its North Sea assets and its involvement with the Flotta terminal. Elf Enterprise Caledonia Ltd, took over the operation and we settled down into another good working relationship with the new owners. It was still a consortium with the other partners being Texaco Britain Ltd, Lasmo North Sea PLC&Union Texas petroleum Ltd. The company took up the challenge of re-establishing the piper field and bringing oil ashore from this ill-fated oil field, it would be a couple years before Piper Bravo came on stream.

I mentioned that we retained the Mt Kintore until our two new tugs Einar and Erland settled into harbour operations. After a couple of months, we realised that perhaps dropping to a two-tug operation was not a wise idea. The main reason being, breakdowns and refit cover. JP Knights did operate tugs in Invergordon, this is where the Keston, our original stand by tug was based.

It was felt, however, that we should not be dependent on outside towage cover and that a new tug be built. This took quite a lot of debate with the senior management at the oil terminal as they were keen to reduce the harbours operating costs, and three tugs would increase this.

However the new operators ELF were eventually in agreement and with their backing, we convinced Orkney Islands Council that a new tug be built. Once again, we sought the assistance of Wijsmuller to design and tender for this new vessel. They were very pleased to be involved and the tender documents were sent out to several shipyards. The successful tender was received from Appledore shipbuilders in Devon. The new tug would be named Harald another Norse Earl with strong Orkney connections.

There seemed to be no end to the new vessels being constructed and this was not to be the last.

The two new ferries for the north isles were settling down to their role but once again, refits and breakdown cover was a concern. The MV Varagen was still laid up in Grangemouth with nothing to do and with the short sea crossing put on hold; something needed to be done with this ferry. We had reports that it was not being well looked after in Grangemouth and that vagrants were sleeping onboard.

I went down to check these allegations but found them not quite correct. The ship however was not in good condition after two years in mothball. A report was submitted to Orkney ferries and the transportation committee highlighting the need for a relief ferry for the north isles and recommended that the Varagen be brought into service.

In August 1991, agreement was reached and the ferry was dry docked and its livery changed to that of Orkney Ferries. This resulted in the company not having to charter in cover during refits and break downs. It was also realised that the Earl Sigurd and Earl Thorfinn were not able to fully provide the ro/ro service to the north isles and the Varagen was an essential addition to the fleet. The Varagen had been purchased by the Short Sea Consortium under a leasing agreement with the British Linen bank and the Council continued with this leasing agreement.

*Varagen*

With Thorsvoe taking over the main south isles service, the Hoy Head was used as a standby vessel. The Lywara Bay was placed on the market and successfully sold. Once again, it was realised that with the Thorsvoe being the relief vessel for the Shapinsay and Eynhallow, the Hoy Head would not be capable of handling the traffic to the south isles on her own and a larger ferry was required.

I submitted a report to Orkney ferries and the transportation committee of OIC outlining the problem. Of course, the cost of another ferry did not go down very well with Councillors. I did point out that the Hoy Head was in fact built in 1973 and maintenance costs would be increasing. Also, she could only carry ten cars.

Agreement was reached on building a new ferry and that the contract would be for a design and build by the successful yard. By this time, we had a very good rapport with Appledore shipbuilders building the Mt Harald and they came up with a very competitive quote and a very basic design. The contract was signed for the new Hoy Head that would arrive in 1994.

After the sale of the Scapa Patrol, I presented a report to the Council for a replacement of the Scapa Pilot similar to the Scapa Pathfinder. The new pilot launch was once again designed by Murray Cormack associates.

The contract was won by FBM Marine in Cowes isle of Wight. The new pilot launch would be named Scapa Pioneer and would arrive in summer 1993.

I took the bold step of arranging the naming of the Scapa Pioneer to take place at the international work boat show in Portsmouth where FBM wished to put the launch on display. As all other naming ceremonies had been carried out by Councillor's wives, I decided without informing the Council that on this occasion my wife, Anna would have the honour of naming the Scapa Pioneer.

I am sure if I had mentioned this to the Councillors, I would have been told that this was not allowed. Anyway, Anna and I drove down to Portsmouth and had a lovely day with the FBM management and our naval architects along with Jim Mitchell, our craft superintendent. Anna was a very proud lady on the day and the naming went without a hitch. A lovely buffet and drinks were enjoyed onboard by all the guest and then a relaxing dinner in the evening.

It was a pleasure to attend a naming that I did not have to arrange. I did, of course, present the yard and our designers with a Council plaque and a bottle of Highland Park whisky. I never did mention the occasion to Councillors although most of the harbour staff were aware of the naming.

*Anna naming the Scapa Pioneer. She pressed a button on the rail, this released the champagne bottle that broke on the deck of the launch into a controlled space so no damage or loose glass lying about.*

On the
Occasion of the
naming of the
SCAPA PIONEER
23 June 1993.

To mrs Sclater

With thanks
from
FBM MARINE LTD
COWES IOW

*A nice bouquet of flowers that eventually reached home after a couple of days driving north. A toast to the new pilot launch.*

The service between Westray and Papa Westray also required some sort of link. We set to and refurbished the Golden Mariana to provide this passenger and small cargo operation previously carried out by a private operator from Pierowal. Orkney Ferries had always provided a weekly service to Papa Westray and this would continue with the new vessels. There were no linkspans in both Papa Westray or North Ronaldsay but with the two Earls fitted with cranes there was no change in the service they had received from the older lift on lift off ferries.

The other addition to our fleet was a small motor launch the Scapa protector for use by our scientific officer, Alex Simpson in our own new biology unit.

I may as well just finish off the new vessels in this section by including the last new build being the MV Graemsay. The existing ferry service was run by a private operator between Stromness and the island of Graemsay and Moaness in north Hoy. This was basically a passenger launch carrying small parcels etc.

Orkney ferries provided a lift on lift off service to Graemsay once a week with the ro/ro ferries. North Hoy did not require this as all the main traffic came via the Houton to Lyness link span. The private operator was only too happy for Orkney Ferries to take over this responsibility and he would then be employed as skipper on the Graemsay and paid a salary.

The Graemsay would not be in service until summer 1996, so I will be back tracking quite a bit with my story as there was a hundred and one things happening within the department during the first six years of the nineteen nineties. Anyway, the naval architects Murray Cormack associates were engaged to design and tender on our behalf for the new ferry.

Dennis Davidson who designed the Kirkwall bay, came up with an excellent design and we went out to tender for the vessel. In fact, the hull was based on the design of the Kirkwall Bay, although looking at the two-vessels, difficult to see this. We also asked that the Graemsay be able to act as a small tug boat to assist the larger P&O ferries operating into Stromness who may require assistance in windy conditions.

The successful tender was received from Alisa Troon shipbuilders. The construction progressed well until the yard went into receivership. This was a big blow to us as the ferry was only about two thirds complete.

On receiving this news, I went down to the yard to meet with the receivers and obtained agreement that work would continue on completing the Graemsay. After a long meeting, we eventually agreed a way forward but of course at extra cost to the Council.

After returning home I once again had to report to the Council on these extras. As we had no alternative but to agree these extras the yard continued with the construction. The yard continued with everyone still employed with no change in the management or staff.

The receivers were still running the yard when the Graemsay was completed and we did have some outstanding payments due that I disagreed with. I arranged for our crew at the yard to take the vessel and head home with it. The skipper was Stevie Mowat, the private operator of the service, now an Orkney ferries employee along with an engineer and two deck hands.

I don't think the receivers were too happy that we just took the boat and left. There was an outstanding payment for the two main engines that I believed we had paid for, prior to the yard going into liquidation and I refused to pay again. My successor Captain Bob Moore succumbed to their demands in 1999 after I retired. The vessel eventually arrived home in July 1996 much to our relief. Another naming ceremony was to take place on the island of Graemsay by Councillor Ann Sutherland on 24 August.

As there was a growing demand for space on the Eynhallow, it was agreed to lengthen her by five metres to meet the requirements on this route. This was carried out during a refit at Jones of Buckie ship yard. As no official naming had taken place when the ferry arrived in 1987, the community on Rousey, Egilsay, and Wyre requested one and they would organise it.

I was happy for this to take place and the community Council arranged everything and a few guests from the mainland travelled over on the ferry on a Friday evening where the ferry was officially named by Mrs Ian Flaws, the skipper of the Eynhallow. After the ceremony a lovely buffet supper and dance was held in the community hall.

The guests from the mainland returned on the ferry just before midnight and the ferry was back in service the next morning. This was another naming with few Councillors invited, on this occasion, nothing to do with me. I don't think we actually received an official invitation as I'm unable to find a copy.

The new HOY HEAD arrived home in March 1994 and of course, once again big naming in Flotta. I will touch on this one in slightly more detail later on.

As we now had all these vessels to look after and the requirement for spare parts was essential, it was once again agreed that new buildings should be constructed at the harbour offices to provide storage and engineering back up for our fleet.

The two oil dispersant tank trailers were dispatched to the airport for storage as they were for aerial spraying and belonged to the department of transport so need for us to look after them. This gave us additional space and we eventually had a very comprehensive set of storerooms and workshops for all three section of the department, harbours, towage, ferries.

*Harbour Authority Building with new storage buildings on right hand side of picture.*

# M.T. "HARALD"

| | | | |
|---|---|---|---|
| **LENGTH O.A.** | 32.0 m | **FUEL CAPACITY** | 91.0 tonnes |
| **BREADTH MLD** | 10.0 m | **F.W. CAPACITY** | 40.0 tonnes |
| **SUMMER DRAUGHT** | 4.78 m | **DISPERSANT CAPACITY** | 12.0 tonnes |
| **TRIAL SPEED** | 12.8 knots | **FOAM CAPACITY** | 12.0 tonnes |
| **B.P. AHEAD** | 55 tonnes | **B.P. ASTERN** | 50 tonnes |

**MAIN ENGINES** – 2 off RUSTON 6RK270M developing 1492 KW each at 900 rpm

**PROPULSION** – 2 off AQUAMASTER US2001/UNIT driven through twin disc M.C.D. units

**GENERATORS** – 2 off 110 KW Alternator driven by Volvo TMD 122A
1 off 220 KW Alternator driven by Volvo TAMD 122A

**DECK MACHINERY** – Norwinch Hydraulic anchor windlass/tow winch (FWD)
tow winch (AFT)

*Details:* 10 m/min at 30 ton pull (40 ton stall)
Brake capacities 160 ton
Auto tension controls with indicators
Effer knuckle boom hydraulic crane 44 tonnes metre

**FIRE PUMPS** – 2 off 360 m²/hour at 135m head each driven by Volvo TMD 122A
supplying 2 remote operated monitors

**LLOYDS CLASS** – 100 A1 TUG LMC UMS; D.O.T. CLASS IX

---

*The details of Harold and naming ceremony invitation, I have spent a lot of time on this subject and it is perhaps not in sequence but it just highlights the work out with normal harbour operations that I was responsible for.*

# THE DIRECTORS OF ORKNEY TOWAGE COMPANY LTD

request the pleasure of the company of

*Capt & Mrs R. C. Sclater*

at the NAMING CEREMONY of M.T. HARALD

at SCAPA PIER on THURSDAY, 12th NOVEMBER, 1992 at 12.30 p.m.
and thereafter to a FINGER BUFFET at the Harbour Authority Building, Scapa

The M.T. HARALD will be named by Mrs H. HALCRO-JOHNSTON

R.S.V.P.
Executive Director
Orkney Towage Co. Ltd.
Harbour Authority Building
Scapa   Tel. (0856) 873636

I certainly spent many days away from home visiting all the shipyards and attending building programme meetings some quite difficult and challenging, getting best value for the Council. Doubt if any other harbour master had such an interesting job. Of course, there is lots more stories to come but hopefully this part is of some interest.

*Scapa Pathfinder and Scapa Pioneer with the Erlend, Harald and Einar alongside the extended Scapa pier. You can see the Yokahama fenders ready for the next ship to ship (STS) lying on the outside of the pier. The four new oil manifolds are just at the bow of the Scapa Pathfinder.*

*Model of our tugs built by skipper of Wijsmuller tug in Amsterdam presented to David Shearer and myself back in 1987 by Sven Aarts.*

When the Einar and Erlend were built, they had overboard exhausts instead of funnels. This was not really suitable for Orkney and corrosion became a serious problem. It was agreed that funnels should be installed and you can see from this photo, the two funnels on the Einar.

The Harald was built with funnels as we were aware of the corrosion problems by the time we tendered for her.

*Golden Mariana*

*The Golden Mariana refurbished to operate on the Westray to Papa Westray route. A much smarter ferry than the original design.*

The Marine Biology Unit's work boat. They carried out monitoring of the waters around Orkney and especially Scapa flow. Over the years, there was very little problems with the environment as the oil terminal was a very efficient operation. We did have small oil spills as can be seen from details on a previous page. After the Eva spill, a new system was put in place where the floating oil pipes at the SPM's were no longer back flushed after loading with sea water.

This had been the cause of several small leakages when the ship's sea valves were open to pump sea water any residual oil from previous cargoes in the line would run out before pumping got under way. The Marine Biology Unit under the control of Alex Simpson commenced drawing up a new oil pollution plan that covered the whole of Orkney. This consisted of every kilometre square of beach photographed and details of beach make up being taken and logged. This took a few years, but in the end, we had the most comprehensive oil pollution plan in the UK, I will cover the oil pollution planning later.

*A fine aerial view of Kirkwall harbour showing the extension, marshalling area,
Shapinsay slip, lifeboat berth and new Orkney ferries offices at entrance to the pier.
New marina would be installed in 2002/04 story later on.*

*Being Presented with a Model Orkney Dinghy*

Captain Max Gunn being presented with a model Orkney dinghy by myself
at the buffet and dance following the Hoy Head naming. Max was due to retire

as Flotta terminal manager shortly after this and I thought it a nice opportunity to mark the occasion with so many Flotta residents at the party.

Max and I had been firm friends since he interviewed me back in 1976 for a mooring masters post. We had both climbed the ladder since then, he being head at Flotta and me in charge at the harbours. Two staunch Orcadian master mariners, a one-off team.

## THE CONVENER OF ORKNEY ISLANDS COUNCIL

requests the pleasure of the company of

*Capt & Mrs R. C. Sclater*

at the NAMING CEREMONY of M.V. HOY HEAD

at

GIBRALTAR PIER, FLOTTA on FRIDAY, 29th APRIL, 1994 at 1930 hours

The M.V. HOY HEAD will be named by MRS MABEL BESANT

**Buffet and Dance to follow**

R.S.V.P.
Director of Harbours,
Harbour Authority Building,
Scapa    Tel. 0856 873636
by 25th April

*M.V. HOY HEAD*
*Dep. Houton 1845*
*Dep. Flotta  0030*
*Bus dep. Broad St. 1815*

*Hoy Head*

The naming ceremony went well but unfortunately, the weather on the day was low cloud and misty. This resulted in several of our guest from south not arriving due to Kirkwall airport being closed by the weather. One being Jim Wilson md of Appledore shipyard and his daughter.

Jim had enjoyed the Harald naming so much he was determined to attend the Hoy Head. Instead, they had to spend the night in Aberdeen and flew back to Bristol the next day. After the bottle of champagne was broken everyone was invited to the "Flotta Hilton" the oil terminal's accommodation and restaurant establishment situated outside the security area of the terminal.

A free bar was available and everyone enjoyed a toast to the new ferry. As usual some enjoyed the free drink a bit too much and when time came to depart for buffet and dance we had a job to get everyone on the bus for the short run to the community hall.

The terminal staff set off the fire alarm which did get everyone out when the terminal fire brigade arrived. The evening went well and everyone eventually caught the ferries back to Houton and Lyness.

## THE CHAIRMAN of ORKNEY FERRIES LIMITED

requests the pleasure of the company of

*Capt and Mrs R.C Sclater*

at the NAMING CEREMONY of M.V. GRAEMSAY

at

GRAEMSAY PIER on SATURDAY, 24th AUGUST, 1996 at 1200 hours

The M.V. GRAEMSAY will be named by COUNCILLOR ANNE SUTHERLAND

**Buffet to follow**

| R.S.V.P. | | |
|---|---|---|
| Executive Director, | *M.V. GRAEMSAY* | *M.V. THORSVOE* |
| Harbour Authority Building, | Dep. Moaness 1130 | Dep. Stromness 1130 |
| Scapa   Tel. 01856 873636 | Dep. Graemsay 1400 | Dep. Graemsay 1400 |
| by 15th August, 1996 | | Bus dep. Council Offices 1045 |

*Just to finish off the new ferries photos of the MV Gramesay naming.*

*Councillor Ann Sutherland*

It was a lovely day for the naming with the MV Thorsvoe being utilised to transport the guests to Graemsay and as the catering vessel with the buffet lunch set on its deck. The Graemsay ferried guests from north Hoy. The naming went as planned with the champagne bottle breaking first time. The photo of Councillor Ann Sutherland is the only photo I have of any of the ladies holding a photo of their named vessel and the spare bottle of champagne.

The Graemsay was built to operate to a link span with a stern door ramp. I tried hard for the rest of my time as director to have a ramp put in place alongside Graemsay pier, as the vessel could operate to the Stromness link span. I could never get the Councillors or the engineering department to accept my proposals. It would have made life much easier for the residents if they had a ro/ro service.

With the Graemsay being the last of our new ferries, I believe we had the most modern and updated fleet in the UK. All our vessels complied fully with the ISM (International Ship Management Code) where applicable.

Over the past 26 years, the department has only built two pilot launchs & two 'of the shelve' tugs and had to lengthen the Shapinsay, Hoy Head and the Graemsay to meet growing demand. In 2020 they purchased a second hand ferry from Norway to replace the Golden Marina ( been a bit of a problem vessel). I had thought that a replacement programme would have been in place by now. In 2003, I became chairman of The Transportation and Infrastructure Committee of OIC and tried my best to get a replacement scenario in place. I did have everything drawn up with the help of consultants and a logical case for replacing the ferries and up grading piers. I, unfortunately, retired fully in 2007 and the documents for this replacement programme were shelved. I will touch on this later in my story.

As I am now up to date with all my ferries, tugs, pilot launches I can get back to more detailed harbour activities. My next chapters will go back to 1990 and cover oil pollution, accidents, cruise ships, HMS Royal Oak, scuttling of German Grand Fleet in June 1919, its aftermath and how it impacted on the harbours department, the Braer incident in Shetland and Lord Donaldson's report, and no doubt a few other issues.

# Part 6

Back in time now after the naming of the Graemsay in 1996. There was a considerable amount of promotional work to be carried out to ensure Orkney harbours stayed prominent on the map as far as further oil activities, cruise liners and general harbour operations were concerned.

Firstly, I will cover the cruise liner industry. Orkney was a popular destination for many years prior to 1990 but the industry was on the up and many other European ports were in the business of attracting liners. In December 1991, an EGM of the budding Cruise Europe organisation was set to be held in Copenhagen.

I was invited to attend along with 20 other port authorities. This was to be our introduction to other cruise port authorities. The main attendees from north of Scotland being Invergordon, Lerwick and Orkney. I travelled over to Copenhagen with Lerwick, port authorities chief executive, Alan Wishart. We met up with a young lady from Glasgow port authority as our flights took us through Glasgow.

I cannot remember her first name but her surname was Montgomery-Smith. I mention this because her father turned out to be a marine architect involved in designing yachting marinas, something I will cover after the cruise section. We arrived in Copenhagen and met up with the other delegates and had an interesting get together and Orkney became a paid-up member of Cruise Europe.

The first AGM was held in November 1992 in Amsterdam and once again, I attended and found it very informative. By this time, I was looking at how best to promote Orkney to further increase our cruise traffic. Most of the Cruise Europe members attended the main cruise industry conference and exhibition in Miami. I was unsure if Orkney Islands Council would allow me to travel to Miami.

After being a member for two years, I felt that we should attend as Invergordon and Lerwick were also attending this prestigious event. I was given permission to attend but reluctantly by some Councillors. With the help of

Captain Bob Moore we designed a cruise Orkney brochure and also obtained copies of the Orkney tourist board's brochure.

I also made contact with the Highland Park distillery and they agreed to send a case of whiskey to my hotel in Miami to use as gifts to various top cruise operator executives. With my case full of brochures, I set off to Miami in March 1994. I should mention that I hired a kilt and all the accessories so I looked as good as the Invergordon delegates who had been attending this conference for many years and always wore the kilt.

The team from Shetland on this first occasion did not wear the kilt but in 1995, the chairman of Lerwick harbour trust did (photos on following pages). The trip was well worthwhile and I made good contacts with various top cruise line executives. On arrival home, I continued my follow up by sending out over 20 copies of Charles Tait's new Orkney guide book to cruise operators.

I attended again in 1995 and once again made some good contacts. The main contact on this visit was the cruise director from Cunard and I managed to persuade him to pencil in a visit of the QE2 one of the most famous cruise ships in the world at that time.

The visit would not take place until 1998 as most of these larger cruise ship itineraries were set a couple of years in advance. I attended four more AGMs of cruise Europe in Guernsey, Bordeaux, Amsterdam, and Invergordon. Had a great time in Bordeaux as Anna accompanied me on that visit.

The one in Amsterdam, we had a reception in the RIJKS museum quite a treat having a drink next to Rembrandts Night Watch. The final one in Invergordon was very handy and once again Anna accompanied me, it was always nice for the wives to attend.

Tim Harris, CEO of P&O Cruises, made a far-sighted remark during his conference speech by forecasting that over the next decade cruising would become a truly worldwide industry though the Caribbean would still remain its main volume base. Moreover John Teets, Chairman, President and CEO of the giant Dial Corporation which owned Premier Cruises, who was one of several executives to visit the Cruise Europe stand thanks to prompting by the president Aris Zarpanely, said he thought that 'Cruise Europe was doing the right thing at just the right time.' Several other cruise executives shared these sentiments and the membership could derive satisfaction that their efforts had placed Northern Europe more firmly the cruising map.

That April, the secretary/treasurer produced a first simple newsletter but production was sporadic and only three of these had appeared before new arrangements needed to be made.

The Cruise Europe message was still fresh in the minds of US-based executives when Mike Meyjes and Gunnar Lepsøe visited them that autumn. They were keen to gather as much information as possible about the new organisation and what its ports and local tourist attractions could offer, expressing a preference for it to be provided on a computer diskette rather than by means of a plethora of individual brochures. At that time the use of computers was still in its infancy but it nevertheless spurred on the Cruise Europe executive to work towards producing one.

### FIRST AGM 1992 - AMSTERDAM

*An interesting speech at the Miami conference in 1992 on the following page, cruising has come a long way since these early days.*

The Orkney Islands Council's Marine Services Department as it is now known, has everything computerised and with up to 170 cruise ships expected in 2019, the above forecast did come true. Things have moved on since I started writing with coronavirus resulting in a complete downturn in 2020/21. The number of cruises liners for 2022 are back up to pre covid. We were certainly the trail blazers back in 1992.

The Scottish tourist board, now Visit Scotland, became interested in the cruise industry and set up a meeting with the Scottish ports members of cruise Europe. I think the tourist board felt a bit left out of this budding industry and it was agreed to set up cruise Scotland.

This was a good idea as the tourist board had considerably more influence and funding for promoting Scotland than the ports. We all became members of cruise Scotland as well and liaised with our own local tourist boards in promoting our areas to the cruise industry. I recall in the early days, there was some disquiet from certain members of the tourist board and general public on the number of liners visiting Orkney in the summer months. The complaint being the number of busloads of passengers visiting Skara brae, ring of Brodgar, Maeshow and the

Italian chapel etc. Compared to today (2019), the numbers then was quite small. As time went on, however, most people accepted the cruise liners and the financial benefit to Orkney.

Next pages, our cruise brochure and a few photos relating to my attendance at cruise Miami, landing pontoons in Kirkwall basin and visit of QE2.

*Iain Dunderdale, myself and Gordon Ireland, looking good in our kilts, on our stand in Miami, March 1994. Iain and Gordon represent Invergordon.*

*Myself, on our stand and with chairman Tom Stove and chief executive Alan Wishart of Lerwick harbour board March 1994. Both Tom and Alan had their wives with them. Had our photo in the sea trade magazine the same year with the Invergordon team.*

# Seatrade Today

*News of the Seatrade Cruise Shipping Convention*     Thursday, March 3, 1994

**Fitness Fun** *Under the direction of marketing director Steve Honigsberg, Anne-Marie Bainbridge tries out a multi-station gym at the Institutional Sales Corporation booth on the Seatrade exhibition floor. Institutional is exhibiting a full line of exercise equipment at booth 214.*

## Cruise Executives Call for Grass Roots Campaign to Defeat Clay Bill in Congress

A call for grass roots support in the cruise industry's ongoing debate against so-called unnecessary government regulation went out to Seatrade delegates from International Council of Cruise Lines President Richard Fain at the "State of the Industry" session Wednesday.

Fain, chief executive officer of Royal Caribbean Cruise Line, and five other cruise executives dealt with the Clay and Gibbons bills and the future of cruising, emphasizing strong market position, brand identification and careful pricing to enable market leaders to remain strong and smaller operators to succeed in their target markets.

**Tim Harris,** chairman of Princess Cruises, said only 10 percent of potential cruise passengers are actually sailing, although the industry has enjoyed a 15 percent sales increase since 1992. He noted the trend to build new, larger-tonnage ships will create more cost efficiency.

*Continued on Page 2*

## New Market Segments, Onboard Activities Cited As Industry Trends

Cruise marketing strategies took center stage Wednesday as Seatrade delegates received an up-to-the-minute briefing on recent innovations to convince more vacationers to choose holidays at sea.

"Our single most important effort must be to entice, invite and educate the millions of prospects in every country that a cruise is the most relaxing, rewarding and best value holiday money can buy," said Paul H. Mundy, chairman of the recently-established Guild of Professional Cruise Agents (UK).

**Carnival Cruise Lines** vice president Marketing Services, Geri Donnelly said there are some 100 million persons who haven't yet cruised. She added potential customers in peak-earning years are more numerous now than at any other time.

**Brian Kravitz,** vice president, Marketing & Sales Promotion, Liberty Travel/Go Go Tours, called for refinements in onboard programs, such as diversity of dining options and more sports activities.

Noting his emerging segment of the cruise industry is "the most price-insulated market in cruising today," Bruce Nierenberg, chairman of American Family Cruises, said family vacations at sea are inherent values and a new trend.

**NCL vice president** of sales, Jacquelyn Johnson, said the company's revitalized marketing includes stylish new advertising that caused a 20 percent increase in reservation calls after it was aired during the Super Bowl.

**Port Party** *Enjoying a fun moment at Wednesday evening's Port of Miami party are, left-to-right, Gordon Ireland, Iain Dunderdale, Seatrade staffer Laura Paris and Robert Sclater. The three men represent ports in Scotland.*

**INSIDE**  Today's conference agenda. *Page 2.*  ·  Key West benefits from Seatrade. *Page 3.*  ·  Experience Miami's attractions. *Page 4.*

*Arriving at 1995 convention with another case of Highland Park whisky. Was a great way to get attention as all delegates were keen to get a bottle.*

*With Tavish Scott, then chairman of Lerwick Harbour Trust, (eventually became a leading MSP) and a lovely Mermaid. Meeting Tavish came in very handy as we had considerable dealings when he became Transport Minister in the Scottish Parliament and I an Orkney Island Councillor. Will cover this later in my story.*

The cruise industry had numerous photographic companies travelling onboard vessels taking photos on every occasion possible. They used many gimmicks to lure passengers to have their photo taken. Photos at the convention were all supplied free of charge.

On next page away ahead with my story showing the 1998 cruise liners visiting Orkney with the QE2 arriving on 1 August. Even back in 1998, we did have numerous liners visiting, in fact, we were the top destination in Scotland. I did not attend Miami after 1995 as I believed I had sowed the seed for the cruise industry to come to Orkney and I had so many other things going on within the department.

*QE2 arriving at Kirkwall pilot station. I boarded with the duty pilot for the trip into Kirkwall Harbour quite an experience.*

*Presenting Captain Warwick with Orkney Islands Council Plaque*

# CUNARD
## Captain R. W. Warwick
*Master*
*Queen Elizabeth 2*

Cunard Line Ltd.

- Mountbatten House, Grosvenor Square, Southampton SO15 2BF. U.K
  Tel: (01703) 716500  Fax: (01703) 225843  Telex: 477577
- 6100 Blue Lagoon Drive, Suite 400, Miami, Florida 33126 U.S.A.
  Tel: (305) 463-3000  Fax: (305) 463-3010  Toll-Free: (800) 5 CUNARD

*Anna and I on the bridge prior to sailing. We were offered a trip to the pilot station but Anna was not sure she could disembark onto the pilot launch so we left the ship before she left the anchorage.*

*Cruise line tender and Viking Longship alongside pontoons Kirkwall Harbour basin.*

Our alongside berths for liners was very limited as they were not deep enough or the piers long enough for the larger cruise ships. This required passengers to be ferried ashore in ships lifeboats. They disembarked at the stone steps on the pier not really very safe as they could be quite slippery. I contacted a company in Morayshire who designed Marina Pontoons and received a quote that I presented to the Council. It was agreed to install one set as a trial alongside the inner basin wall.

It was a great success and we then proceeded to install pontoons the full length of the harbour wall with two gangways one at each end. I had tried to get the engineering department at the Council to assist but they were not interested and said that it was not feasible, how wrong they were.

| Date | Vessel | Max PAX Capacity* | LOA | DRAFT | FROM | ETA | ETS | TO | BERTH | AGT |
|------|--------|-------------------|-----|-------|------|-----|-----|-----|-------|-----|
| 6/7 April | Kong Harald | 691 | 121.8m | 4.70m | Lerwick | 0800 | 1200 | Bergen | Kirkwall Pier | O Line |
| 9/11 April | Nordkapp | 883 | 123.30m | 4.90m | Lerwick | 1000 | 1200 | Bergen | Kirkwall Pier | J Jolly |
| 11/12 April | Kong Harald | 691 | 106.40m | 4.70m | Bergen | 1300 | 1200 | Lerwick | Kirkwall Pier | O Line |
| 27/29 April | Nordkapp | 883 | 123.30m | 4.90m | Lerwick | 1000 | 1200 | Bergen | Kirkwall Pier | J Jolly |
| 15 May | Princess Danae | 420 | 162.31m | 7.80m | Invergordon | 0800 | 1400 | Oban | Kirkwall ± | J Jolly |
| 19 May | Funchal | 460 | 152.65m | 6.18m | Stornoway | 0800 | 1900 | Lerwick | Kirkwall ± | J Jolly |
| 24 May (S) | Funchal | 460 | 152.65m | 6.18m | Scrabster | 0800 | 1900 | Stornoway | Kirkwall ± | J Jolly |
| 25 May | Jason | 310 | 101.60m | 5.50m | Dover | 1300 | 2000 | Lerwick | Kirkwall Pier | J Jolly |
| 29 May | Black Prince | 430 | 143.45m | 6.13m | Bergen | 1100 | 1600 | Leith | Kirkwall ± | J Jolly |
| 5 June | Pacific Princess | 600 | 168.80m | 7.70m | Glasgow | 0630 | 1800 | Invergordon | Kirkwall ± | J Jolly |
| 9 June | Europa | 600 | 199.62m | 8.53m | Portree | 0800 | 1900 | Invergordon | Kirkwall ± | J Jolly |
| 10 June | Caledonian Star | 130 | 89.20m | 6.80m | Flannan Is. | 0900 | 2200 | Noss Is. | Kirkwall ± | J Jolly |
| 14 June (S) | Caledonian Star | 130 | 89.20m | 6.80m | Fair Isle | 0600 | 1930 | Inverewe | Kirkwall± / Shapinsay | J Jolly |
| 14 June (S) | Black Prince | 430 | 143.45m | 6.13m | Leith | 0800 | 1330 | Olden | Kirkwall ± | J Jolly |
| 15 June | Black Watch | 891 | 205.50m | 7.60m | Amsterdam | 0800 | 1400 | Honningsvag | Kirkwall ± | J Jolly |
| 15 June | Clipper Adventurer | 122 | 100.00m | 4.66m | Rhum | 0900 | 1600 | Muckle Sound | Stromness Pier | J Jolly |
| 19 June | Clipper Adventurer | 122 | 100.00m | 4.66m | Edinburgh | 0900 | 2400 | Fair Isle | Stromness Pier/ Kirkwall/ Shapinsay | J Jolly |
| 19 June | Albatros | 751 | 185.39m | 8.94m | Bremerhaven | 0700 | 1300 | Reykjavik | Kirkwall ± | J Jolly |
| 28 June | Astor | 550 | 176.50m | 6.10m | Bremerhaven | 0700 | 1300 | Reykjavik | Kirkwall ± | Elbreck |
| 30 June | Minerva | 300 | 133.00m | 5.75m | Invergordon | 0700 | 1430 | Lerwick | Kirkwall ± | J Jolly |
| 3 July | Jaison | 310 | 101.60m | 5.50m | Lerwick | 0700 | 1400 | Dover | Kirkwall Pier | J Jolly |
| 3/4 July | Hebridean Princess | 50 | 71.63m | 2.75m | Invergordon | 1600 | 1700 | Norway | Stromness Pier | HIC |
| 4 July | Caledonian Star | 130 | 89.20m | 6.80m | Lerwick | 0700 | 2000 | Aberdeen | Kirkwall± / Shapinsay | J Jolly |
| 06 July | Maxim Gorkiy | 600 | 194.70m | 8.27m | Bremerhaven | 0700 | 1300 | Reykjavik | Kirkwall ± | J Jolly |
| 08 July | Caledonian Star | 130 | 89.20m | 6.80m | Aberdeen | 0700 | 2000 | Lerwick | Kirkwall± / Shapinsay | J Jolly |
| 09 July | Vistamar | 300 | 120.80m | 4.49m | Leith | 0900 | 1400 | Thorshavn | Kirkwall Pier | Inch |
| 12 July (S) | Bremen | 184 | 111.50m | 4.50m | Brunsbuttel | 0800 | 1600 | Iceland | Kirkwall Pier | J Jolly |
| 14 July | Astor | 550 | 176.50m | 6.10m | Bremerhaven | 0700 | 1300 | Reykjavik | Kirkwall ± | Elbreck |
| 14/15 July | Hebridean Princess | 50 | 71.63m | 2.75m | Lerwick | 1700 | 1300 | Oban | Kirkwall Pier | HIC |
| 17 July | Berlin | 470 | 139.30m | 4.80m | Torshavn | 0900 | 1700 | Leith | Kirkwall ± | Inch |
| 21 July | Royal Viking Sun | 760 | 204.00m | 7.30m | Tobermory | 0800 | 1800 | Edinburgh | Kirkwall ± | J Jolly |
| 23 July | World Renaissance | 457 | 150.10m | 6.50m | Zeebrugge | 0800 | 1400 | Akureyri | Kirkwall ± | J Jolly |
| 27 July | Black Prince | 430 | 143.45m | 6.13m | Dover | 0700 | 1300 | Reykjavik | Kirkwall ± | J Jolly |
| 28 July | Caledonian Star | 130 | 89.20m | 6.80m | Inverewe | 0800 | 2000 | Fair Isle | Shapinsay/ Kirkwall± | J Jolly |
| 30 July | Astra II | 460 | 130.20m | 5.50m | Oban | 1300 | 1800 | Inverness | Kirkwall Pier | J Jolly |
| 31 July | Delphin | 600 | 156.30m | 6.20m | Leith | 1000 | 2100 | Invergordon | Kirkwall ± | J Jolly |
| 1 Aug | Queen Elizabeth 2 | 1,952 | 293.50m | 10.53m | Bergen | 0800 | 1800 | Leith | Kirkwall ± | J Jolly |
| 1 Aug | Vistamar | 300 | 120.80m | 4.49m | Hamburg | 0900 | 1400 | Thorshavn | Kirkwall Pier | Inch |
| 2 Aug (S) | Silver Cloud | 314 | 155.00m | 5.40m | Amsterdam | 0800 | 1300 | Konigsfjord | Kirkwall ± | J Jolly |
| 2 Aug (S) | Caledonian Star | 130 | 89.20m | 6.80m | Invergordon | 0600 | 2000 | Stornoway | Shapinsay/ Kirkwall ± | J Jolly |
| 13 Aug | Black Prince | 430 | 143.45m | 6.13m | Tobermory | 1000 | 1500 | Leith | Kirkwall ± | J Jolly |
| 16 Aug (S) | Pacific Princess | 600 | 168.80m | 7.70m | Glasgow | 0700 | 1800 | Invergordon | Kirkwall ± | J Jolly |
| 16 Aug (S) | Black Prince | 430 | 143.45m | 6.13m | Leith | 0830 | 1500 | Tobermory | Kirkwall ± | J Jolly |
| 16 Aug (S) | Caledonian Star | 130 | 89.20m | 6.80m | Stornoway | 0800 | 1900 | Invergordon | Shapinsay/ Kirkwall ± | J Jolly |
| 22 Aug | Caledonian Star | 130 | 89.20m | 6.80m | Invergordon | 0600 | 2000 | Stornoway | Shapinsay/ Kirkwall ± | J Jolly |
| 25 Aug | Deutschland | 620 | 175.00m | 6.0m | Bergen | 0900 | 1300 | Leith | Kirkwall ± | Inch |
| 27 Aug | Princess Danae | 420 | 162.31m | 7.8m | Dundee | 0700 | 1400 | Oban | Kirkwall ± | J Jolly |
| 8 Sept | Silver Cloud | 314 | 155.00m | 5.40m | Leith | 1300 | 1800 | Torshavn | Kirkwall ± | J Jolly |

**As at 8 June 1998, 48 Calls in Total**
S = Sunday *Above passenger capacity does not necessarily reflect actual passenger numbers on board

I mentioned the young lady from Clyde port authority who accompanied us to Copenhagen and her father a marine architect dealing with marinas. I had given her my card and asked her to let her father know that I was interested in trying to persuade the Council to install marina facilities in both Kirkwall and Stromness.

I received a letter from him indicating he would be happy to carry out a survey and provide a feasibility report on this subject. I presented a report to the transportation committee and they agreed to meet the costs and fees for the study set at £1000 plus expenses, not a great deal for a consultant. Anyway, Mr Montgomery-smith arrived in March 1992 and carried out his study.

Unfortunately, I do not have any copies of the study but the marina facilities eventually constructed were in the exact position his report detailed. The Council noted my report but would not give the go ahead and it would take another ten years before agreement was reached to construct the marinas. However during the next six years as director, I continued discussion with the small boat operators and sailing clubs in Kirkwall and Stromness.

The local enterprise company were also keen to assist with funding of this much needed facility. This is where I met up with Jock Hourston again, who was the third engineer on the Wairangi, the ship I came home on after breaking my arm. Jock was now chief engineer on the St. Ola and a member of the Stromness sailing club.

I retired in September 1998 but became an Orkney Islands Councillor in May 1999, so was in a great position to help push for the marina project to go ahead. With all the various bodies lobbying for the marinas, the Council eventually agreed to allocate £4.75 million for the project. The marinas were on a much grander scale than those proposed back in 1992 when I submitted Mr Montgomery Smiths report but as I said, both in the same location as his report.

The Stromness marina shown in the photo on the following page was well protected and met everyone's expectations. However, the Kirkwall marina was not completely protected from the north and this soon became apparent after the first northerly gale. The pontoons were battered about and the marina was judged unsafe.

The engineering department had wave studies carried out prior to construction but they were not accurate. By this time, I was chairman of the Transportation and Infrastructure Committee of the Council and responsible for all marine activities in the Council. I knew full well that the original design and the protection for the marina was not up to standard.

It was agreed that further wave studies should be carried out and that full scale tank test would be required. In this case, a Danish company would carry out the work. I was determined to witness these trials so along with the Assistant

Director of Harbours, the Harbour Engineer and a member of the Kirkwall marinas committee, we set off to Denmark.

We met up with the Council's engineering consultant in Edinburgh who designed the Kirkwall marina. After two days of tank testing, a new extension to the north face of the existing pier was agreed to be the best possible protection for the marinas. As the Council had no option but to agree to this, £1.0 million funding was allocated out of the reserve fund with the work commencing as soon as possible.

The marinas were operated under an agreement with the Council's harbours department and Orkney marinas which took the daily running and operation of the facilities out of Council control. This has certainly worked well and the marinas have gone from strength to strength over the years. I was happy to have played a small part in helping with their installation.

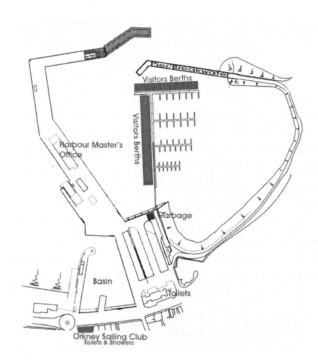

*Sketch of Kirkwall harbour with proposed extension. The final layout of both Kirkwall and Stromness marinas.*

*Kirkwall Harbour Marina*

*Stromness Harbour Marina*

*Tank Testing in Denmark*

John ORR OIC engineering department, consultant engineer, official of Danish tank testing facilities and myself. The testing facilities was a large hanger style building with the whole of Kirkwall bay and harbour laid out in very precise detail and of course, to exact scale. Each test consisted of waves of various heights being directed in to the marina basin. There was no doubt in anyone's mind that the only solution was the extension to the existing pier. Pleased to say the tank test got it dead right.

You can see clearly that prior to the construction of the extension, to the north face of the pier the marina basin was wide open to the sea and wave conditions during any northerly wind. Not sure how the original wave study got it so wrong.

# 50 Square Miles of Opportunity

Department of Harbours
Orkney Island Council

## Department of Harbours

### Orkney Islands Council

#### Orkney

Lying on Latitude 59 North only 6 miles from the Scottish Mainland, Orkney is ideally placed for oil exploration and development in Northern waters. The harbour facilities provide three separate Ro/Ro terminals on Mainland Orkney, giving direct services across the Pentland Firth with other links to the rest of the UK, Continental Europe and Shetland. Throughout the Island group there are several piers used mainly by the inter island trade which are being upgraded for the Ro/Ro ferry service now being introduced.

#### Scapa Flow

This world renowned sheltered anchorage has been a haven for all types of vessels throughout the centuries. Over the years it has been extensively used by the British Fleet. The navies of the NATO countries still occasionally use Scapa Flow during exercises. It was here that the German Grand Fleet was scuttled in 1919, some of these vessels remain and attract leisure divers particularly during the summer months. The main activity now however, is the shipment of Crude Oil and Associated Gas Liquids from the **Flotta** Marine Terminal. The Terminal is operated by ELF ENTERPRISE (Caledonia) Ltd and handles over 15m tonnes of crude oil annually, as well as 0.25m tonnes of LPG. Loading facilities consist of two SPM's each capable of accommodating a 200,000 tonne deadweight tanker. In addition the conventional Jetty at Flotta, which is piped up for both crude oil and LPG exports, can cater for a tanker of up to 150,000 tonnes deadweight. The ex Naval base at **Lyness** offers considerable scope for development with depths of between 8 and 9.5 metres along its 122 metres of berthing face. A 6 hectare site adjacent to the wharf has been zoned for Industrial Development.

#### Kirkwall

Kirkwall Harbour has recently been developed and now offers 780 metres of berthing face with depths of up to 5 metres at LAT. The development also provides additional shelter to the berths on the east side of the pier which were previously exposed to northerly gales. A linkspan capable of taking vessels of up to 110 metres in length and 18 metre beam is located on the west side of the pier. This facility will open up Kirkwall to a wider range of shipping. At present Kirkwall is used mainly for the shipment of livestock, grain, fertiliser and the inter island trade. Kirkwall is a popular port of call for Cruise Liners with forty plus calls expected during the summer of 1991. Due to the harbour improvements it is now possible for the smaller Cruise Liners to berth alongside the pier. The Harbour Authority have on order a dual purpose Pilot boat/Tug with a bollard pull of 9 tons. Delivery of this vessel is expected during the spring of 1992 when it will be available to assist with the berthing of cruise liners.

#### Stromness

Stromness is the main Ferry Port but also handles cargoes of coal and fish farming equipment. It is also at Stromness that most of the leisure diving vessels are based. Plans are well advanced for the development of this busy Harbour. The Ferry Terminal will be extended by 50 metres giving a berthing face of 120 metres. The South Pier will also be extended by 75 metres to a total of 140 metres thereby increasing the quantity of bulk and lift on lift off cargo which can be handled at this port.

#### Scapa

A 35 metre extension to Scapa Pier is currently being constructed. It is expected that this work will be completed by March 1992. Scapa Pier is the base for Orkney Towage Co's Tugs. In the future it is anticipated that all petroleum products will be imported through Scapa Pier.

**Harbour Authority**
Orkney Islands Council
Department of Harbours
Harbour Authority Building
Scapa
Orkney
KW15 1SD

Tel    0856 873636
Telex 75475
Fax    0856873012

**Captain R C Sclater   Director of Harbours**

## Harbour Authority Services

Navigation, pilotage, berthing, port facilities, radio communications, towage, VTS, cranage, fresh water, moorings etc are the responsibility of the Harbour Authority
Tel 0856 873636
Telex 75475
Fax 0856 873012

### Pilotage

In Scapa Flow compulsory for all passenger vessels over 65 metres overall length and all other vessels over 75 metres in length. In the Wide Firth and Shapinsay Sound area compulsory for all passenger vessels over 65 metres in length and all other vessels over 80 metres in length. Pilotage to be arranged at least 12 hours in advance through the Harbour Authority.

### Radio Communications

Operated through Orkney Harbour Radio, which keeps a continuous radio watch 24 hours a day on channel 16 VHF. The ports of Kirkwall and Stromness maintain a listening watch on channel 16 VHF during normal working hours.

### Cranage

2 Jones 355 and 1 Jones 971 mobile cranes capable of lifting up to 40 tonnes are available for hire.

### Towage

Orkney Towage Co. operate a fleet of 3 tugs, two of 52 tonne bollard pull and one of 45 tonne bollard pull. Plans are well advanced to replace the 45 tonne bollard pull tug with a third 52 tonne bollard pull tug. These tugs with twin Aquamaster propulsion units are capable of handling all sizes of vessels within Scapa Flow. All tugs are fully equipped with fire fighting and oil pollution equipment.

## Onshore Support

Aviation Fuel
Bunkering and Lubricants
Chandlery
Cranage and Fork Lifts
Divers
Electrical Supplies
Engineering Facilities
Fresh Water
Marine Electronics
Office Accommodation
Open Storage
Protective Clothing
Refuse Disposal
Ropes
Secretarial Services
Shackles
Stevedoring
Food Supplies
Warehousing
Survey and Debris Clearance
Transport Services

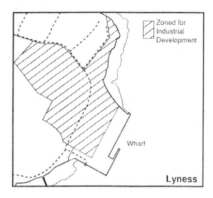

Lyness

Kirkwall

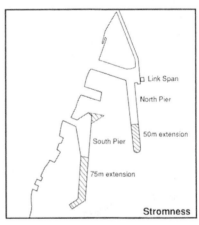

Stromness

# ORKNEY'S NEW CHALLENGE

We continued to promote Orkney to the oil industry and especially the ship-to-ship operations. In this respect, we were contacted by BP Exploration to provide a safe anchorage for the ship-to-ship transfer of North Sea oil from their floating production storage and offloading vessel the FPSO Seillean. This was a very specialised vessel and we were very happy to accommodate this operation.

The first ship to ship took place in December 1992 with another in January 1993. We made sure that this operation was fully publicised by involving the local media both newspaper and TV coverage. All relevant agencies were informed and the operation went without any problems.

Unfortunately, a disgruntled ex-employee of BP who was not aware of the media coverage, contacted a friend at the P&J in Aberdeen and advised that BP were carrying out secret oil transfers in Scapa flow. Of course, this caused great concern as BP were not happy having negative press coverage. I contacted the P&J and advised them to check their own paper from 10 December where they ran a piece on the successful STS in the flow. I also contacted the press complaints commission in London and demanded a full apology from the P&J and a retraction of their story.

It took several weeks but we eventually received our apology. The Seillean carried out two more transfers and then in summer 1993 the vessel was sold. This operation, however, helped to cement our relationship with BP and over the next couple of years, we worked closely with them regarding the new oil fields in the Atlantic and the setting up of the Atlantic Frontier Environmental Forum(AFEF).

# OIC satisfied with ship-to-ship transfers in Flow

18·2·93

Orkney harbours director Captain Bob Sclater has said that the OIC are happy to go ahead with ship-to-ship transfers of oil in Scapa Flow and would be encouraging the practice in the future.

"We are perfectly happy for the ship-to-ship transfers to go ahead, and it will possibly happen again in the next month or so.

"We are quite confident that we can do the job here in a safe and efficient manner. We wouldn't carry it out if we didn't make it a safe practice," said Captain Sclater yesterday.

He said the harbours department were keen to put "an excellent facility" like Scapa Flow to good use for the people of Orkney. "What's the point of having a facility like Scapa Flow, if you don't put it to good use?" he asked.

He made his comments, dismissing a national newspaper story claiming oil company BP had been secretly experimenting with "hazardous" ship-to-ship transfers in the Flow.

It referred to the BP vessel Seillean which visited Orkney in December and again in January and loaded oil into a waiting tanker.

Despite the Aberdeen paper's claims that these were "hush hush experiments," the story was carried in the Orcadian of December 10 and again on January 7.

A BP spokesman said the company had "acted responsibly and the whole process, from initial consultation to detailed planning and successful execution, has always

been carried out properly and openly."

He said: "Before the transfers took place, BP had extensive discussions with the Orkney harbours authority who, in turn, sought the approval of the Orkney Islands Council. The harbour authority also discussed the matter with the RSPB, shellfish growers, Scottish Natural Heritage and Flotta terminal operators at their regular liaison meeting."

"There had been "full and proper consultation" with all relevant authorities and there was never any attempt to secretly experiment."

BP Exploration were very busy with their operations west of Shetland in the deep waters of the Atlantic. These oil wells would be attached to FPSO's and the oil off loaded onto specialised oil tankers to be shipped to oil terminals for onward transportation. The first oil field to be operational was the Foinaven but oil would not be flowing until November 1997.

With our close relationship with BP during 1993-5, negotiations were held to bring this new oil into the Flotta oil terminal. This was no easy task as BP were the main operators of the Sullom Voe oil terminal in Shetland which we thought would be their preferred option. I had several meetings with the Foinaven team and we allowed them to test their highly sophisticated subsea equipment in the shallow waters of Scapa flow prior to going off shore.

The harbour equalisation committee were heavily involved in the negotiations and it was agreed to provide a £7.5 million interest free loan to elf to refurbish two of the 0.5 million oil tanks at Flotta for the storage of the Foinaven crude oil. We also agreed that the shuttle tankers would be allowed into the terminal completely free of harbour dues.

The export tankers would be charged the full harbour charges. We basically were treating the shuttle tankers in the same way as the off shore pipe line from the North Sea fields. All these details were put in place prior to the final proposals being presented by ELF to the BP board.

In May 1995, BP confirmed that Flotta had won the Foinaven contract. We would not have won the contract if some Councillors had their way and lobbied for the shuttle tankers to be charge full harbour dues. Luckily, they were not part of the early negotiations. Following on from our successful bid, I was involved with BP in all aspects of the preparations for the arrival of the shuttle tankers.

It was agreed that our pilots along with the masters of the two shuttle tankers would attend simulator courses at Southampton Nautical College to get hands-on experience on the handling of the vessels and get to know one another. The various environmental bodies, green peace etc. were closely monitoring the Atlantic oil exploration, so BP were determined that everything possible would be done to minimise any oil pollution problems.

As I mentioned above they set up the Atlantic frontier environmental forum AFEF to include all interested parties, oil companies and environmental bodies to discuss the new oil exploration in the Atlantic. The chairman was to be Alasdair McIntyre of the Donaldson enquiry team. I attended all the set-up meetings at BP headquarters in Aberdeen. We also had mock TV interviews in case of problems.

As the Foinaven project took several years to come to fruition, I have covered the progress with some photos, press cuttings and minutes of meeting with ELF highlighting our success story.

The dynamic position vessel, the MV Geomaster alongside Scapa Pier spent several weeks off and on in Scapa flow testing the off shore seabed connectors for the field. We had numerous meetings with ELF and BP management covering all eventualities regarding the operation.

*MV Geomaster alongside Scapa Pier*

# Elf Enterprise

## MINUTES OF MEETING

| Subject | Harbours Meeting | | |
|---|---|---|---|
| Date of Meeting | 30.5.96 | Date of Issue | 5.6.96 |
| File No. | | | |
| Project (AFE if applicable) | Harbours Meeting | | |
| Place of Meeting | Flotta | Dept. | Shipping |
| Persons Attending | Captain R Sclater | Harbours Dept, OIC | |
| | Captain R Moore | Harbours Dept, OIC | |
| | T Newton | ELF | |
| | A Batty | ELF | |

| Further Distribution | |
|---|---|
| | |

| Prepared by | Helen Angus |
|---|---|

| ITEM | DISCUSSIONS | ACTION |
|---|---|---|
| 1 | MINUTES<br>The minutes of the previous meeting were accepted. | |
| 2 | PRODUCTION FORECAST<br>The relevant graphs showing Forecast and actual production for Flotta Crude, Propane and Ethane were circulated. These indicate the effect of the 10 day outage from Piper / Saltire / Chanter to enable tie-in work associated with McCulloch development.<br><br>It was also explained that planned routine maintenance to Gas Plant No 1 may affect Ethane production in September, possibly reducing to 2mb/day. | |
| 3 | FOINAVEN OPERATION<br>The latest information indicates that FPSO Petrojarl is due on station around August 1st with tie-ins and commissioning giving an estimated first oil at Flotta by end of September.<br><br>The manoeuvring and berthing simulator covering the Pentland Firth and Scapa Flow, being prepared by Southampton University, is due for initial testing July 6-7 with final test on July 21st. The anticipated operation of this facility is to be available for August 1st.<br><br>Masters of incoming loaded crude tankers will be initially advised to arrive around slack waters for manoeuvring at the Pilot Station. This advice may be modified after later experience is developed. | AB / RS |
| 4 | FUTURE DEVELOPMENT<br><br>Captain — Final decision and announcement is still awaited from Texaco.<br><br>McCulloch — On course for start up by year end.<br><br>Elgin & Franklin — Formal announcement still not available due to ongoing discussions with Department of Trade and Industry.<br><br>Gailey — Discussions still proceeding with Texaco though no timescale is available.<br><br>Perth — Initial discussions with Amerada Hess / Deminex have begun.<br><br>Elf is currently assessing the associated satellite accumulations close by existing Piper and Claymore reservoirs. This demonstrates the strong determination by Elf to maintain the viability of the 4th Round Joint Venture schemes. | |

The first oil did not arrive until Sunday 7 December 1997 as there were considerable problems off shore as this was pioneering work in the deep waters of the Atlantic. The price of oil in 1997 was at an all-time low, which was also causing problems for the BP exploration team. They persevered and won in the end, as did ourselves and the Flotta oil terminal.

*The photo of the captain of the MV Petrotroll being presented with Orkney Island Council's plaques by myself, on the occasion of the first discharge of Foinaven oil to the Flotta terminal.*

**BP EXPLORATION**

R L Thomson
Ops Manager Foinaven Business Unit

BP Exploration Operating Company Limited
Britoil plc
Golar-Nor House
Howe Moss Drive
Kirkhill Industrial Estate
Dyce
Aberdeen AB21 0GL

Switchboard: 01224 804400

Direct Line: 01224 804425
Direct Fax: 01224 804408

Reference: RLT/amk

17 August 1998

Capt Bob Slater
Director of Harbours
Orkney Island Council

Dear Bob

On behalf of the Foinaven team I wish to acknowledge and recognise the immense contribution that you and your team have made to the success of our operations in Orkney. We are delighted that we based our shuttle tanker operations around Flotta and Scapa flow, you have more than met our expectations and have exceeded them time and again.

Right from the start, one of the things that was most striking is the quality of the relationship between OIC and Elf. This gave us great confidence that things would work out well for us too, which has proved to be the case. There is a great spirit of willingness and a real can do and will do attitude which is refreshing to find. All of this depends on team work and it is the leadership of the team which sets the climate for the relationships. Bob, thanks for being a superb leader.

As you hand "the ship" over to the new crew you should feel content that she is a well found, efficient and happy ship. Have a great retirement and all the best for all your endeavours in your new age. Postpone your dreams no longer.

Yours sincerely

Les

**LES THOMSON**

BP Exploration Operating Company Limited
Registered in England: No. 305943
Registered Office: Britannic House
1 Finsbury Circus, London EC2M 7BA

Printed on Recycled Paper

Britoil plc
Registered in Scotland: No. 77750
Registered Office: Burnside Road,
Farburn Industrial Estate,
Dyce  Aberdeen AB21 7PB

# Foinaven crude flows into Flotta

### by **David Hartley**

HISTORY was made yesterday when the first Atlantic oil arrived at a Scottish oil terminal.

A tanker carrying 60,000 tonnes of crude recovered from beneath the hostile seas 140 miles north-west of Orkney shipped the oil to the islands' Flotta terminal.

As the oil began to flow ashore at 8.45am, staff at the plant celebrated the beginning of a new chapter in the history of the oil industry.

The oil is heavier and thicker than North Sea crude and it had to be heated to 40C aboard the tanker and kept at that temperature in three giant storage tanks at the terminal.

Flotta, opened almost 21 years ago, was built to process oil and gas brought to the terminal by undersea pipeline from the North Sea.

Now it will also act as a storage facility for Atlantic crude shipped by shuttle tanker from the Foinaven field.

The Elf Consortium beat off fierce competition from other terminals in Scotland and elsewhere in Europe to win the contract to handle the oil.

Some £5million was spent adapting the terminal. The work was completed by September last year, when the first Atlantic field was expected to come on stream.

But a series of technical hitches — as BP battled to recover the oil in sea conditions among the most ferocious in the world — delayed the arrival of the crude until yesterday.

Flotta terminal manager Trevor Newton said: "It's been a long wait, but we're delighted to see the first shuttle tanker from the Foinaven field."

The plant is crucial to the economic wellbeing of the islands.

"This is an historic day for Flotta and for Orkney as a whole," added Mr Newton.

"It's new business for us and it adds immeasurable security to all the jobs which depend on the terminal."

Some 30million barrels of Foinaven crude are due to be shipped to the terminal annually over the next five years.

Two shuttle tankers, which take on the oil by ship-to-ship transfer from a floating production vessel anchored permanently over the field, will be used.

The Norwegian-registered Petrotroll was given the honour of making the first delivery after a 10-hour voyage from the Foinaven field.

Her sister ship, the Petrotrym, was anchored in Scapa Flow yesterday waiting to make her first delivery run.

They, and the tankers used to export the oil from Flotta, will make 10 visits to Scapa Flow each month — increasing tanker movements in the harbour by a third.

Orkney's harbours director, Captain Bob Sclater, said: "We are very pleased to see the first shuttle tanker discharging oil at the Flotta terminal.

"History is being made with the arrival of the first Atlantic oil — the first oil ever to be pumped ashore from a ship into the terminal.

"It's very important for us as the harbour authority to have our workload increased by a third.

"The safety record for Flotta is second to none in the world and we hope to continue that with the shuttle tankers operating into the port."

*Foinaven Oil Field operations.*

Two days prior to our second STS with the Seillean, the Mt Braer incident occurred in Shetland. I arrived in my office on 5 January and received a phone call from Orkney coast guard advising that a fully laden tanker was in difficulties in the fair isle channel with no power. They kept me advised on the vessel's situation and just after 11 am informed me that it had grounded at Garth's Ness just west of Sumburgh head. This of course, was in the jurisdiction of Shetland Islands Council and out with our remit.

After discussion with the Flotta oil terminal management, we agreed to contact Shetland Council and advise them that we would provide any assistance required in manpower or equipment to assist with the incident. It turned out that they required no help from us as they had sufficient equipment at the Sullom Voe terminal.

The Department of Transport's oil pollution experts would be taking over responsibility for the situation and in conjunction with Shetland Islands Council's oil pollution plan would attempt to clean up the oil spill. The Braer, by this time, was well and truly holed below the water line and oil was pouring out.

The cargo, however, was not a heavy North Sea crude but a much lighter oil but never the less, still a harmful substance to the seabirds and marine environment. We monitored the situation and watched with interest as attempts were made to spray dispersants from specialised aircraft onto the oil slick.

The weather at the time was atrocious, blowing storm force winds so the dispersant in fact was doing more harm than good as it was blowing ashore on to farm land and houses. They soon stopped the spraying and cleaning of the beaches also ceased due to the weather. After two weeks in conjunction with ELF, we chartered an aircraft and flew up to Shetland to witness the situation.

The wind had never abated during the whole time so we had a bumpy ride up to Shetland. We flew to Scatsta airfield next to Sullom Voe oil terminal and were showing around their oil pollution equipment store. We then flew down to Sumburgh airport to see the onshore operation and past over the wreck of the Braer lying battered on the rocks. The oil, by this time, was nearly all gone due to wave action and the damage to the environment was not so bad as expected.

The situation at Sumburgh airport was still a media circus with TV and newspaper reporters from across the world packing up their equipment as the worst was over. We attended a briefing from Shetland Islands Council on the "clean-up operation" and then headed back to Orkney. The result of the Braer incident brought to light the dangers of loaded tankers getting into difficulties around the UK coast line.

Of course, there had been many incidents worldwide relating to oil spillages, the Torrey Canyon back in 1967 being a prime example when she hit the rocks off Cornwall. Back in Orkney, I had decided to try and ascertain just how many ships along with their cargoes transited the Pentland firth on an annual basis.

With our VTS we were able to acquire every ship and call them on VHF, not every ship replied. Shortly after, we commenced this exercise, the UK government decided to set up an enquiry into shipping around the British Coastline. The chairman of the inquiry would be Lord Donaldson along with his two advisors professor Alasdair McIntyre of Aberdeen University and John Rendle of Shell Tankers (UK) Ltd.

We actually had a vessel run ashore on the island of Stroma in the Pentland firth on Saturday 13 February. The marine officer on duty tried unsuccessfully to contact the Bettina Danica and watched her steam straight onto the rocks on the VTS radar but helpless to do anything. We believe the OOW was asleep 4 on 4 off watch and only awoke just before he hit the rocks and tried to turn the ship but too late.

This was just prior to Lord Donaldson's fact finding visit to Orkney to help with compiling his detailed report to the government. Following Lord Donaldson's visit we set to and drew up our written response to be presented to the enquiry team, which in our case was held in Lerwick Town Hall later in 1993. The main report titled 'Safer Ships, Cleaner Seas' was published in May 1994 and Orkney harbours received a very positive review.

On the Friday evening, Anna and myself were attending the Nautical Institute Annual Dinner Dance in Aberdeen and flew home on the Saturday afternoon. On the Sunday morning, I set off first thing onboard the tug Einar to see if we could tow the vessel off the rocks. The ship was parallel to the shore which indicated she had tried to take avoiding action.

The coast guard helicopter lifted a couple of our crew members onboard the ship to attach a tow line. This was achieved but unfortunately we were unable to tow the vessel off the rocks. A salvage team arrived and were able to take most of fuel oil off the wreck into barrels on the shore and she was left high and dry until the weather eventually broke her up.

As the towage company was involved with the attempted salvage, a salvage payment was due. There were several salvage operations carried out by Orkney

Towage during my time as executive director and later as managing director. I have included some details on salvage on the following pages which may be of some interest. Once again, I have digressed from my story but all very relevant.

Although the Bettina Danica shows a loss, the actual costs would probably have been lower but enhanced during our negotiations with the owners. I attended these negotiations along with David Shearer, the towage marine superintendent at the companies' marine lawyers Holmes Hardingham's offices in London.

Some of the salvage payments are shown on the following pages. I would add that prior to building our own tugs JP Knight's received a 49% share of the salvage whereas after we built our own tugs, this dropped to 25% when their shareholding was reduced and the Council's increased to 75%.

A point of interest with the oil terminals harbour charges based on a compound charge the finance department always showed the towage company operating at as near possible a loss to reduce payments to the shareholders. Of course, in the past with the bare boat charter and annual refit costs JP Knights were not out of pocket.

## SALVAGE

| BETTINA DANICA | Reward | £95,139.75 | |
| | Costs | £106,321.08 | (see attached) |
| | Loss/Gain | -£11,181.33 | |
| | | | |
| ZWARTEMEER | Reward | £189,980.00 | |
| | Costs | £60,334.00 | |
| | Loss/Gain | £129,646.00 | |
| | | | |
| M.F.V. KEILA | Reward | £45,000.00 | |
| | Costs | £15,219.15 | |
| | Loss/Gain | £29,780.85 | |
| | | | |
| M.V. JEVINGTON | Reward | £130,000.00 | |
| | Costs | £38,655.47 | |
| | Loss/Gain | £91,344.53 | |

# ORKNEY TOWAGE COMPANY LTD.

HARBOUR AUTHORITY BUILDING : SCAPA : ORKNEY : KW15 1SD

*TELEPHONE (01856) 873636*
*FAX (01856) 873012*
*MOBILE 0850 709 431*

YOUR REF:

OUR REF:

To: The owners of the "................................", (name of ship) her cargo, freight, bunkers and stores.

"................................" (name of ship) – **Salvage**
**Lloyd's Form of Salvage Agreement** ................................(date)

WHEREAS the contractors under the above-mentioned Lloyd's form of Salvage Agreement (Lloyd's Form) claim salvage in respect of all services performed thereunder by them, their servants or agents and/or by their sub-contractors, their servants or agents (including the owners, masters and the crew members of the tugs or vessels employed by them) NOW pursuant to the provisions of Clause 18 of the Lloyd's Form and in consideration of the said claim for salvage being settled or becoming the subject of an award by the Arbitrator and/or Appeal Arbitrator appointed under Lloyd's Form and in consideration of the said claim for salvage being settled or becoming the subject of an award by the Arbitrator and/or Appeal Arbitrator appointed under Lloyd's Form we do hereby indemnify and hold you harmless against all claims by or liability incurred to the contractors' servants or agents and/or the sub-contractors, their servants or agents arising out of the said services.

Provided always that if any claim for salvage or any other claim is made by any such servant or agent of the contractors and/or by such sub-contractor, their servants or agents, against you as the owners of any such salved property (in rem or in personam or howsoever or wheresoever) you will not admit liability therefor without our prior consent in writing and will further notify us in writing within twenty-eight days of learning of the existence or threat of any such claims and thereafter will, giving reasonable co-operation to us, resist such claims provided that all costs and expenses related to any such claims shall be paid by us.

This indemnity shall be governed by English Law and any dispute arising hereunder shall be submitted to the exclusive jurisdiction of the English Courts.

We hereby irrevocably instruct Messrs. Holmes Hardingham of 22/23 Great Tower Street, London, EC3R 5AQ to accept service of any proceedings arising out of this indemnity.

SIGNED ................................

DATED this          day of          199

Registered Office: Council Offices, Kirkwall, Orkney, KW15 1NY
Registered at: Edinburgh : Registration No. 59843

# HARBOUR AUTHORITY SUMMARY ACCOUNT

This statement shows the trading position of the Harbour Authority and net movement in reserves for the year. This is represented by the trading profit on the Harbour Authority Revenue Account together with surpluses generated on investing activities for the Harbour Authority as a whole.

## Harbour Authority Summary Revenue Account

| 1993/94 Net Expenditure £000 | | Gross Expenditure £000 | Income £000 | 1994/95 Net Expenditure £000 |
|---|---|---|---|---|
| (4662) | Scapa Flow Oil Port | 6264 | 12003 | (5739) |
| - | Miscellaneous Piers and Harbours | 1548 | 1548 | - |
| (98) | Oil Pollution Account | 139 | 292 | (153) |
| (4760) | Profit/Loss to Harbour Reserve Fund | 7951 | 13843 | (5892) |

| Represented by: | Balance at 01/04/94 £000 | Net Movement £000 | Balance at 31/03/95 £000 |
|---|---|---|---|
| Harbour Reserve Fund | 21597 | 2217 | 23814 |
| Harbour Equalisation Fund | 62611 | 4402 | 67013 |
| Relevant Services Contingency Fund | 17135 | 948 | 18083 |
| Conservation Fund | 100 | 6 | 106 |
| Talented Sportspersons Travel Fund | 34 | 2 | 36 |
| Travel Fund | 75 | 4 | 79 |
| Vessel Reserve | 3928 | (377) | 3551 |
| Community Fund | 1 | (1) | - |
| TOTAL | 105481 | 7201 | 112682 |

## HARBOUR EQUALISATION FUND
### COMMITTED INCLUDING FOINAVEN
### (£7.5MM INTEREST FREE LOAN)

JUNE 1995

| YEAR | CRUDE BBLS PER DAY | PROPANE/ ETHANE BBLS PER DAY | CRUDE MBBLS PER YEAR | PROPANE/ ETHANE MBBLS PER YEAR | TOTAL GAS/CRUDE | GRT MM TONNES @11.5 | COST PER GRT POUNDS | HARBOUR DUES £MM | HARBOUR COSTS £MM | SURPLUS/ DEFICIT £MM | DUES PER BBL POUNDS | HARBOUR COSTS/BBL POUNDS | INTEREST EARNED £MM | YEAR END CUM TOTAL £MM | OLG SHARE | BALANCE |
|---|---|---|---|---|---|---|---|---|---|---|---|---|---|---|---|---|
| 1994 | 278,200 | 12,500 | 191,543 | 4,563 | 196,106 | 0.2 | 0.83 | 7.66 | 5.52 | 2.14 | 0.07 | 0.05 | 0.00 | 64.59 | 42.00 | 22.59 |
| 1995 | 232,000 | 12,169 | 84,680 | 4,442 | 89,122 | 7.7 | 0.83 | 6.43 | 5.77 | 0.66 | 0.07 | 0.06 | 3.86 | 61.63 | 43.26 | 18.37 |
| 1996 | 244,000 | 10,358 | 89,060 | 3,781 | 92,841 | 8.1 | 0.84 | 6.80 | 6.08 | 0.72 | 0.07 | 0.07 | 3.70 | 66.05 | 44.34 | 21.71 |
| 1997 | 249,000 | 8,094 | 90,885 | 2,954 | 93,839 | 8.2 | 0.84 | 6.98 | 6.36 | 0.62 | 0.07 | 0.07 | 3.63 | 70.30 | 45.45 | 24.85 |
| 1998 | 221,000 | 6,078 | 80,665 | 2,218 | 82,883 | 7.2 | 0.87 | 6.26 | 5.72 | 0.54 | 0.08 | 0.07 | 3.87 | 74.70 | 46.59 | 28.12 |
| 1999 | 196,000 | 4,756 | 71,840 | 1,736 | 73,276 | 6.4 | 0.88 | 5.61 | 5.86 | -0.25 | 0.08 | 0.08 | 4.11 | 78.56 | 47.75 | 30.81 |
| 2000 | 167,000 | 2,367 | 60,955 | 864 | 61,819 | 5.4 | 0.89 | 4.81 | 6.01 | -1.20 | 0.08 | 0.10 | 4.32 | 81.66 | 48.94 | 32.74 |
| 2001 | 89,000 | 1,712 | 32,120 | 625 | 32,745 | 2.8 | 0.91 | 2.58 | 6.16 | -3.57 | 0.08 | 0.19 | 4.49 | 90.10 | 50.17 | 39.93 |
| 2002 | 52,000 | 0 | 18,980 | 0 | 18,980 | 1.7 | 0.92 | 1.52 | 5.91 | -4.39 | 0.08 | 0.31 | 4.95 | 90.66 | 51.42 | 39.24 |
| 2003 | 44,000 | 0 | 16,060 | 0 | 16,060 | 1.4 | 0.93 | 1.31 | 6.06 | -4.75 | 0.09 | 0.38 | 4.99 | 90.89 | 52.71 | 38.19 |
| 2004 | 34,000 | 0 | 12,410 | 0 | 12,410 | 1.1 | 0.95 | 1.02 | 6.21 | -5.19 | 0.09 | 0.50 | 5.00 | 90.71 | 54.03 | 36.68 |
| 2005 | 31,000 | 0 | 11,315 | 0 | 11,315 | 1.0 | 0.96 | 0.95 | 6.37 | -5.42 | 0.08 | 0.56 | 4.99 | 90.27 | 55.59 | 34.90 |
| 2006 | 28,000 | 0 | 10,220 | 0 | 10,220 | 0.9 | 0.98 | 0.87 | 6.53 | -5.66 | 0.09 | 0.64 | 4.97 | 89.56 | 56.76 | 32.82 |
| 2007 | 26,000 | 0 | 9,490 | 0 | 9,490 | 0.8 | 0.99 | 0.82 | 6.69 | -5.87 | 0.09 | 0.70 | 4.93 | 88.64 | 58.16 | 30.46 |
| TOTALS | | | 689,923 | 21,182 | 711,105 | | | | | | | | | | | |

## ASSUMPTIONS:

1. STATUS OF FUND AT 31 MARCH 1995 IS EQUAL TO STERLING £64.59MM
2. ANNUAL HARBOUR COSTS AS PER INFORMATION RECEIVED FROM OIC FINANCE DEPT – 15/9/93
3. HARBOUR COSTS AS PER INFORMATION FROM OIC AND 2.5% INFLATION FROM 1996
4. INTEREST ON FUND @ 6% 1995/6   5.5% THEREAFTER
5. PORT CHARGES – 83p & HALF RATE OF INFLATION
6. £0.8MM TUG LEASE COSTS REMOVED IN 1999
7. £0.4MM TUG LEASE COSTS REMOVED IN 2002
8. PRODUCTION PROFILES UPDATED
9. INTEREST FREE LOAN OF £7.5 MILLION REMOVED FROM FUND IN 1995 AND REPAYED IN 2001

| | 1 FUND | 2 COSTS | 3 INT. % | 4 INT. % | 5 CHARGES |
|---|---|---|---|---|---|
| | 1995 | 64.591 | 3 | 6 | 0.83 |
| | 1997 | | 3 | 6 | |
| | 1997 & ONWARDS | | 2.5 | 5.5 | |

6/28/95   10:24 AM

## LIST OF COMMITTEES, SUBCOMMITTEE, WORKING GROUPS ETC. WHICH THE DEPARTMENT OF HARBOURS IS INVOLVED WITH

1   Full Council

2   Finance and General Purposes Committee

    (i)   Oil Development Working Group

3   Transportation Committee

    (i)   Pilotage Examining Body

    (ii)   Ship Repair Working Group

    (iii)   Inter-Isles Working Group

    (iv)   Oil Pollution Liaison Committee

4   Harbour Equalisation Fund Committee

    (i)   Oil Pollution Fund Committee

5   Orkney Ferries Ltd Board Meetings

    (i)   Internal Staff Meetings

6   Orkney Towage Company Board Meetings

7   Department of Harbours Monthly Departmental Meetings

8   Elf Enterprise Caledonia Limited/Harbours Department Meetings

9   Chief Officials' Meetings

10   Emergency Planning Forum

11   District Marine Safety Committee Meetings

12   British Ports Association Meetings

    (i)   Marine/Pilotage Working Group

    (ii)   Scottish Ports Committee Meetings

13   United Kingdom Harbour Masters' Association Meetings

14   Cruise Europe Meetings

15   Standing Committee on Pollution Clearance at Sea - COSLA Member

16   MSA Small Passenger Ship Steering Group

17   MSA Regulatory Reform of Merchant Shipping Legislation

61

*A copy of the harbour and harbour equalisation accounts statements from 1995. These highlight the oil pollution and vessel replacement figures at the time, not sure, if they exist anymore. The £7.5 million loan also shown on harbour equalisation account. Also note on various committees that I attended, AFEF came later.*

On 29 July 1993 we nearly had our own Braer incident when the oil tanker MV Nyhval encountered steerage problems in the Pentland firth. The vessel had completed loading 70000 tons of crude oil at the Flotta oil terminal and sailed just before midday bound for discharge in the Baltic. The master decided to proceed down the east side of Swona island and turn to port and head between South Ronaldsay and the Pentland skerries.

The tide at the time was flooding resulting in the vessel steaming with the tide. However, on turning to port to proceed east wards north of the Pentland skerries the ship lost steerage and with the helm hard to starboard, she still kept turning to port and was being pushed sideways towards the skerries.

The duty marine officer phoned me and the towage superintendent and advised us of the situation. He was instructed to turn the two escort tugs around and also the pilot launch with the pilot onboard and proceed towards the tanker. David Shearer and I arrived at the harbour offices within ten minutes and watched the situation on the VTS radar. The ship was still out of control.

We figured that with the strong easterly flowing tide, this was pushing on the stern as she turned to port resulting in the stern being pushed to starboard and the vessels head to port. We were in contact with the master and I advised him to put his wheel hard to port and bring the ship up to emergency full ahead to try and counteract the vessels setting to starboard towards the skerries.

This was achieved and the vessel that had been setting towards the Pentland skerries managed to head back through the firth under control, albeit not at a very high speed due to the strong tide. At one point, we were very worried as the target of the tanker on the radar screen merged with the Pentland skerries. To say we were relieved when we saw the targets moving apart was an understatement.

We then advised the master to proceed west wards until he was in a position to turn his vessel to port and proceed south east between the Pentland skerries and Duncansby head. This was a very frightening scenario and whether the ship would have regained full control proceeding north of the Pentland skerries or ended up ashore is debatable. We were only too happy to see the ship safely on its way.

Following this incident, I took the decision to compile new navigation instructions advising vessels operating into and out of Scapa flow not to use this channel. This decision was endorsed by Orkney Islands Council. I also contacted the hydrographic department of the navy and recommended that additional warnings regarding the tidal flow in the Pentland firth be highlighted on all relevant navigation charts of the area.

I also put forward a request to include designated navigation channels showing the approaches to Scapa Flow from the Pentland Firth. The hydrographer agreed to these request and all charts now have my recommendations included. With the Donaldson inquiry now in full flow, everyone was only too happy to try and improve the safety of all vessels sailing around the UK coastline. The Fair Isle channel where the Braer grounded was also being discussed at meetings with the Department of Transport and the Chamber of Shipping relating to traffic separation zones.

Shetland Islands Council recommended that there should only be one west bound and one east bound track. This would mean all vessels heading west wards would navigate between Shetland and Fair isle and all east bound between Orkney and Fair Isle With these two channels being 20 miles wide with maximum tidal flow of two and a half knots, not really very logical.

I put forward a two-way system in both directions. The department agreed to a two way between Orkney and Fair Isle but the Shetland proposal on one to the north was left. It was very strange how the Shetland Islands Council made out that the Fair Isle channel was a dangerous sea way, illogical when compared to the Pentland firth. They certainly were a bit paranoid about the Fair Isle channel but not in a very seamanship like manner.

On the following pages, copy of tide table booklet issued annually to every vessel operating into Scapa Flow by shipping agents. The recommendations on navigation was included following the MV Nyhval incident. You will note that the tides for Kirkwall and tidal flow based on dover in the Pentland firth are similar layout that I produced by hand, back in 1976-8.

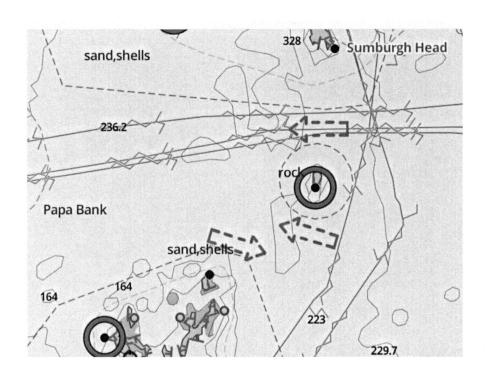

*Vessel traffic routes Fair Isle Channel*

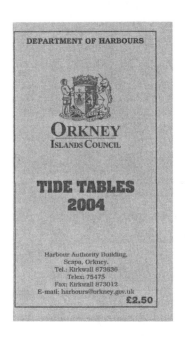

DEPARTMENT OF HARBOURS

**ORKNEY**
ISLANDS COUNCIL

**TIDE TABLES 2004**

Harbour Authority Building,
Scapa, Orkney.
Tel.: Kirkwall 873636
Telex: 75475
Fax: Kirkwall 873012
E-mail: harbours@orkney.gov.uk
£2.50

INDEX

3

363

5 HOURS BEFORE H.W. DOVER

"© Crown Copyright. Reproduced from Admiralty Tidal Stream Atlas
NP 209 by permission of Controller of Her Majesty's Stationery Office;
UK Hydrographic Office."
57

Time Zone–GMT
Times and Heights of High and Low Water

| | Time | m | Time | m | Time | m | Time | m |
|---|---|---|---|---|---|---|---|---|
| 1 Th | 0547 | 2.4 | 1133 | 1.6 | 1745 | 2.7 | | |
| 2 F | 0026 | 1.3 | 0643 | 2.5 | 1244 | 1.6 | 1845 | 2.7 |
| 3 Sa | 0121 | 1.3 | 0734 | 2.6 | 1340 | 1.5 | 1942 | 2.7 |
| 4 Su | 0207 | 1.3 | 0821 | 2.7 | 1429 | 1.4 | 2035 | 2.7 |
| 5 M | 0248 | 1.3 | 0903 | 2.8 | 1515 | 1.3 | 2122 | 2.8 |
| 6 Tu | 0327 | 1.2 | 0943 | 2.9 | 1558 | 1.1 | 2203 | 2.8 |
| 7 W | 0404 | 1.2 | 1019 | 3.0 | 1637 | 1.0 | 2239 | 2.8 |
| 8 Th | 0439 | 1.2 | 1051 | 3.0 | 1714 | 0.9 | 2313 | 2.8 |
| 9 F | 0511 | 1.1 | 1123 | 3.1 | 1747 | 0.9 | 2348 | 2.8 |
| 10 Sa | 0543 | 1.1 | 1156 | 3.1 | 1821 | 0.8 | | |
| 11 Su | 0025 | 2.8 | 0617 | 1.1 | 1231 | 3.1 | 1857 | 0.8 |
| 12 M | 0105 | 2.8 | 0655 | 1.1 | 1309 | 3.0 | 1939 | 0.8 |
| 13 Tu | 0151 | 2.7 | 0739 | 1.2 | 1352 | 2.9 | 2028 | 0.9 |
| 14 W | 0247 | 2.6 | 0830 | 1.3 | 1444 | 2.9 | 2126 | 1.0 |
| 15 Th | 0351 | 2.6 | 0932 | 1.4 | 1548 | 2.8 | 2230 | 1.0 |
| 16 F | 0457 | 2.6 | 1041 | 1.4 | 1705 | 2.7 | 2336 | 1.1 |
| 17 Sa | 0601 | 2.6 | 1155 | 1.3 | 1822 | 2.7 | | |
| 18 Su | 0043 | 1.1 | 0703 | 2.7 | 1309 | 1.2 | 1930 | 2.8 |
| 19 M | 0146 | 1.0 | 0801 | 2.8 | 1414 | 1.0 | 2033 | 2.9 |
| 20 Tu | 0243 | 0.9 | 0854 | 3.0 | 1512 | 0.8 | 2131 | 3.0 |
| 21 W | 0335 | 0.9 | 0944 | 3.1 | 1605 | 0.6 | 2225 | 3.0 |
| 22 Th | 0423 | 0.8 | 1031 | 3.2 | 1654 | 0.4 | 2314 | 3.0 |
| 23 F | 0508 | 0.8 | 1113 | 3.2 | 1739 | 0.4 | 2358 | 3.0 |
| 24 Sa | 0550 | 0.8 | 1154 | 3.3 | 1821 | 0.4 | | |
| 25 Su | 0040 | 2.9 | 0629 | 0.8 | 1235 | 3.2 | 1902 | 0.5 |
| 26 M | 0122 | 2.7 | 0708 | 0.9 | 1316 | 3.1 | 1943 | 0.6 |
| 27 Tu | 0207 | 2.6 | 0748 | 1.1 | 1400 | 3.0 | 2025 | 0.8 |
| 28 W | 0257 | 2.5 | 0831 | 1.2 | 1450 | 2.8 | 2111 | 1.1 |
| 29 Th | 0352 | 2.4 | 0919 | 1.4 | 1549 | 2.6 | 2200 | 1.3 |
| 30 F | 0449 | 2.3 | 1014 | 1.5 | 1656 | 2.5 | 2254 | 1.4 |
| 31 Sa | 0548 | 2.3 | 1121 | 1.6 | 1806 | 2.4 | | |

PHASES OF THE MOON

7 ○ Full Moon     21 ● New Moon

18

We did have another scare on the evening of 18 December 1984 when the tanker MV Channel Dragon lost power between Swona island and South Ronaldsay. I received a phone call advising me of the incident and once again advised the duty marine officer to send the two stand by tugs and pilot to head back towards the vessel.

I arrived at the control room and saw the ship very close to the coast of South Ronaldsay. By this time the master had ascertained the problem and the ship had power restored and was heading on passage. It turned out that the engineer on watch had turned off one of the two generators and then went to pull the switch off the main board. Instead, he pulled the control switch for the generator still running and blackened out the ship.

Thank goodness the chief engineer was still in the engine room and got the electricity back online. Another scary moment. The bridge and engine room standing instructions were included after this incident. It was normal practice on every ship I sailed on for the backup steering motors etc. never to be switched off until well clear of port.

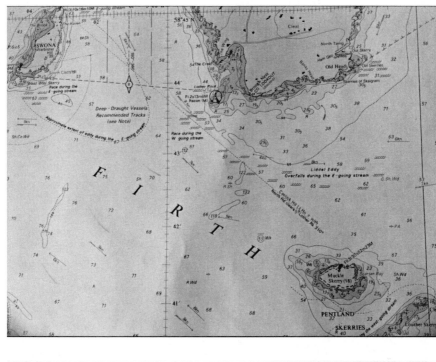

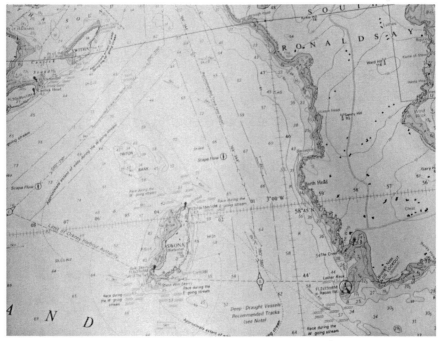

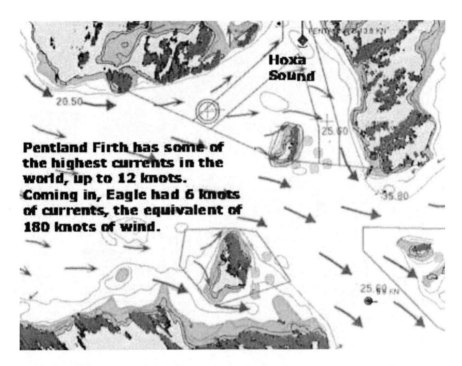

**Hoxa Sound**

Pentland Firth has some of the highest currents in the world, up to 12 knots. Coming in, Eagle had 6 knots of currents, the equivalent of 180 knots of wind.

## DEEP-DRAUGHT VESSELS
## RECOMMENDED TRACKS

The channels and deep-water tracks between the Pentland Firth and Scapa Flow are those recommended by the Orkney Harbours Navigation Service for tankers under pilotage proceeding to or from the Flotta Oil Terminal. Due to possible tidal effects, vessels may need to steer noticeably different courses from those shown in order to maintain the recommended tracks. Radar surveillance of these channels is continuously maintained.

## TIDAL STREAMS

*Tide rip at Lother Rock*

My instructions on the next page were that the duty marine officer was to acquire all shipping passing through the Pentland Firth on our VTS. This was no big deal as it took only a second to click on the vessel and then note its progress if necessary. Nowadays, all vessels use AIS (Automatic Identification System) where ships can be followed worldwide by satellite.

From: Director of Harbours     Date: 4 January 1994

To: Duty Marine Officer,     Ref: 24.S/HK
Operations Room

## MEMORANDUM

### SURVEYS OF VESSELS TRANSITING THE PENTLAND FIRTH

Further to my memo of 15 January 1993 I wish to confirm that the monitoring of vessels transiting the Pentland Firth will cease as from 31 January 1994.

The main reason for continuing the extra two weeks up until the end of January is to take into account days when the radar was out of action and we were unable to monitor the traffic transiting the Pentland Firth.

It will still be a requirement, however, for the Duty Marine Officer to acquire all targets transiting the Pentland Firth to ensure that should an incident occur the relevant information relating to the vessel concerned is available immediately.

Director of Harbours

I have shown on the next page photo of MV Cemfyord, a cement carrier which foundered in the Pentland Firth on 2nd January 2015 with the loss of all eight members of the crew. It was 24 hours later that the photo was taken when the vessel was sighted 12 miles east of the Pentland Firth by a passing ferry. If the harbours still carried out the instructions of the above memo, then perhaps the incident would have been noted much sooner and rescue action taken.

I will admit that the weather conditions were quite atrocious at the time and perhaps nothing could be done to save the crew. This does highlight how dangerous the Pentland Firth can be. The MAIB did state that the captain should not have transited the firth in these weather and tidal conditions something I had known over many years as a pilot.

*MV Cemfyord*

You will note that the entrance to Burwick on the chart is adjacent to the Lother rocks in the area showing eight knots of tide. One of my main arguments about the safety of this port for the short sea crossing. This is the same area that the MV Nyhval encountered steering problems and we turned her around safely. The monitoring of vessels over the 12 months showed over 6000 vessels operating through the firth. This did not include local fishing vessels or ferries operating between Orkney and Caithness.

I mentioned earlier about the Imperial German navy and its involvement with Scapa Flow. After armistice was signed on 11 November 1918 the German fleet was interred in Scapa Flow arriving between 25 and 27 November. This consisted of some 74 ships lying in Scapa Flow with demoralised German sailors onboard.

In command was vice-admiral Von Reuter who was not a very happy man. He decided that prior to the allies taking control of the vessels after the next round of armistice meetings, he would scuttle the fleet. On 21 June 1919, he hoisted a flag signal that all other vessels were aware of instructing them to open their sea cocks and scuttle them.

The main part of the royal navy ships had left Scapa on exercise that morning, so not many other navy ships to take action against the scuttling. After a few hours, 52 of the German ships were at the bottom of Scapa flow with 22 others either beached or still afloat. A great number were eventually salvaged and there has been many books written on this subject.

My main reason for highlighting this is the subsequent interest of sports sub-aqua diving on the remaining wrecks and the harbour departments responsibility regarding diving in Scapa Flow harbour area. In late 1987, three of the wrecks namely the Dresden, Brummer, and Coln, all cruisers were handed over to Orkney Islands Council by the UK government.

As we issued diving permits to allow divers to operate within the harbour area, new permits had to be produced to take into account these acquisitions. Our dive permits now gave permission to dive on these three wrecks but divers must receive authority from owners of other wrecks to dive on them, this fact was included in the original permits. Details of permits issued up to 1997 on following page. Very lucrative business for local dive boat operators mainly operating out of Stromness. Unfortunately, there have been several casualties and deaths over the years of divers so not the safest sporting pursuit.

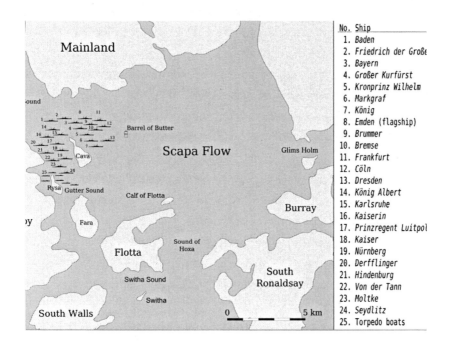

| No. | Ship |
|---|---|
| 1. | Baden |
| 2. | Friedrich der Große |
| 3. | Bayern |
| 4. | Großer Kurfürst |
| 5. | Kronprinz Wilhelm |
| 6. | Markgraf |
| 7. | König |
| 8. | Emden (flagship) |
| 9. | Brummer |
| 10. | Bremse |
| 11. | Frankfurt |
| 12. | Cöln |
| 13. | Dresden |
| 14. | König Albert |
| 15. | Karlsruhe |
| 16. | Kaiserin |
| 17. | Prinzregent Luitpol |
| 18. | Kaiser |
| 19. | Nürnberg |
| 20. | Derfflinger |
| 21. | Hindenburg |
| 22. | Von der Tann |
| 23. | Moltke |
| 24. | Seydlitz |
| 25. | Torpedo boats |

**DIVE PERMITS 1981-1997**

| YEAR | JAN | FEB | MAR | APR | MAY | JUN | JUL | AUG | SEP | OCT | NOV | DEC | Blanket Permit | Total Permits/Year | Total Divers/Year |
|---|---|---|---|---|---|---|---|---|---|---|---|---|---|---|---|
| 1981 | 0 | 0 | 1 | 3 | 9 | 12 | 11 | 13 | 9 | 0 | 0 | 0 | 5 | 63 | 756 |
| 1982 | 0 | 0 | 1 | 5 | 15 | 16 | 16 | 11 | 12 | 0 | 0 | 0 | 2 | 78 | 936 |
| 1983 | 0 | 0 | 0 | 3 | 17 | 18 | 24 | 13 | 11 | 2 | 0 | 0 | 5 | 93 | 1116 |
| 1984 | 0 | 0 | 0 | 8 | 15 | 24 | 26 | 20 | 10 | 1 | 0 | 0 | 3 | 107 | 1284 |
| 1985 | 0 | 0 | 2 | 4 | 24 | 24 | 19 | 26 | 16 | 4 | 1 | 0 | 1 | 121 | 1452 |
| 1986 | 0 | 0 | 1 | 2 | 17 | 12 | 18 | 13 | 11 | 1 | 0 | 0 | 2 | 77 | 924 |
| 1987 | 0 | 0 | 3 | 6 | 20 | 15 | 20 | 10 | 9 | 0 | 1 | 0 | 2 | 86 | 1032 |
| 1988 | 0 | 1 | 3 | 11 | 27 | 21 | 22 | 17 | 12 | 7 | 0 | 0 | 2 | 123 | 1476 |
| 1989 | 0 | 0 | 9 | 11 | 18 | 16 | 25 | 21 | 28 | 8 | 2 | 0 | 2 | 138 | 1656 |
| 1990 | 0 | 1 | 2 | 11 | 17 | 16 | 26 | 27 | 31 | 11 | 1 | 0 | 3 | 146 | 1752 |
| 1991 | 0 | 0 | 12 | 17 | 34 | 41 | 35 | 29 | 33 | 11 | 2 | 0 | 3 | 217 | 2604 |
| 1992 | 0 | 0 | 1 | 21 | 43 | 32 | 30 | 31 | 30 | 13 | 0 | 1 | 3 | 205 | 2460 |
| 1993 | 0 | 0 | 3 | 22 | 37 | 24 | 32 | 34 | 25 | 15 | 0 | 3 | 3 | 198 | 2376 |
| 1994 | 0 | 0 | 7 | 12 | 40 | 37 | 43 | 30 | 28 | 10 | 1 | 1 | 3 | 212 | 2544 |
| 1995 | 0 | 0 | 1 | 17 | 33 | 35 | 37 | 27 | 33 | 11 | 1 | 0 | 5 | 200 | 2400 |
| 1996 | 1 | 1 | 3 | 15 | 26 | 29 | 33 | 40 | 39 | 13 | 1 | 1 | 3 | 205 | 2460 |
| 1997 | 0 | 1 | 5 | 13 | 35 | 35 | 38 | 49 | 35 | 15 | 0 | 0 | 4 | 230 | 2760 |
| Total Permits/Month | 0 | 2 | 46 | 153 | 366 | 343 | 384 | 322 | 296 | 94 | 9 | 5 | 44 | 2064 | 24768 |

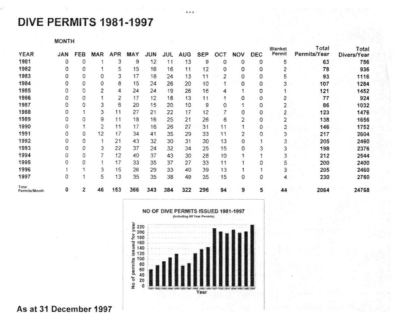

NO OF DIVE PERMITS ISSUED 1981-1997 (including All Year Permits)

As at 31 December 1997

The wrecks of two royal navy ships lying in Scapa Flow were HMS Vanguard that exploded on 9 July 1917 with the loss of 845 officers and crew and HMS Royal Oak sunk by U47 on 14 October with the loss of 833 officers and crew were classed as war graves and diving was prohibited.

371

I will now cover our involvement with HMS Royal Oak torpedoed by Commander Gunther Prien's submarine U47 on 14 October 1939. Over the years, the vessel's oil tanks began to leak oil into Scapa flow. At first, this was only a slight sheen on the surface but by 1995 was becoming more prevalent.

I was quite worried as we were discovering oil tar balls on the beaches which indicated the vessel's oil tanks were deteriorating. I contacted the royal navy and informed them of my concerns. Being the Harbour Master and Oil Pollution Officer for Orkney Islands Council made me the responsible officer. After several meetings both at royal navy headquarters in Bath that dealt with this type of incident and also representation to various visiting senior naval officers' agreement was reached on removal of the oil.

This took several years to achieve which resulted in no further environmental damage within Scapa flow. With several salmon farms situated in Scapa flow, they certainly would not have looked very inviting to prospective customers with oil drifting close by.

During my time in charge at Scapa, I liaised with the local branch of the Royal British Legion and whenever any relatives of those lost on the HMS Royal Oak visited, I made the pilot launch available to take them out to the resting place of the ship.

I also had a Japanese family whose ancestor was lost on board HMS Vanguard taken out to the ship's final resting place. Both the Royal Oak and Vanguard were marked by wreck buoys. We liaised closely with the RN divers who placed a white ensign on HMS Royal Oak in October every year. We were presented with one of these ensigns that we displayed in a glass case in the harbour authority building.

We had many visitors arriving at the harbour offices in connection with the royal navy's involvement with Scapa flow during the two world wars. Also, the royal navy carried out numerous military exercises in and around Scapa which the department was always consulted upon. On the following pages, there is several letters from not only navy personnel but German ambassador and also Japanese visitors interested in our operations.

HM Naval Base Clyde
Helensburgh
Dunbartonshire G84 8HL

Tel: 01436-674321 Ext: 5328
Fax: 01436-674321 Ext: 6249

Rear Admiral J G Tolhurst CB
Flag Officer Scotland, Northern England and Northern Ireland
and
Naval Base Commander Clyde

Captain Bob Sclater MN
Korsgarth
High Street
Kirkwall
ORKNEY

*14* July 1997

Dear Bob,

I was so pleased to have the opportunity to meet you and to talk with you and Hugh at that excellent lunch yesterday about the ROYAL OAK. It was good to hear that you are content that the problem now seems to have been firmly gripped in Bath and I must say that I was very reassured by the briefs that I received before I came up. Nevertheless it is quite clear that there are no easy solutions! I shall write to CESO(N) following my visit and ask that my office is kept abreast of developments as the way ahead emerges. If I can be of any further assistance do please let me know.

I was most grateful to you for the offer of the Pilot Boat to take us across to John o'Groats this morning which enabled me to retain the whole of Sunday's programme, secure in the knowledge that I would be able to get back, whatever the weather; as it was, the trip gave me a great chance to see Scapa Flow on a clear day and it was a bonus to be able to see for myself the sheen of oil on the water in the vicinity of the wreck. The photograph which Gordon Ivol showed me also graphically demonstrated what happens when the oil comes ashore.

I thoroughly enjoyed my all too brief visit to Orkney and hope we may meet again one of these days if I can make my way back there for a rather more leisurely look at the islands.

Yours,

John.

An Agency of the Ministry of Defence

027jul.ra

From: Commodore P C B Canter CBE Royal Navy

The Commodore
Amphibious Warfare
No. 6 House
RMB Stonehouse
Plymouth
Devon PL1 3QS

MOD Network:
Tel:   RMB Stonehouse 36386
Fax:   RMB Stonehouse 36271
Civ:   Tel: (01752) 836386
       Fax: (01752) 836271

HARBOURS DEPARTMENT
Received 8·6·95
File
Attention
Seen

4 June

Dear Bob,

I am now back onboard after my shuttle trip down to London and back and have time to write you a short note of thanks for giving me a really enjoyable and memorable afternoon on Friday. It may have only been a whistle-stop tour of the mainland but you managed brilliantly to give me a real feel for Orkney and its folklore, its history, its rolling countryside and its way of life. As you so rightly pointed out the "How" seems to dominate the Southern Islands and has played such a major part in your history. Thank you so much for giving up your time it was a great way to spend an afternoon.

Please also thank your team for their support to us during our drills period. Scapa seems to have everything we need - space, landing beaches, helpful people and your excellent organisation to provide for all our needs.

With very best wishes

Paul.

DER BOTSCHAFTER
DER BUNDESREPUBLIK DEUTSCHLAND
THE AMBASSADOR
OF THE FEDERAL REPUBLIC OF GERMANY

London, 2 June 1997

Captain R. Sclater
Director of Harbours
Orkney Islands Council
Harbour Authority Building
Scapa, Orkney

HARBOURS DEPARTMENT
Received... 5.16/97...
File ... ........................
Attention...................
Seen.................... P.

Dear Captain Sclater,

Upon my return to London, I would like to thank you again for receiving us and showing us around. It was very kind of you to devote so much time to explaining how you control the ships going in and out of the harbour with the most interesting and modern devices from your control bridge. My wife and I were very impressed to see how all these modern instruments help you to carry out your work.

Thank you again and I do wish you all the best,

Yours sincerely

Jürgen Oesterhelt

(Dr. Jürgen Oesterhelt)

✳

# THE YASUDA FIRE & MARINE INSURANCE COMPANY, LIMITED

FACSIMILE : (03)3348-3041
TELEX : 232-2806 YASUDA J
TELEPHONES : (03)3349-3111

HEAD OFFICE
26-1, Nishi-Shinjuku Itchome,
Shinjuku-ku, Tokyo

TOKYO, 4th November, 1993

Harbour Authority Orkney Islands Council
Department of Harbours
Harbour Authority Building
Scapa
Orkney
KW15 1SD

HARBOURS DEPARTMENT
Received. 15 11 93 .........
File . . . .........................
Attention. . . . . . . . . . . . . . . . . . .
Seen. . . . . . . . . . . . . . . . . . . . . . .

Dear Mr. Slater,

I am now back in Tokyo and wish to take this opportunity to express my
sincere appreciation for the time and all of the kind hospitalities you
extended to me on my recent visit to your office with Mr. John Cooper.

It is indeed difficult in words to express how much I was impressed by your
kind hospitality and how much I enjoyed the time I spent at Kirkwall on the
Mainland.

The story about the sunken battleships in Scapa Flow, the most sophisticated
tugboats and the excellent ferry boats you are responsible for, Beautiful
landscapes and skylines, most charming restaurant on a hill where you invited
me to dinner, the pleasant time and conversation at your house, the St.Magnus
Cathedral, the Italian Chapel by the sea, the "Sinlge Malt Scotch Whisky
Distillery-Highland Park". Everything is unforgettable happy memory I will
enjoy remembering for my life.

I thank you again for all your kindness and I wish you and your family the
very best of health and happiness.

Yours sincerely,

Y.Yamane

One interesting visitor was George Jellicoe who contacted my secretary one day and asked if he could call past for a meeting with me and was I free that afternoon. The name Jellicoe rang a bell but it was not until he arrived that I discovered he was in fact Lord Jellicoe whose father was none other than Admiral Jellicoe who commanded the British fleet during the battle of Jutland.

Lord Jellicoe had a very distinguished career and his life story is something that everyone should read makes my life story pale to insignificance. He told me that he was in Orkney doing a fact-finding tour on behalf of the Churchill association of America.

A group of the association were due to visit Orkney and asked him to organise the visit. They wished to see the Churchill barriers and the Italian chapel built by the prisoners of war during the construction of the barriers. Lord Jellicoe asked if I could assist with this visit. I said no problem and that I would be happy to meet with the group, show them around the harbour buildings and take them out in the pilot launch to the sunken wreck of the Royal Oak.

We agreed he would contact me when the visit was finalised. That evening when Anna and I were taking our dog Sally for a walk, we met Lord Jellicoe on Kirkwall pier, out having a cigarette after his dinner. He was staying in the Kirkwall hotel and he invited us in to meet his family for a drink in the hotel. This we did and had a very pleasant time with them. They said they had taken a taxi out to the Italian chapel and also visited Graemshall Museum situated close to the first barrier.

They mentioned the quaint old lady who showed them around, also their taxi driver. I asked which taxi they used and they said, 'Craigies and the driver was a lady called Norma, another interesting person.' When I told them she was my sister, we all had a good laugh.

They were really good company and very easy to like. We said our goodbyes and looked forward to meeting when they returned with the Churchill association party. Two weeks later, I received an invitation for Anna and I to meet with lord Jellicoe and the members of the association in the Kirkwall hotel.

After introduction, I was asked to give an overview of the planned visit the next day to the harbour offices and a trip out to HMS Royal Oak. I went over the itinerary that I had agreed with Lord Jellicoe and finished by saying that I also owed Winston Churchill a debt of gratitude for building the barriers.

I could see the looks of bewilderment on their faces when I made this comment. I explained that Anna was born and brought up in South Ronaldsay, the farthest away connected island and that if the barriers had not been built our courtship would have been very difficult and perhaps we would never have met, this of course, gave the group a good laugh.

The next morning, they arrived at the harbour offices and we agreed that as there was 20 in the party half would travel out on the pilot launch and the other ten be shown around the harbour control room and have coffee and a talk on Scapa flow in the conference room. Once the first party returned the second group set off. The day went well and everyone enjoyed and appreciated their visit.

I was cordially invited along with Anna to contact the leader of the party if we were ever in Boston. They set off back to London that afternoon and I was presented with a book entitled Winston Churchill, his Wit and Wisdom. Lord Jellicoe thanked me for our hospitality and said that if I was ever in London, I should be sure to get in touch.

Unfortunately, I never did contact him although I was in London on numerous occasions. We seemed to hit it off and got along very well with no airs and graces as he was a down to earth man. I have no correspondence regarding the visit, most of it was done over the phone or meeting face to face. It was one of these visits where no Councillors or officials were involved as Lord Jellicoe wished it to be all low key.

*HMS Royal Oak*

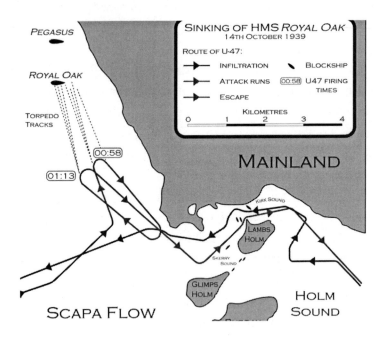

*Commander Gunther Prien onboard U47. Submarine was eventually sunk with loss of all hands of the Irish Coast on 7th March 1941 by HMS Wolverin. ( has been stated that perhaps was sunk by one of its own rogue torpedoes).*

Oil sheen from HMS Royal Oak, the ship is lying in 30 metres of water with the wreck buoy lying to the south marking the war grave. There were a few unsuccessful operations to try and plug the oil seeping from the tanks on the vessel, following my initial representation to the Royal Navy.

It was eventual agreed to cold tap all the tanks and recover the oil into a receiving vessel. This was carried out over several years by Briggs Marine a professional oil service company. Work carried out in fine weather in the summer months.

THIS MARKS THE
WRECK OF HMS
ROYAL OAK AND THE
GRAVE OF THE CREW
RESPECT
THEIR RESTING PLACE
UNAUTHORISED
DIVING PROHIBITED

The entrance had several block ships but the final one was not in place thus allowing commander Prien a route into Scapa flow. After the sinking Prime Minister Winston Churchill ordered that the eastern entrances to the flow to be permanently blocked off. This resulted in the construction of the Churchill barriers blocking off the four entrances between mainland Orkney, Lambs Holm, Glimps Holm, Burray and South Ronaldsay. The construction was carried out by Balfour Beatty with the assistance of Italian prisoners of war. They were eventually completed in 1945.

*Number three barrier between Glimps Holm and Burray, still some remains of block ships in place. The shore line of Glimps Holm is where most of the spilt oil from the tanker MV Eva came ashore and I spent two weeks with the very limited clean up success.*

*The Italian chapel on Lamb Holm built by the Italian prisoners of war. Under the Geneva convention, prisoners of war were not allowed to be used for any military construction that would help their enemies. To get around this, the government stated that the barriers were being built as causeways to join up the four islands to mainland Orkney. This would greatly improve access for these island communities who in the past had to travel by ferry to reach the mainland.*
*The Italian chapel is now a very popular tourist attraction with thousands visiting every year.*

Back to more mundane operational aspects of the Harbours Department. It was essential that we had in place an oil contingency plan in the event of an oil spill. On one of the following pages the number of spills since 1977 are shown. Out of these, between 1977 and 1989, there were 30 reported spillages. From July 1989 until September 1998, only three reported spillages with no environmental damage. This was due to a more vigorous regimen in how the oil terminal operations were controlled.

During this time, we had set to in drawing up a very detailed oil spill emergency plan produced by our own environmental unit under the leadership of Alex Simpson. Alex who had been an employee of Dundee University until the Council took over responsibility for the unit in 1990. He was instrumental in compiling a plan which included a map and photos showing every one-kilometre square of beaches in Orkney.

This gave a record should an oil spill occur not only by the terminal operations but from any other spills out with Scapa flow, and how the beach looked after a spill. This was probably the most comprehensive in the UK at the time. There had been a plan prior to this but not in great detail. We also had set up our Oil Spill Liaison Committee consisting of all interested parties and which met on a regular basis to ensure that everything possible regarding our operations was up to scrutiny.

With our oil spill funding in place, we were able to purchase the necessary equipment, that we hoped would never be used. Also at this time, ELF Caledonia had agreed to set up a fund of £500k to cover any claims from fishermen, fish farmers or any other persons affected by an oil spill to compensate them prior to insurances payments being made.

One point that became clear during our discussions was the fact that clean-up of beaches by mechanical means actually caused more damage to the environment than those beaches that were not accessible to mechanical means. These beaches returned to their natural habitat in a very short period whereas the other beaches took considerably longer if at all. We also agreed that spraying dispersants was really a last resort and we were not in favour of this type of action.

*The local seal population were very happy with our environmental contingency plans, as can be seen basking on the oil pipe lines at the SPM.*

On the following pages details of oil and gas throughput at Flotta Terminal along with Foinaven , STS operations, and also additional cruise liner traffic up to 2004. Bit ahead with these figures in my story but I was in fact Chairman of the Transportation & Infrastructure committee of Orkney Islands Council from 2003/2007 so quite relevant.

The oil pollution incidents along with malfunction/incident list covers a good part of my time as Director and is covered on previous pages of my story.

* * *

FLOTTA OIL TERMINAL (1977-2004)

| YEAR | CRUDE OIL TONNES | No of SHIPS | PROPANE TONNES | No of SHIPS | ETHANE TONNES | No of SHIPS |
|---|---|---|---|---|---|---|
| 1977 | 8,803,282.07 | 121 | 12,438.95 | 1 | 0.00 | 0 |
| 1978 | 15,255,144.56 | 195 | 100,147.14 | 13 | 0.00 | 0 |
| 1979 | 17,364,784.99 | 227 | 145,046.53 | 21 | 32,553.94 | 41 |
| 1980 | 14,967,345.98 | 203 | 214,427.31 | 27 | 32,337.58 | 41 |
| 1981 | 15,166,461.41 | 214 | 248,815.58 | 39 | 49,676.03 | 62 |
| 1982 | 15,384,645.83 | 206 | 285,333.40 | 55 | 62,887.28 | 62 |
| 1983 | 15,623,440.15 | 210 | 255,242.68 | 51 | 61,346.05 | 56 |
| 1984 | 15,579,391.19 | 205 | 276,661.89 | 52 | 67,666.95 | 62 |
| 1985 | 15,589,643.36 | 213 | 279,922.25 | 42 | 71,355.98 | 65 |
| 1986 | 15,412,891.28 | 204 | 212,187.00 | 31 | 51,972.04 | 46 |
| 1987 | 16,633,308.00 | 223 | 244,204.00 | 36 | 74,315.00 | 62 |
| 1988 | 7,714,653.00 | 101 | 127,725.00 | 21 | 29,911.00 | 28 |
| 1989 | 4,268,142.00 | 56 | 23,843.00 | 5 | 0.00 | 0 |
| 1990 | 8,336,225.35 | 107 | 73,791.50 | 14 | 2,411.44 | 3 |
| 1991 | 8,860,241.74 | 119 | 85,420.71 | 22 | 8,632.64 | 11 |
| 1992 | 8,218,496.43 | 106 | 67,924.76 | 18 | 4,391.41 | 6 |
| 1993 | 11,455,689.91 | 133 | 138,397.02 | 37 | 33,715.86 | 42 |
| 1994 | 13,529,630.03 | 154 | 243,410.94 | 52 | 82,579.14 | 96 |
| 1995 | 12,342,693.10 | 146 | 223,194.04 | 49 | 85,534.00 | 103 |
| 1996 | 10,941,380.53 | 131 | 191,788.00 | 55 | 75,265.00 | 90 |
| 1997 | 9,747,674.77 | 119 | 138,257.93 | 53 | 60,679.00 | 73 |
| 1998 | 10,210,854.56 | 122 | 104,606.66 | 32 | 21,633.00 | 27 |
| 1999 | 9,568,002.36 | 115 | 98,611.70 | 40 | 14,322.00 | 18 |
| 2000 | 8,378,324.86 | 98 | 75,736.22 | 29 | 0 | 0 |
| 2001 | 6,824,997.74 | 78 | 63,470.63 | 26 | 0 | 0 |
| 2002 | 6,380,383.20 | 71 | 39,649.82 | 15 | 0 | 0 |
| 2003 | 5,329,570.93 | 60 | 19,740.05 | 9 | 0 | 0 |
| 2004 | 5,070,327.11 | 57 | 18,025.53 | 8 | 0 | 0 |
| TOTAL | 312,957,626.44 | 3994 | 4,008,020.24 | 853 | 923,185.34 | 994 |

# POLLUTION INCIDENTS - FLOTTA TERMINAL

| No | DATE | SOURCE | RESPONSIBLE | REASON | AMOUNT |
|---|---|---|---|---|---|
| 1 | 05.03.77 | Nacella | Ship | V/L broke mooring | 70.00 |
| 2 | 27.04.77 | Fina Norvege | Ship | Tank overflow | 0.05 |
| 3 | 12.06.77 | Fabiola | Ship | Tank overflow | 0.25 |
| 4 | 02.07.77 | Kurushima Maru | Ship | Tank overflow | 2.00 |
| 5 | 31.08.77 | Esso Antwerp | Shore | Sump tank overflow | 0.50 |
| 6 | 17.11.77 | Nacella | Ship | Tank overflow | 2.00 |
| 7 | 25.12.77 | Esso Warwickshire | Ship? | Swivel leak | 0.50 |
| 8 | 05.03.77 | Neverita | Shore | Sump tank overflow | 0.20 |
| 9 | 06.12.78 | Maria | Ship | Tank overflow | 10.00 |
| 10 | 28.12.78 | Process | Shore | Sump overflow | 1.00 |
| 11 | 30.03.79 | Vignemale | Ship | Hull leak | 2.00 |
| 12 | 14.08.79 | Thistle Endeavour | Ship | Tank overflow | 0.50 |
| 13 | 23.07.79 | Cast Puffin | Ship | Tank overflow | 30.00 |
| 14 | 19.06.80 | Texas Getty | Ship | Unattributed | 0.25 |
| 15 | 10.08.81 | Oliva | Ship | Leak at sea suction | 6.00 |
| 16 | 14.06.82 | Fina Belgique | Ship | Tank overflow | 7.00 |
| 17 | 01.07.82 | Terminal | Shore | Valve mal-operation | 7.00 |
| 18 | 18.10.82 | Dallia | Ship | Gas vent | 7.00 |
| 19 | 31.07.83 | Mega Pilot | Ship | Leak at sea suction | 1.00 |
| 20 | 30.08.83 | Jag Laxmi | Ship | Leak at overboard dishcarge | 1.00 |
| 21 | 11.02.84 | Fanny | Ship | Hull fracture | 15.00 |
| 22 | 30.12.84 | Theonymphus | Ship | Camlock release | 5.00 |
| 23 | 02.03.85 | Fanny | Ship | Hull leak | 20.00 |
| 24 | 21.05.85 | Obo Queen | Ship | Leak at sea suction | 2.00 |
| 25 | 06.06.85 | Kittanning | Shore | Leaking "Y" reducer | 1.00 |
| 26 | 19.01.87 | Eva | Ship | Tank overflow | 45.00 |
| 27 | 21.01.87 | Rosario Del Mar | Ship | Leak at sea suction | 2.00 |
| 28 | 07.05.87 | Terminal | Shore | Sump tank overflow | 1.00 |
| 29 | 16.05.88 | Alandia Wave/SPM1 | Unatt. | Slick on surface | 0.05 |
| 30 | 14.02.89 | Terminal | Shore | Heavy wx. At Diesel shed | 0.50 |
| 31 | 28.09.91 | Castillo De Lorca | Ship | Fuel oil overflow | 1.00 |
| 32 | 23.04.92 | Star Westminster | Shore | Loose hose end blank | 1.00 |
| 33 | 13.04.96 | Wilomi Yukon | Ship | Slop tank after loading | 0.50 |
| | | | | **TOTAL (bbls)** | 242.3 |

# MALFUNCTION/INCIDENT LIST - SCAPA FLOW

| DATE | VESSEL | INCIDENT |
|---|---|---|
| 28.02.90 | LOUNDA | Anchored to repair IC System |
| 27.03.90 | SHINOBU | Tow rope parted in high winds, struck Jetty |
| 05.11.90 | EVOIKOS | Power failure in Hoxa Sound |
| 28.09.91 | CASTILLO DE LORCA | Fuel oil overflow, 1 barrel spilled |
| 23.04.92 | STAR WESTMINSTER | Loose hose blank, 1 barrel spilled |
| 25.07.92 | EUROPA | Tender fell from davits, 3 crew injured |
| 29.07.93 | NHYVAL | Lost control North of Pentland Skerries |
| 02.09.93 | TROMAS | Lost anchor in anchorage, recovered 2.10.93 |
| 18.11.93 | NEW ACE | Windlass unable to pick up anchor |
| 11.01.94 | FRONT RIDER | Took shear in tideway |
| 25.02.94 | HANDY SONATA | Problem with main engine, returned to anchor |
| 22.03.94 | SEA EMPEROR | SPM berthing abandoned due to winch problem |
| 20.08.94 | BONA SPRING | Problem with main engine, returned to anchor |
| 18.12.94 | CHANNEL DRAGON | Blackout 2°N of Lother Rocks |
| 26.07.95 | WESTMINSTER | Engine problem |
| 15.09.95 | WINDSOR | Engine problem |
| 09.10.95 | BERCEO | Bow thrust inoperative |
| 15.10.95 | HIRTA | Problem getting SPM mooring on board, berthed Jetty |
| 08.03.96 | OLYMPIC FLAIR | Erratic steering in Pentland Firth |
| 13.04.96 | WILOMI YUKON | Slop tank overflow after loading, ½ barrel spilled |
| 20.04.96 | ALANDIA PEARL | Gyro compass inoperative |
| 11.10.96 | SIDELIA | Turbo blower problem in Pentland Firth |

**FOINAVEN OIL SHIPMENTS (1997-2004)**

| FOINAVEN | IMPORT SHIPS | EXPORT SHIPS | EXPORT TONNES |
|---|---|---|---|
| 1997 | 3 | 1 | 84,893.42 |
| 1998 | 43 | 36 | 2,896,555.00 |
| 1999 | 57 | 35 | 3,574,343.21 |
| 2000 | 61 | 31 | 3,738,239.85 |
| 2001 | 54 | 35 | 3,775,666.00 |
| 2002 | 83 | 46 | 5,280,691.44 |
| 2003 | 58 | 35 | 4,071,671.57 |
| 2004 | 51 | 32 | 3,479,831.46 |
| TOTAL | 410 | 251 | 26,901,891.95 |

**SHIP TO SHIP OIL TRANSFERS (1998 – 2004)**

| YEAR | IMPORT SHIPS | EXPORT SHIPS | EXPORT TONNES |
|---|---|---|---|
| 1998 | 5 | 5 | 572,571 |
| 1999 | 22 | 18 | 2,363,182 |
| 2000 | 41 | 34 | 3,681,855 |
| 2001 | 19 | 17 | 1,812,085 |
| 2002 | 11 | 11 | 926,399 |
| 2003 | 9 | 4 | 575,184 |
| 2004 | 59 | 15 | 2,660,841 |
| TOTAL | 166 | 104 | 12,592,117 |

**CRUISE LINERS (1995 – 2004)**

| Year | Number of Liners | Total GT | Passenger Numbers | Total Income £ |
|---|---|---|---|---|
| 1995 | 47 | 442,916 | 9,843 | 53,320 |
| 1996 | 51 | 651,368 | 14,649 | 82,315 |
| 1997 | 46 | 546,271 | 12,762 | 68,245 |
| 1998 | 48 | 627,703 | 16,356 | 87,970 |
| 1999 | 59 | 632,955 | 15,859 | 93,945 |
| 2000 | 55 | 546,470 | 14,096 | 82,514 |
| 2001 | 52 | 630,492 | 15,970 | 102,383 |
| 2002 | 53 | 722,708 | 16,687 | 109,004 |
| 2003 | 62 | 874,610 | 21,162 | 143,131 |
| 2004 | 56 | 1,007,215 | 22,916 | 210,046 |

The only oil spill that caused concern within my control occurred when a coastal tanker was discharging fuel oil to the local power station and their pipe line ruptured in the middle of the town. A clean-up operation was put in action and most of the oil was cleaned of the street by the Council's roads department with very little finding its way into the rain drainage system.

No environmental damage was caused with this spill and the local hydro board carried out a full inspection of their pipe line and renewed it where necessary. Oil pollution exercises were carried out on a regular basis as can be seen by the programme on the following pages.

I have included a couple of photos of exercises with the coast guard helicopter and the tug Harald. These were required for any salvage operations when lifting crew onto stricken vessels to allow tow ropes to be attached. Exercises with highlands and islands fire brigade were also carried out with the tugs and helicopter in relation to off shore firefighting situations.

*Coast Guard Helicopter and the Tug Harald*

# ORKNEY ISLANDS COUNCIL
# DEPARTMENT OF HARBOURS

# SCAPA FLOW
# OIL POLLUTION
# CONTINGENCY PLAN
# GENERAL GUIDELINES

Contact: Captain R C Sclater MNI
Director of Harbours
Harbour Authority Building
Scapa
Orkney    KW15 1SD

Tel:    01856 87 3636
Fax:    01856 87 3012
Telex: 75475

# SCAPA FLOW OIL POLLUTION CONTINGENCY PLAN
## GENERAL GUIDELINES
## INDEX:

# PROPOSED OIL POLLUTION
# TRAINING/EXERCISE SCHEDULE 1997

**FEBRUARY -** One day refresher course for owners/operators of local vessels listed in Orkney Islands Council (OIC) Pollution Vessel Register reference containment and recovery methods and procedures relevant to Orkney.

**MARCH -** Hoyle Boom deployment ex Orkney Towage Company (OTC) tug with the "HOUTON LASS" and "SCAPA LASS" assisting.

**APRIL -** Boom deployment at Stromness and Kirkwall harbours utilising on-site equipment, OIC and Elf Exploration (EE) participating.

**MAY -** Major deployment exercise Scapa Flow to involve all main players plus equipment.

— Recovered oil discharge exercise ex "FLOTTARIAN" into Flotta terminal dirty ballast system.

**MAY/JUNE -** Desk top exercise involving OIC, EE, BP, MPCU.

**JUNE -** Troil Boom deployment Flotta Terminal Jetty.

**JULY -** Beach exercise at Scapa Beach.

**AUGUST -** Boom anchoring deployment i.w.o SPM, Scapa Flow - OIC and EE involved.

**SEPTEMBER -** Orkneydirect training day on Flotta using EE equipment and facilities

**N.B.** Due to operational requirements, shipping etc. the training programme will be reviewed on a month by month basis and all parties will be advised accordingly.

# ORKNEY ISLANDS COUNCIL
# DEPARTMENT OF HARBOURS

# POLICY STATEMENTS

Contact:      Captain R C Sclater MNI      Tel:    01856 87 3636
                Director of Harbours          Fax:    01856 87 3012
                Harbour Authority Building    Telex: 75475
                Scapa
                Orkney     KW15 1SD

Department of Harbours

Orkney Islands Council

# POLICY STATEMENTS
# CONTENTS

*Oil Pollution Contingency Plans along with other policy documents required for a safe operation were put in place.*

There were a couple of other interesting situations that I found myself involved with, one being the planned arrival of a Russian river cruise ship the 'Maxim Litvinov'. She requested a pilot to take her into anchor in St Margaret's Hope bay. Unfortunately the company who chartered the vessel did not inform the customs or immigration authorities regarding the arrival of the vessel into UK waters. I was advised by the local customs office that should the vessel enter our harbour OIC would be responsible for any infringement of customs or immigration regulations required by them. I therefore advised the tug towing the Maxim Litvinov of these requirements and to anchor in Sinclair Bay off the Caithness Coast until all necessary paper work was in place. As mentioned previously St Margaret's Hope had their own Pier Trusties and out with Orkney Harbour Authority responsibility. Due to weather problems the vessel sailed down to Invergordon to await clearance. This did not happen and she eventually sailed back to Russia and the planned operation did not proceed.

The Maxim Litvinov was to be used as a floating hotel moored in St Margaret's Hope bay. Tourist would be flown into Kirkwall airport and transfer to the ship. It looked like a good scheme but the planning was not really carried out in a professional manner. The logistics was suspect in that the anchorage was not really safe for a permanent mooring for a vessel of this size, especially if the weather conditions deteriorated.

In the end, the owners realised that the planned programme was not up to scratch and took the vessel back to Russia. I had several meetings with the person in charge of the scheme regarding the saga where they highlighted there anger at me for not allowing the vessel into Scapa Flow. One of the big put downs to me was "Your father was a very nice man". Of course, I was not, in there estimation.

*River cruise vessel Maxim Litvinov proposed floating hotel for St. Margaret's Hope Bay.*

A bit forward in time again to 1997 and the proposed tendering of the Northern isles Life Line Ferry services. The Scottish office provided grant funding to the operator of the services at that time being provided by P&O Scottish ferries. P&O operated four vessels on the route namely MV St Clair direct service between Lerwick and Aberdeen the MV St Sunniva between Lerwick, Stromness and Aberdeen the MV St Ola between Stromness and Scrabster, all ro/ro passenger and car/lorry ferries and finally MV St magnus a freight vessel carrying 12 passengers.

They had decided that the franchise should go out to tender and Orkney Islands Council decided that Orkney ferries should tender for the Pentland firth operations between Stromness and Scrabster. The Council appointed a consultancy firm Mds Transmodal to assist with compiling our tender.

At this time, there was an independent operator running a ro/ro freight service between Kirkwall and Invergordon; this service was not operating at a profit and the Council had provided funding to help its operations. I believed that if Orkney ferries was to take over the Pentland firth route then they should also look at operating the Invergordon route as well.

My thinking was that with two ferries, we could provide all the necessary passenger, freight and livestock cover for Orkney, also a backup ferry. Peter Isles, the consultant set up his office in the conference room at the harbour offices and work began on our submission to the Scottish office. Regular meetings were held with Orkney ferries finance director David Robertson and members of the ferries board to come up with the best solution for our tender.

I have included on the following page front cover from our bid. The document was submitted to the Scottish office in July 1997 and a meeting was arranged for the following month in their offices in Edinburgh. The chairman of Orkney ferries Stephen Hagan, David Robertson, Peter Isles and myself attended the presentation of our tender.

The Scottish office officials listened to our pitch but gave no indication if it was going to be successful. We left the meeting and headed to the airport for our flight home. Unfortunately, there was fog at Kirkwall so our flight was cancelled. As it was Edinburgh festival, there was no accommodation available in Edinburgh.

The airline offered us a flight to Inverness and the promise of overnight accommodation there and hopefully a flight home the next day. We took this flight and arrived in Inverness. I decided to check with the harbour office at home on the forecast regarding the fog. The outlook was fog for the next two days. I asked if there was any shipping movement and if the pilot launch was available for a pick up at John O'Groats that evening.

As there were several Council employees on the same flight, I asked the airline if instead of putting us all in an hotel for the night, they could provide a mini bus and run us all to John O'Groats. This was agreed and around seven of us set off in a mini bus. We arrived in thick fog at John O'Groats where my pilot launch was waiting and we arrived at Scapa pier just before mid-night. Kirkwall airport was in fact, closed the next day also, so I did the right thing in getting everyone home and back to work the next day.

# PROPOSAL FOR THE NORTHERN ISLES PASSENGER FERRY SERVICES

Contact:

Captain R. C. Sclater
Executive and Operations Director
Harbour Authority Building
Scapa
Orkney
KW15 1SD
TELEPHONE 01856 873636
FAX.: 01856 873012

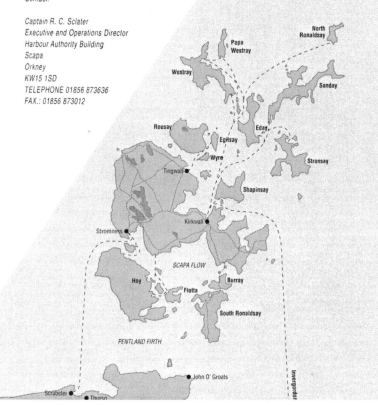

# CONTENTS

As far as the tender process went, the Scottish office had a change of heart and cancelled the whole thing and left P&O with the franchise. However, in 1999 they set up another tendering procedure but by then Orkney Islands Council had changed and did not wish Orkney Ferries to put forward a tender again. On this occasion, P&O lost the franchise and a new company Northlink ferries won the tender.

This was a blow to P&O but the new company were to introduce three new purpose-built vessels for the service that would come into operation in October 2002. I was a Councillor by 1999 and when I saw the design of the two Aberdeen/Orkney/Shetland ferries I said that no way could they operate safely into Stromness on a regular basis due to their size. The only option was to build a new ro/ro terminal in Kirkwall. This was agreed and the new Hatston terminal was built.

Family life also played a big part in my career by having Anna, Esther, Andrew and Joanna keeping me on my toes and making sure I kept my feet on the ground. We made sure that when school holidays came around, we would head off south on holiday and I would get away from the office. With our dog

Sally, we were out every weekend together usually to the beach that she loved. Not the very best-behaved dog but great company.

By 1990, Esther had commenced her studies at Robert Gordon's University in Aberdeen doing a business study degree. Part of the degree course was to carry out a year's work placement with a reputable company. I was in conversation with Captain Max Gunn who asked after the family and I told him about Esther and the need to find a placement in Aberdeen.

'No problem,' he said, 'I will find her a position at ELF headquarters in Aberdeen. This was ideal and Esther had a great year working for them until she returned to university to complete her degree. After graduation Esther started working in the oil industry in Aberdeen but not with ELF. Her work with the oil industry has taken her to Dubai where she worked for eight years, then to London for a few years and now back in Aberdeen working for ConocoPhillips so her year at ELF certainly paid dividends, thanks to the late Captain Max Gunn.

By the time Esther had graduated with her BA, Andrew was ready to head off for his stint at University. He started his degree in engineering at Aberdeen University, a four-year course. This was very handy with his big sister having her own flat for Andrew to visit. I don't think he spent a lot of time there, as being a student he had other fish to fry.

With my position I attended meetings and conferences on a regular basis south and always tried to fly through Aberdeen and have an evening stop over. This was very handy as I was able to take firstly Esther out for meals and then both of them, which we all enjoyed plus the few pounds pocket money handed over before I headed back to my hotel.

Andrew gained a BA hons. in engineering and started his career with the Wood Group working firstly in Broughty Ferry. After a few months, he was asked to work in Dallas, Texas which he really enjoyed. He has had a few different posts working as a turbine engineer, worked with Eon, the electricity company and oil related work as well. Now, he is working in Gloucester with?

Joanna also went to University firstly at Herriot Watt University in the borders where she obtained a 1 class honours degree in Knitwear design.

Then she did two years at Central Saint Martin's school of fashion and design in London and came away with a Master's degree with distinction. She has worked in Italy, Scotland, Shanghai, Columbus Ohio, Seattle and now in Los Angeles. So my children certainly took after their dad as far as travelling is concerned.

*The Family Growing Up*

*Graduation Photos*

I mentioned earlier about the old cannons used as bollards on Kirkwall pier. These were all removed when the harbour was refurbished and new proper bollards were put in their place. We wondered what to do with these five cannons four medium sized and one large. They had probably come of royal navy warships back in Napoleonic times.

It was agreed that the larger be presented to the local TA to be placed outside their headquarters in Kirkwall as they had a similar cannon already on site. They of course, would have to mount it on a new gun carriage, refurbished it to make like new. The other four were recommended to be placed at Kirkwall harbour after they were made to look like new.

Brigadier Robertson in charge of the TA advised me to send them to Chatham dockyard in Kent to be properly restored. This was to cost £4,500 each not including transport. I contacted the local training centre and asked if their apprentices would like to have a go at restoring the cannons. They said yes and designed a model of what the completed cannons would look like. The costs was less than one, if we sent them to Chatham.

The cannons were duly completed and as Kirkwall pier was still undergoing improvements, I recommended that they be placed at the harbour authority building at Scapa until a suitable site was found in Kirkwall. I never did mention them again as I really liked them in front of our building at Scapa where they still remain today. A couple of photos on following pages showing the four in front of the harbour building, the model designed by the apprentices. and last but not least a photo of Anna's grandmother alongside the largest one on the west pier back in the late eighteen hundreds.

*Model of cannon designed by Grain Shore apprentices. The log rotator gives an idea of the scale used.*

*Anna's grandmother Elizabeth Leonard on the West Pier Kirkwall.*

Another issue was the harbour's Equalisation Fund Committee and the relationship between the Council and the oil terminal. This was to change in 1997-8. The Councillors decided that it should be wound up and the largest part of the funds be taken into the Council's coffers. After several heated meetings, it was agreed that the fund be fully taken over by OIC with the oil terminal receiving £20 million to help with the reinstatement of the terminal once it closed down.

It was further agreed that the through put payments of 19p per barrel of oil along with a disturbance fund relating to the terminal would also cease to exist as from January 2000. This fund was used by the economic development department of the Council to provide funding to various bodies and projects over the years, very beneficial to the Orkney economy.

The close financial relationship between both parties ceased and the harbour equalisation committee was no longer required and the fund was transferred into the Council's general reserve fund. This meant that the money raised by the harbours to cover its run down could now be used for all Council services. I did feel it was a backward step but Councillors were happy to take over the fund which in 1998 was around £100 million, the majority being profits made by the efficient harbour's operation.

In 1997, I received the honour of becoming a fellow of the Nautical Institute, copy of letter on the following pages.

The Nautical Institute

11<sup>th</sup> December 1997

Dear *Capt. Sclater.*

202 LAMBETH ROAD
LONDON SE1 7LQ
Telephone: 0171-928 1351
Fax: 0171-401 2817
E-mail: sec@nautinst.org
Web: http://www.nautinst.org

It is my great pleasure on behalf of Council to inform you that you have been elected:-

### A FELLOW OF THE NAUTICAL INSTITUTE

Council recognises the work you have done to promote the nautical profession and your election as Fellow not only reflects the honour which Council wish to bestow upon you but also a new responsibility to ensure that future Fellows meet the same high standards.

As you know, to become a Fellow it is necessary to be proposed and seconded by two Fellows. It is therefore necessary for you to ensure that all applicants who seek your signature, fully meet the criteria set out in the Constitution as printed on the application. You must be satisfied that the subsequent nomination will in no way detract from the high standards set by Council.

I enclose a Certificate of Fellowship with this letter.

It only remains for me to send my warmest congratulations and wish you continued success in the years to come.

Yours sincerely,

N.W.C. Rutherford
Chairman, Fellowship Committee

**CAPT R C SCLATER FNI**

In 1995, the Council had once again decided to look at staffing levels and how to save money. There is no difference in today's world as far as Councils trying to make savings is concerned.

I drafted a full report outlining the Harbours Department Organisation and what I believed was the logical option for our continued staffing levels. My report along with attachments ran into some 300 pages. On the following pages, I have shown the contents page, report is too long to include in my book. I was pleased with the outcome as the majority of Councillors agreed with my recommendations.

**ORKNEY ISLANDS COUNCIL
DEPARTMENTS REORGANISATION**

# PHASE II

# HARBOURS
# DEPARTMENT
# SUBMISSION

## PRIVATE AND CONFIDENTIAL

## CONTENTS OF REPORT
## ORKNEY ISLANDS COUNCIL RESTRUCTURING:PHASE 2

Once I retired they got their way and the post of deputy was dispensed with and replaced with an assistant director. You will also note that I had included on my stationary a logo of the Kirkwall bay in the top right-hand corner to differentiate the harbours from other Council department.

The logo was removed when I retired, as the chief executive stated we were a corporate body and all correspondence was to be on Orkney Islands Council headed paper. I certainly would have fought this decision as I did believe we were a completely different operation from all other departments of the Council. One last point, my depute Captain Bob Moore took over the post when I retired with no interviews held.

Over the next couple of years, things settled down although we continued to promote Scapa flow and Orkney. By early 1998, I was in a position to look at taking early retirement through my membership of the Merchant Navy Officers Pension Scheme (MNOPF). They offered a four-year early retirement package with the pension age dropping from 61 to 57.

I had been a member since 1964 and also had AVC's so with full 75% pension could see no logical reason to continue working. I also had a small pension through my time with P&O. I was not eligible to retire until August and with six weeks leave due, I finally retired in September 1998, 42 years within the marine industry.

Just a couple of interesting people I met in my last year in post.

The Prince of Wales was due in Orkney to open the new Orphir School and also to visit Melsetter house on the island of Hoy. I was tasked with the honour of conducting Prince Charles along with the lord lieutenant and party from Houton pier across Scapa flow to Lyness onboard the Scapa Pioneer.

This was a very interesting trip as I spent the full twenty minutes chatting to Prince Charles and explained the history of Scapa flow from the royal navy involvement, German fleet scuttling, HMS Royal Oak and the Harbours Department and the oil terminal operations. He was very interested and was fully versed in all aspects of the history of Scapa flow. He even knew about the famous poem "Bloody Orkney" written by disgruntled sailors stuck in Orkney during the second world war. On departing the pilot launch, I presented him with a pair of Orkney towage cufflinks in the shape of our tugs and we said goodbye.

*A pleasant trip across Scapa Flow onboard pilot launch Scapa Pioneer with Prince Charles.*

My next interesting meeting was with Kate Addie, the famous BBC reporter. Kate was due to officially open the St. Magnus fair; a fund-raising event organised by the friends of St. Magnus Cathedral to help with restoration work. She was in Nairobi reporting on the bombing of the US embassy and was flying back via London and Aberdeen onwards to Kirkwall.

Unfortunately, it was thick fog in Orkney, so no flights were able to land. I was contacted by Bill Spence and asked if I could help. It was agreed that Kate would get a taxi from Aberdeen to John O'Groats and I would meet her and bring her over in the pilot launch. This was quite a journey, what with her flights and a 5-hour taxi ride.

Anyway, she arrived safely at John O'Groats still in thick fog. We set off to Burwick where Bill would pick her up in his car and head for the opening ceremony. We had a lovely chat on the way over and she was great company. She did arrive slightly late for the opening but no one was worried.

I did, of course, meet countless interesting people during my career and made lots of good friends, some I have mentioned in my story.

On my retirement, I received numerous cards, letters and gifts to thank me for my time as Director of Harbours.

After being retired for just seven months, I realised that I was getting bored and needed a new challenge. As a new Council was due for election in May 1999 I decided to throw my hat in the ring and stand to become an Orkney Island's Councillor. This will be the next chapter in my life.

# Part 7

After eight months into my retirement and having spent two holidays in Tenerife, I knew that this was not what I wished my life to be over the next few years. With a new Council to be elected in May 1999, I decided to put my name forward as a candidate for the Kirkwall Brandyquoy ward of Orkney Islands Council. This being my home town, I thought I may have a chance of winning the seat.

There was one other candidate standing who had been a Councillor prior to this election. This was a new ward so everything to play for, the previous Council consisted of 28 Councillors, now reduced to 21 with new boundaries. I put together my 1-page manifesto, copy on next page and hand posted it into every household in my constituency. This took several days but I was hopeful it would help my case to become their Councillor.

*Orkney Islands Council Elections 6th May*

*Brandyquoy Ward*

*Candidate: Robert C. Sclater*

*I have put forward my name as the prospective candidate to represent your Ward on Orkney Islands Council at the forthcoming elections.*

*I was born and brought in Kirkwall and am married to my wife Anna and have three grown up children.*

*My working career consisted of 20 years in the Merchant Navy from Deck Boy to Master Mariner and 22 years with Orkney Islands Council Department of Harbours initially as Marine Officer/Pilot through to Director, a post I held for 9 years until I retired in September 1998.*

*My reasons for standing are that I now have ample spare time to devote to becoming a Councillor and with my professional background I can bring to the Council an expertise, which already has a proven record with my management of the harbours department.*

*With Orkney dependant so much on the sea for its transport links along with the oil industry, fishing, fish farming, and tourism, my credentials in these fields would I hope be positive for my election as a Councillor.*

*It is not my intention to give you a great electioneering lecture on how I intend to sort out the services provided by the Council as I believe inevitably people who do rarely if ever achieve their aims.*

*Instead I will just say that I would hope to bring a professional, logical and common sense approach to Council business. My goal will be to try to improve the Councils' image where necessary by raising its standards up to the expectations of the people of Orkney. To provide positive leadership in all aspects of the Councils functions to ensure that First Class services are provided at a cost acceptable to the electorate.*

*The main aims of any Councillor should also be to create a positive liaison with the people of the ward they represent to ensure their views and needs are given top priority and where possible and practical are met. I do hope that you will VOTE SCLATER on Election Day.*

*I thank you for you time, and if there are any points which you wish to discuss prior to the election please do not hesitate to contact me on Tel 87 2359 or if you require transport to the polling station on Election day.*

KORSGARTH, HIGH STREET, KIRKWALL 15/04/1999

The election duly arrived and I was very pleased to be elected by a reasonable margin. I know my opponent was not very pleased as he had been a Councillor when I was an official. He was in fact (allegedly) the Councillor who had caused me the problem with the BP ship-to-ship oil transfers by stating it was all done secretly, not true, of course.

I realised once I was elected that becoming a Councillor after being a chief official did not go down well with the Councillors who were re-elected and had been in post when I retired. I was in fact, one of the first ex directors to become a Councillor in Orkney Islands Council. I recall one of the "senior" Councillors saying that being a Councillor was completely different from being an official and I had a lot to learn.

This amused me as he had never been a chief official and also I had produced all the relevant Harbours Department reports for his committee over the past 13 years that he had presented. I realised then that I was in for a difficult time trying to put my points forward in committee with quite a negative attitude towards my election as a Councillor.

This did not deter me and I made sure that my voice was heard. It was not my intention either to undermine my successor Captain Moore, as a member of the harbours committee but more to help him with his task of getting his reports passed in the chamber. I became a member of various committees and was vice chair of the roads and infrastructure committee for two years, chair of the planning appeals committee for two years, vice chairman and then chairman of Orkney tourist board for three years, and director of Orkney ferries wearing a different hat from when I was executive director.

I was also elected as a board member of the Northern Joint Police Board. There was numerous projects and developments in the pipe line relating to the new northern isles ferry contract, new Hatston pier, marinas, new library, pensioners Christmas grant and other smaller items that I made sure my points were raised in committee and at full Council.

I will touch firstly on the Christmas pensioners grant which was set up shortly after oil started to flow into the Flotta oil terminal. This was a grant initially £10 provided out of the oil income received by Orkney islands Council from Occidental the owners of the terminal. The grant was paid to all pensioners, disabled or handicapped persons residing in Orkney.

The reserve fund stood at over £150 million in 1999, mostly generated by oil tanker dues and placed in the Harbour Equalisation Fund. The grant did increase slightly over the years up to £34 by 1999. As it was coming up to the millennium, I thought it would be a nice gesture on behalf of the Council to give a one-off grant of £100 to celebrate the year 2000.

Our friends in Shetland were providing £250 towards their annual Christmas grant. By this time also, our finance department were looking at reducing the grant and eventually doing away with it. I put my proposals forward and it was not met with universal agreement. After many debates and high-profile reports in the local and national newspapers, my proposals were not agreed. The one positive point I did achieve was to maintain the grant and it was not phased out until 2019, long after I stepped down as a Councillor.

Another project which I played a role in was the provision of a new library and archive. The original library in Kirkwall was the oldest lending library in Scotland when it opened in 1683. The library to be replaced, was gifted to Orkney by Andrew Carnegie back in 1903. The debate on the new library had been ongoing for several years and always deferred by the Council for further reports and decisions on where to site it.

It was agreed to set up a library sub-committee to try and progress the project, and I thankfully, was appointed a member. The site was agreed and then the design and layout drawn up and we finally agreed to get on with the construction. I was pleased that I was dogged in my arguments to get on with the project and convince the other committee members that the longer we delayed the more the costs would rise and anyway the old library was no longer fit for purpose.

I should just add that Anna, my wife, worked as a part time librarian so I was fully up to speed on the conditions in the old library. Photos on next pages of old library refurbished by a local entrepreneur and now a first-class coffee house and shop. The new library one of finest in the north of Scotland, on the old auction mark site. Copy of one of my many queries tabled at Council meetings, the main one here relating to the new library project.

I wish to raise the following points at the above meeting.

Recreation & Cultural Services Minutes page 731 item 3 Capital Programme 2001/02

Clarification on the New Library project, I was advised at the meeting on 30th Oct. 2000 that the demolition of the Old Mart will not now take place till later in 2001. I was informed at the meeting on 28th August that in fact this would go ahead early in the New Year. This project has been delayed too long and I wish the Full Council to be advised on when we will see action to get the New Library construction commenced.

Economic Development Minutes page 773 item 8, BVD Complex in Cattle

I still cannot see what benefit will be achieved with only 80% of cattle being tested surely we should still be striving for 100% with the proper safeguards put in place to ensure that Orkney remains BVD free after all cattle are tested and the eradication programme completed.

Page 780/790 item (s) New Creamery

The figure of £3,635,000 contained in this minute at (g) does not correspond with the figure agreed at the Special Full Council on 1st September 1999 which it relates to i.e. Estimated Cost = £3,492,000 + £100,000 equity stake making a total of £3,592,000 amounts to £43,000 less than the minute suggests. Also I note that the capital programme for the project was set at £3.6m I assume that the equity stake cannot be classed as capital expenditure please can I have clarification on these points. Su

Finance & General Purposes page 864 item 21 Orkney ro/ro Services Ltd.

Although I have received a letter from the Director answering my questions regarding this venture they do not clearly stack up and he does confirm "in retrospect that the reports and minutes are not quite as specific on the matters as they might have been".
I believe that the figure of £300,000 agreed in October 1999 is no longer applicable as the cost estimates at that time were a lot higher than what was paid for the vessel along with the repairs. The only asset that the company has is the vessel, value now possibly less than £200,000.

*Old and New Libraries*

In 1999, once again tenders were being sought for the northern isles ferry services between mainland Scotland, Orkney and Shetland. This was similar to the tender that I had been involved with when executive director of Orkney ferries, but was shelved by the Scottish office. The new tender was won by a consortium of Caledonia Macbrayne & RBS out bidding P&O Scottish ferries who had held the contract for many years.

When the Council was presented with the design of their new Aberdeen service ferries, I explained at the meeting that in my opinion they would not be able to navigate safely on a regular basis into Stromness or Kirkwall harbours due to their size and draft. I was, of course, not the director any more just a back bench Councillor.

However, after ongoing debates and reports from the Harbours Department it was accepted that my estimations were correct. This resulted in a decision to construct a new harbour facility out at Hatston with all the necessary infrastructure to suit these new ferries.

Work was also required at the Stromness and Scrabster terminals to suit this part of the ferry links. I was a member of the transportation committee so was in a good position to help the Director of Harbours with progressing these new facilities. The new ferries came into operation in late 2002.

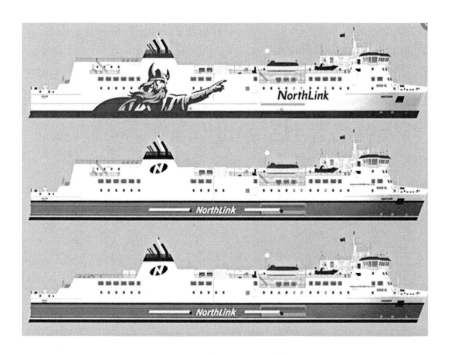

*Photos of MV Hrossey and MV Hjaltland both length 125m beam 20m draught 5.8m and 11720 gross tons speed 24 knots. These operated on the main links between Aberdeen, Orkney, and Shetland. The MV Hamnavoe of length 112 m beam 18.5 m and draught 4.4 m 8780 gross tons, speed 19 knots operated between Stromness and Scrabster. This was classed as Orkney and Shetlands lifeline service.*

Being a member of the Northern Joint Police Board was a very interesting post covering all aspects of police business in the highlands and islands. I attended regular meetings of the board in Inverness. The board members represented Shetland, Western isles, Orkney and Highland Council. There was also members representing these areas on the highlands and islands joint fire board.

The two boards met on the same day, police in the morning and fire in the afternoon, at Highland Councils offices in Inverness. There were two members each from Orkney and Shetland Councils, three from the Western Isles and 12 from Highland Council.

The members from Shetland and the Western Isles attend both boards whereas Orkney had two on the police board and two on the fire board. I thought, what a waste of money having four members flying down to attend meetings where two could cover both as the other island Councils did.

I took this up with the Council's administration department on my return from my first meeting. I was informed that as the Council had made these appointments they could not be changed for the four years until a new Council was elected. I was astounded that we could waste tax payers' money in this way.

It was interesting to note that the Councillors previously on these boards were the ones that lobbied strongly to cut Council expenditure on various essential services but were happy that four of them attended meetings, when two could have covered them. As there was nothing I could do, in 1999, I was determined to broach this subject if and when I was elected to the next Council.

Just to finish this, in 2003, I achieved my goal and it was agreed that only two Councillors would attend both board meetings, with two substitutes to cover. Although travel and expenses were met by both boards and did not come out of Council funds, this did save a considerable sum out of their budgets. Something that should have been done years before.

A slight digress from Council work. In 2001, I was contacted by Tysers our harbour's insurance brokers asking me if I would like to carry out some port works for them. They wished to increase their ports portfolio and thought I might be in a position with my harbours background to assist them. Anna and I were due to fly out to Dallas, Texas in September 2001 to visit our son Andrew who was working for the Wood Group, an Oil Development Company with head offices in Aberdeen.

As we were to fly out from London, I arranged to visit Tysers offices in London prior to our flight to see what the job entailed. After a nice lunch at their head office, we sat down to detailed discussions on what they wished me to do. I agreed to take up the post and would firstly contact the various Scottish ports where I had good contacts. My remit was to carry out a detailed survey of these ports and advise them what Tysers could offer as insurance brokers. This work did not get underway until Spring 2002. I arranged a presentation to the Scottish ports group, part of the UKPA (United Kingdom Ports Association) at one of their meetings to introduce board members of Tyser.

One interesting point; my meeting in London was arranged just prior to the twin towers attack on 9/11. John Lucas one of the Tyser team, had contacted an insurance broker on the 11 in New York to advise him of the meeting taking place the following week. John however, had not taken into account the time difference and phoned his friend at 9 am UK time 4 am New York time.

Due to this early call, his friend slept in and was late for work. Would you believe his offices were in one of the twin towers and were attacked before he arrived at work, lucky escape! Things worked out well and I did provided surveys of several ports but unfortunately, none of then took up the offers provided by Tyser.

They all had well-established insurance brokers and did not wish to change. I think they were set in their ways. They did, however, manage a reduction in their premiums when they received the detailed quotes from Tyser. I carried out this consultancy for four years on a very ad-hoc basis, an interesting post that kept me in touch with the ports industry.

After four years as a Councillor, I decided that I would be happy to stand again when new elections were held in May 2003. I must have done a good job in my first session as no one stood against me and I was automatically returned as the Councillor for the Brandyquoy ward. At last, Councillors accepted me and I was elected unopposed as Chairman of the Transportation and Infrastructure Committee.

This was the committee responsible for all harbour activities plus of course all transportation operation in Orkney. I did have representations from several Councillors and my constituents to go for the top job of convenor but felt I was not really suited to that role, happy to take up the post as chairman. Along with this position came my membership of Hitrans (highlands and islands transport group), covering Orkney, Shetland, Western Isles, Highland , Argyle and Bute and Moray Councils.

I was made Vice Convenor of the group in 2004. I was also appointed as one of the two Councillors on the Police and Fire Boards, with the appointment as vice-convenor of the fire board. Along with my chairmanship, I was automatically a board member of Orkney towage and Orkney ferries. So, back wearing many hats but as a politician as opposed to an official. With my past history, it did hold me in good stead, working with all my old friends in both companies. I was appointed chairman of Orkney Towage in 2005.

*Orkney islands Council in Council Chamber, May 2003. I am sitting at the last chair down the left side, next to the door.*

The funding of the internal ferry services were very relevant with the ongoing running costs well outside the subsidy received from the now Scottish government. I had my job cut out trying to obtain additional funding as you can see from some of the correspondence on later pages. We were also drawing up a replacement program for the ferries as we could not expect to replace them in the short time we had built them.

Since I retired as Director of Harbours, back in 1998, there had been no new ferries built. The Council employed various consultants to help draw up our proposals. I have attached some of the details we presented to the Scottish government during my time as Chairman, trying to progress the replacement programme.

My initial contact with the Scottish government was with Nicol Stephen MSP, then Minister for Transport. He took over as Deputy First Minister in June 2005 and was replaced by Tavish Scott MSP for Shetland. Tavish and I went back a long way as we attended the Miami cruise convention together back in 1995. So this made my task much easier once Nicol Stephen MSP moved on.

**Bob Sclater**

| | |
|---|---|
| **From:** | "Bob Sclater" <bob@sclater.fslife.co.uk> |
| **To:** | "Nicol Stephen" <ministerfortransport@scotland.gsi.gov.uk> |
| **Sent:** | 26 January 2005 12:54 |
| **Subject:** | Inter-islands Ferry/Aircraft Replacement Study |

Dear Nicol

Orkney Islands Council have now received the completed consultants report on the ferry replacement study which also included the inter-islands air services.

I would therefor be very pleased to meet with you and your officials to highlight the findings of this study and to allow the Council to see how we can in conjunction with the Scottish Executive progress the replacement of our internal ferry fleet.

I realise that you have a very busy schedule but would it be possible to meet with you before Wednesday 16th February.

I would be obliged if you could to let me know of any dates which would be suitable to meet in Edinburgh, hopefully within the next three weeks.

I look forward to hearing from you.

Best Regards

Councillor Bob Sclater

Chair Transport & Infrastructure

Orkney Islands Council

**ORKNEY ISLANDS COUNCIL**

## Orkney Inter-isles Ferry Replacement and Air Services Study

by

**Strategic Transport Solutions**

&

**Maritime Corporate Ltd**

December 2004

* * *

Contents

Phase 1

Note: Phase 2 of this study was prepared by Maritime Corporate Limited with specialist input from Burness, Corlett & Partners and Burness, Corlett & Partners (Northern)

**Fact Sheet: Nicol Stephen Transport Minister 9<sup>th</sup> February 2005**

**AEF 2004/05 & 2005/06**

| | Shetland | Western Isles | Orkney |
|---|---|---|---|
| | £74,706 & £77,015 | £90,339 & £93,252 | £52,231 & £54,103 |

**Population June 2002**

| 21,940 | 26,200 | 19,210 |
|---|---|---|

**Allocation per head of Pop.**

| £3405 | £3510 | £3448 £3559 | £2719 £2816 |
|---|---|---|---|

**Difference from Orkney per head of Population**

| £686 | £694 | £729 £743 |
|---|---|---|

Orkney Ferries: Study called for by Scottish Executive following application for replacement of Eynhallow over two years ago. Includes all possible options from High-Speed ferries to passenger only and passenger /vehicles. Alternative routes innovative vessels Fixed links and upgrades to piers and jetties. Also takes into account the internal air service, which is essential to Island life. Full consultation carried out with all relevant bodies who gave full support for the recommendations in the report. Page 113 for Conclusion & Recommendations.

No of Vessels: 9
Insured Value: £23.1 m.

**Orkney Ferries Fleet**

| | Built | Replacement | | Estimated Age at Replacement. |
|---|---|---|---|---|
| Eynhallow | 1987 | £5.5m | 2005/06 | 19 Years |
| Earl Sigurd | 1989 | £8.0m | 2006/07 | 18 " |
| Golden Mariana | 1973 | £2.0m | 2007/08 | 35 " Hard ramp Papay/Westray |
| Shapinsay | 1988 | £5.5m | 2007/08 | 20 " |
| Earl Thorfinn | 1989 | £8.0m | 2008/09 | 20 " |
| Thorsvoe | 1991 | £6.5m | 2009/10 | 18 " |
| Hoy Head | 1994 | £7.0m | 2007/08 | Initial replace by Varagen or Earl Sigurd |
| Varagen | 1988 | £8.0m | 2010/11 | 23 " |
| Graemsay | 1996 | £2.0m | 2012/13 | 17 " |
| Total | | £52.0m | | |

This is based on need for bigger, faster vessels being more passenger friendly (DDA), which the consultants believe will be required for the future.

Present Operating Costs: 1/04/03 to 31/03/04  (02/03)
Wages fuel Repairs etc
£5260m  (£5122m)
Management Admin Costs
£603k     (£567)
Passenger No.  281,000, 277,800, 284000, 290000, 310000
Car     No.                                          75,800,  79,000
Total Costs:  £6098m  (£5689)

Income  2003/04   (02/03)
             £1.684m   (£1.659)

Operating Loss  2003/04   (02/03)
                        £4.414m   (£4.030)
Subsidy for 2004/05 : £4.7m (£4.496m)    Shetland £11.3m on ferries

3 Ferries Earl Sigurd, Earl Thorfinn and Varagen all Class 11A  & 111 MCA Certificates
Ships engaged on voyages of any kind other than international voyages
Other vessels same as Shetland for partially smooth waters or within certain restrictions classes
1V,VI, V1A, & V111A

Airservices

PSO  flights operated by Loganair to 6 Island Airfields.

Costs of PSO's

2003/04 £325,998
2004/05 £441,103
2005/06 £471,474
Loss of Air ambulance contract using Islanders will greatly increase cost for 2006 onwards.

Passenger Nos. 99/00 12889, 00/01 13300, 2001/02 13722, 2002/03 16393 2003/04 18551

Additional costs for the future of the air services relate to up grading at airports new Fire Tenders over next 3 years.
Require lights on runway aircraft can only operate in daylight, which is limited in winter.

Fire Engines £300k over 3 years
Lights £125k for ambulance flights night flying requires considerably more investment.

New Hanger required at Airport for maintenance of Islander fleet. £1.0m plus
Problems with loss of Air Ambulance knock on effect of this on air services and the maintenance team at Kirkwall airport
Few other Transports cost;
Bus Services require at least : £500k to up grade buses Orkney has the poorest bus fleet in Scotland.

New freight Transport building for inter island freight £600k

Ferry Information Boards £400k
Ferry Ticketing and Web sites £100k
New Life Rafts to up grade vessels passenger carrying during winter refit period. £60k

Transport Act 2001 Section 70 could be used for funding Shipping and Air Services out with GAE.

Leave Orkney GAE as is at moment give additional £7m for transport running and replacement programme.

These are all lifeline services, which creates employment for up to 100 persons in ferries alone and about 20/30 in air services. A good number, which are Island, based.

Note: we are using £303k out of our Quality of Life allocation to keep ferries running in 2005/06.
Also received application from Orkney Ferries for additional sum of £118k for second vessel to operate on busy Houton/Hoy route.

My big problem with this first meeting with the Minister was the Convenor and Director of Finance of OIC stated, they had to attend also. Unfortunately, they did not share the same views as me on how to fund the replacement programme, so we achieved nothing. Their attitude was that the Scottish Government should meet all the costs involved. I believed that the Council could have offered to use part of the reserve fund, standing at nearly £200 million at that time, to start the ball rolling.

Additional funding would be sought from the Scottish government and ERDF (European Regional Development Fund) to meet the initial costs of the new ferries and the port infrastructure improvements. The new ferries could be built utilising a leasing agreement with Hambros bank on a similar basis as we used in the past. This would mean payments being paid on an annual basis reducing the capital outlay.

The Council could then lobby the Scottish government to cover the leasing payments through the annual grant as it could be judged as revenue outlay as opposed to capital outlay. The Council always stated that Orkney did not receive the same funding as other island groups as we did not spend as much as them. This surely would have helped greatly in their argument for additional grant aid. I understood at the time, that Shetland Islands Council used this method for replacing their ferries.

I did achieve more by direct contact with Tavish Scott MSP with logical arguments and obtained funding for the various aspects of Orkney ferries operating costs. Copy of some of the correspondence with Tavish Scott MSP on following pages. When dealing with politicians, things can move at a very slow rate. I did believe that we put together a very good case for these transport improvements and we did succeed in obtaining additional funding thanks to Tavish who got things done much faster than most.

26th July 2006

Dear Bob,

Thank you for your letter of 12th June 2006 about the latest approach from Pentland Ferries to lease Burwick Terminal and the request for additional funding to meet the costs of the fire safety sprinkler upgrades to the Class A ferries.

I note that the Council has deferred a final decision on Burwick until such time as Pentland Ferries provides more detailed information on its operations and future plans. I look forward to hearing further updates from you as the proposal develops.

Following a recent review of the transport budget for 2006-2007, I am pleased to announce that I will be making an award of £300,000 to help meet the costs of the ferry upgrades. This will be in addition to the £500,000 allocated for 2006-07 to help the Council meet its other internal transport costs. My officials will contact the Council to arrange the transfer of the funds.

I also hope that my offer to meet some of the costs to engage a consultant to assist the Council with the completion of the STAG will prove beneficial in expediting the production of the final document.

**TAVISH SCOTT**

---

## SCOTTISH EXECUTIVE

Minister for Transport
**Tavish Scott** MSP

Councillor Captain R C Sclater
Orkney Islands Council
Council Offices, School Place
Kirkwall
Orkney
KW15 1NY

Victoria Quay
Edinburgh EH6 6QQ

Telephone: 0845 774 1741
scottish.ministers@scotland.gsi.gov.uk
http://www.scotland.gov.uk

Our ref: 2006/0040060

11th January 2007

Dear Bob,

Thank you for your letter of 4th December 2006 about continuing financial support towards the Council's internal transport costs and the new lairage facilities at Hatson.

I recently met with my officials to discuss the pressures and savings on my transport budget for 2007-08. Although budgets for 2007-08 will not be finalised until next year, I believe that additional funding can be found and I have therefore instructed my officials to flag up £1M for Orkney Islands Council as a pressure on my transport budget for 2007-08, which has received my prior approval.

I have received an update on the implementation of the lairage facilities at Hatson and I am pleased that the funding of the project has now been agreed. I understand that the Council will now be tendering for the construction of the lairage facilities and that it is hoped that the project will be completed in time for the start of this year's peak livestock season. I have asked my officials to keep me updated on the progress of the project.

I hope this is helpful.

Hope to see you in March when in Orkney.

**TAVISH SCOTT**

**Councillor Robert C Sclater**

Council Offices, School Place
Kirkwall, Orkney KW15 1NY
Tel:   (01856) 87 2359    Fax: (01856) 87 2359
Email: bob.sclater@orkney.gov.uk
bob@sclater.fslife.co.uk

ORKNEY
ISLANDS COUNCIL

Tavish Scott Esq. MSP
Minister for Transport
Scottish Executive
Victoria Quay
Edinburgh
EH6 6QQ

20$^{TH}$ January 2007

Thank you for your letter of 11$^{th}$ January 2007 relating to the continuing financial support for the Council's internal transport costs.

I was very pleased to note, as will all my council colleagues within Orkney Islands Council, the details contained in your letter confirming, hopefully an increase to £1M the support for the financial year 2007/08.

Over the next three weeks we will be debating and agreeing our budgets for the next financial year and will take into account the above sum in our final budget setting.

This additional funding will be most helpful to us, as you are fully aware we do have ongoing internal transport costs that we are finding very difficult to meet.

I was also very pleased with the outcome of the Hatston lairage issues and can only thank David Hart and Alan McPherson for the very positive role they played in confirming the capital funding and ongoing revenue costs for the project. The Technical Services Department has confirmed that steady progress is being made with the final design and they hope in conjunction with SAC that they will go out to tender in February with the building completed by end of August.

I attended a meeting with our consultants on Thursday regarding the Ferry Replacement STAG 2 process that appears to be progressing well and hopefully we should have the final draft completed by March.

There is:

I stepped down as a Councillor in May 2007 leaving behind, I thought, a way forward for the new Council. It appeared that this new Council were more interested in restructuring departments within the Council. The Harbours Department along with Orkney ferries and Orkney towage were big on this agenda. The new proposals amalgamated the three entities into the marine services department. The old saying "If it ain't broke, don't try to fix it", very true in this case. It caused considerable staff upheaval and loss of company identity for employees. There was also an endless amount of time and effort spent on promoting a container hub to be constructed in Scapa Flow. Never did think it was feasible and in the end did not come to fruition. Anyway, all our hard work to get movement on our internal ferry services was shelved and to date, very little or anything has been achieved.

Rough idea of new vessels proposed for Orkney's internal ferry service back in 2005.

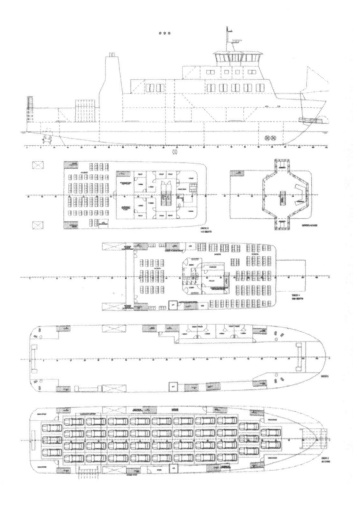

Replacement ferry for North isles.
Length 65.00 metres
Breadth 14.2 metres
Draft. 3.0 metres
Vehicles. 40 cars
Passengers. 200

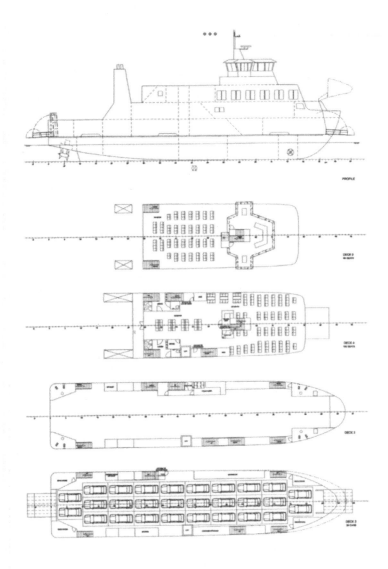

Replacement ferry for South isles
Length. 55.00 metres
Breadth 11.70 metres
Draft. 3.00 metres
Vehicles. 28 cars
Passengers. 125

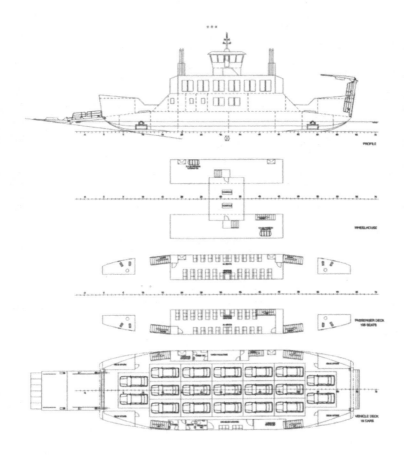

Replacement ferry for inner North isles
Length. 38.00 metres
Breadth. 11.70 metres
Draft. 1.50 metres
Vehicles. 19 cars
Passengers. 100

I mentioned the construction of the new harbour facilities in Kirkwall, with the new deep-water ro/ro ferry terminal with all necessary passenger facilities at Hatston. This was officially opened by Prince Edward, Earl of Wessex, in September 2003. I had the honour of officiating at the opening and showing him round the new pier facilities.

*Introducing Anna to Prince Edward. Official opening of Hatston Pier.*

*We both seem to be enjoying the occasion.*

Hatston pier enabled the larger cruise liners to berth alongside as opposed to anchoring in Kirkwall bay. It made a great difference for passengers and crew to come ashore. Shuttle buses ferry passenger and crew into Kirkwall.

At this time also, we had detailed discussion on transportation of livestock out of Orkney and Shetland, quite a thorny subject with special animal welfare regulations in place, to ensure safe and humane shipping of cattle and sheep by sea. After many joint meetings with Shetland Councillors, farmers union representatives, Scottish government officials, and ferry operators we eventually all agreed that the best shipping method was by animal transporters, known latterly as livestock cassettes.

In the past, animals had been shipped out on the hoof onboard the specialised cattle/sheep carriers the MV Shorthorn Express or MV Buffalo Express during the peak shipping months between August and November. This was a very expensive charter and the Scottish government wished to dispense with this annual burden.

The rest of the year they travelled in trucks or GLT's (general livestock trailers) mainly onboard the dedicated freight ro/ro ferries. Orkney is renowned for its cattle and sheep production with farming being one of the main industries on the islands. The dedicated cassettes along with new lairage facilities at Hatston pier were installed and everyone was very happy with the positive solution to this operation.

The project was jointly funded by the Scottish government, ERDF and the Council. I have attached some details and photos relating to this subject. During our many meetings, I offered to produce some calculations in an attempt to circumvent EU regulations on the shipment of livestock. My figures although useful, were never used as agreement was reached on the preferred method of shipment by the new livestock cassettes.

 SCOTTISH EXECUTIVE   ● ● ●

**Enterprise, Transport & Lifelong Learning Department**   Victoria Quay
Transport Division 4   Edinburgh EH6 6QQ

Councillor R Sclater   Telephone: 0131-244 7277
Chairman of Transportation and Infrastructure Committee   Fax: 0131-244 7444
Department of Development Services   E mail: david.hart@scotland.gsi.gov.uk
Orkney Islands Council   http://www.scotland.gov.uk
Council Office
Kirkwall   Your ref: VC/VC
Orkney   Our ref: THG 12/1
KW15 1NY
   14 June 2005

Dear Bob

**TRANSPORTATION OF LIVESTOCK FROM THE NORTHERN ISLES**

You and Councillor Inkster of SIC wrote to me on 24 May, after the Northern Isles Livestock Shipping Working Group (NILSWG) meeting held on that day, to present the NILSWG sub-group findings on the detailed livestock transport options appraisal and financial appraisal. The Working Group is meeting again on Thursday 16 June in Orkney and I have asked Andrew Maclaren and Catriona Graham to attend. I would have wished to attend but the date clashes with meetings to which I am unavoidably committed at the Scottish Parliament. I would be grateful if you would convey my apologies to the meeting. I thought it would be helpful, however, if I wrote in advance of the meeting on some key issues.

The clear message we have taken from the reports of the meeting on 24 May is that both Orkney and Shetland representatives support a two tier transporter system for transporting livestock from the islands. I understand that there has been a broad consensus of views and I am encouraged by the progress which has been made.

The challenge for us now is how to take these issues forward on the basis of further input by the Group, and we can advise on how this work can best be aligned with the Invitation to Tender (ITT) for the forthcoming contract. I therefore attach a note of issues on which we would welcome the Groups' thoughts and any further clarification about how these issues can be taken forward. Again I apologise that I will not be able to attend the meeting in person, but I look forward to hearing about these and any other issues discussed at the Group.

I am copying this letter to Amanda Pellow and to Councillor Inkster and Graham Spall at Shetland Islands Council.

Yours sincerely

**DAVID M HART**
Head of Division

# SHIPPING AND LAIRAGE FACILITY PLAN FOR ORKNEY

### Report for the
### Northern Isles Livestock Shipping Working Group

### Produced by SAC Kirkwall

September 2004

## CONTENTS

*Livestock carrier used in busy periods August/October. Over 20,000 cattle and 20,000 sheep exported every year.*

*Livestock cassettes now used on ro/ro vessels. Big saving on not chartering livestock vessels in main shipping season.*

*Hatston Pier with ro/ro cargo vessel at linkspan. Outside berth on pier suitable for large cruise liners.*
*Hatson Pier enabled the larger cruise liners to berth alongside as opposed to anchoring in Kirkwall Bay. Made a great difference for passengers and crew to come ashore. Shuttle buses ferry passenger and crew into Kirkwall.*

With the cost of the internal ferry services increasing all the time, the decision to look at fixed links between the islands was to be discussed. This would entail tunnels or bridges. None of these proposal were thought to be financially viable or in some cases too complicated to consider.

I did put forward my view on a tunnel between Orkney and mainland Scotland which did in my mind have more merit than links between the islands. However, once again, my scheme was knocked back. I was involved in a debate at the Stromness debating society and put my arguments forward that were met by some positive/negative responses. I ended up giving a radio broadcast interview with the Falkland Islands radio station on my views on tunnels. Never achieved my goal but gave it a good try. Extract from press coverage on next page.

In Hitrans (Highlands &Islands Transport Group) we looked at all aspects of transport within the region, one being air services provided to all three island groups. Proposals were put forward to try and reduce the cost of air travel by introducing a subsidy for all island travellers. The first proposal was to be a pilot scheme only for Shetland. I had seen in the past that a pilot scheme could result in it lasting for years with other island groups missing out.

Just to highlight this point, at present the Western Isles have had a RET (road equivalent tariff) pilot scheme in place for the past ten years. Shetland have received a 20% discount on fares since last year. RET does not work for them as the road equivalent to their sea route does not equate, as the distance by sea, if too long.

Orkney is still awaiting the RET on the Pentland Firth route that would cut costs by around 40%. So allowing a pilot scheme works fine for the island group that wins it. Back to ADS (air discount scheme) I moved at the HItrans meeting that this should apply to all islands and no pilot scheme be agreed.

Thank goodness we had the Scottish mainland Councillors as they agreed with me that we lobby the Scottish government for the scheme to apply to all Island Council groups. We attended several meetings with Scottish government ministers and officials in Edinburgh to iron out this subsidy. The agreement reached was a reduction of 40% on air fares for those travelling from the three island groups to airports on the Scottish mainland.

*The Hitrans team, 2003. I am third from the left.*

A bit more on airports, the transportation committee was involved in agreeing the provision of a new purpose-built aircraft hangar for Logan Air and also help with a new airport terminal building. One of our best achievements was financial help towards the new instrument landing system (ILS) at Kirkwall Airport increasing the capability of landing aircraft in foggy weather by some 90%.

There were numerous other projects such as a new travel centre in Kirkwall incorporating a bus terminal, tourist office and some rental office space. Also, new passenger facilities at Stromness harbour. The new marinas were being installed at Kirkwall and Stromness that I highlighted earlier on in my story.

One other development that I managed to achieve was a new slipway at Scapa pier. The original small boat slip was really of no use much too small and really only suitable at high tide. I had discussions with the Director of harbours, by this time, the late Captain Nigel Mills and explained that I had tried long ago to get funding for the slipway but to no avail.

I did not want to go through committee as I knew that island Councillors would object and want the funding for some project on their island. He agreed that we could utilise funding from an underspend he had on his maintenance budget which did not require Council approval.

I did eventually report it to my committee and as expected received some objections from other Councillors on our methods. It certainly was much appreciated by the small boat owners who use it on a regular basis. A hard concrete standing was also included alongside the slip for boats to dry out for painting and general maintenance, also handy for the pilot launches.

As vice-convenor of the highlands and islands fire board I substituted for the convenor to chair a disciplinary hearing relating to Stornaway fire station personnel. A group of fire fighters had been suspended due to their non-appearance at a fire call out. It transpired that there was bad blood between two factions on the island relating to a promotion of one of the firemen that one group did not agree with.

The group who did not respond to the call out were in fact having a meal at a local restaurant that resulted in them drinking so not allowed to attend. There tabs on the call out fire board were in place indicating they were available but did not show up.

The other team reported them and they were suspended. I should add that the call out was a false alarm, in fact at the premises of one of the firemen who attended. This had occurred several months prior to the tribunal. There were six members of the fire board along with our legal advisor and highland Council officials. We flew over to Stornaway on the Monday and the tribunal started on the Tuesday morning. The suspended firemen were represented by the fireman's union and the fire brigade by their lawyers.

After four days of evidence, we considered their case and came to a decision. In my mind, it was not clear cut and I believed that the suspended fireman had not been fairly dealt with and there were certainly grey areas regarding the evidence submitted.

However, the majority of board members agreed that they should be dismissed from the service, I along with one other member recommended they receive a final written warning but with the final vote being four to two, they were dismissed. Not a very nice task, chairing a tribunal of this nature.

The fire and police board certainly kept one busy. At this time also, we were involved with the building of a new police station in Kirkwall, the old one some 100 years old past its sale by date. Once again several meetings with police procurement department on the site and construction details. We were also building a new fire station on the islands of Hoy and Papa Westray.

I attended the opening of all three, being the fire board representative at Papa Westray opening. The opening of the Longhope fire station on the island of Hoy was a very different occasion. I mentioned that the fire and police board meetings were mostly held in Inverness at highland Council offices, but once a year we would meet at the various island Councils headquarters.

The fire board agreed to meet in Orkney and would travel over to Hoy for the official opening. As the ferry to Hoy did not fit into our timetable, I contacted the Flotta Oil Terminal to ask if their passenger launch could take us over and back to Hoy. I had a good rapport with the Terminal so they agreed to ferry about 25 of us there and back.

On the morning of the planned opening it was blowing a strong gale. We set off to Houton to catch the M.V. Herston Lass over to Hoy. When we arrived we were told that the normal ferry service had been suspended as were all other ferries operating in Orkney waters due to the worsening weather.

The skipper on the Herston Lass said he was happy take us but not to Longhope but to Lyness Pier as the sea was getting quite rough and this would be shorter distance to travel. Off we set and then we heard that the Longhope lifeboat had been called out to a sailing yacht in difficulties in Scapa Flow due to the now storm force winds.

A number of the lifeboat crew were also part time firemen on the island. After a bumpy ride, we arrived at Lyness pier and were picked up by mini buses for the trip to Longhope, a few miles round the island. We arrived wind swept and witnessed the life boat towing the stricken yacht into Longhope pier. The opening ceremony went well with the lifeboat crew back from their successful rescue in attendance and we had a lovely buffet lunch in the nearby hotel.

Of course, everyone was very concerned about getting back in the launch as the wind was still blowing. I contacted the Flotta Terminal and we agreed to head back as soon as possible and we jumped into the mini buses and headed once again to Lyness. The trip back was even worse with a few of the passengers being sea sick and losing their lovely buffet lunch.

We arrived safely back at Houton where the bus was waiting to take everyone to the airport for their flight back to Inverness and two to Shetland. Luckily, the flights were still flying even with the bad weather. One final point, we later learned that the crew of the lifeboat received bravery commendation on velum for rescuing the crew of the yacht. gives an idea of the weather conditions I took the fire board members on their trip across Scapa Flow. This trip was spoken about for many a day; the opening of the Longhope fire station certainly went down in fire board history.

*Herston Lass on slightly less blustery day in Scapa Flow.*

I enjoyed my time as a Councillor and was involved in many debates and discussions over my eight years and I believe, did achieve some positive results. In 2008, the Council were engaged once again in restructuring and cutting back on staff. This related quite drastically on the Department of Harbours and Orkney towage employees.

Although I had no locus in this, I felt I should write to the chief executive regarding my concerns, and a copy of my letter is on the following pages. This was my final contact with the Council. My predictions were correct. With the number of STS operations, increase in cruise liners along with other harbour related activities the marine services operations are nearly as busy now as when I retired. Never got the Foinaven back though.

Mr Alistair Buchan
Chief Executive
Orkney Islands Council
Council Offices
School Place
Kirkwall
KW15 1NY

Korsgarth
High Street
Kirkwall
KW15 1AZ

02/02/2008

Dear Alistair

Orkney Harbours Operations

I am sure like me your were very surprised to hear in the press yesterday that Forth Ports PLC have decided not to proceed with their Ship to Ship (STS) oil transfer proposals in the Firth of Forth.

This must give Orkney Harbours a golden opportunity to seek this lucrative new business with Scapa Flow, as we all know, being the most suitable, efficient, safe and environmentally run harbour carrying out this type of operations in the UK.

The figures relating to the Ship to Ship transfer of the Russian fuel/crude oil were quoted at some 8 million tons per annum. This would certainly bring the through put of hydrocarbon product into/out off the harbour back up to an acceptable level if this contract can be won.

It must therefor be logical at the present time to put on hold the drastic measures proposed for the run down of the port operations with so many redundancies being sought.

I do not believe I need to spell out to you or to any of the Councillors what an efficient port must provide to the marine industry to ensure that the port is open for business 24 hours a day 365 days a year. In my mind the job cuts highlighted in the press would in fact reduce the viability of the harbour and would not meet their requirements.

Orkney Harbours at present does provide an efficient and well-run harbour and it is essential that the oil industry is aware of this fact. If the proposed reduction in staff goes ahead the Harbours Department hands will be tied in their negotiations to achieve this new business. There is no way that the oil industry will wish to operate into/out of a port that does not provide a full, safe and reliable 24hour a day 365 days a year port service.

Harbour and Towage staff have been fully trained in all aspects of oil pollution clean up techniques. With the proposed reduction by some 27 personnel in the event of an incident (something we hope will never happen) those remaining will have great difficulty in meeting any challenge posed in this aspect of port operations.

The tugs along with the harbour pilot launches have always been maintained to the highest possible standard if you reduce the manpower then I would envisage that maintenance will suffer resulting in the long term to increased costs at refit times, also a possible reduction in reliability.

I read also that BP have made a new oil discover just SW of Foinaven with reserves of some 40 million barrels which will be tied back to the Foinaven FPSO.
It was therefor a great pity to hear we had lost this contract in such a strange and sudden manner something we had won against great odds. BP always seemed very happy with the deal. There is I think more to this than meets the eye and I hope that the council will look at ways of continuing a dialogue with BP to see if anything can be done to try and overturn their decision and have the shuttle tankers return to Scapa Flow.

Finally I do hope also that the Council in conjunction with our MP and MSP have success with your representation to the Scottish Executive to re-instate the £1.0 million Transport Grant

My apologies for the long letter but as one who has been involved with the harbour operations since 1976 I did feel I had to put my feelings down on paper to you and trust you will take account of the above points and accept them in good faith.


Best Regards



Captain Bob Sclater FNI MEI


c.c.
Convener
Director of Harbours
Alistair Carmichael MP
Liam MacArthur MSP



The UK government regulatory bodies MCA, etc and the Scottish Executive who in fact approved new powers enabling ministers to freeze STS operations, have been closely monitoring the Forth Ports situation. They would not look favourably on any request from Scapa Flow to be a designated port for this new STS operation if the Council cannot prove they have the professional capability to do the job. There is I know ongoing debate on this very issue by the UK Government where we will see more stringent regulations coming into force covering STS transfers.
There is no doubt that at the present time we are the best in the business but with the proposed cut backs I doubt if we will continue to be so.

I realise that it may take some time to achieve this new business and that the council is seeking savings on the services they provide. In this case however the ship owner has already paid the council for the ongoing running of the port. The additional harbour dues accrued over the past thirty years for this very eventuality are available in the councils coffers to keep the Orkney Harbours and Orkney Towage staff fully employed for the time being.

There is no reason that over the next few months further studies can be carried out to see if some of the operating practices, natural wastage and voluntary redundancies both within the Harbours Department and Towage Company can be looked at. This would I hope result in a lift in the employees morale which at present appears to be very low.

This is certainly the wrong time to run down what has been one of the top ports in Europe with a safety and environmental record second to none. Here we have the Scottish Executive backing Orkney in its bid for a new container Trans-shipment Hub and we are sending out a message that Scapa Flow will not be open for business in the proper marine sense.

I also read in the press yesterday that J.P. Knight (Caledonia) Ltd have decided to no longer base tugs in the Cromarty Firth. This company as you know provided over the years a back up for Orkney Towage. In fact as recently as a couple of months ago one was chartered in to cover a STS due to the fact that Orkney Towage crew hours were over their working limits and had to be stood down. I am not sure how one can justify reducing the manning by nearly half when only a couple of months ago we could not provide the full service required. Orkney Towage could look at providing towage cover for Cromarty Firth until such time as we have won the Russian Oil contract.

I do have other concerns regarding the proposed run down of manpower in the Harbours Department and Orkney Towage as there will still be the ongoing oil operations carried out at Talisman's Flotta Oil Terminal and hopefully ongoing STS operations.

After several months in retirement, I was contacted by the Sheriff Principal of Grampian highlands and islands to ask if I would be willing to take up the post as an honorary Sheriff in Orkney. This was quite an honour, so I accepted the position. I was duly sworn in on 24 July 2008. With 12 years in the post, I have now conducted around 250 cases and signed numerous search warrants.

So my working life continues, albeit in a very relaxed manner as there is no pressure to attend the court although I do try to attend when requested, if we are not away on holiday. There are four other honorary sheriffs to spread the load. There is no permanently based Sheriff in Orkney, one attends court two weeks ever month and we cover the other two.

Most of our cases result in releasing the defendant on bail or on occasions remanding in custody until the Sheriff could deal with the case himself. Our case load consist mainly of domestic abuse, drink driving, assault, drug misuse and other minor misdemeanours. Each case we deal with relates mainly to the accused being held overnight or the weekend in the local police station cells and by law, their court appearance must be held within 24/48 hours of being remanded. The requirement of using Honorary Sheriffs ceased due to COVID and I have not attended since March 2020, returned to normal Sheriff duties in 2023 carried 5 cases in last couple of months.

**Four honorary sheriffs sworn in**

447

Although I had many responsibilities during my time as a Councillor, this did not restrict Anna and I from taking some well-earned holidays. By this time our three children had left home, Esther and Andrew both graduated and were working in their chosen fields. Joanna continued her studies for seven years, so still at university during most of my time as a Councillor.

Anyway this gave us the opportunity to do a bit more travelling. As a P&O pensioner, I was able to obtain preferential fares on their cruise ships, up to 50% on published fares. Our first cruise was a 14-day voyage in 2000 to the Caribbean sailing from Southampton and flying home from Barbados.

We enjoyed it so much we booked on the maiden voyage of the MV Aurora in September 2000. We set sail from Southampton bound for the Mediterranean but just one day at sea, the ship had engine problems, something wrong with the propeller shaft.

We turned round in the Bay of Biscay and headed back to Southampton. We were refunded our fare and gifted a voucher for the same amount for another cruise. This we took up and booked a half world cruise on the MV Aurora from Sydney Australia back to the UK.

We flew out to Sydney in February 2001. The cruise took us up the Australian coast onwards to Guam, Japan, Hong Kong, Singapore, Thailand, India, Egypt through the Suez canal to Turkey, Spain and back to Southampton after seven weeks away, all for the same price as our cancelled voyage to the Mediterranean.

We did have the P&O concession on this fare as well. Our next voyage was on the MV Minerva flying out to Manaus in the Amazon sailing all the way down the river and onwards via many ports in Brazil, Uruguay, and finally disembarking in Buenos Aires. The cost of this trip was about 65% less than the advertised costs so something we could not resist. After a long flight from London via Sao Paulo to Manaus, we arrived onboard and were provided with afternoon tea. Just as we sat down, two other passengers arrived having flown out on a different flights. They were, in fact, Captain Fred Johnson and his wife Elizabeth from Stromness. Fred, of course, was an ex P&O Scottish ferries master, sailing in command of the MV Sunniva. We were old friends so quite a reunion, they had the same pensioners discount and also could not believe how good a deal it was. We had some good fun with them on the cruise. We had two more cruises, one sailing from Lima back to Southampton via Panama, Caribbean islands and USA.

Our last one was our ruby wedding cruise, a month round the Caribbean and USA in December/January 2011. We flew out and back via Gatwick and Barbados. Our departure from the UK was during the very bad winter of 2010 and our flight was delayed by ten hours due to snow at Gatwick.

Most flights in the UK were cancelled on this day. Thankfully, they opened Gatwick late afternoon and we did get away. The pilot had a job getting the plane away from the terminal due to icy conditions and said that he had one more go as he was nearly over his flying time limits and would have to stand down. There was a big cheer when we did manage to take off.

Our ship the MV Ventura had to wait for our arrival in Barbados and of course, the returning passengers were not too happy being 12 hours late arriving back home. I think that was the end of our desire to do anymore cruises, also P&O had been sold to carnival cruises so no longer pensioners rates. We did, however, travel a great deal as our three children worked overseas.

Esther worked in Dubai for several years in the oil industry, so spent many fine days out there. Joanna spent a year working for Zenya Baruffa, a yarn company in northern Italy, then three years in Shanghai and onwards to Columbus, Ohio and for the past eight years in Los Angeles as head knitwear designer for naked cashmere. So had holidays in Italy, China and the USA visiting her As I mentioned, Andrew spent time in Dallas where we saw the sights.

We have four lovely grandchildren, Noah(13) Finlay(9). Patrick(6) and Erin (6). Esther is back in Aberdeen as a corporate financial recorder for Chrysoar, a new oil company that took over Conoco Phillips operations in the North Sea.

Chrysoar is now the largest operator in the North Sea. Changed its name to Harbour Oil in 2022. Andrew now lives in the Cotswolds village of Winchcombe, and started a new job with Progressive Energy, a carbon recovery and hydrogen related company in February 2020. Andrew is happy to be back in a position where his gas turbine engineering expertise is much more relevant than his last position that related to the production of plastics for air bags in the motor industry. They have certain done us proud I have covered a great deal in my story but there is certainly a considerable amount left untold.

*Happy family Christmas 2018 missing from photo Joana's husband Tyler married April 2019 in San Francisco.*

*A Few of My Business Cards*

*Our Visit to China*

*On the bund Shanghai, Anna enjoying a cocktail on the Bund. standing on Marco Polo bridge, Summer Palace Beijing, and once again standing on the Great Wall of China some 42 years after my first visit in May1965.*

*Captain Bob Sclater FNI. MEI*

So that's my story for now, as I said, it could have filled several more chapters, but I think it covers a good part of my life. When I think back to September 1956, as a young lad of 15 setting off to sea with no prospects, it's not been a bad life.